ROCK THE HOUSE

GROVER G. NORQUIST

VYTIS Press, Inc.
5100 N. Federal Highway #102
Ft. Lauderdale, Florida 33308   U.S.A.

ROCK THE HOUSE

LCCC 95 - 600 - 40
ISBN   0 - 9645786 - 0 - 3

VYTIS Press, Inc.
5100 North Federal Highway   #102
Ft. Lauderdale, FL 33308
(305) 772-1236
*

Distributed by
BOOKWORLD Services, Inc.
1933 Whitfield Park Loop
Sarasota, FL 34243

Printed in the United States of America
Second Edition - Unabridged - September 1995
3 4 5 6 7 8 9 10

(Ordering information at the back of the book)

"After reading ROCK THE HOUSE, I strongly suggest that it be put in the hands of every Republican and every Republican campaign manager. It should be considered no less than the political bible for the Party."

NORMAN WYMBS, AUTHOR
"A Place To Go Back To: Ronald Reagan in Dixon Illinois" - 1987; "Ronald Reagan's Crusade" - 1995

"One of the reasons the Democrats are running like scalded dogs is Grover Norquist. Grover is one of the few individuals that has insight to the inside the Beltway strategy sessions and also has spent a great deal of time outside the Beltway, working for issues that help all Americans. He has a unique quality not often found in Washington, combining intellectualism with effective activism. ROCK THE HOUSE is a true insider's account of the Republican Revolution of 1994."

HALEY BARBOUR, CHAIRMAN
Republican National Committee

"Grover Norquist is one of the conservative movement's most brilliant strategists and most effective grass-roots coalition-builders. His book is full of lessons for liberals who want to understand why they are losing and for conservatives who want to build a permanent governing majority."

EDWIN J. FEULNER, JR., PRESIDENT
Heritage Foundation

"This book does a masterful job in explaining exactly why the nation's politics shifted so quickly, and it does so in an entertaining and accessible way. Grover proves that whoever said Poli-Sci couldn't be fun was wrong."

JOHN H. FUND
Wall Street Journal

"ROCK THE HOUSE is a lively, penetrating account of how the GOP triumphed last November, an election that dramatically underscored the desire of Americans for a fundamental break from the liberal/Beltway politics of the past 30 years. What helps make Norquist's chronicle so superb is that he was absolutely instrumental in helping bring about this positive, seismic shift. Rarely has such a committed, brilliantly effective activist also possessed such a lively pen!"
MALCOLM S. FORBES, JR., PRESIDENT & CEO
Forbes Magazine

"Grover Norquist is one of the conservative movement's most astute political observers. This book is an excellent appraisal of the intellectual wasteland and dishonesty that is American liberalism. I only wish I could share his confidence that the Republican party will once and for all eliminate the regulatory welfare state."
FRED L. SMITH, JR., PRESIDENT
Competitive Enterprise Institute

"Mr. Norquist has become one of the main power brokers in the new Republican majority. His rise helps explain both the power of Newt Gingrich and the ideological makeover of Republicans."
PAUL A. GIGOT
Wall Street Journal
April 1995

"You don't need the major media to know which way the political wind blows. All you need is this book. Grover Norquist uses his refreshing brand of optimistic conservatism to assess America's major political parties and where the emerging Republican majority would take us. ROCK THE HOUSE will make conservatives eager for the political battles to come, liberals nostalgic for an era gone by."
ROBERT S. STEIN
Investor's Business Daily

DEDICATION

To my parents, Warren and Carol, and to
Ronald Reagan and Newt Gingrich,
who have made the
Republican Party worthy of America.

Rock the House

TABLE OF CONTENTS

Dedication v
Acknowledgements xiii
Prologue xv
Introduction and Summary ixx

Chapter One: The 1994 Election 1
Chapter Two: The Republican Coalition 33
Chapter Three: The Collapse of the Democrat Party and
                  the Liberal Establishment 91
Chapter Four: The Failed Clinton Coup 123
Chapter Five: Why Bush Lost 149
Chapter Six: Recapturing the Past:
                  The Reagan Legacy 171
Chapter Seven: Contract With America 191
Chapter Eight: Voices of the Republican Future 219
Chapter Nine: The GOP Future: The Contract
                  With America for 1996 275

Appendices 317
        A.   Taxpayer Protection Pledge 319
        B.   Taxpayer Protection Pledge Takers 323
        C.   Anti-VAT Pledge & Caucus 329
        D.   Conservative Organizations 337
        E.   State Policy Organizations 357
        F.   State Term Limits Leaders 363
        G.   State Tax Activists 371
        H.   Small Business Survival Caucus 377
        I.   American Dream Restoration Pledge 381
        J.   Contract With America Checklist 385
        K.   Contract Scorecard 389

Bibliography 395
Index 409
On-Line Information 439
Americans for Tax Reform Membership Form 441
Additional Books - Ordering Information . . . .
Artistic Credits . . . .
New Publications . . . .

WE SHALL FAIL TO WIN ONLY IF WE FAIL TO TRY

VYTIS

ACKNOWLEDGEMENTS

Just as this book outlines the dynamics of American coalition politics, so did its writing reflect the work and insight of the coalitions it documents.

Literally dozens of people have read all or part of the text, some of them more than once. In the process, errors have, of course, been corrected. More importantly, insights have been imparted which have immensely strengthened the book.

My first thanks to my father, for his meticulous checking of every figure and computation. Then to Gordon Jones, for his work in editing and formatting. He had the help of a legion of first-class assistants, including Maritza Alvarez, Damon Ansell, Jeff Borntrager, Chris Grengs, Jeremy Henry, Kolt A. Jones, Michael Kamburowski, Pamela Nash, Ann Parent, Matt Schubert, and Yarden Weidenfeld.

Melanie Tammen, Gary Maloney, and Heather Higgins provided invaluable comments on the entire text. Peggy Noonan and John Fund made most helpful suggestions. I am grateful for their encouragement.

I wish to thank R. Emmett Tyrrell, Jr. and Wladyslaw Pleszcynski for letting me write the "On Politics" column of *The American Spectator* for the last three years.

To Jack Abramoff belongs the credit for instigating the whole project. Any errors are, as ever, entirely my own responsibility.

Grover Glenn Norquist
Washington, D.C.

PROLOGUE

The Honorable Newt Gingrich
Speaker of the House of Representatives

No activist in America is better positioned to write the description of where Republicans have been and where Republicans are going than Grover Norquist. From the time Grover and I first started to work together in the early 1980's, when he was a leading activist trying to unlock the Soviet Empire and collapse communism, risking his life in places like Angola, Afghanistan, and Mozambique, actively risking his career in places like Washington, D.C., taking on not just communism abroad but the liberal news media at home, Grover has consistently been innovative, insightful, and extraordinarily energetic. He was the founder of the Cost of Government Day movement, which annually reminds us that the federal government costs us too much; and he invented the Taxpayer Protection Pledge, which sets the standard that candidates running for the U.S. House and Senate should pledge in advance not to take more money out of our wallets. The Pledge became a national issue in 1986, '88, '90, '92, and '94.

Grover is very tightly connected to the grassroots activists, the economic conservatives, the social conservatives, and the strong-defense conservatives. In Washington he is in the middle of meeting after meeting involving key activists of all backgrounds.

He has entrée at every level of the Republican Party; he can walk in, explain what he sees happening, listen to the plans and ideas of Republican elected officials, and then help develop a synergistic relationship which matters. In his journalistic role, Grover's explanation of Paul Coverdell's run-off victory in 1992 in the U.S. Senate race in Georgia was a masterpiece. His understanding of how all parts of the coalition came together to put the brakes on the Clinton victory three weeks after the presidential election, by defeating Wyche Fowler, remains to this day the best single study of how the new Republican Party is emerging. He saw how voluntary coalitions came together because each recognized that their future was tied in with the others, and that to get their perfect candidate and then lose was less desirable than to get acceptable candidates and beat the Left. The result was a maturity and a sophistication which had remarkable impact in 1994.

It is fair to say that, through Grover's network of activists and through his understanding of how the Washington liberal news media and Washington liberal lobbyists work, he has an enormous impact on policy and political debates, from the crime bill to the election. Week after week, in a continuing offensive, all of the various social coalitions and economic coalitions come together because they all recognize that the Clinton Administration and the Left are their common opponent, threatening to put an end to their values and their vision of the future. It is, to a large extent, Grover Norquist who has fostered that understanding.

In *Rock the House*, Grover has outlined the framework which made 1994 possible. He has clearly seen the failure of the Left to understand the American people and the rise of a new, younger Republican party committed to new ideas and new approaches. He has seen this new party standing on Ronald Reagan's shoulders, representing the broad stream of conservatives that began with William F. Buckley and Barry Goldwater. And he has seen how to

Prologue

take its various strands, and weave them together into a mechanism for redistributing power out of Washington back to the states, rediffusing power back to individuals, so that families, neighborhoods, communities, places of worship, local voluntary associations and private businesses can once again have the power that legitimately in America belongs to them.

Like Grover, I am an optimist. I believe that the American people are going to prove far more powerful than the bureaucrats and the special interests and dominant news media of the Left. But it is going to be a big struggle, a struggle in which this book will play a significant role. Every person who wants to see freedom prosper and flourish, who wants to see that power is taken out of Washington and returned back home, who wants a federal government that is lean, effective, and smaller, who wants to strengthen the American federal structure, who wants stronger and more effective American volunteerism, who wants more opportunity for more people in their lives, with less power, and less money, and less bureaucracy in the government, every person who is committed to these goals should read this book. They will then understand the recent past and can join with us to create a future that builds upon precisely the successes Grover outlines.

Newt Gingrich
Washington, D.C.
February 1995

Rock the House

Rock the House
by
Grover G. Norquist

INTRODUCTION AND SUMMARY

It's 2:30 a.m., November 9, 1994 at Congressman Newt Gingrich's election night headquarters in Atlanta. The floor is a sea of balloons, the press has filed its last soundbite and Newt Gingrich is speaking to a tired but enthusiastic band of about thirty friends, staffers and advisors. "It's official! We won! There are ice cream bars and some champagne here. Let's take three minutes to celebrate. Then let's get to work on the next two years." Three minutes later Gingrich sits down and for the next two hours listens to thoughts on how best to approach the next 24 hours, the next week, the next two years, and even the next twenty years.

Just as Newt Gingrich turned immediately from the task accomplished to the task at hand, this book will do the same. Since the election of November 8, 1994, we have had our three-minute break. Now it is time to assess how we got here, and, more importantly, where we go from here.

* * * * *

The Republican Party is now the majority governing party in America. The November 8, 1994 elections made this fact clear.

While the Republican Party won control of the United States Senate, 30 governorships, 22 lieutenant governorships, 21 attorneys general, and majorities in 25 state senates and 25 state houses of representatives, the victory in the U.S. House of Representatives and the inauguration of Speaker Newt Gingrich have received the lion's share of the nation's attention.

This attention is well placed. The Republican capture of the House of Representatives is the culmination of a 40-year struggle by a conservative nation to overthrow a liberal political elite that has used gerrymandering, incumbent protection laws, and taxpayer dollars to stay in power. This elite was protected by a collaborating Establishment press that hid Congress's actions and costs from the voters and diverted their attention from its misdeeds.

The Establishment Left is now broken in America, just as the Soviet Union was broken when the first breach in the Berlin Wall opened up on November 9, 1989. The Soviet Empire struggled on for another two years — lashing out murderously at freedom fighters in Lithuania and Afghanistan — and though bloody and vicious to the end, it was finished.

Today, the Establishment Left is lashing out at Newt Gingrich, the American people, democracy itself, and even Bill Clinton, blaming Clinton for its own collapse. But the seeds of destruction of a corrupt, bankrupt and dysfunctional elite predate the arrival in Washington of Bill Clinton and the gang from Arkansas.

This book chronicles the long march through the institutions of the American people, the growth of the Republican Party as a vehicle for this political movement, and the savage defense the Washington Establishment put up to defend the spoils of empire. Those who have viewed the tax dollars of the American people as their own bank account, have despised those they would rule, and who have built up myths to obscure and defend their policy failures, have lost.

Speaker Gingrich correctly refers to the Republican victory as the beginning of an American Revolution. And in America it is no contradiction that the conservative party and the party of traditional values is also the revolutionary, anti-government, anti-establishment party. For unlike Europe, America's tradition and history are revolution. Our nation was created by the American Revolution, a rejection of European "kings, and dukes and other rapscallions", an aristocracy that would rule our lives. America's heritage is one of revolution and the rejection of big government. In America, the nation and the state are two distinct entities: "We" are America; the government (the state) is "Them". American patriots love their country, but distrust their government. Being an American is not a function of race or religion, ethnic background or even birthplace. It is the belief in the Declaration of Independence and the Constitution. A belief that all men are equal before God and the Law, that the government has no right to push us around, that government has no legitimate powers beyond those we temporarily assign to it. We are a nation born of, and united by, these ideas.

SUMMARY OF *ROCK THE HOUSE*

CHAPTER ONE begins by describing what actually happened on election day, November 8, 1994: the size and depth of the Republican victory and the overturning of the old order. The story goes beyond the headlines of 35 defeated Democrat incumbents in the House, including Speaker Tom Foley in Washington, Dan Rostenkowski in Chicago and Jack Brooks in Texas.

It means that more than 50,000 Democrat political activists have lost their hold on taxpayer-supported positions as a result of this election. This Prætorian Guard for the Establishment was swept away as defeated Democrat governors no longer have the tens of thousands of patronage jobs that were the Democrat Party in America. In Washington, D.C. alone, several thousand patronage jobs are gone.

The second half of Chapter One sifts through the wreckage of November 8 and predicts that the wound to the Democrat Party and the Washington Establishment it controlled is mortal. It argues that the interlocking network of power cannot be reconstituted, as the

Democrats lost the ability to extort campaign contributions from individuals and businesses when they lost control of the congressional committees that were such lucrative ports for congressional privateers.

CHAPTER TWO outlines the growth of the Republican Party as a coalition of Americans who wish simply to be left alone. Homeowners, parents, taxpayers, gun owners, small businessmen and women, the self-employed, and the "religious right" have formed a stable coalition that articulates the one thing they have in common: they all want to be left alone.

The victory of the United States in the Cold War, the destruction of the Soviet Empire — that was both evil and an empire — has not stripped Republicans of a unifying issue. The issue of crime now divides the liberal elite from America just as the struggle against Communism once did.

CHAPTER THREE chronicles the corruption and subsequent collapse of the Democrat coalition assembled by Franklin Delano Roosevelt into a collection of interests who see the state as the means of living off the labor of others: government bureaucrats paid by taxpayers, corrupt big city political machines, black "leaders" who have sold their own into a cruel slavery of dependence in return for crumbs from the Establishment's table of money and influence, trial lawyers, teachers' unions, and left-wing intellectuals living off taxpayers. All conspire together to loot the taxpayers and push around American citizens.

But this coalition is collapsing. There are too few taxpayers to loot to feed it. Black Americans are tired of being the guinea pigs for the Left's now failed social experiment. Republican control of the purse strings will cut off hundreds of thousands of parasites who would live off the work of others. The Democrat "tax and spend" coalition is united only in a desire to take money and power from others and

Introduction

greedily shower it on themselves. They have no enduring bond and, like wolves deprived of prey, will turn on themselves in their hunger. **CHAPTER FOUR** examines the last-gasp attempt by the liberal Establishment to save itself at the expense of America. After the 1992 election, Bill Clinton stood astride the American government with all the levers of power, and yet failed to turn America into a European-style social democracy where the majority of the citizens were living off the government. His grab for control of health care was defeated.

Left-wing historians will be kinder to Clinton than his contemporaries are, for he did come very close to changing America into a European-style nation, where elite rulers use the power of the state to fund themselves and control an enfeebled proletariat.

CHAPTER FIVE chronicles the failed Bush presidency and shows how Bush's abandonment of the Reagan legacy cost the Republicans the presidency and gave the Establishment Left one last chance to consolidate power. The Bush failure also demonstrated to the nation that there is only one Establishment in America — the one controlled by the Democrat Party.

Bush hoped to create a bipartisan ruling establishment freed of some of the bizarre cultural excesses of the Left. But the Republican Party he tried to mold would have none of it. The Republican Party from top to bottom, from east to west and north to south, is an anti-establishment party. It is a middle class party that wishes to be left alone, not to rule others or to be ruled by its "betters". The Bush failure and his rejection by the Republican coalition cemented the party as a Reaganite Republican party.

CHAPTER SIX sets the record straight on the Reagan years. The Left has worked very hard to rewrite history. Like Stalinist photographers trying to white out inconvenient people, the Establishment press has worked overtime to "airbrush" from history the Reagan legacy of economic growth, job creation, low inflation, and victory over the Left's vision of the future: the Soviet Empire.

CHAPTER SEVEN focusses on the "Contract with America", the revolutionary agenda endorsed by the Republican candidates for the House of Representatives in 1994. The Contract was the culmination of an almost two-decades-long debate about whether "all politics is local" or whether the Republican Party could nationalize the election by running all its House and Senate candidates on a conservative platform. Republican presidential candidates who campaigned nationally as conservatives were winning landslide elections, but Republican House candidates, running local campaigns, had failed to win a majority. In 1994, the Republican "Contract with America" provided a clear choice between the Republican and the Democrat visions of the future. America voted decisively for a Republican Congress just as it had voted in the past for Republican presidents.

The "Contract With America" is a down-payment on the Republican revolution; its fulfillment will demonstrate that the New Republicans in Congress are not like the Democrats, who dishonestly run moderate campaigns and govern to the left, but instead are a new breed of political leaders who view the politics of campaigns and the work of governing as a seamless garment. The New Republicans believe that strong and specific commitments on the campaign trail help in governing and that successful governing is the surest way to success with voters on election day.

CHAPTER EIGHT is the Republican Party in its own words. The leadership of the Republicans in the House of Representatives and those Republican leaders and thinkers most likely to shape the Republican future were asked to share, for this book, the most important section of their most important speech. These statements of principle, vision and pragmatic action give an unfiltered view of where the Republican Party and its leadership are in 1995.

Introduction

CHAPTER NINE, the last chapter, is the Republican agenda for the future and outlines the Contract with America for 1996. The success of the Contract with America in the 1994 election and as a guide to legislation guarantees that in all future elections the Republican House members will present a new Contract to the voters. Chapter Nine outlines 12 major reforms that Republicans are already pushing in Washington, in the states, and throughout the nation to return America's government to its constitutional and historic role as a servant of the American people.

* * * * *

As this book is completed, in the fall of 1995, we have just completed the first 100 days of the Republican Contract with America. The Republicans kept their word and passed eight critical reforms of the House Rules on January 4, the opening day of Congress. The balanced budget amendment to the Constitution passed the House of Representatives with 300 votes on January 27.

Senator Paul Coverdell said of the 1994 election that Republicans need to remember that they have not won the war. The Washington Establishment is a serious enemy and not lightly conquered. But, Coverdell says, using the analogy of the D-Day invasion of Europe in World War II, we are now on the beaches. Day by day, the Establishment will be beaten back. Day by day, America can restore democratic self-government.

November 8, 1994 was the beginning of the end of Big Government in America.

CHAPTER ONE

THE 1994 ELECTION

On November 8, 1994 the American people went to the polls and made the Republican Party the majority party of the United States.

Republicans won control of the House of Representatives for the first time in forty years by defeating 35 sitting Democrats and capturing a total of 52 new House seats. The Democrat Party had maintained one-party control of the House of Representatives since 1955, longer than Fidel Castro, who seized power in 1959, had ruled Cuba. In this century, only North Korea (1945), China (1949), and Mexico (1929) still have governments with a longer period of one-party control. The fact that these are all essentially one-party states should alert us to the fact that there was something rotten in Washington.

Since 1955, Republicans had elected four presidents (Eisenhower, Nixon, Reagan, and Bush) and controlled the Senate for six years (1981-1987). But all tax measures and all spending bills must originate in the House of Representatives. For forty years, the Democrat Party has thus been able to "govern from below", and maintain effective control through what the drafters of the Constitution envisioned as "The People's House".

1

Rock the House

Winning control of the House of Representatives is as historic a change as the emergence of the Republican Party with the election of Lincoln or the creation of the Democrat Party majority in the 1930-1934 period with the Depression and Franklin Delano Roosevelt. The Republican victory was wider and deeper than simply ending forty years of control in the House.

In the Senate, Republicans won eight seats on election day; with Alabama's Richard Shelby's decision on November 9 to switch from the Democrat to the Republican Party, Republican Leader Robert Dole enjoyed a Senate majority of 53-47. When Ben Nighthorse Campbell, Senator from Colorado, also switched, after Democrat votes killed the balanced budget amendment in the Senate in early March 1995, the Republican edge went to 54-46.

The Republican Party, which was able to win seven presidential elections (including four landslides) between 1952 and 1988, finally brought its majority to the Congress and the state level.

Republicans captured 11 additional governorships for a 30-19 majority of State Houses (the governor of Maine is an Independent). That is the first time since 1969 that Republicans have held a majority of governorships. Republicans gained 108 states senate and 373 state house seats, for a total gain of 481 state legislative seats.

The real shift in power to the Republicans is only hinted at by the total number of new Republican state legislators. Real political power at the state level flows from the control of one or both houses of a state legislature. With one house — the senate or house — Republicans could stop a tax hike or prevent political gerrymandering that would hurt Republicans. Only when they hold both Houses can Republicans actually pass tax cuts. Only with control of two Houses and the governorship can Republicans actually be said to govern a state. Prior to November 8, Democrats controlled 64 of the 98 partisan state chambers (Nebraska's legislature is unicameral and non-partisan) and Republicans controlled only 31. At that point, three chambers, the Alaska Senate, the Florida Senate, and the Michigan House, were tied.

The November election gave Republicans control of an additional 18 chambers, Republicans now control 49 chambers, and the Democrats control 48 chambers. The Nevada House is tied, and as this is written, the California House is fluctuating, though Republicans have a technical majority. The chart on the following two pages shows the changing partisan nature of state legislatures.

Most importantly, before the 1994 election Democrats had the governorship and both houses of the state legislature in 17 states. In only 3 states — Arizona, Utah, and New Jersey — did Republicans control the governorship and the legislature. Today, Republicans have total control of 15 states, and there are only eight Democrat-controlled states. The maps on pages 6 and 7 show these changes.

Republicans won at the federal, state and local levels and in all regions. The scars of the War Between the States have lasted more than 100 years, but after November 8, 1994, Republicans held more than half the governorships of the eleven states of the Old Confederacy, and a majority of the U.S. Senate seats (13-9) and of the U.S. House seats (64-61). For the first time in its history, the Republican Party is a truly national, rather than regional party. The map on page 8 shows the net Republican House gains, state by state

---

CALIFORNIA HOUSE

The November 1994 elections gave the Republican Party a one-vote majority in the California Assembly, but one Republican voted with the Democrats to elect Willie Brown as Assembly Speaker.

That renegade has now been recalled, and Brown is running for Mayor of San Francisco, but Republican woes have not ended. Before leaving, Brown persuaded another renegade Republican to run for Speaker, and she was elected by the Democrats plus her own vote.

She is now the object of a recall petition, but the situation remains fluid. Some politicians will go to great lengths to thwart the will of the voters.

1994 ELECTION RESULTS

STATE	SENATE				HOUSE				CONTROL	GOVERNOR
	DEM	REP	OTHER	CHANGE	DEM	REP	OTHER	CHANGE		
Alabama	23	12	0	+4R	74	31	0	+8R	Dem	Rep
Alaska	8	12	0	+2R	17	22	1i	+4R	Rep	Dem
Arizona	11	19	0	+1R	22	38	0	+3R	Rep	Rep
Arkansas	28	7	0	+2R	88	12	0	+1R	Dem	Dem
California	21	17	2i	+1R	39	40	1i	+7R	Split	Rep
Colorado	16	19	0		24	41	0	+7R	Rep	Dem
Connecticut	17	19	0	+2R	90	61	0	+4D	Split	Rep
Delaware	12	9	0	+3R	14	27	0	+4R	Split	Dem
Florida	19	21	0	+1R	63	57	0	+8R	Split	Dem
Georgia	35	21	0	+6R	114	65	1u	+13R*	Dem	Dem
Hawaii	23	2	0	+1D	44	7	0	+3R	Dem	Dem
Idaho	8	27	0	+4R	13	57	0	+7R	Rep	Rep
Illinois	26	33	0	+1R	54	64	0	+13R	Rep	Rep
Indiana	20	30	0	+2R	44	56	0	+11R	Rep	Dem
Iowa	27	23	0	No election	36	64	0	+13R	Split	Rep
Kansas	13	27	0	+4R	45	80	0	+14R	Rep	Rep
Kentucky	21	17	0	+4R	64	36	0	+7R	Dem	Dem
Louisiana	33	6	0	No election	86	17	1i,1v	No election	Dem	Dem
Maine	16	18	1i	+3R,1i	77	74	0	+16R	Split	Ind
Maryland	32	15	0	+6R	100	41	0	+16R	Dem	Dem
Massachusetts	30	10	0	+1R	125	34	1o	+1D	Dem	Rep
Michigan	16	22	0	+1R	53	56	1v	+1R*	Rep	Rep
Minnesota	43	21	3v	*	71	63	0	+13R	Dem	Rep
Mississippi	36	14	2v	No election	89	29	2i,2v	No election	Dem	Rep
Missouri	19	15	0	+1R	87	76	0	+8R	Dem	Dem

State	Senate D	Senate R	Senate O	Senate Δ	House D	House R	House O	House Δ	Legis.	Gov.
Montana	19	31	0	+11R	33	67	0	+14R	Rep	Rep
Nebraska			Non partisan				Unicameral		NA	Dem
Nevada	8	13	0	+2R	21	21	0	+8R	Split	Dem
New Hampshire	6	18	0	+5R	112	286	2L	+28R	Rep	Rep
New Jersey	16	24	0	No election	28	52	0	No election	Rep	Rep
New Mexico	27	15	0	+1R	46	24	Special Election	+1D	Dem	Rep
New York	25	36	0	+13R	94	56	0	+7R	Split	Rep
North Carolina	26	24	0	+5R	52	68	0	+6R	Split	Dem
North Dakota	20	29	0	+2R	23	75	0	+26R	Split	Rep
Ohio	13	20	0	+5R	43	56	0	+10R	Rep	Rep
Oklahoma	35	13	0	+3R	65	36	0	+10R	Dem	Rep
Oregon	11	19	0	+1D	26	34	0	+5R	Rep	Rep
Pennsylvania	21	29	0	+2R	101	102	0	+2R	Rep	Dem
Rhode Island	40	10	0	+5R	84	16	0	+4R	Dem	Rep
South Carolina	29	17	0	+3R	58	62	4i	+1R	Rep	Rep
South Dakota	16	19	0	No election	24	45	1i	+10R, 3i	Split	Rep
Tennessee	18	15	0	+1R	59	40	0	+3R, 1i	Dem	Rep
Texas	17	14	0	+1R	89	55	0	+4R	Dem	Rep
Utah	10	19	0	+1R	20	61	0	+2R	Rep	Rep
Vermont	12	18	0	+2R	86	61	3i	+6R	Split	Dem
Virginia	22	24	0	No election	52	47	1i	+4R, 1o	Dem	Rep
Washington	26	8	0	+3R	38	58	2u	No election	Split	Dem
West Virginia	16	17	0	+6R	69	31	0	+25R	Dem	Dem
Wisconsin	10	20	0		48	51	0	+10R	Split	Rep
Wyoming					13	46	1u	+4R	Dem	Rep
TOTALS	1,021	905	31,2v	108R, 2D, 1i	2,817	2,603	12i,1u, 2o,2I,3v	372R, 6D, 4i, 1o	18D, 19R, 12S	

* - The outcome of undecided races and filling of vacancies may alter this change.

i - Independent

o - Political party other than Democratic, Republican or Independent

u - Undecided race

v - Vacancy

L - Libertarian

Source: National Conference of State Legislatures, December 7, 1994

5

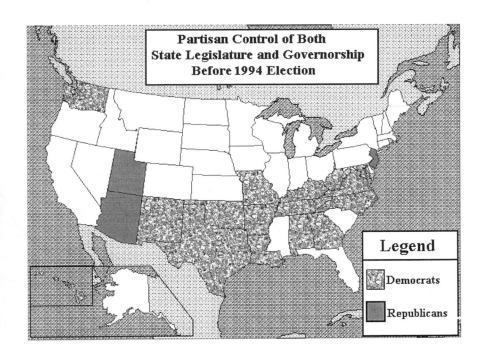

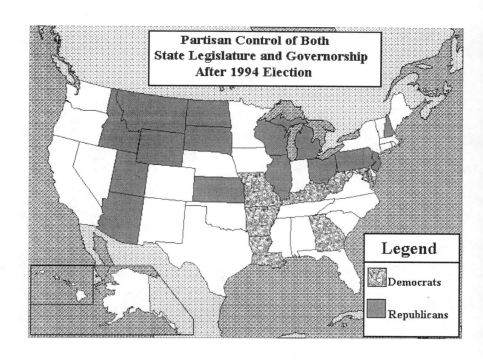

**Partisan Control of Both
State Legislature and Governorship
After 1994 Election**

Legend

Democrats

Republicans

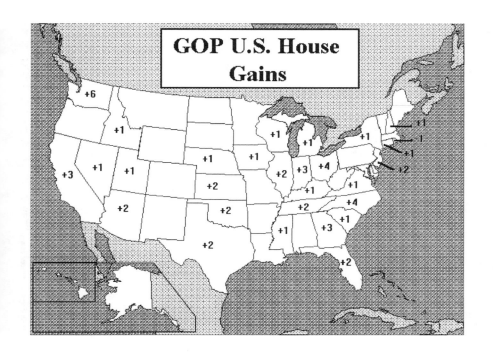

Chapter One

The election of sheriffs, county commissioners and school board officials, along with the gain of 481 state legislative seats (for a nationwide total of 3,509), gives the Republicans a strong farm team for future statewide and national elections (although the Democrats still have an edge in the nationwide totals with 3,838). When new district lines are drawn for state legislative and congressional elections, Republicans have control over redistricting in 15 states and can veto Democrat gerrymandering in all but eight states. (Democrat gerrymandering in California, Texas and other Democrat-controlled states cost Republicans more than a dozen House seats through the 1980's; and a quick look at the number of close votes in Congress shows how this redistricting alone cost Ronald Reagan key defense and foreign policy victories in Congress.)

But politics is more than simply politicians, and the damage to the Democrat Party's infrastructure inflicted by the voters on November 8 is immense. The loss of 52 House seats in Congress, each carrying with it the authority to hire 22 congressional staff, means the loss of 1,144 Democrat patronage positions. There is a total of 18,000 jobs on Capitol Hill. All of the several thousand patronage jobs, such as the elevator operators who manually run the automatic elevators in the Capitol, will be eliminated or given to Republicans. Republicans promised in their "Contract with America" to cut the number of committee staff by a third — all of which will come from the Democrats, who have unfairly stacked hiring positions in their favor for the last forty years. This will eliminate another 1,400 Democrat patronage slots. On the Senate side, roughly 1,000 Democrat staff jobs are disappearing.

Democrat losses at the governorship and state legislative levels will spread out the Democrat job loss across America. Governor Mario Cuomo's loss in New York State will cost more than 12,000 patronage positions, and when boards and various authorities are included, another 20,000 plus positions will no longer be available as goodies for the New York Democrat Party to offer to party activists. In New Mexico, the new Republican governor can replace 1,250 Democrat appointments; in Wyoming, 1,000. Eleven governorships lost by Democrats will cost the Democrat Party more than 40,000 patronage jobs. And if the 476 Democrat state legislators defeated by Republicans have only one staffer each, fully one thousand Democrats will be looking for work from those defeats. The 17 state legislatures taken over by Republicans will replace Democrat committee staff with Republicans: another 1,000 or more jobs.

A conservative estimate is that the Democrats lost more than 50,000 political patronage jobs as a result of the November 8 election.

The liberal Establishments of Washington D.C. and previously Democrat-controlled state capitals are similarly shaken. Dozens of six-figure salary careers in Washington were dependent on a lobbyist's personal friendship with a key staffer for the powerful Ways and Means Chairman, Dan Rostenkowski, or the Speaker of the House, Tom Foley, or the Chairman of the Judiciary Committee, Jack Brooks. All three were defeated. Many reporters at CBS, NBC, ABC the *Washington Post*, the *New York Times*, the Washington bureau of the *Wall Street Journal* and other Establishment news outlets knew only one-half of Washington — the Democrat half that had all the power.

Fortune 500 companies that had hired almost all former Democrat staffers as lobbyists will now find it prudent to have at least 50-50 Republican and Democrat registration in their Washington and state capital offices. There are now more than 10,000 business lobbying groups that will be making this adjustment. Only as this shakeout occurs over time will it become clear how thoroughly and completely the Democrat Party has controlled the entire Washington Establishment over the past four decades. The Democrat majority in the House of Representatives was the tip of a very large iceberg.

Chapter One

Yes, the Republican Party won big in Congress and across the nation. But the election was about a great deal more than patronage. It was about the future. There are two important concepts needed to assess the future: **first**, a grasp of the reasons the Republicans won in 1994 and **second**, determining whether this will be a temporary two-year period of Republican control, as it was in 1947-48 and 1953-54, or a longer period of Republican dominance, as occurred in 1860 and 1894.

WHY THE GOP TOOK BACK THE HOUSE IN 1994

There are **seven major reasons** the Republicans captured the House in 1994.

1. A National Campaign

First, the Republican Party ran an explicitly conservative campaign and nationalized the campaign with the "Contract with America". Unlike previous elections in which every congressional candidate was running a separate, personal campaign for each House seat, the House Republican candidates ran as a team on a common platform.

The failure of the Republican House candidates in past elections to unite with a common agenda and vision explains how Republicans were able to win landslide victories for the presidency — Nixon in 1972 and Reagan in 1984 — without winning a majority of the votes for Republican congressional candidates. When Democrat Speaker Tip O'Neill said all politics is local, he was not expressing a political truism, but rather describing the Democrat Party's strategy to continue its liberal hegemony over a conservative nation. Running as individuals, Democrats in Texas and Ohio could pretend to be independent of the liberal leadership and decisions that flowed from a Democrat Congress. They could run on their records of constituent service, something which will always favor the candidate from the party of give-away government goodies. Republican House candidates running alone failed to capitalize on the popularity of the national Republican message carried by the presidential candidate.

In 1994, Newt Gingrich changed this dynamic with the "Contract with America". Developed under the leadership of Dick Armey, the Contract was written in consultation with all Republican House members and challengers. It contained a list of eight reforms and ten pieces of legislation that the Republican signatories pledged to have the full U.S. House vote on within the first 100 days if Americans elected a majority Republican House. These included term limits, the tax-limited balanced budget amendment, and tax reduction for families and businesses, as well as reduced regulations. The spirit of the Contract can be summarized as: "The federal government is too large and spends too much of your money, and we intend to get the government out of your face and your wallet as much and as soon as possible." (The Contract is discussed in detail in Chapter 7.)

The Republican Party in the post-Reagan era has become so unified that only three incumbents failed to sign the Contract with America. And so powerful was the Contract as a campaign device that only three Republican challengers were successful without it, in this year of unprecedented Republican success.

Exit polling on the night of the election shows why the Republican strategy of running a national campaign for less government worked so well.

● A Fabrizio McLaughlin and Associates poll taken that night found that voters identified themselves as conservatives rather than liberals by a margin of 44 to16 percent, or almost 3 to 1. At the same time, 52.5 percent of voters viewed Clinton as a liberal, while only 6.2 percent believed him to be a conservative.

Asked if they would prefer "smaller government with fewer services or a larger government with many services", voters preferred smaller government over a larger government by 67.8 percent to 20.8 percent.

• A Wirthlin Group poll found 72 percent of Americans agreeing with the statement that "Government is not the answer to our problems. Government is the problem."

• A poll by Luntz Research Companies found that 73 percent of voters believe "the federal government is much too large and has too much power." Only five percent felt the government was too small. And of those who felt the government was too large, fully one-third believed it should be cut in half. Asked if they felt the federal government was more of a partner or more of an opponent in their pursuit of the American dream, by a 59 to 32 percent margin Americans answered "opponent". Fifty-six percent agreed that "the government has limited your rights or threatened your basic beliefs." And a majority (51 percent) could "foresee a time in the near future" when they would have to disobey the law to protect their constitutional rights.

The unified, nationwide Republican message of less government was heard by a nation of voters hostile to the status quo of big government. And with the Democrats controlling not only the House and Senate, but the White House as well, voters fully understood who was in charge of the government.

Dick Armey, the House Republican Majority Leader, argues that Bill Clinton took a nation already wary of government and, by means of his campaign for government-run health care and the 1993 tax hikes, radicalized it against his view of large, activist government.

Armey argues that the Contract with America acted "like a reversal in a wrestling match" where the wrestler on the bottom gains the advantage. Clinton and the Democrats had invested heavily in the claim that Republicans were simply opposing Democrat initiatives, that Republicans were without an agenda, without ideas, and hence responsible for "gridlock". The Contract with America highlighted a Republican agenda that was popular with Americans and that Democrat leaders such as House Speaker Tom Foley and Senate Majority Leader George Mitchell had prevented from enactment (often had kept from being even debated). Democrats attacked the Contract, but in so doing, they highlighted the fact that the Republicans had a political agenda they wanted to share with America and the Democrats while the Clinton White House did not. Worse, the Democrats spent two million dollars in ads attacking the contract funds desperately needed by Democrat candidates. Clinton further compared himself with Reagan and the 1980's, a comparison he fancied, but a debate he could not win. His advisors, such as James Carville, Tony Coelho, and Stan Greenberg, all argued that this would be a winning strategy. It wasn't and couldn't be.

Overall, Democrat incumbents held an overwhelming advantage over their challengers in campaign contributions. But the Republican strategy of nationalizing the election served to overcome a great deal of this advantage. If, as former Speaker of the House Tip O'Neill claimed, "all politics is local", the funding advantage enjoyed by House Judiciary Committee Chairman Jack Brooks and Ways and Means Committee Chairman Dan Rostenkowski would have been decisive. As it was, Steve Stockman spent only $110,000 to defeat Brooks, who spent $1.2 million; Mike Flanagan spent only $107,000 to defeat Rostenkowski, who spent $2.3 million.

The Contract as a political strategy worked like the Battle of Gettysburg. The Contract allowed Republicans to take the high ground. Each of the 10 points of the Contract had been tested in focus groups and had long had strong support among the America people. The Contract forced the Democrats to attack Republicans on their best possible defensive position. And the Republican candidates, both incumbents and challengers, were repeatedly drilled in taking hard questions on the Contract, allowing them further opportunities to get out their message. Only the weakest and least capable buckled.

Voters had a clear choice, a real contrast. For less government, vote for the Republicans and the Contract. For more government, vote for the Democrats and Bill Clinton. That choice was as stark as the choices of Nixon *versus* McGovern in 1972 and Reagan *versus* Carter in 1980. The result was a Republican congressional landslide to match the Republican Party's historic presidential landslides.

2. Incumbents As Party Builders

In addition to running an issues-based, ideological, national campaign, the second factor in the Republican victory was Republican unity and support of challengers by incumbents. Rep. Bill Paxon, the Chairman of the National Republican Congressional Committee, credits the Republican leadership for deciding to make an incumbent's support for other Republican candidates a factor in committee assignments and promotions within the Party. No longer would it be "every man for himself" on election day.

When the Republicans take the House, all incumbents were told, don't count on your seniority to guarantee you that committee chairmanship you have always wanted. We will be looking at how much money you raised for Republican challengers, how many trips you made to support other candidates, and how much of your own campaign war chest you shared with challengers going up against entrenched Democrats.

Republican members of Congress who had coasted along for years in safe districts, raising money only for themselves, taking the weekends off rather than crossing district lines to campaign for struggling challengers in a neighboring district or even in other states, suddenly found themselves energized on behalf of challengers.

Paxon's request — actually a demand for incumbents to become party builders — paid dividends. One hundred twenty-two of the 178 Republican members of the House participated in a drive that raised $3,000,000 for the National Republican Congressional Committee war chest and $3,000,000 directly for Republican challenger candidates. Bill Archer of Texas, with his eyes firmly fixed on the chairmanship of the Ways and Means Committee, reportedly raised $500,000 for other Republicans. (He got the job.) Tom DeLay of Texas, Bill McCollum of Florida, and Bob Walker of Pennsylvania all raised money and traveled extensively for other candidates as part of their campaigns for the job of Republican Whip — the party's chief vote counter in the House. McCollum not only raised money for other candidates, but also helped bankroll a $35,000 independent expenditure campaign against Speaker Foley of Washington. (DeLay won the job in December, and Republicans credited his strong support for challenger candidates as giving him the edge.)

Republican governors also helped their fellow Republicans in other states. Bill Weld of Massachusetts, John Engler of Michigan, and Christine Todd Whitman of New Jersey all helped Republican challengers in Maryland, New York, Connecticut, and Arizona by sending letters endorsing their tax cut proposals to give greater visibility to the challenger candidates and their tax-cut programs. Whitman had been the recipient of similar cross-border support from some of those same Republican governors in her 1993 victory.

3. Role of Coalitions

The third factor contributing to the 1994 win was the strong support of the entire Republican coalition: small businesses, taxpayer groups, the term limits movement, gun owners, and the supporters of traditional family values such as the Christian Coalition. In fact, polling showed that the two groups most likely to vote in 1994 were households with more than one gun in the home and evangelical

Christians.   Both had found themselves targets of the Clinton administration.   The National Rifle Association, Gun Owners of America, and the Christian Coalition worked hard to get their voters out.   Their efforts were bolstered by the Clinton Administration's determination to threaten gun owners and insult Christians.   Anger over Clinton's passage of gun control was a key factor in defeating both Speaker Tom Foley and Judiciary Chairman Jack Brooks and in winning the Senate seats in Oklahoma and Pennsylvania.   All told, according to its president, Wayne LaPierre, the NRA endorsed 276 House and Senate candidates, and 221 of them won.

The Christian Coalition, led by the Reverend Pat Robertson and directed by Ralph Reed, distributed 33 million voter guides just before election day.   Exit polling showed that religious conservatives made up 33 percent of the vote and that their vote went 69 percent for the Republican candidates for the House, 69 percent for Republican candidates for the Senate and 71 percent for Republican governors.   Traditional values conservatives were rewarded with the addition of 45 pro-life/pro-family House members, eight Senators, and seven governors.   The Democrat Party's efforts to stigmatize evangelical and conservative Catholic voters did not work.   In fact, when asked in post-election polls, "Which of the following organizations represents your beliefs all or most of the time?" 32 percent of Americans identified the Republican Party.   The Christian Coalition and the Democrat Party roughly tied, at 17 and 19 percent respectively.

The term limits issue and activists also helped the Republican candidates.   Pro-term limit groups spent more than $1.5 million in independent issue-oriented ads.   Some of those ads reminded Washington State voters that the Democrat Party was leading the fight against term limits and that Speaker Foley was suing the taxpayers of Washington to overturn their pro-term limit vote of 1992.   Six

Democrat congressmen lost in Washington State — the largest one-state turnover in the nation.

A new component in the conservative coalition is the cyberjockeys, those computer technocrats who surf the Internet and operate in cyberspace. The conservative nature of the majority of computer nuts is well known, but this may have been the first time they have ventured into electoral politics. Richard and Mary Hartman, a husband and wife team from Spokane, Washington, posted a complaint about their representative on the Internet and were astounded at the response. The fact that Speaker of the House Tom Foley was their congressman made a difference, of course, but the result was the creation of a national organization to De-Foley-ate Congress (DF8).

The Hartmans hooked up with "Lobo Azul", otherwise known as Jim Bohan, The Blue Wolf of the South Texas Plains, to spread information about the Speaker, collect money (very little), compose anti-Foley ads, and generally "nationalize" that House race. Bohan acted as a clearing house for information posted on his Blue Wolf Network. The result was the narrow defeat of the first sitting Speaker in a hundred years. Foley had enormous resources (he was #1 in campaign contributions from political action committees with $1.2 million, and his total spending was twice that), but he could not overcome his identification with the national Democrat Party, an identification advanced through the latest technology.

With a Speaker's scalp hanging from their belts, the cyber-pols are now monitoring the performance of House Republicans in passing the Contract with America.

4. The Tax Issue

Fourth, the tax issue returned as a powerful winning issue for Republicans after being fumbled by George Bush with his 1990 tax hike. Bill Clinton's massive $241 billion tax increase over five years and his campaign to enact an additional new tax called a BTU tax on the use of energy by Americans reminded all America that Bill Clinton's party was the tax and spend party. Republicans redeemed themselves from the 1990 Bush betrayal by unanimously voting against the Clinton tax hike in the 1993 budget. Not a single Republican in the Senate or House voted for the tax hike.

The tax issue had returned with a vengeance in the race for governor of New Jersey in 1993. Christine Todd Whitman, who had held only local office before nearly defeating Senator Bill Bradley in 1990, challenged Governor Jim Florio. Florio had said in his 1989 campaign that he would not raise taxes. He had then proceeded to push through the largest tax increase in state history — even raising taxes on toilet paper. James Carville, the political consultant who had helped manage the Bill Clinton presidential campaign, returned to New Jersey to work for Florio. Carville announced that he would kill the Republican tax-cut issue once and for all. He believed that Florio could promise not to raise taxes and then turn around and pass a massive tax hike. Yes, the voters would be outraged, but if some of the new money could be used to buy enough votes, and if over time voter rage cooled sufficiently, then Florio could be re-elected. And if Florio could be re-elected, then certainly Bill Clinton could be forgiven his 1993 tax hike when re-election time rolled around. Florio's re-election would prove to all Democrat governors and U.S. senators and representatives that it was safe to raise taxes early in their terms; voters would have forgiven, forgotten, or been paid off before the next election. Carville still believed in the old Rooseveltian model of "tax and tax, spend and spend, elect and elect". The 1993 New Jersey gubernatorial election would prove that the model still worked.

Certainly Christine Todd Whitman did her part to make Florio's re-election a possibility and Carville's job easy. With only a month to go, Ms. Whitman was 20 points down in the polls because she had moved to Florio's left on crime and welfare. Florio supported a New Jersey law that cut off additional welfare benefits to women on welfare who have a third child. Ms. Whitman criticized this rather modest and popular welfare restriction. Whitman then called for "weakening" a law against drunk driving. She proposed to allow those convicted to drive solely for the purpose of getting to and from work. Though this is actually a reasonable position, it sounded sinister and "soft on crime" by the time Florio's ad men got through with it.

Whitman turned her campaign around with the help of *Forbes* magazine CEO Steve Forbes and economist Larry Kudlow, who advised her to make a bold proposal for a one-third cut in the New Jersey income tax over a three-year period. She spelled out spending reductions to match the tax cuts and her poll numbers rose slowly, enough for her to win in a photo finish.

The New Jersey lesson was learned by Republicans running for governor in 1994. Arizona's Fife Symington, down in the polls, announced that if re-elected in 1994, his platform would be to eliminate the state income tax over four years. He put forward a spending restraint and economic growth plan to back it up and won in a come-from-behind victory. In New York, George Pataki, who had won his state senate seat by defeating an incumbent Republican who had taken the "no-tax-increase" pledge and broken it, received the GOP nomination despite being virtually unknown statewide. Pataki ran an aggressive campaign calling for a 25 percent cut in the state income tax and overcame the tremendous power of incumbent Mario Cuomo's fundraising machine in a Democrat-leaning state. In Connecticut, John Rowland, a former congressman, won his race for the governorship with his campaign pledge to eliminate the income tax imposed by former Republican (now Independent) Lowell Weicker. In Maryland, Ellen Sauerbrey kicked off her campaign with a call for a 25 percent cut in the state income tax. With that as a platform, she overcame her lack of campaign funding and her low name recognition to battle the heavily favored Parris Glendening to a dead heat. The closeness of this race and questionable ballots in Baltimore will leave Glendening's win always in doubt.

The powerful tax issue, first introduced to the national Republican Party by Rep. Jack Kemp in the late 1970's and embraced by Ronald Reagan in the 1980 presidential campaign, was temporarily lost by Republicans as a result of the Bush Administration's 1990 tax hike. It was recaptured as a result of Clinton's rapacity for higher taxes (and Republican unanimity in opposing them) and confirmed by Christine Todd Whitman's victory in 1993 and the sweep of Republican gubernatorial victories in 1994.

5. Momentum

The fifth factor in the 1994 November victory was momentum from the string of Republican victories in 1993 and the two special elections in 1994 for House seats in Oklahoma and Kentucky.

When Republican Kay Bailey Hutchison won the June 5, 1993 special election in Texas to replace Senator Lloyd Bentsen, who had left to become Bill Clinton's Secretary of the Treasury, it sent a strong signal that Bill Clinton's administration was not moving the Democrat vote beyond its base. In other 1993 elections, Republicans won the governorships of Virginia and New Jersey and the mayoral races in New York City and Los Angeles. These victories were important in and of themselves in building the Republican Party. Control of the nation's two largest cities is particularly important in cutting down on vote fraud in future elections for governor and U.S. senator in each state. Republican election experts in New York believe that proper policing of the polls in that city will prevent 80,000 stolen votes each election cycle. This is a tremendous savings for Republican statewide candidates, who will no longer have to spend money for advertising and get-out-the-vote efforts in the suburbs and upstate New York to overcome an 80,000 vote deficit in the city.

The resignation of Rep. Glenn English of Oklahoma to run the National Rural Electric Cooperative Association and the death of Rep. William Natcher of Kentucky in early 1994 provided two more opportunities for Republican victories in special elections. Republicans made the most of them, winning both seats in a preview of the Border State gains to come in the November general elections.

6. The Edge to Good Candidates

The sixth factor is candidate recruitment and training. In the contest for the U.S. House of Representatives, the 1993 Republican victories and the seven Democrat elected officials who switched parties that year were doubly important because they came during the 1994 candidate recruitment season. Good news for Republicans encourages stronger candidates to run challenger campaigns. It is a real sacrifice for an individual to leave a job for a year or more and spend a tremendous amount of time away from the family to take what is historically a very big gamble — that he or she can overcome the fundraising and other incumbent advantages of the Democrat in office. The 1993 election victories brought forward, in National Republican Congressional Committee (NRCC) Chairman Bill Paxon's view, "one of the best fields of candidates in recent history."

The Republican National Committee and the sister Republican House and Senate campaign committees have stressed training and education of candidates and campaign staff. Joe Gaylord, Norm Cummings, Ed Brookover, and Barry Hutchinson have designed and led campaign training seminars ranging from a single afternoon to three months in length.

In 1994 alone, the Political Education division of the RNC, run by Evelyn McPhail, conducted campaign training for almost 6,000 candidates, campaign staff, and volunteers in 43 states. More than

150 campaign managers in 1994 took Joe Gaylord's famed Campaign Management College, which lasts five days.

RNC vice-chairman Jeanie Austin organized four "Women Who Win" seminars for women candidates. As a result, Republican women did well in 1994, with a record number taking seats in the House in the 104th Congress.

7. A Changing House of Representatives

Lastly, the strong field of candidates in 1994 coincided with record numbers of Democrat incumbents retiring to produce a strong Republican year. This result contrasted with two previous elections in which Republicans had high hopes of winning many House seats: 1982 and 1984. In 1982, the Republican candidates were strong, as the successes of the 1980 election encouraged good candidates to take the plunge. However, 1982 was a recession year and also the first election year for the new congressional districts gerrymandered by the Democrats after the 1980 census. That gerrymandering cost Republicans 17 seats across the nation. In 1984, the opposite occurred: the low rate of success in 1982 was discouraging, and the GOP was caught without its best candidates when 1984 turned out to be a very strong year, as a result of the Reagan landslide. In 1996, after two years in the minority and the prospect of sharing the ballot with Bill Clinton, a large number of Democrat incumbents may choose the better part of valor, fold their tents and quietly steal away.

WHY 1994 WAS A "PERMANENT" REVOLUTION

The Republican victory in November 1994 was large, nationwide and at all levels of government. It was driven by a desire for smaller government. There are **six reasons** to believe this victory signals a long period of Republican political and ideological dominance:

1. Voting Patterns

First, the Republican Party will most likely increase its majority in the House of Representatives in 1996. Looking at the voting patterns of key districts and the closeness of the 1994 races, there were 43 Democrats elected with less than 55 percent of the vote in 1994 (see table on next page), and 42 Republicans (see table on page 26). Moreover, fully 35 of these Democrats won in districts that were won by George Bush in 1988, the last two-party presidential election. Only nine Republicans who won in 1994 with less than 55 percent of the vote represent districts lost by Bush in 1988.

In addition, as the table on page 26 shows, 18 Democrats were re-elected by double-digit margins in 1994, but from districts which are strongly Republican: Bush carried each of them in 1992, and with a few exceptions, by 56% or more of the vote in 1988.

DEMOCRAT WINS IN CLOSE RACES			
State & District	Name	'94 %	Margin
Alabama 5	*Cramer*	50.5	1.0
Arkansas 1	*Lambert*	53.6	7.2
California 3	*Fazio*	48.8	1.8
California 17	*Farr*	51.7	6.7
California 24	*Beilenson*	49.3	1.9
California 36	*Harman*	47.7	0
California 42	*Brown*	51.1	2.2
Connecticut 2	*Gejdenso*	42.5	0
Florida 11	*Gibbons*	51.6	3.2
Illinois 3	*Lipinski*	54.0	8.0
Illinois 17	*Evans*	54.5	9.0
Illinois 20	*Durbin*	54.8	9.6
Indiana 9	*Hamilton*	51.9	3.8
Indiana 10	*Jacobs*	53.4	6.8
Kentucky 3	Ward	44.4	.3
Maine	Baldacci	45.7	5.0
Michigan 9	Kildee	51.2	4.1
Michigan 12	*Levin*	52.0	5.4
Michigan 13	Rivers	51.9	6.8
Minnesota 2	*Minge*	51.8	6.5
Minnesota 6	Luther	50.1	0.2
Minnesota 7	*Peterson*	51.3	2.6

DEMOCRAT WINS IN CLOSE RACES			
State & District	Name	'94 %	Margin
Missouri 9	*Volkmer*	50.7	5.9
Montana AL	*Williams*	48.6	6.4
New York 26	*Hinchey*	49.1	.6
No. Carolina 7	*Rose*	51.7	3.4
No. Carolina 8	*Hefner*	52.4	4.8
No. Dakota AL	*Pomeroy*	52.3	7.3
Ohio 13	*Brown*	49.1	3.6
Ohio 14	Sawyer	51.9	3.8
Oregon 1	*Furse*	48.2	.2
Pennsylvania 15	*McHale*	47.7	.2
Pennsylvania 18	Doyle	54.8	9.6
Pennsylvania 20	Mascara	53.2	6.4
So. Carolina 5	*Spratt*	52.3	4.6
Tennessee 6	*Gordon*	50.6	1.2
Texas 5	*Bryant*	49.8	2.2
Texas 17	*Stenholm*	53.7	7.4
Texas 25	Bentsen	52.3	7.3
Vermont AL	*Sanders*	50.1	3.5
Virginia 5	*Payne*	53.3	6.6
Wisconsin 4	*Kleczka*	53.9	9.3
Wisconsin 7	*Obey*	54.3	8.6

Incumbent seats in *italics*; **bold** shows Bush '88 district loss.
Columns show winning vote percentage and margin of victor

These are districts where Republicans can win; however, many of these Democrats vote conservatively and have strong personal ties to district voters. Beating them in 1996 will require good, well-financed Republican candidates. In any event, six of these 18 are over 60 (their average age is 60.2), and history suggests that when they retire they will be replaced by Republicans.

STRONG DEMOCRATS, REPUBLICAN DISTRICTS				
District	Name (Age)	'94 Margin	'92 Margin	Bush '88 %
Alabama 3	Browder (52)	28	23	62
Alabama 4	Bevill (73)	Unopp.	40	56
Georgia 9	Deal (52)	16	18	70
Indiana 3	Roemer (38)	10	14	58
Kentucky 6	Baesler (53)	18	22	58
Michigan 10	Bonior (49)	24	9	61
Mississippi 3	Montgomery (74)	36	57	67
Mississippi 4	Parker (45)	36	44	61
Mississippi 5	Taylor (41)	20	28	71
Missouri 4	Skelton (63)	36	40	59
Pennsylvania 6	Holden (37)	14	4	61
So. Dakota AL	Johnson (48)	23	42	53
Texas 4	Hall (71)	19	20	63
Texas 11	Edwards (43)	18	34	57
Texas 14	Laughlin (53)	12	41	53
Utah 3	Orton (46)	19	22	68
Virginia 2	Pickett (64)	18	12	65
Virginia 4	Sisisky (67)	24	36	60

2. "The Mother's Milk of Politics"

Second, the above analysis of how many Republicans and Democrats are vulnerable in 1996 does not take into account the fact that the Democrat Party's loss of committee and subcommittee chairmanships radically changes the balance of power in fundraising. The Clinton administration and leading Democrat chairmen squeezed millions out of corporate America for the 1994 elections. Now, stripped of their majorities in both houses, the Democrats cannot continue the strategy of extorting campaign cash from businesses terrified of what could be dropped into the hidden recesses of a 1,300 page tax or regulatory bill. This strategy was perfected by former House Democrat Whip Tony Coelho, now a senior adviser to the Democrat Party.

How fierce a fundraiser will former chairman of the Commerce Committee John Dingell (D-MI) be now that he cannot threaten CEO's, businesses and whole industries? Or former terror of the telecommunications industry Ed Markey (D-MA)? True, Clinton can abuse the powers of the federal regulatory agencies as fundraising tools, but a Republican Congress will have the subpoena power and the power of the purse to defund abusive agencies.

No longer can Democrat congressmen carry "juice" bills in their pockets, threatening to introduce punitive legislation if corporate America doesn't pay them off in campaign contributions. *Honest Graft*, an entire book written by former *Wall Street Journal* reporter Brooks Jackson, highlights examples of how the Democrats have played "hardball politics" in their fundraising. Such politics frequently falls under the legal definition of extortion, or at best the solicitation of bribes.

At the state level, control of governorships is central to a party's ability to fundraise. It is no coincidence that several of the successful Democrat primary presidential candidates — Dukakis in 1988 and Clinton in 1992 — have been sitting governors, because they have a tremendous fundraising advantage in being able to target all those who benefit from government contracts.

3. Redistricting

Third, the loss of 481 state legislators and control of 18 state legislative chambers will weaken the Democrat Party in 1996 and beyond because redistricting can no longer be used to cluster all Republican voters into a handful of districts and spread out the Democrat votes to assure narrow but predictable Democrat victories in more seats. Louisiana has already redistricted, and court challenges to congressional districts in Texas and North Carolina may force redistricting. A half dozen other states, including Pennsylvania, Illinois, New York, and California may redistrict as soon as 1995. Kentucky may have to re-draw its state legislative districts. All states will redistrict for federal and state offices in 2000.

4. The Farm Team

Fourth, the loss of so many state legislative seats reduces the Democrat farm team from which stronger candidates for Congress can emerge in 1996 and beyond, and at the same time dramatically increases the potential Republican field.

5. An Anti-Government Tide

Fifth, the clarity of the ideological defeat for the Democrats is increased when one looks not only at the wins and losses of candidates, but also at the successes and near-successes of initiatives and referendum questions placed on the 1994 ballot by citizens. Voters made their anti-government message clear in voting for term limits, tax limitation, victims rights and anti-crime initiatives.

● Term limits of three terms for U.S. House members and two terms for U.S. Senators passed in seven states: Colorado, Maine, Nebraska, Idaho, Oklahoma, Nevada, and Alaska, and in Washington, D.C. Massachusetts passed a four-term limit for U.S. House members. A term limits measure was defeated in Utah only because it exempted all present politicians and because a congressional candidate stuck a provision for run-off elections onto it. (Utah already has a statutory term limit.) This brings the number of states with term limits to 22, covering 40 percent of the House of Representatives, 44 percent of the Senate and 40 percent of the nation's population.

In addition, more than 250 cities, towns and counties have imposed term limits on their local officials.

● On the tax front, Ohio voters repealed recently-enacted taxes on soft drinks. For the fifth time, Massachusetts voters rejected an attempt to impose a graduated income tax to replace their present flat tax of 5.95 percent. Colorado voters rejected an increased tax on cigarettes by a margin of 62 to 38. California voters rejected a gasoline tax to fund mass transit by a margin of 80 to 20, and delivered the *coup de grâce* to advocates of government-run health care by voting 73.4 percent to 26.6 percent to reject a single-payer plan paid for by higher taxes on tobacco and businesses. Nevada voted 78 to 22 percent to adopt a constitutional requirement that any tax increase in the future must be passed by greater than a two-thirds margin of the legislature. Montana voters narrowly failed to place such a supermajority requirement for tax increases into their constitution, and taxpayer groups there have already begun organizing for the 1996 ballot.

● Even Massachusetts, once tarred as "Taxachusetts" for Dukakis's constant tax increases and believed hopelessly liberal since 1972 (when it was the only state to vote for George McGovern), cast a vote for individual liberty by abolishing rent control in the state (51-49) and kicked the nanny state in the shins by voting to end the blue laws that made it a crime for a store owner to open on Sunday mornings and state holidays.

Across America voters voted to toughen penalties against violent crime, reduce the legal loopholes available to murderers, protect the rights of victims of crime, and strengthen the rights of law-abiding gun owners.

• In Georgia, voters voted 81-19 to establish a "Two-Strikes" amendment, which sets mandatory minimum sentences for first-time violent offenders and life without parole for second-time violent offenders.

• Wyoming voted 68-32 to require the legislature to create a sentence of life imprisonment without parole for people convicted of serious crimes.

• California passed "Three Strikes and You're Out", a state constitutional amendment pushed by Mike Reynolds, whose daughter was murdered, and by U.S. Senate candidate Michael Huffington, a Republican politician who joined the tough-on-crime measure's board before it became popular in the wake of the Polly Klaas knifing in the spring of 1994. Three Strikes passed by a strong 71.9 to 28.1 percent.

•Colorado toughened its bail requirements for felons by a margin of 77 to 23 percent.

•Ohio, Idaho and Alaska voted to enact certain "victims' rights" measures granting victims standing at various times during a trial, sentencing and parole hearings, so that judges and jurors can be reminded of the nature of the criminals. These votes bring the number of states with such victim's rights amendments to nine.

• Alaska voted by a 72.7 to 27.3 percent vote margin to amend its state constitution to prohibit any attempts to limit a person's right to own guns.

Even where conservative initiatives were defeated, the seeds of the next fight were planted.

- Taxpayer groups will return in Oregon and Missouri, where poorly-drafted measures to require a vote of the people to raise taxes were defeated. A flood of tax dollars was spent against both measures.
- Voters in Florida voted in November 1994 to forbid the state courts from interfering in the next drive for tax limitation that will come to the ballot in November of 1996. In the past, Democrat-appointed judges have ruled that an initiative limiting "taxes" (plural) violate the state's "single subject" rule.

6. The Democrat Bourbons

The final reason to believe that the Republican capture of the House is likely to last for forty rather than four years is that Bill Clinton, the Democrat Party, and the entire Establishment have learned nothing from their defeat November 8th. Their first reaction was to deny the polling data that showed from mid-summer at the latest that a Republican landslide was coming. They then explained that the coming cataclysm was an undifferentiated primal scream of anger against Washington and all incumbents. This excuse holds no water, as not a single Republican incumbent House member, senator or governor lost the election. Thirty-five Democrat House members, two Democrat senators, and nine Democrat governors did lose. And if the public was only anti-Washington, why did the Republican victory sweep out so many Democrat governors, attorneys-general, state legislators, and local office holders?

The explanation/excuse presented by the president after the election was that the American people were so frustrated by Congress's refusal to pass his tax on energy, his government takeover of health care, and his $16 billion stimulus package to spread pork barrel spending throughout big cities that they paradoxically rose up as one and elected a Republican leadership which had fought *against* all these Clinton initiatives!

Only those on the White House payroll bought this nonsensical line. By the time of the Republican inaugural of Gingrich and Dole, Clinton had settled into comfortable denial, calling the election an "aberration" and reiterating his belief in big government. Ted Kennedy, re-elected in Massachusetts over a political neophyte of uncertain political convictions, weighed in with the advice that Democrats should stick to the principles that had just cost them the rest of the nation.

Establishment Washington is in shock and disbelief. The Afrikaaners in South Africa turned over power to Nelson Mandela with more grace and dignity. Sullen, confused, and lashing out at an American people they don't understand, the Democrat minority walks the halls of Congress.

Outside of Washington — outside the Beltway — people are not asking why the Democrats lost, but why it took a people hostile to big government so long to reject the party of big government. It is a historic coincidence that the day America awoke to find the Democrat Party's grip on Washington and America broken was November 9, 1994, exactly five years to the day after the Berlin Wall was first opened. Americans carried the burden of fighting Soviet imperialism for almost fifty years. This defense requirement called for an historically large federal government and commandeered the time, energy and finances of the American people. Liberated five years ago from the fight against foreign statism, Americans turned finally to the task of reducing the size, scope, and power of our own imperial city.

And on the first Tuesday after the first Monday in November, the walls of Washington were breached.

CHAPTER TWO

THE REPUBLICAN COALITION

The Republican Party is a coalition of individuals who want to be left alone. It is growing every day.

Hiding the True Cost of Government

As the federal and state governments have increased in size, power, and cost over the past 40 years, the number of Americans whose lives have been damaged and restricted by runaway government, taxes, and new regulations has increased dramatically. Despite the best efforts of politicians and bureaucrats to hide the ever-growing tax burden and costs of regulation, Americans are increasingly aware of both.

The growth of government was accomplished by the politicians through a deliberate strategy of concentrating benefits and spreading costs. Let me illustrate:

The United States has a population of about 260 million people. If the government takes $1 from each of them, no one will miss it, especially if the politicians tell them it is for a worthy cause, such as "aid to the arts". Washington can then parcel out that $260 million to its friends.

THE REPUBLICAN COALITION: A Partial List

● **Small businessmen** who are harassed and damaged by government regulation and taxes ● **Homeowners** threatened by rising property taxes ● **The self-employed** who face regulations and taxes written for large companies with tax accountants and lawyers ● **Property owners** threatened with expropriation by environmental law ● **Parents** who oppose efforts by politicians to hand out condoms to their children in public school ● **Home schoolers** who do not want the politicians who have destroyed public education to extend their regulations and bright ideas to their children in their homes ● **Parents** who send their children at their own expense to private schools in order to flee the failed government schools they are still forced to pay for ● **Gun owners** who resent politicians who will not execute criminals or imprison repeat felons but instead decide it is easier to regulate law-abiding citizens and violate their Second Amendment rights ● **Taxpayers** ● **Computer users** who oppose the "clipper chip" that would allow the politicians to eavesdrop on everyone's computer communication ● **Evangelical Christians, conservative Catholics and Orthodox Jews** who are insulted by a government that takes their money in taxes and then proclaims that anything paid for with "government" — no longer "taxpayer" — money cannot be tainted by religious belief or values ● **Believers** who find it wrong to have their money forcibly taken to pay for such works of art as "Piss Christ" — a jar of urine with a crucifix in it ● **Workers** whose sense of justice is offended and whose careers are damaged by a government policy of racialism that includes "affirmative action," quotas, and set-asides for government programs where contracts are awarded not on merit but on the basis of race, sex or some other government-determined preference ● **Younger Americans** who cannot afford to save for their retirement because of Social Security taxes taken from their paychecks to pay for those already retired ● **Veterans** and those now serving in **America's armed forces** who resent Bill Clinton and the Democrat Party's undisguised "loathing" of their profession and sacrifices ●

Chapter Two

If the politicians give $100,000 to each of 2,600 favorites, they will have created a strong lobby for keeping that program going. And since it is costing each citizen only $1 a year, it is not worth the trouble for any single American to send a letter — which now costs 32 cents — to his representative to demand an end to it. It is certainly not worth the cost of a phone call. But for the 2,600 beneficiaries, defending this "worthy program of national importance" is a full-time project. They will be willing to fly to Washington to personally meet with their elected representatives. Who knows, they might each, in return for their $100,000, be willing to give back $1,000 in campaign contributions to a representative who promises to continue to vote for such a program.

At the end of the year, Members of Congress will have heard from, and received checks from, 2,600 happy constituents who feel this program is very important to the nation. The same Members of Congress will have heard not a word against this program from taxpayers. The 2,600 recipients will form an association and set up an office in Washington to make it easier to communicate with their Congress. They will have a newsletter. They will hire a press secretary so that Dan Rather and Connie Chung can receive regular updates on the value of this federal initiative. Mr. Rather will be invited to speak to this association's annual meeting. He may even receive an honorarium — which will not bias CBS's evenhanded coverage of the issues, of course. At dinner parties in Georgetown, sophisticated columnists and news producers will share cocktails with the beneficiaries and their trade association representatives. No representative of the taxpayers will be at these dinner parties to ask annoying questions.

This strategy worked reasonably well when there was only a handful of such programs. Five such programs would only cost every American five bucks each. A hundred programs of this size would boost every American's taxes one hundred dollars — still not enough

35

to make a rational taxpayer devote a great deal of time to thinking about this petty larceny. And certainly not worth a plane trip to Washington to complain.

But by 1994, the federal government was spending a trillion and a half dollars each year. This means that more than twenty percent of the nation's economic output is being taken by the federal government annually. Another 17 percent is taken and spent by state and local governments. The Tax Foundation calculates that the average American works until May 3 to pay taxes for all this good government. Every single dollar an American earns in January, February, March, April, and the first three days of May goes to pay for government.

Today, Americans spend on taxes (that is, they have taken from them) more than they spend on food, shelter, and clothes combined.

THE TAXPAYERS RESPOND

As this burden grew, taxpayers began to organize in self-defense. In 1969, James Dale Davidson formed the National Taxpayers Union to lobby *for* taxpayers and *against* the thousands of lobbying groups defending existing "programs" and pushing for more spending. Since that time, hundreds of taxpayer groups have sprung up around the nation. In 1978, Howard Jarvis and Paul Gann used California's initiative process to place Proposition 13 on the statewide ballot. Prop 13 was a state constitutional amendment to cut property taxes roughly in half and to require that any future tax hikes in California receive a two-thirds vote of the legislature rather than a simple majority. Proposition 13 brought taxes down and made it harder to raise them.

Prop 13 was violently opposed by the Democrat governor Jerry Brown and by the entire Establishment. Dozens of major corporations contributed to defeating Prop 13; none supported Jarvis and Gann.

Still, the property tax burden had become so great that Prop 13 passed, 65 percent to 33 percent.

Inspired by this victory, other states began to organize. In Massachusetts, Citizens for Limited Taxation placed an initiative on the 1980 ballot to cut property taxes in half (to 2½ percent of assessed valuation) and to forbid the state from passing unfunded mandates on to local government. "Proposition 2½" passed in the Commonwealth of "Taxachusetts" in a two-to-one landslide. In Idaho, activists took the language of Proposition 13, whited out California, typed in Idaho, and introduced it. It passed easily.

Since 1978, the fledgling taxpayer movement has grown. State and local taxpayer groups have placed dozens of tax reduction and tax limitation measures on the ballots of the 24 states with the initiative process. In the 26 states that still deny voters the right to put measures on the ballot, taxpayers are forced to petition state legislatures. In Iowa, one of the stronger taxpayer groups was formed by David Stanley and his wife Jean. Iowans for Tax Relief now has 50,000 members and has defeated repeated efforts to raise taxes.

Today, Americans for Tax Reform, a national taxpayer group, works with 800 state and local taxpayer groups asking candidates for federal office to take the "Taxpayer Protection Pledge". A candidate is asked to sign a pledge to oppose any and all income tax increases. In the wake of the 1994 elections, the 104th Congress opened on January 4, 1995 with eight House members and 31 senators who have taken the pledge.

The pledge is now also being circulated in many states where state and local taxpayer groups ask candidates for governor and state legislator to oppose tax increases of any kind.

Both the federal and the state Taxpayer Protection Pledge have spaces for two witnesses so that candidates for office recognize the importance of keeping the pledge. The pledge itself, of course, became a central campaign issue in 1988 when George Bush took the pledge and made the "read my lips" commitment at the New Orleans Republican Convention. When he broke the pledge with his 1990 tax increase (which cost him his re-election), he became an object lesson as to just how seriously taxpayers view the pledge. As a result, in 1993, when Clinton demanded that the House and Senate increase taxes again in his tax and budget increase program, not a single pledge-taker broke his/her word. While Clinton won his tax increase of $241 billion over five years and a spending increase of $300 billion a year by 1998, not a single Member of Congress who had taken the pledge was willing to support him. All remained true to their pledge and voted against the tax hike.

Now, with the victory of the Republicans in the House, Republican leaders from Speaker Gingrich to National Congressional Campaign Committee Chairman Bill Paxon have taken the pledge. Responding to the power of the tax issue and the organized taxpayer movement, on the first day of the 104th Congress, Republicans adopted a new rule for the House of Representatives (part of the Contract with America) that requires any income tax increase to win 60 percent of the vote in the House to pass. A simple majority of 50 percent plus one will no longer suffice. This will make it more difficult for the House to pass any tax increase, and since 43 percent of the House had signed the Taxpayer Protection Pledge at the beginning of 1995, no income tax rate increase can pass in the 104th Congress (1995-1996).

In response to the self-defense efforts of taxpayers, the spending interests have developed three counter-strategies: **First**, politicians have worked hard to hide tax increases and make them less visible. **Second**, politicians have found that passing mandates on to state and local governments forces another level of government to enact the hated taxes. And **third,** politicians have used regulations to force costs onto individuals and businesses so that they show up in higher costs of products and services — not in visible taxes.

38

Chapter Two

1. Hiding Taxes

The technique of concentrating benefits and spreading costs was discussed above. Another technique of hiding taxes combines a graduated tax system with inflation, so that taxpayers are pushed into higher and higher tax brackets, where they pay a higher proportion of their income in taxes, even though no tax increase has been enacted. During the 1960's and 1970's, politicians were even able to vote for repeated tax *cuts*, earning themselves a lot of credit with the voters, while inflation undid all the good of the cuts and more. "Bracket creep" was ended during the Reagan years, when the tax brackets were "indexed" so that they now go up to match inflation. But the repeal of indexing is constantly on the minds of the taxers in Washington.

Automatic withholding of taxes by employers also hides their impact on workers. This technique will be discussed further in Chapter Nine.

Still another temptation for revenue-hungry politicians is to use business to collect taxes instead of government. The best way to do that is through a value added tax (VAT) or a national sales tax. These options are always on the lips of politicians when "tax reform" is in the air. They will be discussed further in Chapter Four.

2. Unfunded Mandates

As resistance to taxes grew, the Washington politicians moved in the direction of "mandates". These are requirements imposed by the federal government on state and local governments and on companies and even individuals. The Clean Air Act, for example, requires enormous expenditures by local governments and companies to upgrade facilities, provide inspections, and change behavior, all without respect to the gains in air quality that will follow. The Americans with Disabilities Act of 1990 similarly requires modification of government facilities, the employment of additional personnel,

39

training in sign language for government workers, all without any money from Washington to defray the expenses.

The Resource Conservation and Recovery Act requirements might hit a rural county with $500,000 in new annual costs, to be paid for by as few as 10,000 residents; the Safe Drinking Water Act, which could cost an urban area 12¢ per tap, might cost a rural area as much as $86 per tap.

States are not shy about imposing mandates on cities and towns, either, and all levels of government seem to be willing to afflict individuals with them. The mandatory recycling laws passed so cavalierly by town councils across the country involve enormous expenditures of time and energy by families and individuals.

The Contract with America promised relief from unfunded mandates, as will be discussed in Chapter Seven.

3. Regulations and "Takings"

The third strategy for hiding the cost of government is the use of regulation and the "taking" of private property by regulation of its use. Unfunded mandates are often imposed by regulation, of course, but the regulations are often more directly destructive of individual and corporate economies.

The total cost of federal regulations today is estimated to be as much as $500 billion a year. Adding the regulatory burden to the tax burden puts the total cost of government at 52 percent of the economy. Thus, Americans for Tax Reform added the cost of regulations to the cost of taxes and found that Cost of Government Day occurred on July 10, 1994. That is, Americans are working until July 10 just to cover the tax costs and hidden regulatory costs of government. And Cost of Government Day still underestimates the cost of government, as it does not take into account many state and local regulations.

Chapter Two

One of the advantages of regulations from the point of view of Washington politicians is that the higher costs of a car or home or washing machine can be blamed on businessmen and women. Politicians can create the regulatory burden, shift it onto consumers, and then stand up as the defenders of consumers and blame nasty businessmen for higher costs. Policing this "rapacious" business community requires still more power and money in Washington, of course, to run yet more agencies, bureaucracies, and regulatory bodies. The spiral continues of government-created problems that demand yet more government to "solve" them, creating still more problems.

Yet, just as the tax burden became too obvious, too large, and too destructive of the economy, so too has the cost of government regulations. This has led to the demand of the new Republican Congress that there be a moratorium on new regulations and a further demand for a roll-back of those regulations that were held back prior to the 1994 election and dropped on the American people only after the election. Clinton knew that these 614 final and 98 proposed regulations would be unpopular, and his completely politicized regulatory agencies worked to support the Democrat Party's need to delay any discussion of the true cost of Clinton's government until after the election. Such coordination by supposedly independent regulatory bodies demonstrates the political nature of today's behemoth government. It also demonstrates that those putting out the regulations well understood that the American people do *not* want more government. If they thought for one minute that the American people wanted these regulations, they would have announced them before — not after — the election. While the politicians insist that Americans want more government "protection", bureaucrats make decisions and act as if they believe precisely the opposite. Watch what they do, not what they say.

When the tax and regulatory burden got high enough, the politicians had to look for other ways to take property and wealth from the real economy and transfer it to the government. The environmental movement provided such a mechanism. From it come such "issues" as "wetlands".

Using the legitimate concern over needless destruction of true wetlands, which are the source of much marine life, environmentalists, with help from their friends in government, have created a bureaucratic monster with arbitrary and extensive powers. Temporarily wet ground that has never seen a duck or a cattail has been declared "a wetland", and its use by its rightful owner forbidden under severe penalty of law. Property owners have been fined and imprisoned for draining mosquito breeding grounds. Unfortunately, "wetlands" is only one of a number of environmental programs which have the effect of depriving property owners of their constitutional rights.

In response to the growing size and greed of the government, taxpayers have organized at the federal and state levels, as have small businesses and property owners. Today there are more than 800 taxpayer groups and almost 1,000 property rights groups across America. Groups like the Small Business Survival Committee, headed by Karen Kerrigan, have led the fight against the regulatory and tax burden on small businesses.

DEMOCRAT MISJUDGMENT

Taxpayers, homeowners, and small businessmen form the backbone of the Republican/conservative coalition in America. The Republican Party has also had the support of social conservatives and foreign policy conservatives. "Social conservatives" include the pro-life movement and parents who oppose Washington's social experiments in the public schools.

Chapter Two

"Foreign policy conservatives" include Cuban-Americans who fled Castro's Communist dictatorship, Vietnamese-Americans who know the truth about Jane Fonda's friends and the concentration camps they ran in Southeast Asia, and refugees from Lithuania, Latvia, and Estonia and their children. In addition, many supporters of a strong and safe Israel see in American liberals' demands for American military weakness a death sentence for the Jewish homeland.

Together, this coalition of economic, social and foreign policy conservatives has given the Republican presidential candidates a solid 60 percent of the vote, election after election. The Establishment Left has fought hard and successfully over the past forty years to keep this presidential majority for conservative candidates from becoming a congressional majority that would take over the entire federal government, and to keep it from establishing itself at the state level as well.

Gerrymandering congressional districts (discussed in Chapter One) was one way to keep the growing conservative majority from taking the House of Representatives. But it was equally important to pit conservatives against each other.

In 1992, the Establishment was optimistic for two reasons: **First**, with the victory of the United States in the Cold War over the Soviet Union and the scattering of the USSR into 15 independent nations, the Establishment hoped that foreign policy conservatives would no longer be repelled by the weakness of the Democrat Party on defense and no longer attracted to the Republican Party. **Second,** the Establishment predicted that social conservatives would inevitably fight with economic conservatives. After all, they reasoned, economic conservatives want small government while social conservatives want the government to make everyone observe traditional values which means more, not less, government. Abortion in particular must divide the Rightist coalition, as enforcing a ban on abortion gets the government into people's lives, not out, as economic conservatives wish.

Neither of these events occurred, as the Reagan coalition held together and actually strengthened its cohesiveness over the past four years.

* * * * *

To begin with, the U.S. victory in the Cold War did not rob Republicans of a powerful, unifying issue, as Bill Clinton and Democrat strategists hoped.

1. Crime Replaces the Cold War as a Bedrock Issue

For half a century, the views of candidates on Soviet Communism were paramount to many, many voters. Cuban-Americans would not even listen to a candidate's position on health care if they thought he viewed Castro as a misunderstood progressive. Polish-Americans would write off candidates who did not consider Soviet occupation of their ancestral lands an American concern. The Left could not appeal to refugees from Communism's advance in Asia, Latin America, and Europe because the American liberal's faith in the good intentions of socialism and antipathy to American strength horrified voters. The Left was unwilling to recognize evil where it reared its head, and could not even ape Republicans when they simply voiced the legitimate fears and resolve of ordinary Americans.

George Bush's loss in 1992 was thus due to more than his betrayal of taxpayers with the 1990 tax increases and the regulatory explosion born of the Clean Air Act revisions and the Americans with Disabilities Act. It was also due to the collapse of the Soviet Union, which made a vote for Bill Clinton less dangerous. Clinton's corporate statism might cost the United States a few points in economic growth, but he could not lose Europe or Latin America to Soviet control the way Jimmy Carter, Walter Mondale, or Michael Dukakis might have.

It is difficult to imagine a Bill Clinton winning the presidency in any year prior to 1992. His "loathing" of the American military, his demonstrating against America's defense of South Vietnam (but not against the aggression of the Communists), his dissembling to avoid the draft, and his lack of *gravitas* in world affairs would have made Mike Dukakis astride his tank look like General George Patton.

But as the worldwide struggle against Soviet imperialism faded, another issue began to replace it in the conservative arsenal: crime. In November of 1992, five states passed initiatives that assure victims of crimes a hearing at various stages in criminal justice proceedings. The power of the crime issue was demonstrated by the overwhelming popular support for ratification. In Kansas, the amendment received 84 percent of the vote; in Illinois, 81 percent; in New Mexico, 69 percent; in Colorado, 80 percent; and in Missouri, 85 percent.

In 1990, Oregon passed, with 74 percent support, an anti-crime initiative promoted by former Rep. Denny Smith that requires a criminal convicted of a second violent offense to serve the entire sentence — no parole, no probation.

Apart from confounding liberals who hoped conservatives had lost their anti-Communist trump card, the crime issue offers **five important opportunities** to the conservative movement and to a Republican Party smart enough to act quickly.

First, crime is a real issue, not a symbolic one. It affects millions of Americans. Every year nearly 5 million people are victims of violent crime: murder, rape, robbery, or assault. Another 19 million are victims of property crimes: arson, burglary, or theft. Just as Polish-Americans and Cuban-Americans had first-hand knowledge of Soviet imperialism that made liberal platitudes about negotiations and peace talks ring hollow, so too have millions of Americans come to know that our present judicial system serves lawyers, bureaucrats, and criminals rather than the victims and their families.

Second, crime is an issue on which the Democrat Party is institutionally incapable of following — or even mimicking — the opinions of the American public. Just as the far Left hobbled efforts within the Democrat Party to take a sensible view of the Soviet threat, so does the criminal rights lobby make it impossible for the national Democrat Party to take a sensible stand on stiff sentencing and more prisons. The financial reports from the Clinton campaign contain pages of contributions from defense lawyers and trial lawyers. It is indicative that Janet Reno, Clinton's Attorney General, devoted more public comment to the rights of criminals than to defending the legitimate rights of crime victims and the community at large.

Third, the crime issue gives the Republican Party a tremendous opportunity to reach out to minority communities that have traditionally voted Democrat. Black Americans are disproportionately victims of violent and property crimes, and they cannot look to Democrats or the traditional black leadership for a serious attack on crime and criminals. Crime allows Republicans to speak directly to the real experiences and needs of black Americans in cities where Democrats refuse to protect their lives and property. Crime is also an issue that concerns women sufficiently to make them a fast-growing market for gun sales. Arresting, convicting, and incarcerating criminals has become a *true* "women's issue". And just as the issues of abortion, special privileges for homosexuals, and prayer in school allow Republican candidates to reach deep into the New Deal coalition, crime speaks to many traditional Democrats who find few modern Democrat leaders willing to take criminals off the streets.

Fourth, the crime issue will increase in importance for Republicans in the next two years because its battles will be fought largely in the states, where Clinton has no veto. Victories can be won through the initiative process in the those states with initiative and referendum laws. State legislators can be targeted for support or defeat based on their positions on crime.

Republicans can take advantage of national organizations that already exist. CrimeStrike, affiliated with the National Rifle Association, is working with hundreds of state and local groups to enact victims' rights constitutional amendments and tougher sentencing laws. It has already had great success in getting legislation enacted and in using the press to highlight efforts to release career criminals prematurely. The Safe Streets Alliance, meanwhile, was founded by activist Jim Wooten to enact truth-in-sentencing laws. Today, criminals serve an average of 27 percent of the sentences imposed on them. The Safe Streets Alliance model sentencing act reads: "Notwithstanding any other provision in state law a convicted felon shall serve at least 85 percent of the sentence imposed by the judge or jury, which shall hear from the defendant's victim(s) on the issue of sentencing before being eligible for...early release".

Fifth, the conservative solution to crime — putting violent offenders in prison for longer periods of time — works, is cost-effective, and is easily understood by anyone who has not graduated from Yale Law School. In a report released by the National Center for Policy Analysis, Texas A&M economist Morgan Reynolds points out that crime has increased as the expected costs of committing crimes has fallen. Today, for a burglar, for example, the chance of arrest is 7 percent. If he is unlucky enough to be one of the 7 percent arrested, not to worry. Only 87 percent of arrestees are prosecuted. Of those, only 79 percent are convicted. Then only 25 percent of those convicted actually go to prison. When all these probabilities are factored in, a burglar has just a 1.2 percent chance of going to jail for any particular crime. Reynolds points out that "Once in prison, a burglar will stay there for about 13 months, but since more than 98 percent of burglaries never result in a prison sentence, the average sentence for each act of burglary is only 4.8 days".

Similar calculations yield an expected punishment rate in 1990 of 1.8 years for murder, 60.5 days for rape, and 6.7 days for arson.

For every crime, the expected punishment has declined over the decades. When punishments rise, crime falls. California increased its prison population 314 percent between 1980 and 1991, and the crime rate fell by 13 percent over that period.

A National Institute for Justice study found that putting a criminal in prison for one year costs roughly $25,000. A Rand Corporation study of 2,190 professional criminals found that the average career criminal commits 187 to 287 crimes a year. The Rand study calculated the total costs to society at $430,000 a year for every career criminal left on the street. Thus society is $405,000 better off for every career criminal kept behind bars an additional year. In December 1991, there were 823,414 convicts in state and federal prisons, and another 422,000 in local jails. Meanwhile, 530,000 were on parole and 2.7 million on probation. That is 3.2 million convicted criminals walking the streets. Thirty percent of all murders, 25 percent of all rapes and 40 percent of all robberies are committed by persons on bail, probation, or parole.

With the implosion of the Soviet Empire, the greatest external threat to American lives is the American criminal. Former Attorney General William Barr points out that more than 6,500 murders are committed each year by criminals on bail, probation, or parole. Since World War II, more people have died at the hands of criminals who should have already been in jail than died in Vietnam and Korea.

There remain two opportunities for Republicans to lose control of the crime issue.

First, Republicans cannot afford to follow the illusory path of gun control. Just as liberals sought to focus not on Russian Communism but on negotiations over the number of missiles we had, today they argue that the problem in America is not criminals but guns. The Left wishes to discuss guns because they do not wish to discuss crime.

The widespread ownership of guns is not only not a problem but also in fact, a large part of the solution to crime.

Several studies have confirmed that more than 600,000 Americans each year deter a criminal by brandishing or using a firearm. Cities that have publicly trained and armed women have seen rapes decrease. A National Institute of Justice study found that 56 percent of criminals would not attack someone they thought was armed; 39 percent of the felons had actually decided not to commit a crime because they thought the victim might be armed.

Conservatives must avoid suggesting that gun control might be even one percent of any anti-crime initiatives, for the Left will then insist on gun control first. George Bush's Budget Director Richard Darman said "some" taxes might be acceptable and ended up with a package that contained many tax hikes and increased spending and deficits. "Gun-control-too" means "gun-control-only".

Second, conservatives must call the bluff of the Left, which tries to avoid discussing the victims of crime by labeling any discussion of crime "racist". The Bush campaign fatally hurt itself in 1992 by not responding quickly to charges arising from the William Horton ads in 1988. As governor of Massachusetts, Michael Dukakis let murderers sentenced to life in prison go free on weekend furloughs. That was a very real, fair, and telling issue. Sadly, every state has several William Horton stories, stories of those released too soon who kill or rape again. If the Republicans decide to be as serious, determined, and unapologetic about locking up criminals as they were about destroying the Evil Empire, the streets of America can be liberated, and those who have built and defended the present unacceptable and dysfunctional judicial system at the state and federal levels can be swept into the dustbin of history.

Gun Control: the Democrat Party's Self-Destructive Boomerang Issue. The power of the gun issue played itself out in the 1993 and

1994 elections, demonstrating that gun owners are an important part of the growing Republican coalition.

Gun owners joined with anti-crime activists to vote Republican to punish criminals rather than law-abiding gun owners.

In a two-week period at the end of 1993, President Clinton won passage of the North American Free Trade Agreement (NAFTA), defeated the bipartisan Penny-Kasich legislation that would have mandated $90 billion in real spending reductions over a five-year period, and won passage of the "Brady Bill", which requires a five-day waiting period for handgun purchases. Afterward, Clinton's staff bragged that they could win "anything" if they focused on it for a two-week period. The White House optimism then degenerated into giddiness. Joycelyn Elders called for the legalization of drugs. White House strategists decided to postpone welfare reform (the planned feint to the right in preparation for the 1994 congressional elections) to concentrate on health care. Clinton announced his opposition to a balanced budget amendment proposed by Senator Paul Simon (D-IL) that would require a 60 percent vote of both houses of Congress to borrow money and a simple majority to raise taxes. The ideological mask of "New Democrat" was being cast aside, not only by Clinton's staffers and cabinet members, but also by the president himself.

Nowhere was the Democrat Party's hubris more evident than on gun control. As a candidate, Clinton had robbed the Republicans of the issue by soft-pedaling his support for the Brady Bill and rejecting suggestions that he supported Michael Dukakis's stated goal of disarming the civilian population. For his part, George Bush lost the gun issue in 1989 when he pushed through an executive order banning the importation of some "assault rifles". In 1992, the National Rifle Association — which had played a key support role in the GOP presidential victories of 1980, 1984, and 1988 — sat out the presidential election.

Chapter Two

Key Democrat strategists and President Clinton believed that gun control would be a political winner, and the polls seemed to support that idea.

An April 1993 Harris poll showed 89 percent of Americans supporting passage of the Brady Bill "to require a waiting period for the purchase of handguns so that the authorities can check who is buying a handgun". Harris found 82 percent of Americans supporting a proposal that all handguns be registered by the federal government. Attorney General Janet Reno was calling for federal gun registration and licensing ("just like cars").

But reading such polls literally is a mistake.

First, these numbers were not new. Asked a stand-alone question on guns, the public has always overwhelmingly supported gun control. The hitch is that people who "support gun control" in polls seldom vote on the basis of that issue; gun owners often do. In October 1988, one month before George Bush crushed Michael Dukakis, Gallup released a poll showing 91 percent of Americans supported a federal waiting period for gun purchases.

Second, such data is almost always misleading because the questions are asked in a vacuum. Frank Luntz, pollster for the Ross Perot campaign, found that 88 percent of Americans believe a citizen has the right to own a gun, 78 percent oppose a gun ban, and 83 percent believe citizens have a right to self-defense. More importantly, asked whether new gun control measures or "stricter penalties for criminals and reduced parole" would best fight crime, 75 percent of Americans favored tougher sentences and only 20 percent favored more gun control. Forty-six percent of Americans believed the Brady Bill would "not reduce gun-related crimes significantly", against only 33 percent who believed it would.

Elections in 1992 and 1993 provided a reality check on the gun control issue for those paying attention. The gun issue cost the Democrats one Senate seat and two governorships:

• In a Georgia runoff three weeks after Clinton's 1992 win, the gun issue elected Paul Coverdell over incumbent Senator Wyche Fowler. Coverdell's 17,000-vote margin is more than accounted for by the National Rifle Association's decision to mail its 90,000 Georgia members three times in support of Coverdell and then to phone each member to get them to the polls. NRA ads ran ten times a day on sixty-eight radio stations during the days leading up to the election.

• In the 1993 New Jersey governor's race, incumbent Jim Florio failed in his attempt to pillory the NRA itself for opposing his vaunted ban on so-called assault weapons. Although Florio's Republican opponent Christine Todd Whitman lost the NRA's open endorsement by backing the Brady Bill and the Florio assault weapon ban, the NRA made more than 300,000 get-out-the-vote phone calls to likely Whitman voters, and on election day Whitman won by only 27,000 votes. (It was an expensive loss for Clinton and the Democrats. The New Jersey governor is the most powerful in the nation, with roughly 4,000 political appointments. If these appointees spent only four hours a week on their own time doing political work, that would have created the equivalent of 400 full-time political activists for the 1994 and 1996 elections. This is a larger political army than the combined staff of the Republican National Committee, the National Republican Senatorial Committee, and the National Republican Congressional Committee — all deployed in one state.)

• In Virginia in 1993, Attorney General Mary Sue Terry was 19 points ahead in the gubernatorial race when her campaign began to run pro-gun control ads across the state. (Terry's gun control ads actually ran on Rush Limbaugh's radio show!) Republican candidate George Allen came out in favor of stricter sentencing and opposed parole for violent offenders. He won by 17 points.

It's a useful rule: *The crime issue always trumps the gun issue.*

Neal Knox, a member of the board of directors of the National Rifle Association, argues that eight years of Ronald Reagan and four years of George Bush, both NRA members, had lulled some gun owners into a false sense of security. "No more", he says. "Now people are waking up to the danger". But sleeping or not, the NRA is a giant. With more than 3.3 million dues-paying members — 900,000 of them added in 1994 alone — the NRA dwarfs other political organizations. The U.S. Chamber of Commerce has 215,000 members; the National Federation of Independent Business has 600,000 members; the Republican National Committee roughly 300,000. Handgun Control Inc., the leading organization supporting gun control, has 300,000 members. History should have warned Clinton, or at least congressional leaders, of the dangers of reading raw poll numbers in "support" of gun control. Two Democrat senators paid for their "yes" votes on the Gun Control Act of 1968 by losing their seats: Joe Clark of Pennsylvania in 1968 and Joseph Tydings of Maryland in 1970.

Reagan's turnaround primary victories in North Carolina and West Virginia in 1976 were aided by strong NRA mailings criticizing then-President Gerald Ford's support for handgun bans. That same year, Massachusetts gun control advocates put on the ballot Measure 5, which would have banned many handguns; it was defeated, 69 to 31 percent. The gubernatorial victories of John Dalton in Virginia in 1977 and Bob Martinez in Florida in 1986 are attributed, by the candidates themselves, to the gun issue. In 1982, a California gun-control measure on the ballot brought a flood of gun owners to the polls and helped Republican underdog George Deukmejian defeat

Democrat Tom Bradley for governor. In 1992, gun opponent Beryl Anthony, a member of the House Democrat leadership, was defeated in a Democrat primary by gun-owner activism.

Gun-control advocates point to the primary victories of Democrats Tom Andrews of Maine in 1990 and Mike Synar of Oklahoma in 1992 as proof of the power of gun control politics, although Synar *was* beaten in a 1994 primary, which undercuts their case somewhat. In any event, to these two instances of anti-gun incumbents defeating pro-gun primary challengers can be added no examples of pro-gun incumbents being defeated by primary challengers on the wings of anti-gun sentiment or resources.

One loss for gun owners did occur in Maryland, where a referendum to kill a commission set up to ban certain weapons was defeated in 1988. But it took electoral skulduggery to do it. The get-out-the vote offices of the repeal campaign were raided by the police, and the phone banks stopped on election eve in a purported effort to stop the use of "walking around money". However, the gunowner's campaign did help George Bush carry this normally Democrat state that November.

Meanwhile, state constitutional amendments have strengthened the rights of gun owners in North Dakota, Maine, West Virginia, Utah, and Nebraska. Savvy Democrat politicians understand the implications, particularly those who — like former House Speaker Tom Foley of Washington and former Senate Majority Leader George Mitchell of Maine — come from rural and gun-owning states. They may try to slow the liberal clamor for gun registration and confiscation. But they'll have to reckon with the president's willingness to get more gun control today at the expense of fewer Democrats in the House and Senate tomorrow. Speaker Foley apparently put party loyalty ahead of his understanding of this issue by supporting gun control in 1994. His loss on November 8, 1994 confirms his understanding if not his wisdom.

The Establishment Left indeed made a grave error in trying to sell "gun control" to an America that wants "criminal control". But perhaps a more serious error was its misjudgment of the effect of "traditional values" on the Republican coalition. Even the savviest of Democrat political advisers were certain that the Religious Right and its moralism would force a split in Republican ranks between "moderate" Republican women and pro-lifers, between secular libertarians and traditional-values believers.

2. The GOP Civil War That Never Happened

In fairness, George Bush's defeat on November 3, 1992 did raise real questions about the future of the Reagan coalition that had won three national victories and governed the nation for 12 years.

Had the coalition splintered? Had the "Religious Right" frightened away suburban Republicans? Was the abortion issue destroying the party by driving away young voters, women of all ages and the libertarian wing of the party? Maybe the abortion issue helped Reagan in 1980 and 1984, but now that the Supreme Court was backing away from the absolutism of its 1973 *Roe* v. *Wade* abortion decision, perhaps the pro-choicers and their checkbooks were getting as active and agitated as the pro-life vote had been in reaction to *Roe* v. *Wade*'s pronouncement.

Should the party purge Pat Robertson, evangelicals, Phyllis Schlafly and Pat Buchanan? Many commentators suggested that they were losing more votes for Republican candidates than they gained. Would the Republican presidential primary contest for 1996 be a civil war?

A sober analysis of the 1992 and 1994 elections — both candidates, initiatives and referenda — answers important questions and calms nervous conservative stomachs. The anti-tax, small government instincts of the American electorate are secure and continuing. First a look at 1992, and in particular, the Georgia Senate race between

Republican Paul Coverdell and incumbent Democrat Senator Wyche Fowler.

An ABC News exit poll on November 3, 1992 found that 55 percent of American voters wanted fewer government services and lower taxes against only 36 percent of voters who preferred more government services financed by higher taxes. Six state tax limitation and tax-cutting initiatives were approved by the voters that day. Tax hike initiatives and referenda were defeated in 10 of 11 attempts. New spending was rejected for schools, infrastructure and environmental clean-up. "Tough on Crime" initiatives passed in 6 states. In electoral contests, Republicans picked up 10 seats in the United States House of Representatives, and 155 state legislative seats (54 senate and 101 house). On election day, 60 percent of Americans identified themselves as conservatives and only 35 percent called themselves liberals.

Initial panic among the ranks was quelled, but a distant fear remained. Could Republicans find a presidential candidate and, above all, a platform in 1996 that could pass between the Scylla and Charybdis of the Christian Right and an increasingly pro-choice electorate? And, if not, who was going to tell Pat Robertson and his local counterpart in each state and county that, "while the last few years together have been great, and your votes a great help, would you please now go away and be quiet until asked to vote for candidates we select for the Party"?

Alternatively, who was going to tell the 57 House Republicans who voted to support research on aborted fetuses that their actions disqualified them from the Republican Party?

This mutual suspicion, with factions keeping their backs to the wall as they circled, wondering who was planning to purge whom, could have continued for months and even years, but the party was quickly put to a real challenge — the run-off election for Georgia's U.S. Senate seat held by Democrat Wyche Fowler and contested by Republican Paul Coverdell.

This was no drill; this was real combat!

With the Georgia seat up for grabs because neither Fowler nor Coverdell received a majority of the vote on November 3rd, the Senate partisan lineup stood at 57 Democrats and 42 Republicans. The Republican Party's ability to stop radical and non-reversible changes in labor and election laws was in jeopardy. Forty-one votes are required to sustain a filibuster and the Establishment press was hinting to Republican Senator Bob Packwood of Oregon that collaboration would be the better part of valor. Vermont's Jim Jeffords often lines up with the Democrats already. The Georgia Senate vote on November 24, 1992, exactly three weeks after Clinton carried Georgia over Bush, might well be the difference between stopping the Clinton honeymoon and watching a replay of the Lyndon Johnson/Democrat Congress creation of yet another Great Society spending explosion.

On November 3rd, Georgians had cast two million votes, with Fowler receiving 49 percent of the vote, Coverdell receiving 48 percent and Libertarian Jim Hudson receiving three percent.

Three weeks later, the runoff saw 1.2 million votes cast, with Paul Coverdell winning the election by just over 17,000 votes.

It is important to note that Georgia is an exception to the recent history of Republican successes in the South. Since Reconstruction, Georgia has never elected a Republican governor. It is the only state in the nation that has not elected a Republican governor in the last 100 years. Coverdell's election to the Senate made him only the second Republican ever elected U.S. Senator from Georgia. The first, Mack Mattingly, was elected in 1980 under rather unique circumstances: the Reagan landslide helped, as did a recent "denunciation" by the Senate of his opponent, Herman Talmadge, on ethics charges.

Talmadge's wife, who was divorcing him, provided a key piece of evidence when she announced that she had found a coat in his closet stuffed with dollar bills.

In 1992, in contrast, the runoff vote between Fowler and Coverdell followed the Clinton win in Georgia and saw both Clinton and Vice-President-elect Al Gore come into the state to campaign for the Democrat. Despite this history, on November 24, three weeks after the Bush defeat, Paul Coverdell won 50.8 percent of the vote.

How did Coverdell win in a state so inhospitable to Republican statewide candidates?

For starters, the Reagan coalition showed up firing on all cylinders. The National Right to Work Committee, with two million members nationwide, mailed their Georgia membership, highlighting the fact that Coverdell supported Right to Work laws while Fowler was a wholly-owned subsidiary of the union bosses. Newspaper ads seconded the message of the mailings. Georgia is a "Right to Work" state.

The National Rifle Association also showed up in force. The NRA mailed three times to its Georgia membership of 90,000. They also sent out 250,000 flyers to gun dealers and gun clubs so that they could share factual information on the stands of Coverdell, the friend of gun owners, and Fowler, the gun-grabber. For the last four days of the run-off, the NRA ran ads on 68 radio stations.

All Georgia members of the NRA also received bumper stickers reading "Sportsmen for Coverdell", and six campaign activists came into the state for the runoff to join 30 volunteer activists who ran a phone bank for the final six nights, calling all 90,000 Georgia NRA members.

Charlton Heston, who has championed both the Right to Work issue and gun owners' rights, flew into Georgia, his boyhood home, for a day of non-stop campaigning for Coverdell.

Chapter Two

The sustained, targeted, and professional campaigns run by the National Right to Work Committee and the National Rifle Association on behalf of Coverdell had been denied to George Bush in the general election. Bush's administration had sided with union bosses against workers in key cases and banned the importation of some so-called "assault rifles", implying that crime is caused by inanimate objects rather than by criminals.

Bush's cringing concessions to the union bosses and gun control zealots did not win him any support, money, votes, or even a kind word from those he was trying to placate. He simply convinced two parts of his natural base — those concerned about monopoly union power and gun owners — that he could not be trusted to protect them. On November 3, 1992, they had better things to do — electing U.S. Senators and Representatives, a governor, and state legislators who understood their issues. But they were there on November 24, because they had candidates with clear differences on their issues.

The small business community, the backbone of the Republican Party, was active for Coverdell. The National Federation of Independent Business (NFIB) mailed to its 17,000 Georgia members a piece that contrasted the stands of Coverdell (himself a successful small businessman) and Fowler, who never met a federal regulation or tax hike he didn't like. NFIB also established a phone tree highlighting the importance of this campaign to small businessmen. Political hacks in Washington foolishly compare the political clout of labor unions and Fortune 500 businesses. The real comparison is between the 17 million union members — many of whom are in the union because of compulsory union laws — and the 11 million small business owners in the nation who must carry the weight of every regulation, law, and tax that Congress passes in the certain knowledge that General Motors can afford "this little extra regulation or tax".

The advocates of term limits, every national taxpayer group, the Perot state organizers, and the Libertarian Party endorsed and campaigned for Coverdell.

Coverdell commanded this support as a result of his history as a low tax, small government, traditional Republican, opposed to intrusive and expensive government and willing to confront the powerful labor unions and pro-spending interests.

But what about the Religious Right?

Coverdell was also pro-choice on abortion. Very much so.

Coverdell had supported George Bush over Ronald Reagan in 1980. And Bush over Pat Robertson in 1988. And Bush over Pat Buchanan in 1992. In every case he had lined up against the stronger opponent of abortion and against the stronger proponent of traditional values.

In the 1992 primary, Coverdell defeated first, John Knox, a pro-life advocate and then, in a runoff, former U.S. Attorney Bob Barr, a pro-life candidate who had earned the support of the Right to Life movement by his service in the Reagan and Bush Administrations.

This is where the rubber hit the road. What would the Christian Coalition do about a candidate who had campaigned against their leader, Pat Robertson, in 1988? What would the pro-life forces do, faced with pro-choice Democrat Wyche Fowler and pro-choice Republican Paul Coverdell? Coverdell, while forcefully supporting *Roe* v. *Wade*, was willing to countenance some state legislation requiring parental notification and perhaps other restrictions. This was not black and white, good versus evil. It was a very nuanced difference.

Leaders of pro-life organizations, pro-family groups and traditional-values evangelicals caucused. Coverdell would not be a vote for the Human Life Amendment to ban almost all abortion — the touchstone of the electorally-active, pro-life community for almost twenty years. But Fowler would vote for the Freedom of Choice Act (FOCA), and Coverdell would not.

The Freedom of Choice Act, billed as simply "codifying" *Roe* v. *Wade*, actually goes much further. It would forbid *any* restrictions on abortion *at all*. Not for sex selection. Not to require parental notification or permission for minors. Not even five minutes before full-term delivery. Paul Coverdell favored some common-sense state restrictions and therefore would vote against FOCA. This was the critical divide. As Lenin would have said, Fowler was "objectively pro-abortion" and Coverdell "objectively pro-life".

The decision was made and the die cast for Coverdell. The Christian Coalition, the political organization formed in the wake of Pat Robertson's 1988 presidential bid, sprang into action. More than 1.2 million voter guides were printed and delivered to evangelical activists throughout Georgia. The Georgia Christian Coalition Chairman, Pat Garland, put thousands of miles on his van, personally handing out the voter guides that contrasted the positions of Coverdell and Fowler on FOCA, prayer in school, and taxes. The Christian Coalition then phone-banked 40,000 calls to get out the vote of their identified supporters. (The margin of Coverdell's victory was only 17,000 votes.)

The Committee for a Pro-Life Congress spent some $30,000 in radio advertising highlighting the difference between the candidates on the Freedom of Choice Act. Pro-lifers distributed literature. Phyllis Schlafly, the founder and leader of the Republican National Coalition for Life, the group committed to keeping the pro-life language in the GOP's national platform, mailed to pro-lifers, hitting hard on the threat posed by FOCA.

The Focus on the Family radio news program, "Family News in Focus", appeared on 54 radio stations with a special on the Coverdell/Fowler face-off. The abortion difference was emphasized.

Returning from the campaign trail, Pat Garland of the Christian Coalition reported to candidate Coverdell his county-by-county assessment of the upcoming vote. Pat Garland, who had become the leader of the Georgia Christian Coalition only two months before the general election, called each county correctly. Coverdell's victory gave the Republican Party in the Senate the key vote it needed to protect the filibuster against the worst Bill Clinton had to offer.

A moderate's moderate had been elected with the necessary, critical, enthusiastic, and cheerful support of the so-called Religious Right.

Writing in the *Atlanta Journal Constitution*, Q. Whitfield Ayres, the pollster for the Coverdell campaign said, "The Coverdell campaign showed traditional Republicans and religious conservatives could submerge their differences in the common cause of defeating a liberal Democrat. Religious conservatives who had generally supported other candidates in the primary became an important component of Mr. Coverdell's winning coalition".

"Nothing stops infighting like the prospect of victory," Ayres adds.

Paul Coverdell, who had frequently clashed with conservatives and evangelical activists over the years, speaks with great respect of Christian Coalition leaders such as Pat Garland, and calls national Executive Director Ralph Reed "a national leader who understands politics". From the trenches, Coverdell praises the "significant pragmatism" of the evangelicals who "worked against me in the primary and again in the Republican runoff". In the subsequent runoff, they made the "mature, nuanced and principled decision to support me over Fowler".

Coverdell dismisses the predictions and assertions of a division between evangelicals and moderates as "media driven" by "those who have an agenda...[I]t is hogwash".

Chapter Two

The Georgia runoff experience was exactly duplicated a few months later in Texas, when pro-choice Republican Kay Bailey Hutchison was elected to the Senate seat vacated by Lloyd Bentsen, appointed by President Clinton to be Secretary of the Treasury. Once again all elements of the Republican coalition came together, putting aside minor differences to assure an electoral victory. The election to the U.S. Senate of pro-choice Republicans in Georgia and Texas, with the help of pro-life and evangelical groups, confirms what the poll data indicate: the Religious Right is not a drag on Republican candidates.

Roger Stone, an early Reagan backer who helped form the Republican Majority Coalition (which is committed to removing the present anti-abortion plank from the Republican platform), believes the lessons of the Georgia race are very encouraging. "The great war [over abortion] everyone expects doesn't have to happen".

Stone does believe that a "perception of an abortion litmus test" in the Republican Party hurts the party, although he admits that "the economy was the driving force" in the Bush loss to Clinton — not intra-party division over the abortion issue.

Could it be that the pro-life stand in the Republican platform cost Bush and other Republicans more votes than it gained for them? After all, the platform was pro-life in 1984 and 1988, and those were two very good years for Republican candidates.

Did a faltering economy, a Bush campaign lacking the "silver bullet" of the tax issue, and a Supreme Court divided by one vote on the constitutionality of the *Roe* v. *Wade* decision of 1973 change the dynamics of the abortion issue?

Two polls say no.

First, a Wirthlin Group poll of November 13, 1992 found that only 16 percent of all voters said that abortion was one of the one or two issues that mattered most in deciding their vote. Of those 16 percent, Bush won 68 percent to Clinton's 25 percent.

Thus, 10.9 percent of voters voted for Bush and 4 percent of voters cast ballots for Clinton based on their views on abortion. This gave Bush a net gain of 6.9 percent on the abortion issue.

Second, an exit poll commissioned by the four major networks and run by Voter Research and Surveys (VRS) also found abortion cutting for Bush. VRS found 13 percent of voters listed abortion as "one of the one or two issues that mattered most" and that this 13 percent broke for Bush 55 to 36 percent. This translates to 7.2 percent of the electorate voting *for Bush* because of his pro-life stance and 4.7 percent of the voters voting *for Clinton* for his pro-choice stance (a net plus of 2.5 percent for Bush). The VRS poll also asked about the importance of family issues generally, and found a 6.5 percent advantage for Bush there.

The argument that the abortion issue hurt Bush appears to come from three sources: **First**, anecdotal evidence from friends and relatives "like my Aunt Bertha who has voted Republican since Wendell Willkie, but this time. . .". **Second**, those Republicans who have always been uncomfortable with the anti-abortion position of the rest of the party and find Bush's loss a convenient reason for reopening the debate. **Third**, media observers, like *Newsweek*'s Eleanor Clift, who are smart enough to read polls, yet Machiavellian enough to urge the Republican Party to abandon a proven vote winner.

The lesson here: Republican activists and candidates would do well to look at real-time polling data rather than listen to cheerful advice from their political enemies, who would love to see them fail.

Even when the Establishment press was willing to concede that the abortion issue cut for Bush with a narrow band of voters, it was most insistent that the overall effect of the "Religious Right" and social conservatives was negative. Exhibit A for the prosecution was the Houston Convention, pilloried as "too mean-spirited and extreme". The poll numbers tell a different story here as well.

Chapter Two

The *Washington Post* poll, commissioned on the Sunday before the convention, found George Bush trailing Bill Clinton 57 to 36 percent. Seven days later, after Ronald Reagan, Pat Buchanan, and Pat Robertson had supposedly spooked America, the Bush campaign had closed the gap by sixteen points — although Bush was still down 47 to 42 percent.

* * * * *

The Georgia and Texas special elections were welcome victories for Republicans, carrying three powerful messages that portended further good news for the 1994 elections, when the Democrats had to defend 22 Senate seats and the Republicans only 12.

First, working together, the Republican/conservative coalition of small businesses, taxpayers, pro-lifers, right to work supporters and pro-family activists can defeat the get-out-the-vote efforts of politicized black churches and labor unions.

Second, the tax issue is back and cutting for the Republicans. Paul Coverdell blanketed the state with attacks on Wyche Fowler for his vote for the 1990 budget deal that raised taxes and caused the recession. Tom Perdue, Coverdell's campaign manager (described by *Atlanta Journal* writer Dick Williams as "Atwater and Carville combined"), said the tax message was central to the campaign. Fowler tried to defend himself by pointing out that the 1990 tax hike was, after all, a Bush proposal. Coverdell, who had managed Bush's Georgia 1980 race, was not fazed, hammering relentlessly against Fowler's pro-tax vote. Democrats in the House and Senate who naively supported the 1990 tax increase in the belief that Bush's support made it "bi-partisan" and gave them the necessary cover, now find, in the post-Bush era, that they will have to take the rap alone for one of the most economically destructive votes in history. Fowler was unable to use Bush as a shield for his pro-tax vote. If George Bush was Budget Director (and architect of the 1990 Budget Deal) Dick Darman's first victim, Wyche Fowler was his second. The Senate and the House are full of more targets. It is worth remembering that Senators were still losing elections four and six years after they voted for the Panama Canal Treaties.

Third, the Coverdell election was the first where pro-life groups focussed on preventing passage of the Freedom of Choice Act (which Bill Clinton had promised to sign), rather than on an unlikely Human Life Amendment.

In the past, a candidate was accepted as pro-life only if he or she supported one of the Human Life Amendments that would outlaw almost all abortions. Today, a candidate is "objectively" pro-life if he or she will only oppose the Freedom of Choice Act as too permissive. Simply supporting parental notification or opposing abortion for sex selection or when the baby is viable puts one at odds with FOCA. Incidentally, the extreme pro-choice position, as embodied in FOCA, is supported by only 12 percent of the American people. Despite this fact, the National Organization for Women (NOW) and the National Abortion and Reproductive Rights Action League (NARRAL) *require* support for FOCA of candidates they support.

In short, a candidate favoring the Freedom of Choice Act is at odds with 88 percent of the American electorate. The scramble by liberal Republicans to rewrite the 1996 platform is unwarranted. The threat of a Bill Clinton signing FOCA changes the entire terrain upon which the abortion wars are being fought. Now, pro-lifers are willing and effective allies of many "moderate" Republicans who have always been "pro-choice with exceptions". Under the threat of FOCA, which eliminates the exceptions, "moderate" Republicans take their place on the opposite side of the barricades from NOW and NARRAL. And they welcome their new political allies, as Paul Coverdell and Kay Bailey Hutchison did.

Chapter Two

Will the Republican coalition built by Ronald Reagan continue to have tensions, arguments and primary battles? Certainly. So did the governing Democrat coalition of Franklin Delano Roosevelt. But, at the end of the day, Republicans must remember that those outside the enduring, inclusive GOP coalition wish our nation harm and that intraparty struggles are best waged after successful elections.

THE CLASS WARFARE CARD

If abortion could not divide the Republican Party, perhaps a sense of class could. Democrats hoped that the new Republicans, fresh from Bible class and quoting scripture, would be off-putting to country club, Main Street Republicans. The hope was that some Republicans would rather lose elections than attend meetings with déclassé Sahara of the Bozart Bible-thumpers.

The Democrats decided to gamble everything on this hope in the summer of 1994.

Vic Fazio, the chairman of the Democratic Congressional Campaign Committee, held a press conference in Washington, D.C. on June 21, 1994 to signal his party's strategy for the 1994 elections: stimulate voter turnout from the Democrat base and divide Republicans. Fazio attacked the Religious Right, identifying them as conservative Protestants, traditional Catholics and Orthodox Jews and portraying their beliefs as radical and out of the mainstream.

Are religious Americans an asset or a liability for the Republican Party? Are they too inflexible? Will they divide the party? Will they support candidates who are not "pure"? Can the Democrats energize their voter base by raising the fear of Religious Right policies?

Truth to tell, we knew the answers to these questions well before the election of November 8, 1994. Fazio's announcement of a campaign to vilify conservative religious parents involved in politics was not a new strategy, but a restatement and an intensification of a strategy employed in 1993 and in the special elections of 1994. There was a track record. Let us re-examine it.

Georgia: The Georgia Senate runoff in November 1992 was discussed in detail above. Suffice it to say here that Republican Paul Coverdell won by 17,000 votes and cheerfully credits conservative churchgoers for his margin of victory.

Texas: In June 1993 Kay Bailey Hutchison, a moderate Republican with a history of support for legalized abortion, defeated two pro-life candidates in the primary. The Religious Right gave her strong support in her 67 to 33 percent special election victory over appointed incumbent Bob Krueger.

Los Angeles and New York City: Republicans won the mayoral races in both cities with strong support from traditional Catholics and Orthodox Jews. In Los Angeles, the Democrat Michael Woo ran television ads attacking Pat Robertson and claiming that his opponent, Republican Richard Riordan, was a pawn of the Religious Right. Riordan won the mayor's race for the Republicans for the first time in 30 years by a margin of 54 to 46 percent. In New York City's school board elections, the Christian Coalition joined with Roman Catholic Cardinal John O'Connor to distribute 300,000 fliers in support of conservative candidates — 51 percent of whom won. New York reminds both parties that attacks on the Religious Right energize not only white Southern fundamentalists, but also Hispanic Protestants and Catholics, Orthodox Jews, and many churchgoing blacks.

Arkansas: The Republicans won the Lieutenant Governor's race for the first time in over 20 years, electing Mike Huckabee, a former president of the Southern Baptist Convention. Attacks on his "religious" background and heavy artillery from the Arkansan in the White House failed to prevent this Republican upset victory.

Wisconsin: In May 1993, Republican Mark Neumann campaigned against Democrat Peter Barca to replace U.S. Senator Les Aspin, whom President Clinton had appointed Secretary of Defense

Neumann, running as an economic conservative, responded to media pressure by publicly distancing himself from the Religious Right saying, "I go to church on Sundays, but that's a far cry from being a religious fanatic". Disowned by their candidate, religious and pro-life supporters lost any enthusiasm for the GOP candidate, and Neumann failed to win this Democrat-held seat by 49 to 50 percent.

Conversely, in 1994, when Neumann again ran against Barca, he did not disavow the social conservatives, and he was victorious, as will be discussed below.

Virginia: In 1993, Democrats launched an all-out attack on Republican candidates for governor, lieutenant governor, and attorney general for their support from evangelical Christians and specifically from Pat Robertson, whose evangelizing and broadcasting empire is located in Virginia Beach. The Democrats had held all three offices for 12 years, and their candidate for governor, Mary Sue Terry, was leading by 29 points when the Democrats attacked. A backlash brought voter turnout by evangelicals to 38 percent of the total vote (up from 19 in the 1992 general election), and Republican George Allen won the governor's race with a 20 percent margin.

Democrats claim their strategy of attacking religious conservatives paid dividends in the defeat of Mike Farris, the Republican challenger to incumbent Lieutenant Governor Don Beyer. Farris was even attacked by Republican Senator John Warner for having eight children that he home schooled. Democrats criticized his defense, as a lawyer, of parents' rights to control what their children read in public school.

Virginian political observers counter that Beyer's victory was due more to his spending margin than to Farris's ties to the Religious Right. Beyer outspent Farris by almost three to one. They point out that Farris did, after all, garner more votes than Democrat Mary Sue Terry, who lost the real prize of the governorship.

Oklahoma and Kentucky: Special elections held for the House seats in Oklahoma's Sixth District and Kentucky's Second saw

Democrats attack Republicans on religion. Democrat Joe Prather in Kentucky sneeringly referred to his opponent, a pastor and owner of a Christian bookstore, as "the Reverend" Ron Lewis. Republicans won both seats by about ten points.

Of the nine major elections between Clinton's 1992 victory and the 1994 elections, Republicans won eight, losing only the Neumann race in Wisconsin. Trashing religious conservatives did not once fell a Republican candidate. Neumann's loss in Wisconsin shows that Republicans who repudiate their church-going backers lose their enthusiastic support — and lose elections. The Virginia 1993 races show that elevating Christian-bashing to new heights increases Republican turnout. In Virginia, it cost Democrats six state legislative seats, the governorship, and the attorney generalship and succeeded only in defeating an underfunded first-time candidate for lieutenant governor.

The 1994 Congressional Elections: Any remaining concern about electoral drag from the Religious Right should have been put finally to rest by the outcome of the November 1994 elections. Vic Fazio and other Democrat strategists (and their acolytes in the media) identified several Republican House challengers as "poisoned" by their identification with the Christian evangelicals. These included Helen Chenoweth in Idaho, Andrea Seastrand in California and Jon Christensen in Nebraska. All three won in November. In addition, Van Hilleary of Tennessee, Mark Souder of Indiana, Zack Wamp of Tennessee, and several other candidates, had close ties to the Religious Right which did them no harm. In general, the 104th Congress is substantially more evangelical, more conservative, and more pro-life than was the 103rd. Thirty-five pro-choice Democrats were defeated or retired in November, while over 50 firmly pro-life Republicans were elected.

Chapter Two

Republican candidates should not be afraid that the Democrats will continue and augment attacks on them for religious associations. The interesting question is why, given the failure rate of this strategy, Vic Fazio and Democrat candidates would rather discuss religion than Bill Clinton's plans for America.

LEAVE US ALONE

The reason the Christian Right and the economic conservatives are not at each other's throats is that they both fit comfortably into the "Leave Us Alone" coalition. Liberals, when they have found some eternal truth — whatever it is this week — seem to feel a need to make everyone else see this truth and believe it. Religious conservatives, on the other hand, have focused on being left alone.

To understand why religious conservatives are so comfortable in a coalition dedicated to being left alone, it is helpful to remember how the Religious Right came into being. Conservative activist Paul Weyrich, now a media maven with his own cable television network, National Empowerment Television, reminds us that the Christian Right was not started or organized in response to the 1962 Supreme Court decision banning prayer in school. It was not even started in response to *Roe* v. *Wade*, the 1973 Supreme Court decision that struck down all state laws regulating abortions. Rather, the Religious Right was organized in response to two attacks on their essential interests by the federal government under Jimmy Carter in 1978.

The **first** was a threat by the Internal Revenue Service to declare that religious schools that did not have enough minorities in them would be presumed discriminatory and have their tax deductibility taken away. This effort was driven by the National Education Association, which wanted to destroy its private school competitors. Parents with children in private schools were not trying to tell other parents how to raise their children. They just wanted to be left alone by the federal, state and local governments and the teachers' unions. It is ironic that liberals, who maintain that they have the right to specify what books are read in public schools, and the right to keep religion out of the schools, attack parents who simply wish to be left alone as "intolerant". Sadly, the Establishment media, such as the *New York Times*, will never criticize such attacks by those who wish to manage the lives of others in the name of progressive liberalism.

The **second** event that sparked the creation of an organized Religious Right was the threat by the Carter Administration to use the Federal Communications Commission to attack Christian radio stations. To this day, the FCC bureaucrats deny this goal, but politicians had been using the FCC to attack conservative radio stations as far back as the Kennedy and Johnson years, and listeners to Christian radio stations began a letter-writing campaign in defense of their stations.

The Christian Coalition, led by Executive Director Ralph Reed, continues this tradition of religious conservatives who wish to be left alone by the government. The Christian Coalition's major issues in the 1994 election cycle were: support of welfare reform, a balanced budget amendment, term limits, and opposition to higher taxes. In short, these issue priorities positioned the Christian Coalition very comfortably within the "leave us alone" camp that has become the Republican Party coalition.

Home Schoolers: Ten Days That Shook Washington

The best example of the power of the so-called Religious Right and the "leave us alone" nature of their world view is the home schooling movement. Its size and power, invisible to the myopic eyes of the *New York Times*, is a good example of why liberals are so surprised whenever they run into America by accident.

They did so emphatically in 1994 during congressional consideration of the Elementary and Secondary Education Act, H.R. 6 (ESEA). The encounter left deep scars on liberal sensibilities and an important lesson in the hearts of astute Republican strategists.

At 10:30 a.m. on Monday, March 14, 1994, Dean Clancy, the education staffer for Rep. Dick Armey (R-TX), called the National Center for Home Education to ask if an amendment offered by Rep. George Miller (D-CA) might be interpreted to require that all parents who teach their children at home be "certified" by the government.

Within an hour, Mike Farris, (Republican candidate for lieutenant governor of Virginia in 1993, and also president of the Home School Legal Defense Association [HSLDA]), determined that the Miller Amendment could easily be interpreted by states or the Department of Education (or later by the courts) to require home schoolers to be licensed — a longtime goal of the National Education Association. To date, despite vigorous lobbying by the teachers' unions, not one of the 50 states has required such teacher licensing for parents. Miller refused to alter his language, and Rep. Armey's attempt to strip the amendment out was defeated on a party-line vote in the House Education and Labor Committee.

These events set the stage for a fight between the National Education Association (NEA) and home schoolers — parents who believe their children are best educated at home. The NEA is the largest union in the country, with 2.5 million members, an annual budget of over $700 million a year, and unionized teachers in every congressional district in America.

Ten days later, at 3:38 p.m. on March 24, Congress voted 374 to 53 to pass the Armey amendment, which not only exempts home schoolers from the threat of teacher certification by the government, but also goes on to exempt home schoolers and *all private schools* from the entire 715 pages of H.R. 6 and further protects home schools by rewriting the federal definition of "school" to exclude home schoolers.

From a standing start, the National Center for Home Education waged a grassroots campaign of phone calls, faxes and personal visits to Congress that defeated the most powerful lobby in America in a week and a half. *Roll Call*, the newspaper that reports on Congress, wrote that more than 800,000 calls rained in on Members of Congress. This response was greater than the outcry over gays in the military, the Clinton tax increase, or NAFTA. A ten-year veteran of Congress reported that he had "never seen anything like this before".

The home schoolers' defeat of the NEA and the Democrat leadership in the House will be studied for its lessons about where power lies in America and how it will be exercised in the future. Like the Battle of Gettysburg, it will be relived, refought, and documented, and future political fights will use it as a reference point. In this unexpected victory of David over Goliath were signs of what was to come in November 1994.

Mike Farris estimates that there are between 700,000 and 1,000,000 children presently being schooled at home. These children are members of 250,000 to 300,000 families, and since virtually all home schoolers belong to two-parent families, there are 500,000 to 600,000 parents who home school. This is one-fifth the number of dues-paying NEA members, but these parents are fighting for their children, not for a cost of living increase.

Farris's own group, a legal defense fund for parents who are harassed by local school districts, has 38,000 members who pay $100 in dues each year. His newsletter is mailed six times a year, and his emergency faxes go out to 140 groups that in turn connect with 3,000-4,000 city groups that reach 250,000 to 350,000 families. While home schooling in the 1960's and 1970's was largely a liberal phenomenon (parents who were taking their children out of the conformist, rigid public schools), the growth in home schooling since the late 1970's has been primarily among religious conservatives and Catholics.

Farris believes that the present trends will continue over the next four years, and that while home schoolers represent two percent of all school-aged children in America today, this proportion will grow to five percent before leveling off. He argues that five percent is a likely maximum, as home schooling requires that a family have a high enough income level (or a great willingness to sacrifice) to allow the family to get by on one income while one parent remains at home to teach.

One of the forces driving the home school movement is a desire to escape the militantly secular, values-free NEA. That is what gives the battle over H.R. 6 its salience and makes it worth careful study. It is also what drives the growing private school movement. Twelve percent of children are in private schools, and this number is growing, despite some reduction in the number of Catholic parochial schools. The reason is the creation of two to three new evangelical schools in America every day.

What follows is a blow-by-blow account of "Ten Days that Shook Washington", the home schooler/NEA battle royal.

Monday, March 14, 1994. Within an hour of discovering the threat to home schooling, Dick Armey offers an amendment in committee to exempt home schoolers and private schools from the licensing requirement. George Miller, while insisting he has no hidden agenda to regulate home or private schools, leads the entire Democrat side of the committee in voting down the Armey language. Miller's intentions are now clear.

The printing company that puts out Farris's Home School Legal Defense Association newsletter tells him that it will take five days to get a newsletter out with a warning for home schoolers. Farris decides this is too long and finds several local printers who can prepare 38,000 letters to HSLDA's members. A letter to all members of Congress outlining the home schoolers' fears is hand-delivered to every member within 30 hours of the original alert.

Within 56 hours, 38,000 letters are out the door to all HSLDA members, and the national fax alert has begun.

Wednesday, March 16. Mike Farris tapes an interview with "The 700 Club", Pat Robertson's television show. An hour later, Marlin Maddoux, the host of the nationally-syndicated television show "Point of View", interviews Farris on the home school issue for a full two hours. The interview is broadcast to 4 million viewers.

4:00 p.m. Congressional staffers begin calling HSLDA, promising that their bosses will vote for the "Home School/Private School Freedom Amendment" and asking that the calls from their district stop.

Thursday, March 17. The wave of calls into Washington builds. By noon, Rep. Miller has his staff stop answering calls and puts on an answering machine.

1:00 p.m. Farris tapes an interview with James Dobson for Dobson's radio show that will go out over 1,500 stations on Monday, March 21.

The chief of staff for a Democrat Congressman tells home school leader Doug Phillips, "My office has received 600 calls today. We have decided to vote for your amendment. Please tell your people to stop calling. Don't get me wrong. I believe in democracy. It's just that we have had about as much democracy as we can handle for one day."

Within 48 hours of the fax alert, more than 1,000 Christian radio stations have covered the story. Within 72 hours, a majority of evangelical churches in the country are alerted.

Friday, March 18. Rep. Armey announces that he will sponsor the Home School Protection Amendment on the floor of the House. More than 70 Congressional offices have promised to support the Armey amendment as of 7:00 p.m. that evening. Problems arise as some congressional offices (mis)inform home schoolers calling in that there is no problem with the ESEA. A small coalition of moderate or liberal home school groups tries to negotiate compromise language. Another fax is sent out from HSLDA, making clear that Miller's language remains unacceptable.

Over the weekend, many members of congress are met by home schoolers in their districts. More importantly, Tom Foley, Speaker of the House, is confronted by dozens of home schoolers and promises to support the Armey amendment.

Monday, March 21. Miller is unrepentant, although his phones are still kept off the hook. Miller sends out a petulant "Dear Colleague" letter denying the obvious power grab he attempted and urging fellow members not to be angry with him for the telephone blitz, but to blame "the far right". Two private school groups, the Association of Christian Schools International (ACSI) and the American Association of Christian Schools (AACS), join the effort and send out mailings and fax alerts. Armey's language is updated, and a national fax alert goes out to home schoolers with the most recent language. Rush Limbaugh discusses the home school telephone blitz of Congress.

10:00 p.m. A 1,000 person rally is held in Dallas, Texas, in support of home schooling.

Tuesday, March 22. The phone wave continues. A number of congressmen instruct staff to stop answering all calls. Limbaugh revisits the issue. Rep. Bill Goodling (R-PA), the ranking Republican on the Education and Labor Committee, is still denying that the Miller amendment threatens home schoolers. Miller refuses to back off.

Wednesday, March 23. An ice storm hits Washington, but the phone calls continue. Home schoolers arrive on Capitol Hill from Georgia, Missouri, Virginia, Pennsylvania, and West Virginia.

12:30 p.m. ACSI reports that it has contacted its 3,000 schools in the nation. Mike Farris appears on the Pat Buchanan show for one hour.

The Catholic Conference remains on the sidelines, complaining that the Armey amendment might jeopardize federal funds going to their members. While many parochial schools and home schooling Catholics join the fight, the Catholic Conference — dubbed the "Chamber of Commerce of the Religious Right" for its unwillingness to challenge the Democrat Leadership — refuses to help fight against teacher certification or to fight for the independence of its schools. Instead, it works with the Democrat Leadership to undermine Armey and cut out real protection for home schoolers and private schools.

Thursday, March 24. Dick Armey sends around a "Dear Colleague" letter explaining that a "compromise" amendment by House Education and Labor Committee Chairman William Ford will not protect home schoolers.

9:00 a.m. The Democrats who control the Rules Committee introduce an out-dated version of the Armey amendment for the day's votes. Michigan Democrat Dale Kildee solicits and then sends out a letter from the Catholic Conference attacking this Armey Amendment. Armey will need to update his amendment to the correct language (language that answers the concerns of the Catholic Conference). Massachusetts Democrat Joe Moakley, Chairman of the Rules Committee, is the only person who can allow this last-minute, on-the-floor revision. Home schoolers in Massachusetts call Moakley, and within an hour Moakley's staff agrees that Moakley will support the Armey's update.

1:54 p.m. The Ford "compromise" amendment passes with 424 votes. Only Miller votes no. This compromise is regarded by the home schoolers as a fig leaf for those unwilling to complete the job.

Chapter Two

1:57 p.m. Armey asks for unanimous consent of the House to modify his amendment. A single Member could object and stop Armey from presenting the amendment he wants. Silence.

2:00 p.m. Debate begins on Armey's final language of the "Home School/Private School Freedom Amendment".

3:38 p.m. Ten days after Armey and home schoolers went into action, the Armey amendment passes by 374 votes to 53.

How did the home schoolers win? Dick Armey notes that they were prepared. "They knew the Clinton Administration would make a move against home schoolers on behalf of the NEA. They didn't know when, but they were ready". Farris adds that home schooling is the central organizing principle of the lives of hundreds of thousands of parents. They were defending their homes and their children. "They are exhibiting enormous personal responsibility in their families, and they want enormous personal freedom".

Farris adds that while this strong reaction was a surprise to members of Congress, home schoolers are battle-tested veterans of lobbying at the state legislative level, where there have been 50 major assaults on private and home schooling over the past 10 years. Six years ago in Connecticut, a state legislator pulled a power grab just like Miller's, and four hearing rooms were filled with home schoolers. State legislators told the bill's sponsor to "pull your stupid bill". In Montana, an attempt by the teachers' union to gut the law protecting home schoolers brought out 600 protesters and the law was instead even improved.

Other members of Congress who watched the precision drill of Dick Armey in the House and Mike Farris and the home schoolers on the outside note several key factors in the home schoolers' success.

First, they picked the right champion. Armey was willing to fight it out. He refused to compromise. He would not trade getting the home schoolers to go away for some inside-the-beltway reward. Armey knew that every member of Congress — including the Speaker

— had promised home schoolers in their districts that they would vote for the Armey Amendment, and that false compromises like the Ford Amendment would not suffice.

Second, the home schoolers went for total victory. That is, they did not simply protect themselves from attack, but rolled back the other threats to home schoolers in the bill and protected private schools as well.

Third, home schoolers and Armey did not fall for the classic ploy of "get them to stop calling and then I'll vote for you" (*i.e.*, put down that gun, and we'll talk). The pressure continued unrelentingly.

Fourth, over ten days Farris sent out five faxes to his fax network, including all of the nation's Christian radio stations so that his home schoolers knew the exact state of the evolving battle on Capitol Hill, what procedural votes were important, etc. It takes a high level of sophistication to prevent Congress from fooling voters with meaningless votes that are canceled out by procedural motions.

Home schoolers had several advantages. Among these was the major advantage that they were defending a freedom they already enjoy. Dick Armey notes that it is always easier to get people to fight to protect a liberty than to acquire new freedoms. These were, Armey observes, "real people who saw their personal liberties at risk. They understood that if they didn't act in the next few days they'd be out of the home schooling business".

Round one was over, and the NEA power grab went down for the count.

THE PERMANENT REVOLUTION

There are three reasons why the Republican capture of the House of Representatives in 1994 will not be swept away by harsh winds in 1996, or even the year 2000.

Chapter Two

1. The Conservative Arsenal

First, the conservative coalition has built up a number of strong organizations in Washington and around the nation that support the Republican agenda. These include Washington-based foundations like The Heritage Foundation, with an annual budget of $22 million and 150 employees; national organizations not based in Washington, such as Dallas's National Center for Policy Analysis and the Reason Foundation in Los Angeles; and more than 30 policy institutes and regional networks based in states across the nation.

Had Barry Goldwater been elected president and swept GOP majorities into the House and Senate in 1964, the incoming Republicans would have had nowhere to turn for conservative ammunition. There did not exist at that time conservative activist groups to echo the Republican agenda and push it forward. There were, to be sure, ample theoretical and philosophical studies, articles and symposia being produced by the Foundation for Economic Education, the Intercollegiate Studies Institute, *National Review,* and *Human Events,* but for hard research in defense of the conservative position in those days there was only an occasional study from the Rand Corporation and the recently-established American Enterprise Institute.

The *New York Times* and the three national television networks would have denounced the Republican agenda, and publicized opposing studies produced by the liberal Brookings Institution, Harvard and Yale Universities, and America would have heard no response, both because the media was controlled by those with a liberal world view and because the resources to support a conservative political movement did not exist.

Today, a far-flung host of conservative groups throughout the nation supports the Republican agenda.

The **National Rifle Association** has 3.5 million members and opposes gun control at the federal and state levels. The **Christian**

81

Coalition has more than 1.5 million members and is ably led by the youthful-looking political veteran Ralph Reed and a top-notch Washington operation in Marshall Wittmann and Heidi Scanlon. The **National Right to Work Committee** has millions of members who fight for the rights of working Americans against abuses by the labor union bosses. There are more than 800 state and local taxpayer groups and some 850 property rights groups. Karen Kerrigan's **Small Business Survival Committee** organizes small businessmen at the state and local levels to fight against higher taxes. Reed Irvine's **Accuracy in Media** and Brent Bozell's **Media Research Center** put out well-documented studies on the liberal bias in the major television networks and news magazines.

Public interest law firms such as the **Pacific Legal Foundation**, the **Washington Legal Foundation**, and the **Institute for Justice** bring legal expertise to the fight for constitutional guarantees of the rights of parents, students, businessmen, and taxpayers. The Washington, D.C.-based **Center for Individual Rights**, under the direction of Michael Greve and Michael McDonald, and the California-based **Individual Rights Foundation**, led by David Horowitz, provide legal assistance specifically to students who run afoul of the "political correctness" Gestapo on college campuses. Along with the **Home School Legal Defense Fund**, the **Rutherford Institute** helps parents who have problems with the public school establishment. The **National Association of Scholars**, with Steve Balch as president, provides a counterweight to the liberal American Association of University Professors.

Paul Weyrich's **Free Congress Foundation**, founded in 1974, is a general headquarters for conservative activism. His weekly strategy lunches with senators, congressmen, and conservative activist groups bring focus and coordination to the conservative coalition. In 1993, Weyrich, together with Burton Yale Pines, a former editor at *Time* magazine, embarked on an ambitious campaign to bring a serious conservative and populist voice to national television with the introduction of **National Empowerment Television**. NET now broadcasts 24 hours of programming daily, including 8 hours of live programming and is now available to 11 million viewers across America by full-time cable and satellite broadcasts. Some of its programming reaches as many as 20 million viewers. With its steady stream of congressmen, senators and activists as guests on its regular programs, NET keeps Washington and the nation in constant communication. Paul Weyrich is also involved in the work of **The Krieble Institute**, which provides political training to freedom-oriented activists in the countries that once made up the Soviet Union. In fact, it was Bob Krieble's vision of what could be done behind the Iron Curtain, a vision which matched that of Ronald Reagan, which led to the victory of the forces of freedom in many of these societies emerging from serfdom. **The Heritage Foundation**, under its current president, Edwin J. Feulner, has grown to be the largest and most influential of the conservative think tanks in Washington. Focussing primarily on defense, foreign policy, and economic issues, Heritage also pioneered networks among regional and state-level think tanks and within the international conservative movement. With an emphasis on congressional policy-making, Heritage also engaged in an extensive training program for executive branch managers in the first Reagan term. The **Cato Institute**, a libertarian, free-market think tank that provides quick turn-around and principled position papers for congressmen and the media, moved to Washington, D.C. from San Francisco in 1981. Led by Ed Crane, Bill Niskanen, and David Boaz, Cato has become one of the leading producers of sound ideas and ground-breaking innovations in free-market thinking. The **National Center for Policy Analysis**, founded by John Goodman and head-quartered in Dallas, Texas, has grown so rapidly in size and impact that it has opened a Washington office run by Peter Ferrara. Ferrara is the father of so many conservative initiatives, from privatization to enterprise zones and tax reform, that he constitutes his own one-man war against big government. Pete du Pont, the former governor of Delaware who ran a principled campaign for the presidency in 1988 is now NCPA's national chairman. **Eagle Forum**, the 60,000 member-strong women's group led by Phyllis Schlafly, has chapters in every state and by the late 1970's was strong enough to single handedly defeat the feminist movement, the leadership of both political parties, all three networks and the labor unions by stopping the passage of the so-called Equal Rights Amendment. Susan Hirschman, Eagle Forum's Washington Director, has now moved to Capitol Hill as top staffer to an incoming freshman representative. The new director is Amy Reed.

In short, the conservative movement can now draw upon a substantial network of experienced think tanks and activist groups that will arm it well for the many pitched battles that lie ahead.

While conservative organizations do not have anything like the foundation support that buttresses the Left, there are some far-seeing grant-making foundations willing to come to the aid of economic and social conservatives. Without financial support from foundations such as **Olin, Bradley, Scaife, Anschutz, Ahmanson, Earhart, Liberty Fund, Koch, Smith Richardson, Grover Hermann, Brady, Roe**, and **Coors**, the conservative arsenal would be decidedly short of weapons. In addition to their financial support, the directors of these foundations, people like Mike Joyce, Dick Larry, Jim Pierson, Bill Simon, Bob Krieble, Paul Rhoads, David Kennedy, and Vic Porlier, have been a constant source of the ideas that have built the modern conservative movement.

2. We Are Legion

Second, beyond institutional strength, the modern Republican movement also has something that eluded President Richard Nixon and even President Ronald Reagan: *thousands of highly trained and active personnel.*

84

Chapter Two

It is correctly said that the Democrat Party has only one Rolodex, and therefore it matters little whether you elect Gary Hart or Walter Mondale: the union bosses will still run the Labor Department. And it does not matter whether the Democrats choose Jimmy Carter or Ted Kennedy. In either case, Cyrus Vance and his cronies will run the State Department. But it was also true until the 1980's that conservative Republicans did not have the legions of trained, credentialed, conservative personnel needed to staff a White House, a federal bureaucracy or even Congress.

Morton Blackwell, the founder of the **Leadership Institute**, has trained more than 10,000 young Americans to become candidates for political office, student newspaper publishers, congressional staff, State Department officers, and campaign managers. Since 1983, Blackwell has run these schools in virtually every state in the nation.

GOPAC, a Republican candidate training and education organization founded by Pete du Pont and chaired by Newt Gingrich since 1988, has run over 400 tele-training seminars for Republican congressional candidates and over 100 one-to-two-day seminars for state legislative candidates in 28 states. Every month, under the direction of Executive Director Lisa Nelson, GOPAC sends out 9,000 audio-tapes that help educate and train Republican state legislators and Republican state legislative candidates in policy and politics.

The **Federalist Society**, run by Eugene Meyer, is a society of libertarian and conservative law school students — and now lawyers — active in 135 of the 177 law schools in the country and in 45 cities. This organization of constitutional scholars and lawyers is the Right's answer to the National Lawyers Guild, which has been so helpful to the Left over the years. Since it was founded in 1982, more than 10,000 law students have joined the Federalist Society.

3. Boy Named Sue Trounces Little Lord Fauntleroy

The third advantage the modern Republican Party has, in addition to its new and stronger institutions and its credentialed personnel, is the quality of its cadre.

Conservatives going to college in the 1960's and 1970's benefitted from the "Boy Named Sue" school of character building. Universities were hostile to conservative activism, scholarship, and thought. A student who expressed a pro-free market idea was grilled ruthlessly by the professoriate and by liberal students.

In the same period, by contrast, liberal students who explained away the death marches of the Khmer Rouge Communists in Cambodia by saying that "the Khmer Rouge are moving people from hospitals in the city to rural health care clinics" were listened to with nodding heads.

Ed Feulner, now the president of **The Heritage Foundation**, was an early editor of the *Intercollegiate Review*, a publication of the Intercollegiate Studies Institute; Angelo de Codevilla, now a conservative foreign policy scholar at the Hoover Institution, wrote as an undergraduate for a campus quarterly called *Politæa*, published at Princeton University; and Gordon S. Jones, now president of the Association of Concerned Taxpayers, went through the campus wars as a writer for *The Arena*, an alternative paper published at Stanford University at the height of the Vietnam War protests. These examples could be multiplied many times over.

A younger generation had not only the antipathy of a liberal ideology to contend with, but also the additional problem of "political correctness". Thus it is no surprise that some of the best young conservative activists came from the *Dartmouth Review*, one of the first conservative alternative newspapers on a college campus. Authors Ben Hart and Dinesh D'Souza, editorial writer Greg Fossedal, Reagan speechwriter Peter Robinson, Kevin Pritchett in the Senate Majority Whip's office and Laura Ingraham, who clerked for

Chapter Two

Supreme Court Justice Clarence Thomas, were all *Dartmouth Review* students roughed up by the politically-correct college scene (Hart was actually bitten by a liberal professor). All have become strong, competent and activist opponents of the welfare state. Can anyone name a Dartmouth liberal — professor, administrator, or alumnus — whose contributions to liberalism compare with the contributions of the *Dartmouth Review* alumni to the Reagan Revolution? Coddled and unchallenged, the American Left on campus has profited from "ideological affirmative action". Their writings, ideas and thoughts were given a free ride, or even bonus points in the competition with their classmates.

But in the real world, the conservatives annealed in the liberal furnace have a real advantage over their mollycoddled liberal opponents. Dartmouth is now a breeding ground of revolutionaries of the Right and whining, inconsequential non-combatants of the Left.

One can see this by comparing conservative columnists today with liberal columnists. George Will, William Safire, Thomas Sowell, and Joe Sobran are solid intellectuals who, as columnists, are continually marshalling historical or economic evidence in support of creative new ways of assessing the actions of government. Their liberal counter-parts, such as Anthony Lewis, Flora Lewis, Richard Cohen, and Judy Mann, are so predictable as to be completely unnecessary. If any of them has ever had a thought outside the canon of Liberal Orthodoxy, they have kept it carefully concealed. Look at Herblock, who has been the editorial cartoonist for the *Washington Post* since 1946. He cannot draw. He isn't funny or particularly insightful. His cartoons are so predictable — fat cat Republican robber barons chomping expensive stogies and helpless, downtrodden welfare mothers — that there is really no point in looking at them. Jeff MacNelly or Steve Benson produce cartoons with consistent bite and wit to them, because their talents were forged in the campus fires of the 1960's and 1970's.

Black conservatives get special treatment from the Left, so it is no surprise that black Republicans like Ohio State Treasurer Ken Blackwell are top notch. Ambassador Alan Keyes, who worked at the United Nations with Jeanne Kirkpatrick for Ronald Reagan, was so competent and knowledgeable that liberal black activist Randall Robinson of TransAfrica refused to debate him on television. Keyes was literally chased off campus in his undergraduate days, in an incident recounted by Allan Bloom in *The Closing of the American Mind.* The two black Republican congressmen, Gary Franks of Connecticut and freshman J.C. Watts of Oklahoma are special targets of the left and have become stronger as a result.

David Brock, the conservative investigative reporter with the *American Spectator,* scooped the entire press corps with his article (and later book) entitled "The Real Anita Hill". Liberal activists Jill Abramson and Jane Mayer tried to do a rebuttal to Brock's book, but the quality of their liberal reporting was so laughable that even with the entire Establishment press rooting for them, the book was a flop, exposed as error-ridden and disingenuous.

Brock went on to break open the story ignored (actually stone-walled) by the entire Establishment press: Bill Clinton's misuse of Arkansas state troopers and other taxpayer-funded resources to conduct his personal affairs of the heart. The Establishment press rose as one to denounce Brock and his writing, but today there is no one who denies the basic truth of Brock's story (in fact, as this is written, the *Washington Post* is finally running excerpts of a new book by a *Post* reporter confirming everything Brock said). Most in the Establishment press are now jealous that Brock was there first with more investigative savvy and more physical courage than they had. Where is the liberal equivalent of David Brock? What liberal investigative reporter has broken as many hidden stories so well? The ideological blinders of modern Leftists keep them from becoming competent reporters.

Chapter Two

The Republican Party represents a coalition of individuals who wish to be left alone by the government. Every part of the coalition is now growing in size, power, and political effectiveness. It has taken a great deal of time and effort to organize individuals who would prefer not to think about or deal with the government.

In his two years as president, Bill Clinton has, in dealing with the "leave us alone" majority of Americans, acted like a Spanish *banderillero*, the person in the bullfight whose job it is to stick *banderillas* — decorated, barbed darts — at the bull to irritate and anger it. He personifies the bloated, haughty, and self-important government, whose growth and power have served to irritate, enrage, and motivate Americans to organize in self-defense against the state.

(L) John Boehner, House Republican Conference Chairman
(R) Grover G. Norquist

CHAPTER THREE

THE COLLAPSE OF THE DEMOCRAT PARTY AND THE LIBERAL ESTABLISHMENT

The Democrat Party is a coalition of organized interest groups seeking to use the coercive power of government to accumulate power and money from others. It is shrinking in size and power.

The foundation stones of the Democrat Party are labor unions, corrupt big-city political machines, government workers, teachers' unions, left-wing intellectuals, and activists in the feminist, environmentalist, homosexual and "peace" movements. When it comes to financing the party, the trial lawyers and, again, the unions play the most critical role.

THE DEMISE OF THE ROOSEVELT COALITION

The present Democrat coalition is a shadow of its former self. The Rooseveltian New Deal coalition included Southern whites, blacks, unionized workers, Catholics, Jews, recent immigrants, aging and economically insecure Social Security recipients, and corrupt big city machines.

Rock the House

In the 1950's, '60's and 70's, the Democrat Party began to add new groups to its coalition, groups that often drove out existing components of the Roosevelt coalition that were larger in number.

Disaffected Democrats

The Democrats' embrace of a pro-abortion (not simply pro-choice) agenda offended Catholics and, later, evangelicals. The addition of the anti-American Left during the Vietnam War pushed World War II and Korean veterans, patriotic southerners and those who served in Vietnam away from the Democrats. Adding the most radical excesses of feminism to the party doctrine insulted women who value parenting and husbands. Using the schools to promote the gay lifestyle (not just tolerance of homosexuals) drove evangelicals, Orthodox Jews and even non-political homosexuals away from the Democrats. Raising taxes to pay for welfare state bureaucrats drove away small businessmen and taxpayers.

The present Democrat Party is like a frenetic hostess inviting any vagrant in from the street while the invited guests flee out the back door in larger numbers.

What's worse for the Democrats, the inherent contradictions in their coalition are now coming to the fore. Under Democrat presidents like Franklin Delano Roosevelt and Harry S. Truman, Southern whites could stay in a party drifting leftward, but time and greater mobility mean the memories of the Civil War no longer serve to bind Southern whites to the Democrat Party. The inner-city immigrants of the turn of the century, willing to trade votes for patronage and pork, are now suburbanites with no interest in paying the costs; nor do they need the "benefits" of big-city machines.

Teachers' unions demand that Democrat politicians oppose school choice voucher proposals that would allow all parents the right to have their children attend the public or private school they prefer.

Such freedom is of particular importance to parents in inner city areas with poor public schools. In fact, black and Hispanic parents are even more supportive of school choice than are white parents, who back school choice with 70 to 80 percent support. The Democrat Party, when confronted with a conflict between the political needs of the leaders of the National Education Association and the hopes and aspiration of black parents, has not hesitated for a moment: the Democrats side with the teachers' unions against black parents.

Democrats always choose the needs of the government workers' unions over those supposedly served by the programs administered by those workers. This presents the Democrats with a definite dilemma because, while the unions provide money, black parents provide votes. How much longer can black inner city parents continue to be cannon fodder for the financial interests of the labor unions and, derivatively, the Democrat Party?

The national debate over the North American Free Trade Agreement (NAFTA) and the General Agreement on Tariffs and Trade (GATT) revealed the new power relationships between labor unions and the Democrat Party. In the 1930's, the Democrat Party represented the wants of labor unions in the private sector. By the early 1950's, some 35 percent of all workers in the United States were unionized. The Democrats passed the Wagner Act, forcing many workers to join labor unions and pay dues to keep their jobs. Workers paid dues to the unions, which in turn kicked back money to the Democrat Party. Every additional union worker meant more money and a wider volunteer base for the Democrat Party at all levels — state, federal and local. (At that time, government workers were mostly soldiers, non-union school teachers, and police.)

Now, the percentage of private-sector workers who are unionized is down to no more than 11 percent of the real economy's workforce.

Only in the public sector (the government workforce) is union membership growing. Roughly one-third of government workers are unionized. Among all workers, only some 16 percent are unionized.

The NAFTA and GATT treaties would have been opposed by a Democrat Party representing the perceived interests of the leadership of the United Auto Workers· and the United Steel Workers of America. But Bill Clinton, Speaker Tom Foley, and Senate Majority Leader George Mitchell did not hesitate for a moment before plunging full steam ahead in support of those trade treaties. Why?

The answer is that there is only one group in the nation that is absolutely certain its economic interests are not threatened by NAFTA or GATT. That is the government unions. No one in Germany can compete with the NEA membership for a teaching job in Newark or a social worker's job in Los Angeles. Government workers would see lower prices for consumer goods due to expanded international trade, without the slightest risk of job loss.

NAFTA and GATT made it official. The Democrat Party sees itself as the party of government and government workers, not of private sector union workers, and certainly not of all American workers.

Disappearing Democrats

The aging population also presents problems for the Democrat Party. While the Civil War is less and less a reason for Southerners to stay with the party of Jefferson and Jackson, now that it is run by Bill Clinton, the more recent New Deal still holds sway with older Americans who came of age during the presidencies of Roosevelt and Truman. An American who turned 21 in 1930 is 85 years old in 1995. The New Deal generation is now, literally, passing away. Two million Americans die each year, and if the New Deal generation leans roughly 60-40 Democrat *versus* Republican, there are 1.2 million

Democrat deaths each year and only 800,000 Republican deaths. This is a net loss of 400,000 Democrats each year. Thus Bill Clinton in 1996 will have, due to age attrition alone, 1.6 million fewer Democrats within his presumed "base" than he had in 1992. This disproportionately-disappearing Democrat base will continue for another decade. Worse, those young Americans voting for the first time are trending Republican as they compare the Reagan and Clinton years and decide which party to join.

The Democrat Party also underwent a crisis in the spring of 1993 with the discovery that there are millions fewer homosexuals than was previously thought. Serious Democrat political operatives, when asked how many homosexual voters there were in the nation, would give the traditional response of 10 percent. Some liberal groups actually argued for 15 percent. These numbers are extrapolated from "findings" first published in the Kinsey Report on human sexuality that provoked a lot of press in the 1950's.

To Democrat strategists who believed these numbers, it made political sense for the Party to force the military to accept open homosexuals in the Army, even despite the views of the Joint Chiefs of Staff, and over the personal objections of General Colin Powell. They figured that the Democrats were winning 85 percent of the gay vote and this was 85 percent of 10 percent of the national vote, or 8.5 percent of the total vote on election day. This was as large a vote as the black vote and worth any amount of controversy.

But in 1993 the Alan Guttmacher Institute (research arm of Planned Parenthood) published a study demonstrating that the real number of homosexuals in America is one percent of the adult male population and one-half of one percent of the female population. This study was quickly corroborated by several other reputable surveys. In other words, there are perhaps one million male homosexuals and 500,000 lesbians in total. Therefore, the months of bad press and the alienation of the 8,000,000 veterans of World War II, the 4,000,000 veterans of Korea, and the 8,000,000 Vietnam veterans was all to win a portion of 1.5 million votes. (And the *New York Times* exit poll after the 1994 election reveals that Republican candidates for Congress received 40 percent of the gay vote anyway.)

Overnight the consultants whose political-correctness blinders would not allow them to question the 10 percent number, despite its unlikeliness (and despite earlier studies, such as a 1991 National Opinion Research Center survey), now had to recalculate the balance between Republicans and Democrats. Clinton's vote-expensive, anti-military and pro-homosexual campaign bought at best 85 percent of one percent of the voting public. This reduction from 10 percent of the population to one percent is a problem ten times larger for the Democrat Party than the disappearance of all the Cuban-Americans in the United States would be for the Republican Party.

The Machine Breaks Down

The big-city machines of the Democrat Party are also in decline. First, higher taxes and the Democrats' refusal to take the crime issue seriously have driven millions of Americans, and hence voters and taxpayers, out of America's largest cities. Detroit has lost 200,000 citizens over the last ten years; New York City has declined in population from its peak of almost eight million in 1950 to just about seven million now, with most of the decline coming since 1970; the population of Washington, D.C. peaked at almost 800,000, but is down to a little over 600,000 now.

Just as labor unions raised wages and wrote inefficient work rules that killed millions of jobs, so have Democrat-run cities killed the geese that laid the golden eggs — or at least driven them twenty miles outside of the city into the suburbs and former rural areas. Cellular phones turn commuting time into part of the work day for Americans, not dead time, making longer commutes more acceptable.

Chapter Three

It is becoming harder for the Democrat Party to get federal funds into their big city machines to pay back the mayors for their get-out-the-vote campaigns. Bill Clinton pushed a $16 billion payoff to big city political machines as soon as he got into the White House. He called it a "stimulus package", but it was simply a wish list of social welfare spending requests from Democrat mayors.

Worse for the Democrats, New York City and Los Angeles both now have elected Republican mayors. So too have Raleigh, North Carolina and Jersey City, New Jersey. The Republican campaign for choice in education and for tough anti-crime measures is capitalizing on the Democrats' failure — now inability — to loot the upper and middle classes in the city to pay for more welfare. Without anyone to loot, without workers and a business base to tax, and unwilling to face up to the issue of crime, or to ask the teachers' unions to care as much about education as about their pay and benefits and work rules, the Democrats will certainly lose more cities. And without complete control of cities, the ability of the Democrat Party to *steal* votes is greatly diminished. An honest vote count in New York will, according to Republican poll watching experts, cost the Democrat candidate for president as many as 80,000 votes in 1996. Those same votes will be lost to any Democrat candidate for senator or governor. Democrats fear that after the fall of Ways and Means Committee Chairman Dan Rostenkowski, even Chicago might vote for a good-government Republican candidate for president.

The collapse of the Democrat Party was not simply one of organizational decline. Democrats have also been losing the battle of ideas. Liberalism was dealt a body blow with the destruction of the Soviet Empire from 1989 to 1991. Socialism, long the cousin of American liberalism, had been shown to be a miserable failure and a blood-soaked failure at that. American liberal muckraker Lincoln Steffens wrote of the Soviet Union, "I have been over into the future

97

and it works." Jane Fonda assured us in the early 1970's that if we really understood what Communism was, we would "get down on our knees" and beg to become Communists. Harvard Professor John Kenneth Galbraith wrote in *The New Yorker* as late as 1984 that the Communist economy of the Soviet Union was making "great material progress", arguing that, "Partly, the Russian system succeeds because, in contrast with the Western industrial economies, it makes full use of its manpower." Nobel Laureate economist Paul Samuelson, in the 10th edition (1985) of his textbook *Economics* (this book's use by millions of students has made him rich), wrote that "it is a vulgar mistake to think that most people in Eastern Europe are miserable...What counts is results, and there can be no doubt that the Soviet planning system has been a powerful engine for economic growth."

The American New Left that organized against America's defense of Southeast Asia from Soviet imperialism was full of disdain for America and America's servicemen and women, but silent on the terrorism of the North Vietnamese and full of faith that a Communist victory in Cambodia, Laos and Vietnam would usher in a democratic paradise. The death marches in Cambodia and the re-education (concentration) camps of the Vietnamese Communists did not faze Jane Fonda or others in the hard Left, but did have a corrective impact on more honest Leftists such as folk singer Joan Baez and others who had believed the lies of the Communists and felt betrayed by the dictatorship and bloodshed that followed. Some of these disillusioned radicals have become the most effective critics of Communism and its apologists in the U.S. Democrat Party.

The myths of American evil and the good agrarian reformer communists in Southeast Asia collapsed, and the image of the American liberal was undermined for having sided with economically incompetent murderers against their own nation. It is a little hard for American liberals to claim the moral high ground, having been so wrong about the murderous nature of the Soviet Union, the Vietnam-

Chapter Three

ese Communists, and the Red Chinese. It is fashionable for liberals today to suggest that "no one knew" about the nature of these early totalitarian regimes, but in fact many refugees and independent observers told the truth about the early Soviet Union, the Chinese and Vietnamese Communists, and Castro's Cuba.

When Poland and Hungary threw off the Soviet Union, liberals had to face freedom fighters they had spit upon for 40 years. When Ronald Reagan characterized the Soviet Union, the oppressor of Eastern Europe, as an "Evil Empire", he was attacked by the likes of liberal reporter Sam Donaldson for having made a socially impolite gaffe. "What was the problem?" asked astonished Poles. When liberals like Donaldson saw a Soviet army of occupation in Poland, did they not see an empire? And seeing the empire and the Red Army astride Eastern Europe with orders to machine gun to death all who attempted to flee it, why should anyone have trouble with the word "evil"?

The collapse of the socialist dream shattered the belief of liberals in the inevitability of socialism. One of Lenin's greatest weapons was the belief by many western liberal intellectuals that the world was moving "scientifically" through history towards socialism and that conservatives opposing this movement were simply "standing athwart history yelling stop".

Now that the Communist Party has collapsed in Russia itself, it is obvious that the leftward drift of history in the 20th century towards larger government and more government power in National Socialist Germany and Bolshevik Socialist Russia was an aberration, and that the totalitarian régimes were abject failures rather than beacons of the future. Big-government liberalism's ideological proximity to statist socialism has become an embarrassment rather than a sign of progress.

Liberalism sacrificed the moral high ground on issue after issue. Today, spending on welfare is no longer a sign of how compassionate one is. Rather, in the light of exposés by scholars such as Charles

99

Murray (*Losing Ground*) and George Gilder (*Wealth and Poverty*), welfare is now seen as responsible for the expensive and counterproductive destruction of an entire part of America. Welfare spending is increasingly viewed not as a good thing that liberals want lots of and conservatives a little, but as a positive evil that breaks up families, breeds dependency, cripples futures, and loots those who work for a living.

Foreign aid was exposed as the enemy of reformers in poor nations. Dictators who sat on top of failed economies, but could send their children to Harvard with cash supplied by the U.S. State Department, saw no need to liberalize their economies and allow property rights, low taxes and the emergence of a real economy. One need only compare Tanzania, recipient of much government-to-government compassion (fueled by taxes taken from ordinary Americans) to South Korea or Taiwan. American liberals demanded an end to aid for these "pariah" nations in the 1960's, and even made it difficult for them to buy needed military equipment. Cutting off "aid" to South Korea and Taiwan turns out to have been the best thing we could have done for them.

Throughout the 1960's, '70's and '80's, the myths and claims of liberalism and socialism collapsed for all to see. "I'm from the government and I'm here to help you" became a clichéd joke, as in "the check is in the mail" or "I'll still respect you in the morning". The idea that the government could create jobs by taking money out of the pockets of working Americans, sending it to Washington, and then paying it out to other Americans, made as much sense as the idea that one could raise the water level of a lake by taking a bucket of water out of one side, walking around the lake, and pouring it back in (less spillage). In the case of government, many Americans began to get the idea that the spillage was the point.

Chapter Three

Politicians try to get the media to focus on the water pouring into the lake and to ignore the fact that the bucket is filled from the same lake.

Why, Americans asked when Clinton wanted to "stimulate" the economy by taking tax dollars and giving them to big city mayors to spend, would this "stimulate" the economy? Where was the money coming from in the first place? The only thing stimulated here were campaign contributors who would be expected to "repay" part of the largesse they got.

The Democrat Establishment was built on five C's: crisis, complexity, cross-subsidization, compassion, and civil litigation.

● **Crisis** means that we must act now. There's no time to consider calmly the merits of a potential new program or regulation. We must act. There was an oil *crisis* in the 1970's when the price of oil rose, and Democrats told us that we must tax gasoline to solve this *crisis*. Then, in the early 1980's, when Ronald Reagan's decontrol of oil resulted in a *crisis* of falling oil prices (rather than the *increase* promised by the liberals), that *crisis* could only be solved by higher gasoline taxes. And in the late 1980's when oil prices stayed the same — and therefore we were using too much gasoline — that *crisis* could only be fixed by higher taxes on gasoline. After a while Americans came to feel that the answer — higher taxes on gasoline — was the real goal rather than the answer to any particular *crisis*.

● **Complexity** is the squid ink "answer" the Establishment emits when citizens ask common sense questions, such as why the United States should subsidize with foreign aid countries that attack us in the United Nations and do business with our enemies. The American people, we are told by our betters, are too stupid to understand the *complexities* of certain subjects, like international relations, so we should sit down, shut up, and send more money to Washington. Oddly, there is never a *crisis* that requires a tax cut, or less spending or anything so *complex* that we must have lower taxes.

● **Cross-subsidization** is a liberal game in which we rob from Peter to pay Paul, and then take from Paul to help poor Peter. It works well when the costs to those paying the freight for higher spending can be hidden. It works until the tax burden is so high that individuals can calculate that they are receiving nothing like what they are sending in to Washington.

Of course there is the inevitable "spillage", which is where the bureaucrats and politicians in Washington do well by doing good.

● **Compassion** is an honorable virtue that Democrats have long evoked in support of all manner of social programs that taxpayers now recognize have actually hurt those they aim to help. In the 1984 Mondale-Reagan campaign the Democrats bragged — and their allies in the press trumpeted — that they were winning the *compassion* issue. Voters did indeed, when asked, agree that the Democrat Party was the more *compassionate* party. However, after the election, analysts found that when asked to define *compassion*, voters said, "that's when the politicians steal our money and give it to bums." Many people offered answers like this one: "Yes, the Democrat Party is the more 'compassionate': that's why I voted Republican, because they won't waste my money."

The Democrats are caught between a rock and a hard place. They can feed the welfare state and the unionized bureaucracy that provides them with campaign funding and campaign workers or they can serve the needs of the poorest Americans in whose name they created the unionized, bureaucratic, welfare state. They cannot do both, for the welfare state bureaucracy displaces and consumes the private sector activism and resources that might help the poorest Americans help themselves. And a liberated underclass does not need, and cannot afford, the welfare state bureaucracy.

● **Civil Litigation** is another major building block of the Democrat Party. The trial lawyers, who make their living suing people in civil cases, provide a great deal of the money the Democrat party and its front groups need. These are the lawyers who talk you into suing McDonalds when you spill a cup of their coffee on yourself driving away from the drive-thru. Given the present state of the law, a good trial lawyer can convince a jury that McDonalds should pay you $3 million because they made the coffee too hot. Never mind that the three million must come from the pockets of low-wage-earning McDonalds workers or from higher prices to McDonalds customers.

● **Trial Lawyers: Ready Cash for Democrats**
How significant is the trial lawyers' money? Very significant indeed! A study by the American Tort Reform Association found that in the four years from June 1990 to June 1994, trial lawyers gave candidates $17.3 million in political contributions in Alabama, California and Texas alone. This compares to total contributions to candidates from the Democratic National Committee and the Republican National Committee of $12.4 million and $10.8 million, respectively.

As early as the late 1970's, trial lawyers were giving twice as much to Democrat candidates as to Republican candidates, but by the 1990's, Democrats were receiving 90 percent of all trial lawyer contributions.

Trial lawyers are not just one of the key money machines for the Democrat Party. They also fund liberal groups in the Establishment that in turn promote liberal and Democrat causes. "We are what supports Nader", says Fred Levin, who earned $7.5 million in one year as a trial lawyer. "We all belong to his group. We contribute to him, and he fundraises through us ." Trial lawyer Herb Hafif adds, "I can get on the phone and raise $100,000 for Nader in one day." Pat Maloney, another trial lawyer, says, "We support him overtly, covertly, in every way possible."

In 1990 and 1992, when the Democrat Party tried to destroy Newt Gingrich in retaliation for his role in the resignations of Speaker Jim Wright, Whip Tony Coelho, and Budget Committee Chairman Bill Gray of Philadelphia, they turned to the trial lawyers and Ralph Nader. The lawyers laid out more than $100,000 towards an independent expenditure campaign savaging Gingrich in the 1990 primary contest.

Texas Republican activist Karl Rove identifies the trial lawyers as the single largest source of campaign funds for Ann Richards in her campaigns for governor and for the Texas Democrat Party generally.

There are only about 50,000 members of the professional group, the Association of Trial Lawyers of America. They are dwarfed by the 2.5 million members of the National Education Association. But political consultant Gene Ulm, who specializes in state legislative races, rates the trial lawyer lobby as "second only to the teachers' unions in power at the state level ". Although short on membership, the trial lawyers are long on cash and willing to spend it directly for the party or indirectly through the party's front groups, such as the so-called "consumer groups ". Trial attorney B.B. Spence is quoted in a ground-breaking investigative report in *Forbes* magazine by Peter Brimelow and Leslie Spencer on trial lawyer financing of politics: "I probably give them [Ralph Nader front groups] five percent of my income. " Mr. Spence is reported to have earned $2.5 million in 1988.

Chapter Three

The very size of the cash awards won by the trial lawyers and public awareness of this abuse have begun to shake this pillar of the Democrat coalition.

Public opinion is turning against the trial lawyers. A March 1993 poll in Alabama found that 80 percent of Alabamians would be more likely to vote against a candidate for the legislature or state court who took large contributions from trial lawyers. Seventy percent would be "more likely to vote against a candidate if he or she were endorsed by plaintiffs' trial lawyers ". Polls in Louisiana found 71 percent would vote against a candidate endorsed by the trial lawyers. Polls in Texas and Mississippi produced similar results.

In 1989, pro-reform activist Victor Schwartz was quoted in *Forbes* as saying of the trial lawyers, "They've never lost on an issue before Congress." But in 1994, public revulsion over the greed of the trial lawyers and the political power flowing from their contributions to the Democrat Party forced both the House and Senate — then still run by Democrats — to pass legislation that put the first limits on product liability abuses in the airplane construction business. Bill Clinton was forced to sign the bill, although he was a major recipient of trial lawyer money. As they raised millions for him in the 1992 election, he bragged that he had always served their interests as governor of Arkansas.

Yeshiva University's Cardozo School of Law Professor Lester Brickman estimates that trial lawyers' total income from contingency fees exceeds $10 billion annually. If the trial lawyers are only one fifth as generous as Mr. Spence, they are kicking back one percent of this amount, or $100 million a year, to the Democrats and their front groups.

Rock the House

FALSE FLAG CONSERVATIVE DEMOCRATS

In a nation that has consistently told pollsters it would prefer smaller government to larger government, whose entire history is one of revolutionary anti-establishmentarianism, the Democrats could only maintain majorities in the House of Representatives and the Senate with a "conservative" wing of the party that could run in Southern, rural and Midwestern districts and states telling the folks back home they are conservative Democrats and distancing themselves from the ever-leftward drift of the "national party ".

These "conservative" Democrats had three responsibilities:

● **First**, to get themselves elected in districts that would never elect liberal Democrats.

● **Second**, to vote for the liberal leadership of the House and Senate, guaranteeing liberal Democrat control.

● And **third**, to cast just enough conservative-looking votes to keep themselves in the good graces of the rubes back home, while loyally and unswervingly voting with the Democrat leadership whenever it really mattered on procedural matters.

This false-flag recruitment of conservative voters to elect phony conservative Democrats in Southern and Midwestern districts had been faltering in recent elections, but it collapsed completely in the 1992 and 1994 elections. It happened when Rep. Charlie Stenholm of Texas, the Kim Philby of conservative Democrats, was exposed as serving the interests of the liberal leadership on a consistent basis and could no longer serve as protective coloration for endangered "conservative" Democrats. Without his cover, many were defeated in 1994, and Stenholm unabashedly led the charge against adding a tax limitation provision to the balanced budget amendment in January of 1995. Instead, he strongly supported a balanced budget amendment that liberal Illinois Senator Paul Simon admits is a backdoor effort to force ever-higher spending and tax increases.

Key incidents in the unmasking of Charlie Stenholm occurred in 1993, during consideration of the first Clinton budget, and during the 1995 battle for a balanced budget amendment with a tax limitation safeguard in it.

Outing Liberal Democrats

On Thursday afternoon, May 27, 1993, Rep. Charlie Stenholm voted in favor of Bill Clinton's budget reconciliation package, which increased taxes by $241 billion over the next five years and increased spending from $1.5 trillion in 1993 to $1.8 trillion in 1998. More than a dozen moderate Democrats followed Stenholm's lead, giving Clinton his first major legislative victory by a margin of 219 to 213. Both Republicans and Democrats agree that without Stenholm's support and influence Clinton's package would have died in the House.

Only days before the final vote, taxpayer groups and business lobbies believed they had the votes to defeat the package. That would have forced Speaker Tom Foley to withdraw the bill from consideration until after the Memorial Day recess. Opponents hoped that once representatives were in their districts, they would feel the growing anger of taxpayers and reject the package. That had actually happened over the April recess: Senator Bob Dole was then leading a filibuster against Clinton's $16.5 billion "stimulus" package. His efforts were immensely strengthened by voter reaction during the recess, and the package was killed. So too, it was thought, would the anti-tax forces in the House gain strength through any delay.

One reason people believed that Clinton's package was in serious trouble was Stenholm's announcement that he would insist on real caps in entitlement spending. The Washington press corps frequently called Stenholm for the "moderate" or "conservative" Democrat spin on issues, and for ten years, Democrat congressmen who had wanted to distance themselves from the party's liberal ideology had looked to Stenholm as their standard-bearer. If Stenholm had stood his ground, demanding real spending reductions and real caps on entitlements, Clinton would have lost that May 27.

But Stenholm caved. The Democrat leadership allowed him to attach a toothless "entitlement review process" that even Ways and Means Chairman Rostenkowski belittled as "bells and whistles". Stenholm's collapse was so total that it led tax activist Peter Roff to complain, "After a dive like that, someone should call the boxing commissioner."

The fury of conservative members of Congress at Stenholm's betrayal was unprecedented, not simply because of the size of the package Stenholm allowed through, but because it was the latest in a series of efforts to cut spending that Stenholm endorsed and then undermined. Members were angry at Stenholm, but also at themselves for being fooled — yet again — into thinking Stenholm would stand firm. Sadder and wiser, one member likened Stenholm to the "Peanuts" cartoon character Lucy, who each fall holds the football for Charlie Brown to kick, only to pull it away at the last instant.

Some argued that Stenholm was simply weak, unable to stand up to pressure. Republican consultant Richard Billmire recalls that when the winds were blowing from the Right in the early 1980's, Stenholm, was "terrified of Ronald Reagan" and could be counted on as a sure vote in support of the Contras and the Reagan tax and budget cuts. "Bush did not scare Stenholm", Billmire says, but Foley and Clinton did. Or it might just be that Stenholm's double-dealing stemmed from his own drive for power, which required that he please the Democrat leadership.

Rep. Newt Gingrich, now Speaker of the House but then House Republican Whip, saw Stenholm as an active part of the Democrat leadership's strategy, providing cover for Democrats in swing districts who have to pretend to be moderates. Gingrich likened Stenholm to the Washington Generals, the basketball team that barnstorms with the Harlem Globetrotters. "Their job is to make it look interesting, make it look close even, but in the end to lose gracefully."

Stenholm's usefulness to the Democrat leadership was underscored in 1989, when he was given the post of deputy whip. A whip's job is to line up votes for the leadership's position — an odd job for an honest dissident. Stenholm had also been rewarded with a plum assignment on the Budget Committee. By contrast, when then Democrat Phil Gramm bucked the House leadership in the early 1980's to co-sponsor Reagan's first tax cuts, he was stripped of his committee assignments.

Former New Hampshire Rep. Chuck Douglas led the fight for a balanced budget amendment in 1990 — which Stenholm purportedly supported — and has vivid memories of the "help" Stenholm offered. Because the Democrat leadership would not allow the amendment out of committee and onto the House floor, Douglas circulated a discharge petition, a little-used parliamentary mechanism that forces a vote on a piece of bottled-up legislation if a majority of members sign on. "When we were within two votes of forcing the discharge", Douglas recalls, "we saw Stenholm up at the front desk talking with the Speaker. Throughout the entire process Stenholm was always trying to slow us down; we were certain he was warning Speaker Foley, and so I rushed up two more signers, and we discharged the balanced budget amendment. This is what we had been working on for months. Charlie's reaction — he was livid!"

Stenholm performed similar "mediating" functions during consideration of funding for the National Endowment for the Arts and the line-item veto. By offering "compromise" amendments, which made cosmetic changes only, Stenholm provided "conservative" Democrats with votes they could take to the voters, while at the same time making certain that there were no substantive changes in the status quo.

One reason given by Stenholm himself for his efforts at "moderation" was that the Democrat leadership would not tolerate open votes on the most conservative alternatives. The falseness of that argument is now apparent. Since the 1994 election, the House is under the control of conservative Republicans, who are anxious for those clear-cut, up-or-down votes. But Stenholm continues to try to play a "mediating" role.

With the defeat in November 1994 of dozens of "conservative" Democrats, Stenholm now finds himself general of an army with no troops. His strategy of providing cover did not work, and his opposition to the plans and programs of their successors brands him as the fraud he has been all along. There is no "conservative wing" of the Democrat Party. There are, however, some Democrats who still represent conservative districts. Those Democrats, such as Nathan Deal of Georgia, Jimmy Hayes of Alabama, Billy Tauzin of Louisiana, and Bill Orton of Utah may vote conservative to save their seats, but with a Republican majority in the House, their pretense is much harder to maintain. They sense impending defeat in 1996.

THE COLLAPSE OF THE LIBERAL MEDIA MONOPOLY

The Democrat Establishment in Washington maintained effective control over the nation from 1932 to 1994 while only being able to garner 40 to 43 percent of the vote for president since 1964. (Democrat Jimmy Carter's victory in 1976 does not disprove this statement. Carter ran not as an Establishment Democrat, but as a Southern moderate and to Republican President Gerald Ford's right on social issues as well as the issue of Poland's national independence.) Maintaining this control required more than the money and manpower of the labor unions, the trial lawyers, the corrupt big city bureaucratic machines, and a smoke and mirrors "conservative wing". It also required control over the communications to and from Washington. The completeness of that control rivalled that of the communications organs in totalitarian states. When the collapse came, it came as fast as in those dictatorships.

For example, in Albania, the Communist party slogan for 1960 was, "We are the light of Europe". Albanians, cut off from normal communications, believed it. But by the 1980's, when broadcasts of Italian television were reaching across the Adriatic Sea, many Albanian families could watch Dynasty and Dallas on television. The Albanians knew perfectly well then that their Communist backwater was not the light of Europe and that capitalism, not communism, was providing prosperity for the masses. Once the Big Lie of Communism was exposed, the system fell quickly and virtually without defenders in 1990.

So too in the United States. As late as 1969, 90 percent of Americans got their television news from ABC, NBC, or CBS. There were no CNN, and no C-SPAN covering what actually happened on the floor of Congress. There were no fax machines, no VCR's. Producers at the three networks would read the *Washington Post* and the *New York Times* and then decide what was and what wasn't news. The American people would see and read only what made it through this rather dense filter.

If CBS said something was "a jobs bill", it was. There was no voice asking just where the tax money to "create" these jobs was coming from, or what jobs were being destroyed by taking the tax money out of the economy in the first place. Liberalism was the world

111

view of those who wrote the news for the wire services and the television anchors. It was thus the only world view available to most Americans.

Slowly this monopoly on information broke up.

First came little cracks, such as the establishment of the *National Review* in 1955, edited and sustained by William F. Buckley, Jr.

In the early years, circulation hovered around 20,000-30,000. It spiked up to around 140,000 during the Goldwater years, then steadily declined. When Ronald Reagan was elected, circulation hopped up to about 100,000. Starting in the mid-1980's, it climbed again until by January of 1992 it was 160,000. By 1994 it had jumped to 250,000-260,000.

Human Events, a feisty weekly newspaper based in Washington, has provided a consistent conservative outlook since the 1950's, but its circulation was low. Editorial and reportorial excellence, provided by Tom Winters and Allan Ryskind, attracted the attention of Phillips Publishing which has finally brought <u>HE</u> the financial resources it has needed, and its circulation is now growing rapidly.

The *American Spectator* grew from humble beginnings in Indiana. Originally called *The Alternative*, it was indeed an alternative campus newspaper at the University of Indiana, edited by R. Emmett Tyrell and published by John Von Kannon ("The Baron"). The *Spectator*'s circulation in 1992 was 30,000. It jumped to 100,000 in 1993 and to 330,000 today — the largest circulation political monthly of the Left or Right in the United States.

The *Washington Times* became the second Washington, D.C. daily newspaper in 1982. Almost immediately the <u>*Washington Times*</u> presence weakened the <u>*Washington Post's*</u> monopoly on information in the nation's capitol. The <u>*Post's*</u> ability to censor by omission disappeared. Republican initiatives could not be ignored. Democrat contradictions were highlighted. Suddenly there were two sides to each issue. Editor-in-Chief Wes Pruden and editorial page and commentary editors Tod Lindberg and Mary Lou Forbes have brought the paper increasing stature, influence, and (importantly for any newspaper) advertising revenue. Above all, the *Times* provides a forum for conservative intellectual and policy ideas that are completely shut out of the pages of the *Washington Post*. The *Times'* circulation is now almost 100,000.

In addition to these periodical publications, there is always a need for what A.A. Milne called "the relative permanence of stiff covers ". That means books. Needless to say, the major publishing houses have been hostile to the ideas of modern conservatives, until very recently, when the growing market for conservative books made the potential profits impossible to ignore. Two small publishers nourished that market through the lean years: Regnery-Gateway, founded by Henry Regnery and now run by his son Al, and Arlington House, founded in the 1960's by the late Neil McCaffrey, Jr. At the same time, McCaffery established the Conservative Book Club, which has made thousands of classic and contemporary titles available to modern readers. Only his vision and tenacity could have made such a project work.

The telecommunications revolution has greatly increased the number of options Americans have for receiving news and entertainment. From 769 broadcast TV stations in 1967, there are now more than 1,600. The number of broadcast radio stations increased from 5,249 in 1967 to 11,700 today. Cable is now available to 96 percent of American homes and subscribed to by 65 percent (up from 3 percent in 1967). Now, over 85 percent of American homes have VCR's. They did not exist in 1967.

The growth in specialized channels is phenomenal: CNN, C-SPAN One and Two, Arts and Entertainment, Discovery, the Learning Channel, Bravo, the History Channel and many others. Direct Broadcast Satellite is now available throughout the 48 contiguous states with more than 150 channels of "digital" video and audio programming.

And satellite communications make it possible for radio talk shows to be syndicated throughout the nation. Today, Rush Limbaugh's three-hour radio talk show is heard on 659 stations. Twenty million Americans listen to Rush in the course of a given week. His show also appears on 250 television stations, and a half-million people subscribe to *The Limbaugh Letter*. The 73 Republican freshman members of Congress paid tribute to Rush Limbaugh's towering presence in the 1994 campaign when they asked him to be the keynote speaker at the Freshman Orientation week hosted by The Heritage Foundation and Empower America. The freshman women gave Rush an award consisting of a target with Rush's prediction of Republican victories in the bull's eye and the ABC, CBS, and *New York Times* predictions (and hopes) falling wide of the mark The freshman class voted to make Rush an "Honorary Member" of the Class of 1994.

G. Gordon Liddy, the conservative talk show host, is on 230 stations, with three million listeners.

The Michael Reagan show, hosted by President Reagan's son, is now carried on 100 stations (including WHO, "Dutch" Reagan's old station in Iowa) from 6 to 9 p.m. Pacific Time, from Los Angeles, California.

The *Wall Street Journal* editorial page, managed by Robert Bartley, a solid economic conservative and brilliant writer, puts out two million copies of the finest editorial work in the nation five days a week. With writers such as John Fund, Paul Gigot, David Brooks, Amity Shlaes, Tim Ferguson, Tom Bray, Adam Meyerson, Jude Wanniski, and Melanie Kirkpatrick, reading the editorial page of the *Wall Street Journal* keeps two million households abreast of exactly what is happening in America. Its excellent economic analysis was praised by economics writer Melanie Tammen, who observed that, "If you read the *Wall Street Journal*'s editorial page for one year, you will have a sounder grasp of economic policy than if you pay for a Harvard Ph.D. in economics."

Investor's Business Daily, with a circulation of 186,000, has a front page and news section that rivals the *Wall Street Journal*'s editorial page.   Tom McCardle, Bob Stein, Claude Marx, John Merline and Martin Wooster contribute timely and accurate news articles on state and national news.

The Heritage Foundation, Cato Institute, 30 state policy foundations, the Competitive Enterprise Institute, and Americans for Tax Reform all put out regular policy briefs by fax and computer to radio talk shows and local newspapers. The National Taxpayers Union has made available on-line to computer users its database of congressional spending, so that constituents can know in a minute how big a spender their own congressman or woman is. The Heritage Foundation's "Town Hall" is an on-line area within CompuServe where conservatives all over the country can share information and access the latest news. Americans for Tax Reform now operates "Homepage" on the Internet, to provide information to political activists and others who want to participate in the movement to down-size government. See the back of this book for more information on "Homepage".

Audio and video tapes are another channel for news and information. State Rep. Bill Richardson of California made a video tape detailing the judicial atrocities of California Supreme Court Justice Rose Bird, who was running for re-election. The tapes were given free of charge to video rental stores, where individuals checked them out for neighborhood anti-Rose parties. As early as 1976, Orrin G. Hatch, then an unknown lawyer in Salt Lake City, distributed audio tapes free of charge to delegates to the Utah Republican nominating convention. So impressed were the delegates that they voted him into a primary election, which he won, before going on to unseat 18-year incumbent Democrat Frank Moss. Phyllis Schlafly used video tapes to derail the Equal Rights Amendment in Vermont and other states.

GOPAC uses monthly audio tapes to keep its members informed of developments in Washington, and makes its training tapes available to state political parties for the edification and motivation of candidates at the local level.

Americans for Tax Reform was one of the pioneers of conference calls among activists all over the country. A regular monthly call dealing with initiatives and referenda is supplemented by special ad hoc calls dealing with specific issues like school choice in Arizona or New Jersey. On these calls, local workers can share their best ideas and techniques and can summon support for their efforts from others with experience all across the nation. GOPAC also used one-way conference calls to provide campaign training beginning with the 1992 election.

In short, there are now dozens of ways around and over the Maginot Line of liberal Establishment control of information. In fact, Republican candidates who once feared a negative editorial in the *New York Times* or the *Washington Post* now report they don't even read those dinosaurs of the information age. They are much more interested in what G. Gordon Liddy, Rush Limbaugh and Michael Reagan are saying to their much larger listenership.

But the revolution in communication has not been simply, as the Establishment Left believes, the coming of Rush Limbaugh. The fax machines, CNN, and C-SPAN are what make Rush Limbaugh and talk radio so important. Any American in the nation watching C-SPAN can be as well-informed about what is happening on the floor of Congress as the highest-paid lobbyist in Washington or the most "important" news reporter for the *Washington Post*. In fact, by watching what is really happening on the floor of Congress and participating in radio talk shows with other Americans and talk show hosts armed with immediate faxed information from think tanks and congressional offices, the American people know what is happening before the talking heads bob knowingly before us on the 6 and 11

Chapter Three

o'clock news. Why stay up to watch "film at eleven" when C-SPAN allowed you to watch the entire speech by Newt Gingrich as it happened? Who needs the Establishment's edited version? And after Americans have watched an entire Gingrich speech and then seen Dan Rather's or Bryant Gumbel's description of what was said, they conclude that Rather and Gumbel do not accurately report the news.

American distrust of the media does not stem just from famous instances such as NBC's decision to show a faked truck crash on national television or publicize phoney alarmism about battered wives on Super Bowl Sunday. Day after day, Americans can watch C-SPAN, listen to talk radio, and read alternative news sources and conclude that the America of Bryant Gumbel's imagination is just that: what the liberal Establishment would like America to think of itself rather than what is real.

The Establishment Left's ability to sell us their version of what is happening in Washington has collapsed. When NBC is reduced to simply reporting what happened in Washington, it no longer has power. When the Establishment press tries to slant the news, it is caught immediately. It is no longer any fun to be Dan Rather at CBS. He has been reduced to being a reader of the news and no longer serves as an interpreter.

The difference for American politics can best be understood by looking at the very different reporting of the Vietnam and Gulf wars.

In Vietnam, an American general would give a briefing, and the three networks and the *New York Times* could decide what to cover from an hour's talk. Thirty seconds of footage would emerge. A reporter could badger the general with hypothetical questions and twist words around to get the general to appear to have changed his position. Headline: *General Admits Error*. No one who was not in the briefing room would understand the context of the final report. The reporters in the room had complete freedom to choose what to

117

focus on. Americans wouldn't have a clue how to judge the fairness of the reporting.

But during the Gulf War of 1991, CNN gave live coverage to the military briefings. An Army spokesman would speak for 20 minutes, giving a compete rundown of the day's events. Then the press would start in playing "gotcha ". Questions the military had repeatedly said it would not answer were asked. The reporters put the same question again and again, hoping to elicit some misstatement. But this time the America people saw the press at work. They were able to decide for themselves how forthcoming the military was being, how honest the reporters' questions were, how important, or how silly. "Saturday Night Live" reflected the nation's reaction to the press in Iraq when it featured a skit of the military briefer offering a serious report, and reporters following with ridiculous questions such as, "Would you give us some of the secret passwords?" and "What wouldn't you want the Iraqi high command to know?"

Now that there were alternative sources available to average Americans, the evening news on ABC, NBC, and CBS had to be written with the knowledge that many American already knew what had happened by watching CNN or listening to the radio. There could be no slanting of the news. No selective coverage. No trashing of American troops. Oddly enough, the United States won this war handily.

The defeat of the Democrats in the House, Senate, governorships, and state legislatures was not simply a rejection of Bill Clinton or even of the Democrats. It was a rejection of the entire Washington Establishment, and that certainly includes some of its most powerful members: the *Washington Post, Newsweek, Time,* the *New York Times,* and the three old networks.

The Establishment media have revelled for decades in being part of Washington's power structure. They have been part of the party scene and enjoyed the perks and privileges of being "in the know" and sculpting public opinion. No more. They are as dethroned by technology and a better-informed electorate as Tom Foley and Dan Rostenkowski were by the 1994 election. And they are less graceful in defeat.

Peter Jennings, who anchors ABC's "World News Tonight" had the following reaction to the election results on his daily ABC radio commentary:

> "Some thoughts on those angry voters. Ask parents of any two-year-old, and they can tell you about those temper tantrums: the stomping feet, the rolling eyes, the screaming. It's clear that the anger controls the child and not the other way around. It's the job of the parent to teach the child to control the anger and channel it in a positive way. Imagine a nation full of uncontrolled two-year-old rage. The voters had a temper tantrum last week...Parenting and governing don't have to be dirty words; the nation can't be run by an angry two-year-old."

Steve Roberts, a senior writer for *U.S. News and World Report* (and formerly a reporter for the *New York Times*), actually said on CNBC's "Equal Time" on election night, "They are not voting Republican tonight, Mary. They are voting against the unhappiness in their own lives...This is not an anti-government vote tonight ".

Newsweek Washington Bureau Chief Evan Thomas summed up the election results on "Inside Washington" on November 12, 1994 with the following: "This is a rotten time to be black. Blacks are just going to take it in the chops. "

Seeing the Republican victory coming, *Newsweek* Senior Editor Joe Klein wrote in an October 31 news story, "The Republicans have resorted to demagoguery and transparent bribes (like lower taxes). " After the election Klein wrote, for the November 14 *Newsweek*, "A truly awful election year. Dismal, depressing and despicable.

Especially after 1992, which was pretty good (as these things go). Serious ideas were discussed in 1992. "

Just four days before the election, *USA Today* columnist and Pacifica Radio talk show host Julianna Malveaux had this to say about Supreme Court Justice Clarence Thomas on the government-funded Public Broadcasting System's "To The Contrary": "I hope his wife feeds him lots of eggs and butter, and he dies early like many black men do, of heart disease. "

These are not the angry and disappointed comments of people whose friends have just lost an election. They are the voices of rage of people who see the election results as a very personal rejection of them, of everything they have been saying and doing for ten years. These are the rantings of jilted lovers who believed in their hearts that the American people liked them, believed them, needed them. And now they discover they have no power over the American people. And they hate America for it.

The Establishment press, courtiers to the old order, once-feared knights of the liberal round table, lash out like the Red Queen upon finding out that "off with their heads" is no longer feared. No one is taking orders from this crowd any longer.

New technologies and new sources of information had a direct impact on the election of 1994. A poll by Frank Luntz found that Americans who got their television news from CBS voted Republican by a 44-43 margin. In explanation, the Center for Media and Public Affairs found that "CBS gave Republicans four times as much bad coverage as good (20 percent positive *versus* 80 percent negative evaluations), while Democrats were praised by 44 percent of CBS sources."

Those who viewed NBC voted Republican 45-39, and those who watched ABC voted Republican 52-36. "World News Tonight" on ABC was the most balanced (43 percent positive for Democrats *versus* 39 percent positive for the GOP).

Those who primarily got their news from CNN, which uses a debate format to present both sides of issues, voted 57 percent to 32 percent for Republicans. The fourth network of CNN has broken up not only the financial monopoly of the three old networks, but also their monopoly on political information.

Talk radio is even less controlled by an elite, as listeners themselves call in and direct the discussion of issues. There is plenty of competition. Those Americans who listened to no talk radio voted Democrat by a razor-thin margin of 42-41 percent. Those listening to 1-4 hours a week voted 53 percent to 35 percent Republican over Democrat; those listening to 5-10 hours per week voted Republican 59 percent to 35 percent Democrat; and those listening to 11 hours or more a week voted Republican 68 percent to 23 percent Democrat. The more directly voters get their news, the less the Washington filter, the more likely the voters are to vote Republican.

* * * * *

As the tumbrels pass though the town, taking away the failed and rejected Establishment, Harvard University joins the talking heads of the old networks and *Newsweek* and *Time* on the scrap heap. Since 1972, Harvard's Kennedy School of Government has run a week-long seminar on issues for incoming freshmen elected to the House of Representatives and the Senate. In 1981, The Heritage Foundation and the Free Congress Foundation tried to schedule a conservative alternative to the liberal indoctrination workshop. House Speaker Tip O'Neill deliberately moved the Harvard seminar so that members had to choose. In those days, The Heritage and the Free Congress Foundations lost.

Not any more. In 1992, the two foundations, along with the Family Research Council, organized a training conference for congressional freshmen. This time, 33 Republicans attended the conservative seminar, and only a handful went to the Harvard seminar (a few went to both and pronounced the Heritage-FCF-FRC program superior). Even in 1992, Harvard's pull on Congress was waning. Six freshman Democrats committed to the conservative workshop, but the Democrat leadership bludgeoned them into going to Harvard instead.

By November of 1994, the 71 incoming Republican freshmen announced they were *all* attending the Heritage introductory seminar on Congress and *none* would be going to Harvard. Indeed, why would Members of Congress who were elected to tear down the present Establishment wish to sit at the feet of those who built, defended and still believe in it? Why try to learn from those whose creations have destroyed so many families and killed so many futures? Why listen to those still living in the 1960's? Left with only a pool of 17 freshman Democrats to even invite to listen to its liberal world view, Harvard capitulated and cancelled its seminar.

CHAPTER FOUR

THE FAILED CLINTON COUP

Bill Clinton won the presidency with only 43 percent of the popular vote on November 3, 1992. Exit polls taken that day showed that 55 percent of Americans wanted a smaller government with fewer services and lower taxes. Only 36 percent wanted more services and higher taxes. Looking specifically at the 43 percent of Americans who voted for Clinton, however, the exit polls found the exact reverse. A full 55 percent of Clinton voters wanted larger government with higher taxes and more services, and only 36 percent wanted smaller government, fewer services and lower taxes.

Bill Clinton's political base was a minority of 43 percent of the American electorate, a minority opposed to the rest of the country on the central issue of the size and scope of government. In fact, Bill Clinton's coalition was a photographic negative, the exact opposite, of the rest of the nation.

How could he possibly govern and get re-elected in a two-man race in 1996? How would he avoid the pitfalls which had trapped other Democrats?

Bill Clinton was armed with critical insights that Jimmy Carter, Walter Mondale, and Michael Dukakis never grasped.

First, Bill Clinton knew that the Democrat Party coalition was shrinking, cracking, and self-contradictory. He knew that it could not survive without massive infusions of taxpayer dollars. He did not believe, as Walter Mondale did, that the union boss-black leadership-liberal intellectual-ethnic coalition still existed in a form or size sufficient to win majorities at the national level. To survive, Clinton knew he would have to drastically expand the Democrat coalition within four years.

Second, Clinton knew that most of the American electorate was uncomfortable with who he was and what he represented. The average American voter listening in on one of Bill Clinton's bull sessions with his friends at Yale or Oxford would be sickened, and Clinton knew it. Michael Dukakis, living in an upscale suburb of Boston, actually thought that vetoing legislation requiring teachers to lead the pledge of allegiance every morning in school would win public support. It always had in Cambridge and Brookline, Massachusetts. But Bill Clinton had lived in Arkansas and, while he shared Dukakis's cramped view of the world and America's place in it, he knew perfectly well that Americans as a whole rejected that view. Clinton had learned from the failures of Carter, Mondale and Dukakis. He had learned to hide his disagreements with America.

WHEN YOU'RE LOSING, CHANGE THE RULES

As Clinton took the oath of office on January 20, 1993, the Democrat coalition was shrinking and the Republican coalition growing. To keep his congressional majorities and win re-election he would need to bump his support up from 43 percent to 51 percent and kneecap his opponents' political organizations.

He had a working model in the 1974 Watergate-driven election of 75 freshman Democrats to the House of Representatives. Like Clinton in 1993, this band of radicals did not represent a stable electoral coalition commanding the support of a working majority of American voters. Like Clinton, they were smart enough to know it. Many were elected in districts that traditionally voted Republican. Like Clinton, they were certain of the righteousness of their cause, certain enough that they were willing to change the rules of the House of Representatives to lock in their hold on power.

The "Watergate Babies" and their older and younger left-wing allies in the Democrat caucus firmly controlled the House for 20 years (1975-1994) with the exception of, at most, only the first year of the first Reagan Administration, when tax cuts and some spending restraint were enacted.

Clinton had observed that the Democrat members of the House maintained this control in the face of the Carter failure, the twin Reagan landslides, a George Bush victory, Speaker Jim Wright's and Whip Tony Coelho's corruption scandals, check bouncing, drug sales in the House Post Office, Rep. Gerry Studds' sexual assault on a young male page, Rep. Barney Frank's formal reprimand by the House of Representatives for lying to protect a homosexual who was running a prostitution ring run out of Frank's house, and polling data consistently rating congressmen well below all other public figures. How did they do it? They simply changed the rules. They stacked the deck. They cheated. This would be the model for a successful Clinton coup.

The Watergate Babies went to work fast to dig a moat around their incumbency and pull up the drawbridge. First, they surrounded themselves with political bodyguards — staffers, researchers and (legal or not) campaign aides. The number of staffers in the House jumped from 5,280 in 1972 to 6,939 in 1976. By 1986, it had crept up to 7,920. They also showered themselves with larger budgets. Appropriations for the legislative branch jumped 18.6 percent in 1975 and 20.6 percent in 1976.

In addition, Democrat Members of Congress who were in formerly Republican districts found that voters learned to appreciate and understand them better when the amount of "franked" (that is, taxpayer-funded) direct mail from Congress increased in number from 321 million pieces in 1974 to 401 million in time for the 1976 election year, and to 430 million for the 1978 election. In 1980, when the heavy artillery was brought out during the general election with Ronald Reagan at the top of the ballot, 511 million pieces of taxpayer-funded direct mail filled voters' mailboxes, burying the hopes of many Republican challengers.

Rules were changed in other ways. Almost every Democrat in the House received his or her very own subcommittee chairmanship — the better to exhort (read: extort) campaign contributions from the industry under that subcommittee's jurisdiction (read: control). Other powers were seized from the executive branch, such as rescission and impoundment. And, by micromanaging federal contracts and grant-making, Members delivered to their home districts billions of dollars in pork barrel projects that produced campaign funds and votes. Small wonder that by the end of the 1980's voters were beginning to notice that re-election rates were at historic highs and that one was more likely to lose an election in Mexico's choreographed "balloting", retire feet first from the British House of Lords, or be physically removed from a Soviet Politburo than to lose a re-election bid to the U.S. House of Representatives.

If Clinton and Gore could learn from their House brethren and mimic their rites of self-protection, they would not be needing to order any change of address kits in 1997.

A president cannot "gerrymander" his district, but Clinton immediately did the closest thing available to him. He supported a power grab in the House of Representatives to allow, for the first time in history, the delegates from Guam, American Samoa, the Virgin Islands, the District of Columbia, and the Resident Commissioner of

Puerto Rico to vote on the floor of Congress when Congress meets — as it usually does — as the Committee of the Whole. This maneuver cut in half the 10-seat gain House Republicans won in the 1992 election.

Clinton also pushed hard to make Washington, D.C. a state, which would have given the Democrats another two Senate seats.

To stop voters from learning directly about what was happening in Washington, the Democrats moved to stop the C-SPAN coverage of "special order" speeches from the floor of Congress. House Republicans, led by Newt Gingrich and Pennsylvania Rep. Bob Walker, had effectively used these special orders to speak directly to the American people about what was happening in Washington. The gambit failed, but it highlighted the fact that the Democrats under Speaker Tom Foley and President Bill Clinton well understood that news from Washington, if unfiltered by the Establishment press, was a real danger to their power.

Clinton went to work immediately — not to cut taxes on the middle class, as he had promised during the campaign — but to cement his own power base.

His "stimulus package" was both a $16 billion payback to the big city mayors who delivered the vote for the Democrats in 1992 and a down payment on their doing the same in 1994 and 1996. This payoff was stopped by a Republican filibuster in the Senate and largely withdrawn in embarrassment when the pork barrel nature of the spending was exposed by researchers at The Heritage Foundation and the Cato Institute.

Big labor unions were paid off when Clinton overturned George Bush's executive order implementing the Supreme Court's decision in *Beck* v. *Communications Workers of America.*

In 1988, the Court had ruled that the Constitution prohibited labor unions from using union dues for purposes other than collective bargaining. Routine union practices such as voter turnout and candidate endorsements were forbidden, unless the union member agree. According to the Court in the *Beck* decision, any union member could ask to have returned all dues money not being used to pay for the legitimate bargaining function. In the case of the Communications Workers of America, only 21 percent of the money was being used legitimately, and Harry Beck was entitled to have 79 percent of his dues money returned to him.

The problem was that very few unionized workers understood the *Beck* decision, and it was certainly not in the interests of the unions to tell them. Many employers were likewise reluctant to publicize this decision, since doing so might precipitate union strikes and violence. After all, since dues paid by the 16.6 million private sector union members totals $7.3 billion a year (average dues are $440), the unions stood to lose $5.8 billion a year if all workers asked for their money back under the *Beck* decision. Even if only ten percent asked for the illicit 79 percent back, it would cost the unions $580 million a year.

As soon as the *Beck* decision was delivered by the Supreme Court, Republican activists pleaded with the Bush Administration to issue an executive order requiring employers to post information for workers about their "Beck Rights". After all, the Department of Labor requires information about many labor issues to be posted in workplaces. But the Bush Labor Department dragged its feet until just before the 1992 election, when it did, finally, agree to an executive order from the president. This is the order that Bill Clinton repealed at his first opportunity. By cancelling the Bush executive order, Clinton told his supporters that they would be paid off, regardless of what the Constitution says about workers' rights.

Clinton also fought hard to pass a law that would have given the labor unions tremendous leverage in strikes: the "Striker Replacement Act". This legislation would, in effect, have made it almost impossible for businesses to oppose labor unions willing to go out on strike for long periods of time. And with a friendly Labor Department run by

Clinton allies and appointees, any business would be foolish to believe it could not be smashed with some trumped-up charge of "unfair labor practices". Striker Replacement failed of passage only because of a Republican filibuster in the Senate, led by Orrin G. Hatch of Utah.

Next, Clinton went to work to repeal the Hatch Act, which had been passed in 1939 to stop blackmail by government workers who, by engaging in partisan political activity, abuse their positions to extort campaign contributions from fellow workers, those regulated by the government, and anyone who might feel it "wise" to make a contribution when a local bureaucrat demands one.

With Clinton's cooperation, Democrats on the Hill quickly repealed Hatch Act abuse-preventing restrictions on the three million civilian government workers. They are now free to contribute to, demand contributions for, and work "after hours" for the party of government. This development has serious implications, since the bureaucracies of Washington are already largely closed to outside influence.

Prior to action on the Hatch Act, Columnist George Will pointed out that already, "Today's government is a monologue, wherein government convinces itself there should be more of itself." Will cited James Payne, a scholar who found that in 14 House and Senate committee hearings on spending issues, of some 1,060 witnesses who testified, 47 percent were federal administrators, ten percent were state or local government officials, and six percent were senators or congressmen themselves. *Fully 63 percent of the witnesses speaking to the government were the government itself.*

The gutting of the Hatch Act allows the government that talks to itself to run and finance the campaigns of the politicians. Government will now also elect the government. This was a giant step by Clinton to strengthen the power of the government against a possible election challenge by taxpayers in 1994 or 1996.

Of course, Clinton's liberalization of the Hatch Act did not include members of the armed forces. They, after all, are probably Republicans. Or at least less than sympathetic to a president who told the world he "loathes" them and demonstrated it by having men in uniform serve hors d'œuvres at a White House event for his friends. (Apparently, to Bill Clinton, everyone in uniform looks alike. Soldiers, waiters, whatever.)

After turning the government into a big lobby for more pro-government policies, the next step for Clinton was to make sure that every beneficiary of welfare spending be organized to vote for more of the welfare state. This was why the Democrats made the "Motor Voter Bill" one of their top priorities, despite the fact that voter registration has always been the domain of the states.

Congress passed the National Voter Registration Act, commonly known as "Motor Voter", and it was enthusiastically signed by Bill Clinton on May 20, 1993. This bill requires the states to offer immediate voter registration to anyone — illegal alien, alien resident, or citizen — applying for a driver's license. Registration must also, under Clinton's law, be encouraged at all welfare offices, unemployment offices, and other state offices — to all potential voters, in short, other than taxpayers. This requirement was inspired by the successful program run by Mayor Marion Barry of Washington, D.C., who demanded that anyone receiving a government check from his summer youth program first show proof that they had registered to vote (and were therefore in a position to be grateful for the government check).

Of course, many illegal aliens have driver's licenses. Zoë Baird, whom Clinton nominated for the Attorney General's job, had an illegal alien as a chauffeur. Presumably, he had a license to drive. Reportedly, the assassin of Mexican presidential candidate Luis Donaldo Colosio, a Mexican citizen named Mario Aburto, was registered to vote in not one, but two cities in California.

"Motor Voter" was designed to facilitate voter fraud and to ensure that anyone in America who gets a welfare check can pay for it later with his or her vote.

While Clinton was changing the rules to ensure his success in 1996, he also began building around his presidency a wall made of sandbags filled with special interest cash. The *New York Times* reported on October 1, 1994 that in 20 months Clinton had personally raised $40 million — nearly half the amount the entire Democrat Party had reported it raised during that period. Clinton and his wife, Vice-President Al Gore and his wife, and top White House and Cabinet officials appeared in 1994 at almost 300 fundraising events. The *Times* reported that, "Bill Clinton has flattered big money donors with private White House parties and seats at state dinners and momentous events. He has freed Cabinet officers, their aides, and White House officials to give private briefings on business and politics to especially generous supporters."

At the same time, Bill Clinton moved to kneecap the independent sector of American volunteers who compete with his welfare state bureaucracy and thereby commit two deadly sins. **First**, they embarrass the entire government because private charity actually helps people and is demonstrably more efficient. **Second,** individual volunteers who help their neighbors thereby put the lie to the Democrat claim that only the virtuous, non-greedy government worker and politician care about people. Of course, most effective social work is done through churches and religious organizations; the transformation of alcoholics, drug addicts and others comes largely through commitment by the individual deciding, perhaps with help, to fix his or her own life. No government program is allowed to have any religious base, and none can individualize help.

Such a threat to the welfare state had to be marginalized, so Clinton invented AmeriCorps, a government program to replace real volunteers with government workers who can only work in secular, non-religious organizations. The high cost of these workers, estimated at $37,000 per "volunteer" each year, can only dampen enthusiasm for real volunteerism through churches, synagogues, and private organizations. In the AmeriCorps program, "volunteers" will be paid the minimum wage and will then receive scholarship money for their college education.

The antipathy to private charity evidenced by the AmeriCorps program is now endemic in the Democrat Party. Michael Dukakis dripped venom at the idea of "A Thousand Points of Light" — Bush speechwriter Peggy Noonan's evocative phrase describing what Alexis de Tocqueville first observed in the 1830's: that America's genius was its many independent associations which solve local problems, independent of any state or aristocrat. The fact that volunteer activity increased dramatically during the Reagan and Bush years is an embarrassment to the Democrat Party and a threat to its vision of a completely statist, bureaucratized welfare state.

Although budget constraints limited the number of AmeriCorps volunteers to 10,000 the first year, that is still twice as many as the Peace Corps employs, and the program can easily balloon in future years as more and more "volunteers" agitate to get on the gravy train. The Peace Corps, of course, is the model of a government program paying Americans to do with taxpayers' money what others do for true volunteer motives. The Peace Corps was an effort to secularize and bureaucratize the missionary impulse that had sent thousands of Americans abroad to do useful work at no expense to the taxpayer and with no credit to politicians.

Along with the attempt to crush the voluntary sector of the economy came Clinton's efforts to cartelize the rest of it, sweeping

132

aside small businesses and seducing the big business community into an alliance with him and the Democrat Party.

The Clinton Administration enjoyed considerable success during its early months of pushing for higher taxes and government-run health care, in picking off individual firms. Fortune 500 companies were told bluntly that if they endorsed the tax increases *in toto* or backed Hillary Clinton's government takeover of health care, they could be part of the inside operation to write the actual tax package or health care plan. Many companies decided to subordinate their general interest in lower taxes and a free market in health care for a place at the table. Apparently they believed that, since some tax bill and some health bill would pass, they might as well be cutting the best deal their firm could get. In fact, many of the Fortune 500 companies that met secretly and — we now know, illegally — with Hillary Clinton and Health Czar Ira Magaziner were planning to profit enormously at taxpayer expense if the government-run health care plan was passed in the form they would help to shape.

Still, Clinton needed to break the independent spirit of the general business community, not just co-opt one company at a time.

HOW CLINTON SEDUCED CORPORATE AMERICA

Since his election, Clinton has worked hard to court American business. He has had more meetings with Fortune 500 CEO's than either Bush or Reagan did. In his first year, he addressed the annual meetings of the U.S. Chamber of Commerce and the National Federation of Independent Business, and he personally lobbied Saudi Arabia to buy American planes.

Just as Clinton's health care scheme was based on Germany's national health system, so too was Clinton's vision of the proper relationship between the government and large corporations patterned on the European model of government-industry partnerships. Success in increasing such partnerships in America would certainly change the balance of political power by capturing — or at least neutralizing — American business, long presumed a reservoir of conservative — or at least Republican — support.

The American Left and the former Soviet Union always had an exaggerated view of the power of American business. In their view, the capitalists had all the money and property, and since political power, they thought, necessarily flows from economic power, America must be run by and for corporate interests.

It was not an implausible theory. In America today there are more than 18 million businesses, including sole proprietorships, partnerships, farms, and small firms. America has more businesses than it has union members. In the 1991-92 electoral cycle, business-associated political action committees (PAC's) contributed $127 million while union PAC's raised and spent only $43 million.

A simple inventory and comparison of political arsenals suggests that corporate America should be running Washington and the state capitals. Nevertheless, business has lost repeated fights over the Clean Air Act to environmentalists. Business also lost to the civil rights groups on legislation dealing with hiring quotas. The 1990 Americans with Disabilities Act is costing business billions right now. George Bush signed the minimum wage increase, and Bill Clinton signed a mandated family leave policy. Business's supposed muscle has been losing to the bad — actually silly — science of the environmentalists, losing to emotionalism, economic illiteracy, and slogans.

Free-market congressmen and staffers, frustrated by the inability of business to translate its resources into political victories, identify **five reasons** why business muscle has not translated into political strength.

1. Access, Influence, or Power

Business leaders too often confuse access, influence, and power. *Access* means that if your PAC contributes to a politician, he will allow you to drop by and visit while you are in Washington. *Influence* is being in the room when the politicians decide to raise taxes on your industry but, due to your large contributions to the committee chairman and all his friends on the committee, the raise is only half as much as first threatened. *Power* is the ability to defeat elected politicians.

Only power matters in Washington. The late Jesse Unruh, the former California state treasurer, distilled the contempt politicians have for those who buy access into this colorful aphorism: "If you can't take their money, screw their women, and still vote against them, you don't belong in this business."

While business PAC spending is three times as great as labor or union PAC spending, fully 79 percent of business PAC contributions goes to incumbents to buy access or protection. Business PAC's give only eight percent of their donations to challengers and a mere 12 percent to candidates in open seats. Labor unions spend only 64 percent on incumbents, 18 percent on challengers, and 29 percent on open seats. It often happens that union giving to challengers will elect a Democrat in a marginal district, and that business giving to incumbents will keep him there. Labor sows, business cultivates and fertilizes, labor reaps.

Moreover, business contributes in a much more bipartisan way. Fifty-three percent of business PAC money flowed to Democrats and 47 percent to Republicans in the 1991-92 election cycle. The less bipartisan, but more effective, union PAC's gave 94 percent to Democrats and only six percent to Republicans.

2. Staffing with the Enemy

In their quest for access rather than power, trade associations and corporations often hire Democrat staffers from Capitol Hill. The theory is that the staffer will provide access and influence with his former boss, but the relationship usually runs the other way. Joe

O'Neill, a former staffer for U.S. Senator Lloyd Bentsen, was hired by the National Retail Federation to influence this important Democrat on the Finance Committee. But in 1988, when others in the business community asked the Retail Federation to join a campaign against the value-added tax, the Federation refused because Bentsen was running for vice-president and O'Neill didn't want any anti-tax efforts hurting the Dukakis-Bentsen campaign. Bentsen had colonized the National Retail Federation, not the other way around.

That Democrat staffers are expected to maintain their loyalty to the party and not to the corporation or association they temporarily draw a paycheck from was highlighted in cold relief in early 1993. Word went out from the Democratic National Committee that any Democrat working in industry who provided serious opposition to the Clinton health plan (as opposed to visible but toothless opposition) would be kept off all Democrat campaign work now and in the future. Any Democrat with hopes of one day working on a future presidential race or on lucrative House and Senate campaigns or being hired by the Commerce Department was unlikely to fight against government-run health care with any real enthusiasm.

3. Feeding the Alligators

The business community allows itself to be divided. The distilled spirits industry does not oppose higher taxes on beer and wine. The American Gas Association, which represents natural gas producers, has no objection to gasoline taxes. But the most unnecessary and damaging division is when small business groups temper their opposition to mandates, regulations, and taxes if there is an exemption for businesses with fewer than 10, 25, or 100 employees. Ironically, small business groups then complain when General Motors is indifferent to burdensome rules or costs that devastate small business, but are only annoying to GM. Exemptions are carved out only when the politicians are convinced they cannot pass the bill without the exemption.

Solidarity between large and small businesses would have stopped a lot of bad legislation.

4. Hanging Separately

Business fails to build coalitions, not simply with other firms, but with outside groups. When the government wanted to increase the Corporate Average Fuel Economy (CAFE) standards that force cars to be smaller in order to achieve higher gas mileage, the strongest opposition came from pro-family groups who value large cars for their families for reasons of both safety and comfort. But one leading lobbyist for the car companies said openly, "If we have to win with 'those folks,' do we really want to win?" Dick Lesher, the President of the U.S. Chamber of Commerce, had not even met Phyllis Schlafly until 1984. Schlafly had defeated the entire Establishment drive for the Equal Rights Amendment with fewer resources than most Fortune 500 companies spend on their Washington offices in a year — to lose gracefully.

5. Blackmail and Greenmail

Industries subject to regulation (and that means almost any industry) can be blackmailed into supporting regulation on other industries. They may actually seek regulation of other industries in order to "level the playing field".

On the other hand, any industry that benefits from one government program can be cross-pressured into neutrality or even support for bad policy elsewhere. We may call that "greenmail", as opposed to the more common blackmail.

If Rep. Dick Armey of Texas is ever successful in cutting off agricultural subsidies, three million farmers will be liberated to become a tremendous lobby against higher taxes and regulations.

THE BATTLE FOR BUSINESS

When the U.S. Chamber of Commerce endorsed the Clinton budget on February 22, 1993, it looked as though Clinton would succeed in domesticating the business community. The U.S. Chamber was the one business group that had stood against TEFRA, Ronald Reagan's tax increase of 1982, and again against George Bush's tax hike of 1990. Richard Lesher, the president of the Chamber, had been a solid bulwark of principle against the strongest pressures of political Washington. So the business community nationwide shook to its foundations when the mighty Chamber caved in to the political pressure from Clinton's White House. What threats had been made to the Chamber and to individual board members could only be imagined. In 1990 it was reported that John Sununu, then George Bush's chief of staff, threatened (figuratively, one presumes) to attack Lesher's private parts with a chain saw. If that threat had not moved the Chamber, Clinton's boys must have really been *mean*.

Worse, in the fall of 1993, the U.S. Chamber submitted testimony to Congress favoring a law requiring all businesses to provide health insurance as a part of a worker's compensation package. This law would override the wishes of individual workers and of businesses.

The struggle for the business community's soul was on. A Clinton win would mean capturing tens of millions in campaign contributions and finishing the job started by the Democrats in the 1930's when they launched a concerted effort to drive business away from its alliance with the Republican Party as the party of industry and growth. Since 1930, the business community has swayed in the political breeze with only a sporadic attachment to principle on the part of some individual companies and a handful of trade associations. A victory in this titanic struggle would capture the business community and not simply neuter it, but turn it into a powerful opponent of its own best interests.

Chapter Four

When the U.S. Chamber endorsed the Clinton tax hike, the Conservative Opportunity Society, the caucus of activist Republicans led by Rep. John Boehner (R-OH), began a year-long campaign to turn the Chamber around. Republican congressmen boycotted a U.S. Chamber awards event. Boehner and leading House GOP activists such as Tom DeLay and Dick Armey of Texas, and Chris Cox of California communicated the U.S. Chamber's treason to hundreds of state and local chambers. Conservative activist Bob Krieble, the founder of Loctite Corporation, a Fortutne 500 firm, funded two hour-long television shows on National Empowerment Television outlining the Chamber's perfidy. One of the videos, featuring Krieble and former U.S. Chamber Chief Economist Richard Rahn, was mailed out to almost 1,000 state and local chambers. The *Wall Street Journal* weighed in editorially and with fine columns by Washington correspondent Paul Gigot.

Later, when the Chamber endorsed mandated costs of health insurance on companies and workers in the fall of 1993, Boehner organized a phone and mail blitz to the U.S. Chamber Board of Directors and local chambers. While other business groups waited silently with their fingers in the air, the Small Business Survival Committee, led by veteran activist Karen Kerrigan, organized a letter from previous Chamber board chairmen to the entire Chamber board, arguing that the costly mandate would damage smaller firms. Kerrigan sent out a critique of the Chamber's pro-mandate position to 800 radio talk shows and spent a month talking to radio audiences so they would know what their business dues were paying for.

After a year's campaign, the U.S. Chamber of Commerce fired Senior Vice President Bill Archey on April 5, 1994. Archey had been the chief supporter within the Chamber of Bill Clinton's industrial and tax-and-spend policies and an architect of business community collaboration with the Clinton Administration. He had come to personify the Chamber's temporary abandonment of its strong pro-free-market principles in favor of "pragmatism" and "being in the room when the decisions are made". One collaborator-businessman, Robert Patricelli, whose business stood to gain from a government takeover of health care, resigned from the Chamber board.

Following Archey's humiliating dismissal, the U.S. Chamber went on to repudiate its previous statements in favor of a government mandate on health care and further stated its strong opposition to the Clinton government-run health care plan, even as a starting point for debate on health care reform.

The seduction of the U.S. Chamber of Commerce by the Clinton Administration had been reversed after only 15 months. The Chamber's decision to come in from the cold was an important milestone in the Clinton presidency. The nation's largest business association had decided it was safe, desirable, and necessary to oppose Clintonism and all its works.

Clinton lost this battle for **three reasons**.

First, Republicans learned that Congress is just the last stop on the long march through the institutions. The Left has captured many universities and most of the major grant-making foundations, such as Ford, Rockefeller, MacArthur, Robert Wood Johnson, Pew, Carnegie, and now Heinz. The Left came perilously close to seizing the commanding heights of the U.S. Chamber, from which vantage point it would have pressured all of Washington's business leaders. If the Republican Party wanted a pro-market business community, it would have to continually fight for it. Republicans came to understand that the leftward drift of the U.S. Chamber was not the fault of Bill Archey alone.

As early as 1983, the Democrats had begun a concerted campaign to intimidate and neutralize the U.S. Chamber.

Tony Coelho (D-CA), at that time head of the Democratic Congressional Campaign Committee (DCCC), urged Democrat congressmen to boycott the Chamber's television shows to protest the

Chamber's endorsement of pro-business Republicans. The then Majority Leader Jim Wright called Dick Lesher to his office and shouted colorfully, "Don't piss on my leg and tell me it's raining." (Translation: stop endorsing so many Republicans just because they are pro-growth and the Democrats are pro-tax.) Republicans had never systematically fought back.

What was remarkable about 1993 was not that politicians were lobbying the U.S. Chamber, but that the Republican Congressmen finally joined the battle as a counterweight to Democrat pressure.

The **second** factor was the radicalization of the small business community.

As Karen Kerrigan, the president of the Small Business Survival Committee points out: "In Bill Clinton's vision of the future there is only big government and tamed, subsidized, and regulated big companies. There is no role for small business, because small businesses are independent and want nothing from the government other than what Bill Clinton will not give — to be left alone."

The Small Business Survival Committee worked with businesses large and small to oppose any and all mandates, regulations and tax increases. It worked with conservative taxpayer and property rights groups, strengthening the small business lobby by linking it with principled coalition partners. Its leadership has helped unify the business community.

Third, the radical nature of Bill Clinton's anti-business positions became clear to all — even to the leaders of larger firms who might have been tempted to sign a separate peace. *Forbes* magazine commissioned a Gallup poll of leading CEO's which found that fully 75 percent disapproved of Clinton's performance, and only 21 percent approved. That poll was taken in April of 1994 when Clinton's approval/disapproval rating among the general public was a more positive 51-42 percent. (Since losing the CEO's of large firms,

Clinton has tried to make some headway with their "inside the beltway" lobbyists.)

Speaker Newt Gingrich points out that throughout 1993 and 1994 businessmen gradually learned that Clinton speaks the words of Middle America, but his actions are those of the hard Left. Even if Clinton suddenly decided to govern as a "New Democrat" after all, he could not easily do it. His appointments are off the national Democrat Rolodex, which contains nothing but liberals.

In the 1950's and 1960's, business fought against labor unions that wanted a larger share of the pie. It was an honest fight. Throughout it, the unions were tempered in their demands by a real interest in a growing pie. In Clinton's America, by contrast, the business community faces the twin threat of unions substantially made up of government workers, often allied closely with Vice-President Al Gore's environmental activists. These government unions actually want to see some companies and whole industries (tobacco, lead, Western grazing, timber, and mining) driven out of business. An energy regulator, for example, doesn't need a vibrant energy industry. In fact, his job security is enhanced when the industry is weak, because weakness indicates a need for "help".

A business community facing such uncompromising enemies had to decide: either it would lose, or it would learn to build the coalitions necessary to fight — not for access and influence, but for real political power.

THE HEALTH CARE BATTLE

There has been a great deal written and said about the Clinton Administration's health care reform effort.

Economists teach us that government has never taken over any industry and made prices go down. All efforts to keep health care prices or costs low without competition — and a government monopoly is the surest way to eliminate all competition — can only come through rationing care, resulting in long waiting lines for operations and reduced quality (as in Canada).

But the health care debate was never about health care any more than Jimmy Carter's moral equivalent of war — the oil crisis — was about energy or oil. The purpose of Hillary Clinton's 1,300-page secret health care plan was the seizure and maintenance of political power.

Remember, Bill Clinton won with only 43 percent of the vote. To get re-elected, he needed something that would put at least ten percent of the middle class on the government payroll. Health care was it. Health care was fully 14 percent of the economy and growing. Once the government got its hands on it, it would grow faster; and with everyone in the country required to look to the government for health care — for their children, for their parents, for themselves — there would be no more of this "rugged individual" nonsense.

Clinton Care would provide a sense of false security with its promise of government-paid universal coverage for everything and everybody. When expectations had been raised to that point, and self-reliance destroyed along with habits of restraint and careful choice, there would be no going back.

Once a return to a private system was impossible, Americans would learn to wait patiently in line, deferring to the orders of bureaucrats in order to get the medicines and surgery they needed to stay healthy and alive. It would take time, but Americans could learn to wait in line as Russians once did for bread and toilet paper and health care, no matter how shoddy the quality — because that would be all there was available.

In one great leap forward, an America with government control of health care would become a European social democracy. America would cease to be America.

America is not like other nations. We are not one religion. Or one ethnic group. Or even one race. We are united in our belief in the Declaration of Independence and the Constitution, documents testifying to the limited role of government in a society whose highest political goal is individual liberty. All men and women are to be equal before the law. Government is the servant of the people, granted only those powers delegated to it temporarily by the people.

A government that decides who gets a heart transplant and who does not, a government that decides whether an operation will be performed today or next year, is a government with life and death power over all citizens. It is a government which will have to make choices and develop preferences; it cannot possibly treat all individuals the same.

Knowing the nature of America — but not liking it — the Clintons hid their plan for government control first in secret planning meetings that were only opened up to public scrutiny as the result of a direct court order from a federal judge, after the fact. Then they camouflaged their intentions in the complexity of 1,300-page plan whose length and complexity masked the complete government takeover of health care it contained.

The real agenda did surface from time to time, as when Sheila Copps, Deputy Prime Minister of Canada, said on the floor of Canada's parliament that "Yesterday I had the privilege of discussing with the wife of the President of the United States their health reforms. She was asking me how they could put in place a system which would mirror or be similar to the system we have in Canada. The Americans are coming to this country to see a system that works."

144

Chapter Four

THE SEARCH FOR A PERPETUAL MONEY MACHINE

Along with the drive for health care, the Clintons ran a parallel, though muted, campaign for a value added tax, or VAT. Bill Clinton three times denied that his administration was pushing for a VAT. Hillary Clinton three times called for a VAT. A value added tax is a national sales tax that is applied at every level of production and sale of a product. Virtually every nation in Europe has a VAT. VAT's fund the expensive welfare states from Sweden to Italy. Britain's VAT is 18 percent. Sweden's is 25 percent. While many VAT's are introduced with the promise of *replacing* existing taxes, in Europe none has permanently replaced the personal income tax, or corporate income tax, or social security taxes.

A value added tax would be a money machine for big government.

Support for a VAT was dropped by the Clinton administration only because fully 178 members of the House and Senate had joined the Anti-VAT Caucus run by Reps. Tom DeLay and Dick Armey, both of Texas. The Republican platforms of 1988 and 1992 had both denounced the European VAT as a job-killer and inflationary. Thus Clinton would have had to introduce this new tax without bipartisan cover. Even Clinton's BTU (energy) tax — a small version of a VAT that would have hit only one industry initially — could not pass both houses of Congress.

The VAT failed, but the Clinton tax and spending plan passed. It was designed to damage independent small businesses and increase spending on Democrat constituencies. No economic theory argued for a tax increase and a spending increase at a time of budget deficits and slow growth. But Clinton was listening to his political advisors, not his economic advisors, when this plan was drawn up.

The Small Business Survival Committee has calculated that the Clinton tax hike killed more than 700,000 jobs in small businesses, as

145

the so-called tax on "the rich" actually fell heavily on small businesses which file their income taxes as Subchapter S corporations, that is, as if they were individuals. Fully two-thirds of the tax on "the rich" was paid by small businesses. Actually it was paid by every American who buys a sandwich or a lug wrench from a small business. Businesses don't pay taxes; they only collect them from consumers and send them on to Washington. Only people pay taxes.

The Clinton tax hike (and the jobs killed by it) explains why economic growth during the first two years of the Clinton Administration (which were also the first two years of the economic recovery from the Bush recession caused by *his* tax hike) was only half as strong as in the Reagan recovery in 1983 and 1984, exactly ten years earlier. Reagan cut taxes and grew the nation's economy at four percent; Clinton raised taxes and the growth rate slowed to two percent.

* * * * *

The Clinton coup attempt failed. He was not able to turn America into a European-style social democracy. But he came close. He tried his damnedest. Liberals who have turned viciously on Clinton for his failure should remember that while he failed, he did not betray them. He tried hard, and he almost won. But by making it explicit, with his health care scheme, just how big he and the Democrats wanted government to get, Clinton brought on a voter backlash. In the words of a *Washington Post* lead editorial, this backlash produced a change that "went almost uniformly in one direction and that was against liberalism and toward the right...Mr. Clinton has done worse than fail at restoring government's legitimacy."

Michael Barone, writing in *U.S. News and World Report* on September 5, 1994, two months before the Republican electoral victories, wrote that:

Chapter Four

"Far from making the country admire and embrace boomer liberalism, the Clintons are hurting the ideas and movements they are associated with and threatening the boomer liberals' hold on other parts of society.

Why? Both Clintons embody, in exaggerated form, the attractive traits of boomer liberals: They are articulate and bright, exuding empathy and interest in moral issues. But at the same time, they also symbolize the unattractive boomer liberal traits: self-righteousness and selfishness (the rhetorical condemnations of greed and the real-life commodities trading), self-indulgence (Clinton's profligate appetites) and bossy social engineering (the Clinton's health care plan)."

Bill Clinton's presidency and the grab for the brass ring of an American socialism were the high-water mark of statism in the New World. Like Gettysburg, the battle of 1993 and 1994 will be studied by liberals and Americans for years to come. How did the social democrats get so close to taking America? How did such smart inhabitants of the White House, with control of the Senate and House, fail to pass a health care program that could have ensnared America in a Gordian knot of intergenerational subsidies that would never come undone? At what moment was the battle to turn America into what it was not — a European-style social democracy — lost?

The liberals will turn on Clinton and blame him for this failure as some historians blame Robert E. Lee for the South's defeat at Gettysburg. But Clinton, like Lee, was in a now or never situation.

The better analogy may be Soviet Russia's Mikhail Gorbachev. When he came to power in 1988, Gorbachev tried to save communism, first by intensifying the war in Afghanistan, then by spasmodic efforts at reform that would not, he hoped, undermine the Communist Party's monopoly on power.

He failed, and in his failure lost everything: power, party, and nation. Clinton was tasked with saving the liberal establishment and the Democrat Party's political power. His failure hastened the collapse of the old order in Washington. Both Gorbachev and Clinton were dealt losing hands. Each could have delayed failure, but in taking risks to maintain power, each lost control of the situation and prematurely lost power for his respective Establishment.

CHAPTER FIVE

WHY BUSH LOST

In A Choice, Not an Echo, *Phyllis Schlafly wrote in 1963 of the struggle between the Eastern Establishment of the Republican Party and its more conservative, western base. Every presidential election reflected this contest for the soul of the Republican Party: Senator Robert Taft of Ohio versus Governor Thomas Dewey of New York in 1944 and 1948, Taft versus Dwight Eisenhower (from Kansas, but the candidate of the Eastern Establishment) in 1952, California's Richard Nixon versus New York's Nelson Rockefeller in 1960, and Rockefeller versus Arizona Senator Barry Goldwater in 1964.*

By 1980, the conservatives had established the firm control over the presidential nominating process for the Republican Party that had eluded them in 1940, 1944, 1948, and 1952. But Reagan remembered well the willingness of the liberal Republicans to betray Goldwater's candidacy in 1964. Reagan protected himself from such attacks by choosing George Bush as his vice-presidential candidate.

Even after eight years of success with a conservative president, some liberals in the Republican Party argued that a president without conservative credentials, who was pragmatic, "kinder and gentler" to the demands of the party of government, and who moved to the center would be even more successful.

Rock the House

The Bush Presidency exposes as a dangerous failure the idea that a Republican Party can maneuver devoid of conviction and principles. One cannot move a tree without tearing out its roots. And the GOP is now rooted in a popular vision of limited government. Just as the Carter and the Clinton administrations have exposed the dream of a "conservative", "reasonable", "new" Democrat as an illusion, the Bush Presidency cemented the Republican Party not as a majority conservative party, but as a wholly conservative, small-government party that gains its strength from commitment to principle.

On Tuesday, November 3, 1992, the Bush Presidency died of multiple, self-inflicted wounds.

George Bush inherited from Ronald Reagan a vigorous economy and a powerful Republican coalition of Americans committed to limited government, a strong national defense, and respect for traditional values. Bush lost because he reversed Reagan's economic policies and because he abused the successful political coalition Reagan had built.

When Bush was inaugurated in January 1989, the economy was in its 75th month of continuous growth. Eighteen million jobs had been created since the Reagan tax cuts took effect on January 1, 1983. Inflation stood at 4.6 percent — down from 13.5 percent in 1980. As a result of economic growth and Reagan's restraint of domestic discretionary spending to 1-percent growth per year, the deficit had fallen three years in a row and was forecast (by the Democrat-controlled Congressional Budget Office) to fall from $153 billion in 1989 to $135 billion in 1992, two percent of the Gross Domestic Product (GDP).

After eight years of Ronald Reagan, almost as many voters were calling themselves Republicans as Democrats. The under-24 vote was strongly Republican. Reagan Democrats were becoming regular voters for Republican presidential candidates. The Reagan Republican Party was the party of economic growth at home and strength abroad, and the party most likely to protect taxpayers from the federal government. Left on automatic pilot, the nation and the Republican coalition were poised to reach new heights.

Yet 45 months later, George Bush was rejected by 32 states and 62 percent of the American people. Voters told pollsters they trusted Bill Clinton rather than Bush to create jobs, restore economic growth, and act in the interests of people like themselves. Young voters turned harshly against Bush, voting 43 percent to 34 percent for Clinton over the president. The Reagan Democrats went home. Republican Party identification plummeted, and of those Republicans who remained, Bush lost 27 percent. Over a third of conservatives voted for Clinton or Ross Perot. Most Americans who marked their ballots for the president did so more out of fear of Clinton than enthusiasm for Bush.

Masterful Foreign Policy

In understanding what went wrong, it is important to recognize where President Bush built on the Reagan legacy and where he strayed from it.

Continuing Reagan's pressure on Moscow and its colonies, George Bush led the Free World to final victory in the Cold War, leaving a united Germany in NATO and a Soviet Union fractured into 15 independent republics. He skillfully commanded a military strengthened by the Reagan buildup and managed a global coalition to defeat the fourth largest army in the world in its nearly successful bid to control two-thirds of the planet's oil reserves. He negotiated a trade agreement with Mexico (one of Reagan's first proposals) that will strengthen the U.S. economy and keep our southern neighbor on the path of peaceful reform.

Ronald Reagan brought the Soviets to the end game, but George Bush continued to push Gorbachev down the path of political reform and liberalization until there was no turning back. Granting aid too early might have ended the reforms, and pushing too hard would have alerted Gorbachev to the final destruction he was hurtling towards while trying to hold together his socialist empire. Moreover, by keeping America strong, by keeping the Western alliance together, by showing in the Persian Gulf that the U.S. was willing and able to resist aggression, and by not giving premature economic aid to the Kremlin, Bush reinforced Reagan's signal to Soviet military leaders that they could not get the West once again to exchange a relaxation of pressure for meaningless words, reversible reforms, or a handful of immigrants. It was on George Bush's watch that the single greatest external threat to American life, liberty, and the pursuit of happiness withered away.

The paradox of the 1992 elections is that a president with so many achievements could not convince even his supporters that he deserved a second term. George Bush's three fatal mistakes were to undermine the entrepreneurial economy, to alienate important parts of the Reagan coalition, and, through a foolish distinction between politics and governing, to keep his distance from the American people.

Return of Over-Regulation

George Bush's most serious mistake was to reverse the Reagan economic policies.

Although Clinton tried to describe the stagnation of 1991-92 as the result of "12 years of trickle-down economics", Bush's economic performance was a failure precisely because he rejected the Reagan economic policies, not because he continued them. Reagan created 18 million new jobs, increased the Gross National Product (GNP) by 30 percent, and enlarged total wealth in the nation through his cuts in marginal tax rates, deregulation, and restraint in spending. Bush followed the opposite policies, with predictably opposite results.

One of these departures was a return to the regulatory excess of the Richard Nixon and Jimmy Carter years. Bush expanded the number of federal regulators from 100,000 back to the Carter level of 120,000. His banking regulation penalized healthy banks and starved small businesses of credit, without solving the underlying problem of federal deposit insurance — the incentive for banks and savings and loans to make risky investments when deposits are guaranteed by taxpayers. He proudly signed a Clean Air Act, which, for uncertain environmental benefits, added $25 to $40 billion *a year* in regulatory costs on top of the $120 billion America was already spending on environmental regulation. He appointed as director of the Environmental Protection Agency William Reilly, who saddled small businesses with billions in higher costs, paperwork, and criminal penalties for honest errors; he also jeopardized the life savings of thousands of small-property owners with a capricious set of wetlands regulations. Bush boasted of the Americans with Disabilities Act, whose vague language and draconian penalties do more to benefit lawyers than the handicapped.

A study by the Republicans on the Congressional Joint Economic Committee found that between 1989 and 1992, the regulatory burden on small businesses rose by more than 34 percent.

The Great Tax Betrayal

The most dramatic departure from Reaganomics was the budget deal Bush negotiated in 1990 with the Democrat Congress. Bush had overcome a 17-point deficit in the polls in 1988 when he declared himself a Reaganite with his "read my lips" commitment to "no new taxes". His betrayal of this commitment destroyed his personal credibility and cemented Bush's image as an insider who, unlike

Reagan, was part of corrupt, official Washington, not the tribune of the taxpayers, defending "us" from "them".

It is hard to overestimate the damage the tax hike did to the Republican Party and George Bush. Bush's job approval rating dropped from 75 percent in September 1990 to 51 percent in October when he signed the budget deal. His disapproval rating rose from 19 percent to 37 percent. Republicans lost eight House seats in 1990. The number of Americans who thought the country was "generally on the wrong track" jumped from 54 percent to 73 percent.

The no-new-taxes pledge was the Republicans' central unifying principle. Bush threw it away and gave the Democrats political cover by signing a deal with them. He thus muddied the distinction between the two parties on the issue on which Democrats were most afraid of the voters' wrath. Later, in 1992, Clinton would laughingly say "read my lips" every time Bush tried to call him a tax-and-spend liberal.

The damage to the economy was also serious. The budget deal raised taxes by $175 billion, aggravating the recession. The budget deficit doubled from 1990 to 1992 in part because of slowing revenues, but also because there was no longer any effective spending restraint. The budget deal increased both taxes and spending.

Inflation-adjusted domestic spending rose by over eight percent a year under the budget agreement — nearly three times as fast as it did during the Carter administration. Spending for 1991-1995 has been $500 billion higher than what Office of Management and Budget Director Richard Darman projected in the budget deal.

Reagan reduced domestic spending from 14.8 percent of the GDP to 12.2 percent. Under Bush's budget deal, domestic spending climbed back up to 14.9 percent. The only effective constraint in the budget agreement applied to supply-side Republican members of Congress. Pro-growth tax cuts had to be offset by entitlement cuts or tax increases elsewhere.

Chapter Five

The Sequester Road Not Taken

Darman and the media establishment now say Bush's big mistake was to make a tax pledge he never could have kept. This is nonsense. There was a way for Bush to stick with his tax pledge, but it would have required getting better strategic advice and better economic forecasting than he got from his budget director.

The alternative to the budget deal was to enforce a full or, more likely, a partial Gramm-Rudman sequester. The Gramm-Rudman law, passed by bipartisan majorities of Congress in the Reagan years, had reduced the deficit from 5 percent of the GDP in 1985 to 3.2 percent in 1989. Combined with Reagan's and, for one year, Bush's refusal to raise taxes, Gramm-Rudman had proved a very effective lever for restraining federal spending.

Under Gramm-Rudman, Congress had to pass a budget for Fiscal Year 1991 with a deficit of no more than $74 billion, or face an automatic sequester according to a pre-arranged formula. The problem for Bush was that it looked as if he'd have to begin enforcing a sequester of $83 billion in October 1990. Half of this sum would come from defense. A 30-percent cut — $41.5 billion — would have been required from the $125 billion in domestic spending programs that Congress did not shield from sequestration, including such popular services as air-traffic control, childhood immunizations, and the FBI.

A less draconian option existed for Bush. This was to insist on a partial sequester of less than $83 billion, allowing Gramm-Rudman targets to slip a little, as had been done for Fiscal Year 1988. Bush could then have proposed alternative budget cuts, which would have been distributed more broadly and therefore less painfully than the Gramm-Rudman formula.

155

Even a partial sequester would have guaranteed a bloody fight between Republicans and Democrats in Congress.

Distinctions between the parties, obscured by the budget deal, would have been clarified. Bush would have kept the pledge that got him elected. The deficit may have risen modestly, but it would not have doubled.

Instead, Darman sold President Bush on three things: a negotiating strategy, a budget deal, and an enforcement mechanism — all of which weakened the Republican Party, strengthened the Democrats in Congress, destroyed the president's credibility with the American people, and miserably failed to solve the deficit problem.

Warnings Not Heeded

The souring economy and the popular turn against Bush and the Republicans following the tax-and-spend increase of 1990 might have been a warning shot for the Bush administration and nascent campaign, but the growing crisis in the Gulf masked the damage done to Bush and his governing coalition.

As Bush's popularity numbers skyrocketed with the onset of the air war, those around the president crowed that the economists and conservatives had been wrong. The people loved George Bush. They would soon forget — if they had not already forgotten — the budget deal. The people were lucky to have such a great leader of men and nations.

Basking in his 90-percent approval ratings, an overconfident Bush turned down numerous opportunities to undo the damage caused by the budget agreement. In early 1991, pro-growth Republicans in the House and Senate put together a jobs creation package — the DeLay-Wallop legislation — which would cut the Social Security tax, cut the capital gains tax, and speed up depreciation schedules for business investment, all written to fit within the budget deal's constraints. The Bush White House opposed the measure, saying "We don't need it."

Even if the bill had failed to pass the Congress, it would have served the president and the GOP by provoking a partisan fight over the idea of cutting taxes and creating growth.

Paul Craig Roberts, assistant secretary for tax policy in the Reagan Treasury, pointed out in early 1992 that the president has the unilateral ability to index the taxation of capital assets by re-defining the word "cost" to include a correction for inflation. An executive order to this effect would have helped long-term capital formation and boosted the economy in the short run by freeing up assets now subject to punitively high taxation at sale. The Bush administration discarded this chance.

Misuse of the Veto

Nor did Bush use his veto powers to reinforce a Harry Truman-like strategy of running against Congress on economic policy. Until the cable-regulation legislation of October 1992, every single one of George Bush's 35 vetoes was upheld. Thus no piece of legislation, no tax, no regulatory burden was placed on the American people between 1989 and 1992 without George Bush's signed support. Had Bush vetoed more bad legislation, and been overridden, as Ford, Truman, and Reagan were, he could have made the case that he was not in complete control. He could then have made the case for a Republican Congress. Instead he was part of every error, every perceived and real betrayal of the taxpayers, every problem that flowed from Washington.

In turning aside requests for action, White House aides kept assuring outside friends that the president would soon give a speech to outline his vision of the solution to America's economic ills. That speech was to have been the 1992 State of the Union. Then it was to be the March 20 "Deadline" speech complaining that Congress had not acted on his State of the Union proposals. Neither lived up to the promise.

In his acceptance speech at the Houston convention in the summer of 1992, Bush did articulate a program of tax relief contingent on spending and deficit reduction. And in September of 1992, at the Detroit Economic Club, he offered a strategy for free trade areas as well as a more complete vision of tax and spending limitation. But then he ignored these themes in the rest of his campaign. Offered the opportunity in the debates to speak directly to the American people about his economic plans — without having his message distorted by the media — all Bush could come up with was that he would put James Baker in charge of economic policy.

Bush needed more than talk, in any case. When the president broke his word on taxes, he rendered his word impotent. Only actions, unilateral and unambiguous, could redefine and save the Bush Presidency. With his most memorable words shown to be a lie, he could not talk his way out of trouble and back into the hearts and trust of the American people.

Rooting Out Reaganites

The president probably could have weathered a recession if he had maintained the enthusiastic support of his political base. Had he hung on to the Reagan Democrats and the 27 percent of Republicans and 35 percent of conservatives who voted against him, the 1992 election would have had a much different outcome.

From the first, though, George Bush engaged in an unseemly and inexplicable effort to distance himself from Reagan and the Reagan coalition. Political appointees who had supported Reagan in 1980 were rooted out of government jobs with no consideration of competence or past service. Samuel Skinner, later Bush's Chief of

Staff, openly boasted at an early Bush Cabinet meeting that he was the first cabinet secretary to completely purge his department of Reaganites.

White House aides began to leak disparaging remarks about Reagan and the Reagan staff. "The cowboys are gone," they chirped. The ideologues are gone. Now watch us, the serious pragmatic professionals. "Our people don't have agendas. They have mortgages," a Bush aide was quoted as saying in the *Washington Post* two days before the Bush inaugural.

In 1980, Ronald Reagan had recognized that there were two wings of the Republican Party and had reached out to the Establishment, liberal, and smaller wing in choosing George Bush as his running mate. Reagan allowed Bush to bring hundreds of his campaign supporters into the administration, from Chief of Staff James Baker on down.

Bush made an initial gesture to party unity in adding a conservative, Dan Quayle, to his 1988 ticket, and by choosing John Sununu as chief of staff and Jack Kemp and William Bennett for cabinet positions. For the most part, though, the political appointees in the Bush administration were chosen not to represent parts of the party coalition, or to transcend ideological differences, or even to provide for geographic balance. This was to be a government of George and Barbara Bush's personal acquaintances: loyalists and friends from college, business, government, and party. Most Reagan conservatives soon learned they were not wanted. And those who had key positions, such as Kemp and Bennett, were neutralized and ignored.

* * * * *

Mistreatment of Reagan

A greater miscalculation was Bush's mistreatment of Ronald Reagan and the 1980's. The Bush White House allowed the press and the Democrats to attack the Reagan Presidency without recognizing that the portrayal of the 1980's as a "decade of greed" when only "the rich got richer" was an attack on the low-tax, deregulatory strategy of the modern Republican Party. Darman and Treasury Secretary Nicholas Brady actually promoted the argument that Bush's economic problems resulted from Reagan's legacy. While Bush did inherit some problems — among them the savings and loan fiasco and a high but shrinking budget deficit — he also inherited a dynamic entrepreneurial economy, where the vast majority of the American people, not only the rich, were becoming more prosperous. Bush's failure to defend those Reagan policies that worked was strongly resented by the Reagan coalition; it was serious political, as well as economic, misjudgment. The Reagan legacy is treated more fully in the next chapter.

Resented even more was Bush's failure to give credit to Reagan for playing such an important role in winning the Cold War. Bush did not even mention Reagan by name on Christmas 1991 in his five-minute report to the nation on the fall of the Soviet Empire. On that day the red flag was removed from the top of the Kremlin and all the sacrifices of Americans — from the cold hills of Korea to the rice paddies of Vietnam, to the taxes paid for the defense of America and our allies — were finally rewarded. That was the time for a speech that told the history of the past 40 years. The lies of the Left that apologized for Soviet imperialism and terror were naked before the world. All that Reagan and the conservatives in the GOP had fought for was upheld. Yet, to avoid crediting Reagan, Bush gave equal credit to both parties for the successful conclusion of the Cold War.

Chapter Five

Bush's failure to give Reagan proper credit haunted him in the 1992 campaign. By denying the world-changing differences between Carter and Reagan, Bush was unable to explain why Clinton would be a worse choice.

Bush could have avoided remaining in Reagan's shadow by standing on his shoulders and building the low-tax, small-government, strong-defense coalition that was the 1988 Republican Party.

Truman had succeeded domestically by building on Franklin Roosevelt's coalition. Bush instead ran away from Reagan's policies and, in the process, his political base.

Alienating Key Constituencies

As Bush pointedly separated himself from Reagan, he also alienated virtually every constituency in the Reagan coalition. The sharpest blow, of course, was the budget deal. Bush's "no-new taxes" pledge was his contract with economic conservatives. He broke that contract and was two years late in his grudging apologies.

Bush was equally cavalier with smaller but very important constituencies. In 1988 he was endorsed by the three-million-strong National Rifle Association. The NRA mailed three million magazines endorsing Bush and vilifying the pro-gun-control position of Democrat candidate Michael Dukakis. Then, in his first year in office, Bush banned the importation of some semi-automatic rifles and flirted with signing the Brady Bill. Bush fell for the media-driven fallacy that semi-automatic rifles are "assault" rifles. To the millions of American gun owners, Bush demonstrated that he didn't understand the issue and culturally was divorced from their lives.

As a result, in 1992 the NRA refused to endorse George Bush, and he lost the gun control issue that had worked so decisively for Republicans in 1980, 1984, and 1988. The White House thought individuals and organizations concerned with the rights of gun owners had nowhere else to go. But they did go somewhere else — into House and Senate races where gun control advocates such as Joan Kelly Horn, Beryl Anthony, and Tom Coleman were defeated.

The National Right to Work Committee, with a membership of over two million, had mailed heavily in 1988 in support of Bush's commitment to protecting Section 14(b) of the Taft-Hartley Act, which guarantees the rights of workers not to be coerced into unions. Bush and his Labor Department responded by failing for four years to enforce the Supreme Court decision in *Beck* v. *Communications Workers of America*. The *Beck* decision, handed down in 1988, forbids unions from extracting more in compulsory dues than they needed to negotiate and maintain an individual worker's contract. In the case of the million-member CWA, fully 79 percent of union dues could be refunded to workers if requested.

If Bush had acted immediately to enforce *Beck*, every union member could have requested and received up to $350 from his or her union each year. (Union dues average $440 annually, and the CWA refund figure of 79 percent is a conservative estimate of the financing of other unions.)

If only one percent of the nation's 16.6 million union members had asked for refunds, unions would have been denied $58 million a year they spent on behalf of Democrat candidates and other political causes. But the regulations necessary to enforce *Beck* — requiring unions to keep books so members could tell how their dues are being spent and requiring the posting of notices explaining the rights of workers — did not become final until a few days before the '92 election.

Republican members of the House repeatedly wrote letters to Secretary of Labor Elizabeth Dole, and later to her successor, Lynn Martin, urging them to enforce the *Beck* decision. Dozens of Republicans were narrowly defeated in 1990 and 1992 with union help that could have been reduced if *Beck* had been enforced.

Worse, the Bush Administration lobbied the Supreme Court in legal briefs to impose union-only hiring discrimination on a $1.6 billion project to clean up Boston Harbor. The September 1992 newsletter of National Right to Work, which was sent to two million donors, did not focus on the threat of Bill Clinton campaigning to repeal Taft-Hartley but instead had a banner headline: "Bush Slaps Right to Work in the Face; Sides with Union Officials on Boston Harbor Dispute".

Citizens concerned about the abuses of labor unions and the misuse of compulsory union dues also had other options besides supporting Bush. They, too, focused on House and Senate races to ensure the ability to defeat the unions' wish list of legislation.

Offending the Religious Right

Through his court appointments and his unwavering opposition to abortion and fetal-tissue research, Bush did end up winning the overwhelming support of pro-family activists and conservative evangelicals and Catholics. Even here, though, Bush offended this large constituency so often that at the Republican convention in Houston in 1992, Bush had to shore up support from pro-family conservatives, something that should never have been in doubt. Although the show-casing of pro-family activists at the convention was well-received at the time, their prominence was used later in the campaign by the media to "prove" that Republicans were bigoted and mean-spirited. There should have been no need to provide this opening. Bill Clinton, in contrast, was able to keep his supporters in the cultural Left mostly off-stage during the Democrat convention.

Religious conservatives had been outraged by the National Endowment of the Arts' use of tax dollars to fund obscenity and blasphemous works such as a jar of urine containing a crucifix.

The Endowment's chairman, John Frohnmeyer, eventually was dismissed, but for months the White House defended him. The message was twofold: (1) the cultural elite could practice religious sacrilege and mockery of middle-class American values, using the tax dollars of working men and women; and (2) the Bush White House feared irritating the arts community more than it feared upsetting evangelicals and Catholics, many of them Reagan Democrats, who were understandably offended by this taxpayer-funded bigotry.

Voters who turned to the Republicans as their champion in the struggle against violent crime watched in confused horror as George Bush joined liberal opinion leaders in responding to the Los Angeles gang-led violence with calls for more government social-welfare programs. The man who knew instinctively how to deal with Saddam Hussein offered appeasement and tribute to our domestic terrorists.

Even in his strongest suit, foreign policy, the president antagonized an important constituency — East European ethnics. The captive-nations organizations have been stalwarts of the Republican coalition. Many Americans of Lithuanian, Latvian, Estonian, Ukrainian, and to a lesser extent Polish origin blamed Franklin Roosevelt for Yalta and the McGovernized Democrat Party for its failure to oppose Soviet colonialism militarily or even rhetorically.

Yet when the moment arrived to achieve the Eisenhower/Dulles promise of a "rollback", the Bush administration repeatedly sided with Mikhail Gorbachev and Moscow against democratic forces in the republics. Bush delayed recognition of the newly independent Baltic states and gave a speech in Kiev, the capital of Ukraine, in which the most memorable sentence was a condemnation of "suicidal nationalism". The result was that Baltic and Ukrainian voters, concentrated in key battleground states like Illinois, Ohio, Michigan, and Pennsylvania, turned sharply against the president.

A similar turnaround occurred among the 2.5 million Croatian-Americans, who were appalled by Bush's insensitivity to Croatian national aspirations. James Baker traveled to Belgrade in 1991 to tell the Communist government of Yugoslavia that America valued stability and a unified Yugoslavia over the freedom and independence of Croatia, Slovenia, and Kosovo. Croatian-Americans saw this as an open U.S. invitation for Serbia's aggression and massacres in their homeland. Before this betrayal, Croatian-Americans were about as Republican in their voting and financial contributions as Cuban-Americans.

It was Clinton who would reach out for captive nations and Croatian votes with his compelling observation at the Los Angeles World Affairs Council on August 13: "From the Baltics to Beijing, from Sarajevo to South Africa, time after time this president has sided with the status quo against democratic change; with familiar tyrants rather than those who would overthrow them; with the old geography of repression rather than a new map of freedom."

Pride of Coriolanus

Bush's third great error was his specious distinction between politics and governing. This distinction, shared by top advisers such as Sununu, Baker, and Darman, set the tone for his administration and damaged him in two fatal ways: (1) He suffered as a president, because he didn't realize that effective governing requires strengthening one's political allies and keeping one's political enemies on the defensive; and (2) he suffered as a campaigner, because he considered politics as something dirty, to be stooped to only for a few months every four years, rather than as the high art of honest persuasion.

Bush seemed to exhibit the pride of Shakespeare's Coriolanus, the brave Roman general who believed he deserved the consulship, but would not lower himself to ask the people for their votes. Where Reagan talked with the American people, Bush made deals with foreign leaders or, behind closed doors, with the Democrat congressional leadership. He supported many excellent domestic policy proposals — school choice, capital gains tax cuts, and term limits — but he never made his case for these policies before the American people. As a result, Congress set and controlled the agenda.

Bush's refusal to explain his goals in the Gulf War went beyond inarticulateness. He wielded slogans that did not communicate. Another Hitler. New World Order. Ozone Man. Tension City. He began his presidency by getting rid of the talented Reagan speechwriters and making it obvious to all inside the White House the low regard with which he viewed their replacements. When he was accused of running a racist campaign in 1988, he made no effort to set the record straight. When a man is accused of pandering to and manipulating the American people, and he doesn't consider it a grave insult, it speaks volumes about how he views the American people and how lightly he judges his commitment to them. His disdain for rhetoric was clearest in his casual breaking of his "no-new-taxes" oath. There was no sense of shame, no apology to the American people for the betrayal of their trust. Why bother? It was just something he had said to get elected.

"Dirty Politics"

Because Bush didn't take political rhetoric seriously, he was willing to call Clinton a "bozo", and to imply — without evidence —that Clinton as an Oxford student had been a dupe of the Soviets. Unsubstantiated charges such as this delegitimize valid charges, and give serious anti-Communism a bad name. But anything goes in politics, Bush implied.

Absent the late Lee Atwater, the campaign strategist for 1988, Baker and Bush did not understand the positive, pro-growth, pro-jobs message of the Reagan years, and thus thought the 1988 victory over Dukakis stemmed from a few gut punches judiciously, if sometimes unfairly, thrown. So they saw no need to have a positive vision in 1992, and expected to knock Clinton out in a few rounds: after all, with his draft and womanizing problems, Clinton was even more glass-jawed than Michael Dukakis.

Conversely, Bush allowed the press and Democrat politicians to paint his 1988 campaign as unfair, negative, and racist. The 1988 discussion of William Horton's furlough highlighted Dukakis's weakness on the crime issue. It was, in fact, a very fair and hard-hitting criticism of an indefensible act by Dukakis as governor. But by wincing whenever "Willie Horton" was thrown at them, Bush and his aides gave credence to the idea that this was somehow an underhanded code word for racism.

Only the humorist P. J. O'Rourke correctly threw the Horton issue back at the Democrats. On the now-defunct Fox program, "Off the Record", Democrat activist Bob Beckel used "Willie Horton" as slang for a dirty trick. O'Rourke responded, "Now wait a minute, Bob... What about the issue bothers you? Do you think William Horton was not guilty of murder? Do you think it is a good idea to let murderers out of prison on weekends for a vacation?" Beckel immediately backed down and stated his preference to "not dwell on the past".

The failure to defend the 1988 campaign as honest and legitimate led to the paralysis of the 1992 campaign. The Democrats could simply assert, "We know they campaign dirty," and they defined every fair shot, every telling blow as unfair. Since the Bush people thought all politics was dirty, they had no strategy for hitting cleanly and then defending their attacks.

No Mandate for Clinton

Bush White House and campaign aides offer two excuses for their failure to bring home a Republican victory in 1992: (1) We were up against a tide for change, and (2) the social conservatives hurt us. The media offers a third — the voters gave Bill Clinton a mandate.

All three are false. History was running with Bush. Brian Mulroney in Canada in 1988, Helmut Kohl in Germany in 1990, and John Major in Britain in April 1992 all pulled off unexpected center/right victories.

The Republican platform on abortion was unchanged from the winning platforms of 1984 and 1988. If the Republican convention in Houston was perceived as more directed to social conservatives, it was because Bush had failed to consolidate his traditional-values base over three years and because he gave insufficient emphasis at the convention to a serious and believable pro-taxpayer, pro-growth, pro small business agenda.

Finally, Bill Clinton did not win a campaign of ideas and issues. He campaigned against term limits, and they passed overwhelmingly in all 14 states where they were on the ballot — with an average of 66 percent of the vote. Term limits got a total of 20 million votes in those 14 states to Bill Clinton's 14 million votes.

Clinton offered four major domestic planks: (1) raise taxes on the rich; (2) spend billions on the nation's infrastructure (read: union-controlled construction projects in big, Democrat-controlled cities); (3) government-controlled health care; and (4) more expensive environmental regulation.

On Election Day four state initiatives spoke directly to these four themes. Voters in California voted on Measure 167 — an initiative that would have raised taxes on businesses and individuals making more than $250,000. It was defeated by a 16-point margin, 58 percent to 42 percent. Also in California, a "Clintonesque" mandatory government health care regime was defeated 69 percent to 31 percent. In New York state, an infrastructure bond that promised thousands of government jobs in return for additional state debt was defeated 55 percent to 45 percent. And while carrying Massachusetts, the green ticket of Clinton-Gore watched a mandatory recycling bill be rejected 60 percent to 40 percent.

Voters in Colorado rejected a one percent sales tax increase to pay for education billed as "pennies for the children", and demanded that all tax increases be voted on by the people. Arizona passed an initiative to require a two-thirds vote of the legislature to raise taxes. Californians repealed part of Governor Pete Wilson's record tax hike, and Connecticut required a limit on state spending increases to a level below inflation.

In all, 10 out of 11 statewide ballot questions that would have raised taxes were defeated. Six out of eight measures to cut or limit taxes and spending passed.

Kinder and Gentler

George Bush lost his presidency, but the establishment is not yet finished with him. One can already see the outlines of the bargain that liberalism offers Bush: repudiate Reagan and all his works, blame the slow economy on Reagan's tax cuts and deficits, apologize for appealing to evangelicals and Catholics, and then we will rehabilitate you by splitting the credit for the end of the Cold War between your managerial skills and Gorbachev's vision and courage. Reagan will be left out of the new and improved history of the end of the Cold War.

Bush should refuse this deal; for history will rightly credit him with great successes as well as great failings.

History will be kinder and gentler than the voters of 1992 to the president who helped liberate 450 million people and one-sixth of the territory of the Earth.

(L) Grover G. Norquist
(R) Haley Barbour, Chairman
Republican National Committee

CHAPTER SIX

RECAPTURING THE PAST: THE REAGAN LEGACY

The Italian leftist Antonio Gramsci, leading communist strategist and drama critic of the Socialist paper *Avanti!*, differed from Karl Marx in the latter's focus on the economy, or "the means of production". In his *Prison Notebooks*, Gramsci argued that those who would change society must first "capture the culture", the institutions that shape our view of ourselves: the universities, the press, the churches and the molders of public opinion.

It was his follower, the German student leader Rudi Dutschke, who coined the phrase, "The Long March Through the Institutions", referring to the process of bringing universities, the press, and the mainline churches under radical control as, over time, the radicals get established.

The American Left has followed Gramsci's vision and Dutschke's strategy rather than pure Marxism. The Left has great sway in Hollywood, the multi-billion dollar film industry, the music industry, the Establishment press, book publishing, the arts and theater. They never got their hands on the steel mills, the auto plants and the coal mines, where Marx would have directed their efforts. They knew they didn't need to.

One of the reasons for believing that the Republican Party's resurgence is more than temporary is the growing understanding by conservatives of the importance of "capturing the culture". Richard Grenier, a brilliant writer who has served as a film critic for *Commentary* and a correspondent for the *New York Times* and now writes for the *Washington Times*, published *Capturing the Culture: Film, Art, and Politics* in 1991, teaching a generation of conservatives about Gramsci and the politicization of the culture by the American Left.

Grenier's tutorial has had a great deal of impact. For when the Left began to use its power in the commanding heights of the culture torewrite the history of the 1980's, even as we were living through that decade, conservative intellectuals did not concede, as they had with the decades of the 1930's, 1950's and even 1960's.

THE REAL REAGAN RECORD

Ronald Reagan took office in the second year of double digit inflation, with interest rates over 20 percent, with the per capita income of Americans falling, unemployment increasing, the misery index (inflation plus unemployment) at just under 20 percent, and the Soviet Union and its surrogates on the march in Latin America, Asia, and Africa. Europe was paralyzed by American weakness and Soviet threats.

Reagan cut marginal tax rates across the board for all Americans by 25 percent, slowed the growth of the money supply, reduced the regulatory burden on Americans, strengthened our nation's defenses, confronted the Soviet Union, made plans to build the Strategic Defense Initiative, and began appointing judges who thought criminals were bad and society worth defending.

And it worked!

Chapter Six

The economic boom that resulted lasted 92 months, from November 1982 to July 1990 (that is, from the time the tax cuts took effect to the month George Bush said he would raise taxes). This was the longest period of uninterrupted economic growth during peacetime in American history. It was twice as long as the average economic expansion since World War II. The American economy grew by one-third, and the real growth rate from 1983 to 1990 was 3.5 percent a year: twice that of the 1973 to 1982 average of 1.6 percent.

Even with (I would say because of) lower tax rates, total revenues still rose from $599 billion in 1981 to $1,031 billion in 1990. Income tax revenue alone rose from $244 billion in 1980 to $466.9 billion in 1990.

The prime interest rate fell from 18.87 percent in 1981 to 10.01 per cent in 1990 (and fell further to 6.25 percent by 1992).

The output of American manufacturing increased by 38 percent in real terms (taking inflation into account) from 1980 to 1989. This meant that manufacturing was 23 percent of the American economy in 1989, up from 21 percent in 1980. In 1988 and 1989, manufacturing was a larger percentage of the total gross national product than any year since World War II.

The stock market tripled in value from 1980 to 1990.

Real personal assets increased from $15.5 trillion in 1980 to $21.1 trillion in 1990.

Clinton's pollster Stan Greenberg pointed out that the Left would have to completely rewrite the history of the 1980's if it was ever to win the presidency. After all, how could a Democrat candidate for president run against the true history of the 1980's?

The success of Reaganomics sparked a binge of tax cutting around the world.

The table below, based on data compiled by Alan Reynolds, compares marginal tax rates in other countries in 1979 with the rates in 1990. These cuts have produced the world-wide economic boom over these years.

MAXIMUM MARGINAL TAX RATES ON INDIVIDUAL INCOME		
Country	1979	1990
Argentina	45%	30%
Austria	62%	47%
Belgium	76%	55%
Bolivia	48%	10%
Botswana	75%	50%
Brazil	55%	25%
Canada (Ontario)	58%	47%
Chile	60%	50%
Colombia	56%	30%
Denmark	73%	68%
Egypt	80%	65%
Finland	71%	43%
France	60%	53%
Germany	56%	53%
Greece	60%	50%
Guatemala	40%	34%
Hungary	60%	50%
India	60%	50%
Indonesia	50%	35%
Iran	90%	75%
Ireland	65%	56%
Israel	66%	48%
Italy	72%	50%

MAXIMUM MARGINAL TAX RATES ON INDIVIDUAL INCOME		
Country	1979	1990
Jamaica	58%	33%
Japan	75%	50%
Korea (South)	89%	50%
Malaysia	60%	45%
Mauritius	50%	35%
Mexico	55%	35%
Netherlands	72%	60%
New Zealand	60%	33%
Norway	75%	54%
Pakistan	55%	45%
Philippines	70%	35%
Portugal	84%	40%
Puerto Rico	79%	43%
Singapore	55%	33%
Spain	66%	56%
Sweden	86%	65%
Thailand	60%	55%
Trinidad /Tobago	70%	50%
Turkey	75%	50%
United Kingdom	83%	40%
United States	70%	33%

Source: Alan Reynolds, *Fortune Encyclopedia of Economics*, 1993.

Chapter Six

The Reagan "flattening" of the income tax code did not have the effect of increasing the tax burden on the poor, as is so often charged. As the table below shows, as the Reagan economic program worked itself out, the top income classes paid a larger share of the total taxes collected than they had before (from 18 percent in 1981 to 25 percent in 1991). At the same time, the share of total taxes paid by the bottom 50 percent of taxpayers declined (from eight percent in 1981 to five percent in 1991).

SHARE OF FEDERAL INCOME TAXES PAID BY INCOME GROUPS, 1981-1991

Fiscal Year	Top 1%	Top 5%	51st-95th Percentile	Bottom 50%
1981	18%	35%	57%	8%
1982	19%	36%	56%	7%
1983	20%	37%	56%	7%
1984	21%	38%	55%	7%
1985	22%	39%	54%	7%
1986	25%	42%	52%	7%
1987	25%	43%	51%	6%
1988	28%	46%	49%	6%
1989	25%	44%	50%	6%
1990	26%	44%	50%	6%
1991	25%	43%	51%	5%

Sources: Richard McKenzie, *What Went Right in the 1980's*; Christopher Frenze, *The Federal Income Tax Burden, 1981-1987*, Joint Economic Committee.

Nor did the poor suffer from effective income tax rates. The table below shows that the lowest 20 percent of taxpayers received a massive cut in rates, mostly because so many of them were removed from the tax rolls entirely due to an increase in the personal exemption. The table shows that effective tax rates dropped for all income classes, but that the drop was greatest for the poorest Americans and smallest for the high-income brackets.

REDUCTIONS IN EFFECTIVE INCOME TAX RATES, 1980-1992			
Income Group	Effective Tax Rate Under 1980 Law	Effective Tax Rate Under 1992 Law	Difference 1980-1992
Lowest 20%	1.7%	-2.8%	-263.6%
2nd Lowest 20%	7.3	2.6	-64.1
Middle 20%	11.7	6.3	-46.3
2nd Highest 20%	15.6	8.7	-44.2
Highest 20%	25.2	16.3	-35.2
Top 1%	33.9	23.7	-30.2
Source: Richard McKenzie, *What Went Right in the 1980's*.			

Chapter Six

Spending Continues

The one area President Reagan could not control was the growth in federal spending. There, Congress refused to put on the brakes. While Reagan pushed for a balanced budget amendment, Congress failed to pass one despite Republican-led attempts in 1982 and 1986.

FEDERAL SPENDING DURING THE 1980's

Fiscal Year	Total Federal Expenditures (Billions of current dollars)	Total Federal Expenditures (Billions of FY 1987 dollars)	Total Federal Expenditures (as a Percent of GNP)
1980	$590.9	$832.1	22.3%
1981	678.2	867.7	22.9%
1982	745.8	891.1	23.9%
1983	808.4	921.1	24.4%
1984	851.8	933.5	23.1%
1985	946.4	1,001.3	23.9%
1986	990.3	1,017.3	23.5%
1987	1,003.9	1,003.9	22.5%
1988	1,064.1	1,027.1	22.1%
1989	1,143.2	1,057.2	22.1%
1990	1,252.7	1,110.2	22.9%
1991	1,323.8	1,122.8	23.3%
1992	1,380.9	1,132.1	23.3%

Source: *Budget of the U.S.*, FY 1993.

While taxes remained at roughly 18 to 19 percent of GNP during the 1980's, as the table above shows, federal spending crept up from 22 to 23 percent of the GNP. Congress's increased spending created enormous deficits and added to the national debt. (The Left's complaint that the higher deficits were Reagan's fault and not the fault of Congress does not explain their panic now that Congress is in the hands of Republicans, and Reagan has retired. Perhaps now they are willing to admit that Congress controls the purse strings, something that pleased them in the Democrat '80's, and displeases them in the Republican '90's.)

It was this binge in spending which caused the deficits so often attributed to Reaganomics. Total tax revenue increased every year after the Reagan tax cuts took effect, by tens of billions of dollars. This result is not surprising, given the stimulus to the economy provided by the tax cuts, and the job-creating force of that economic boom. But Congress created more new spending every year than the Internal Revenue Service collected in new revenue. That is a prescription for massive deficits, and massive deficits we got, as the table on the next page shows.

"THE SEVEN FAT YEARS"

Reaganomics produced an economic boom unprecedented in world history. During the Reagan years, almost 20 million new jobs were created. Contrary to an oft-repeated criticism, these were not "McJobs", flipping burgers in fast food outlets. Actually, only 12 percent of the new jobs could be characterized as low-skilled (and the value of a low-skilled job to a low-skilled person ought not to be minimized). The rest were technical, managerial, and professional, jobs in law, advertising, computers, and medicine.

Over the years, some popular indexes have been developed to measure economic performance of presidents. The best known is the "misery index", which adds unemployment and inflation. On this index, Ronald Reagan does very well.

FEDERAL DEFICITS DURING THE 1980'S			
Fiscal Year	Total Federal Deficits (Billions of Nominal Dollars)	Total Federal Deficits (Billions of FY '87 Dollars)	Total Federal Deficits as a Percentage of GDP
1980	$73.8	$104.0	2.8%
1981	79.0	101.0	2.7%
1982	128.0	152.9	4.1%
1983	207.8	236.8	6.3%
1984	185.4	203.2	5.0%
1985	212.3	224.6	5.4%
1986	221.2	227.3	5.2%
1987	149.8	149.8	3.4%
1988	155.2	149.8	3.2%
1989	152.5	141.0	2.9%
1990	221.4	196.2	4.0%
1991	269.5	228.6	4.8%
1992	290.4	238.1	4.9%
1993	254.7	202.7	4.0%
Source: *Budget of the U.S.*, FY 1993			

Rock the House

In fact, of all the administrations since the end of the Second World War, the two Reagan administrations score best, as the table below shows. Another index, called the "expanded misery index", adds figures on interest rates and economic growth. On that index too, Reagan scores at the top, as the table shows.

ECONOMIC REPORT CARD OF THE PRESIDENTS								
Administration	Inflation Change	Unem-ployment Change	Interest Rate Change	Shortfall in GNP Growth	Misery Index Change	Rank	Expanded Misery Change	Rank
HST II	-0.4	0.4	0.3	-2.6	0.0	4	-2.3	4
Ike I	0.3	1.6	0.6	0.7	1.9	9	3.2	9
Ike II	-0.8	1.3	0.5	1.1	0.5	5	2.1	8
JFK/LBJ	-0.5	-0.8	0.3	-1.7	-1.3	3	-2.7	3
LBJ II	2.2	-1.1	1.5	-1.4	1.1	7	1.2	6
RMN I	0.0	1.6	0.0	0.0	1.6	8	1.6	7
RMN II/Ford	4.8	1.5	0.8	1.1	6.3	11	8.2	10
Carter	3.9	-1.3	5.5	0.3	2.6	10	8.4	11
RR I	-5.7	1.4	-0.7	0.7	-4.3	1	-4.3	1
RR II	-0.6	-0.8	-2.1	-0.2	-1.4	2	-3.7	2
Bush	-0.2	1.0	-2.1	2.1	0.8	6	0.8	5
Source: Richard McKenzie, *What Went Right in the 1980's*.								

Chapter Six

The Reagan tax cuts left more money in the hands of Americans to use as they saw fit. It is often charged that the result was an orgy of selfishness, characterized as "The Me Decade". Nothing could be further from the truth. As Richard McKenzie writes in an article in *National Review*:

"...total charitable giving, in real terms, more than doubled [between 1955 and 1980], increasing from $34.5 billion...to $77.5 billion...or at a compounded annual growth rate of 3.3 percent. [But] between 1980 and 1989, total giving in real dollars expanded by 56 percent to $121 billion, or by a compound growth rate of 5.1 percent. *The annual rate of growth in total giving in the 1980's was nearly 55 per cent higher than in the previous 25 years.*" (Emphasis in original.)

Despite the racial rhetoric of the Democrats, economic progress was not restricted to whites. As Ed Rubenstein shows clearly in an article in *National Review*, while the number of poor blacks had increased by two million in the last years of Jimmy Carter's economy (1978-1982), between 1982 and 1989 the number of poor blacks fell by 400,000. Overall, the fraction of people of all races living in poverty actually fell in the Reagan years.

RECLAIMING HISTORY

In general, the Reagan economic record is something to be proud of. As we shall see below, there were those ready to make the defense when the misinformation and "factoids" of the media began to be used by politicians.

Chicken Little Democrats

The Democrat Party predicted the opposite results for every one of Reagan's policies. Deregulation of oil would increase prices, they said. Prices actually fell. Tax cuts would fuel inflation, they said. Reagan cut the 13.5 percent inflation rate he inherited from Jimmy Carter in 1980 to below 3.2 percent in 1983. America didn't have a recession; we had a seven year boom.

In foreign policy, we were told that the robust Soviet economy would allow the Soviets to more than match our defense build up, that their sophisticated technology would outwit our Strategic Defense Initiatives, and that their happy Eastern European sister socialists would cheer them on in this contest with a declining America that could not feed her children. Remember Paul Kennedy's 1989 book predicting America's collapse, *The Rise and Fall of Great Powers*?

Exactly the opposite happened. The Berlin Wall came down in 1989, the Romanians shot their dictator Nicolae Ceausescu, the East German dictator Erich Honnecker resigned and fled to Chile, and in 1991, the Soviet Union ceased to exist, which meant independence for the peoples of Lithuania, Estonia, Latvia, Ukraine and other occupied nations.

These developments were the result of Ronald Reagan's firmness in foreign policy and his success in building up America's defenses, depleted during the Carter Administration.

The Big Lie

The Democrats, fearing that Reagan's record of success and their own record of being wrong about everything might lead the American people into electing more Republicans, began a smear campaign against the 1980's. It was, they said, a decade of greed, its policies premised on the lie that supply-side tax cuts would "pay for them-selves". They described America as mired in debt, with a prosperity that was fleeting and false. In fact, they said, the economic boom had

Chapter Six

never really happened. All the new jobs were lousy and low paying. And besides, everyone always knew socialism was stupid and that the Soviet Union was a paper tiger.

Every Democrat, liberal columnist, writer and Establishment Left media personality was enlisted in trashing the 1980's. The "hive", as columnist Joe Sobran describes the liberal Establishment, buzzed as one.

And yet, this time when they probed with a bayonet, they met steel.

In 1992 Robert Bartley, the editor of the *Wall Street Journal*, published *The Seven Fat Years*, which set the record straight in a way that the Left has never successfully combatted. In 1994 Richard B. McKenzie wrote *What Went Right in the 1980's*, rebutting slogans with charts, graphs and real data. *National Review* magazine put out a special issue on August 31, 1992: "The Real Reagan Record". *National Review*'s economic columnist Ed Rubenstein published *The Right Data*. Paul Johnson, the British historian extraordinaire republished his work *Modern Times* in 1994 with a special supplement on the 1980's, upending the entire liberal mythology. Some of this information has been presented above.

In a February 1991, a *Commentary* magazine article, "What Everyone 'Knows' About Reaganomics", by Paul Craig Roberts, answered once and for all the slander that the Reagan tax cut policy had been based on false claims. Roberts writes:

"President Reagan's economic program was set forth in an inch-thick document, 'A Program for Economic Recovery', made available to the public and submitted to Congress on February 18, 1981. Tables in the document make it unmistakably clear that the administration expected the forthcoming tax

183

cut to reduce revenues substantially below the amounts that would be collected in the absence of such a cut. Without the tax cut, revenues were projected as rising from $609 billion in 1981 to $942 billion in 1986. *The total six year revenue cost of the tax cut was thus estimated at $718.2 billion.*

As the tax-rate reduction was expected to slow the growth of revenues, receipts as a percentage of GNP were expected to fall from 21.1 percent in 1981 to 19.6 percent in 1986. *Accordingly, the document spelled out the necessity of slowing the growth of spending in order to avoid rising deficits* [Emphasis added]."

The books and articles spelling out the truth of the economic growth in the 1980's armed columnists, radio talk show hosts, candidates and individual Americans with an ability to refute the counter-historical rantings of such economic luminaries as Bryant Gumbel and Peter Jennings.

Bill Clinton and his friends did not notice that the trashing of the 1980's that went unchallenged in the pages of *The Nation* and at Georgetown cocktail parties was not working with an American electorate, much of which was alive — and employed — in the real live decade of 1980-1989.

As a result, when Republicans put forward their Contract with America on September 27, 1994, pre-Reagan politicians like Tony Coelho told the Democrats that a really clever strategy would be to attack the Contract as a return to the tax-cutting policies of Ronald Reagan.

Every Republican candidate had a briefing book, *Issues '94*, put out by The Heritage Foundation, whose first chapter was a 22-page outline of the successes of the 1980's compiled by the insatiably brilliant Peter Ferrara. Ferrara brought together the graphs, tables,

Chapter Six

insights and numbers of Rubenstein, Bartley, McKenzie, Christopher Frenze, Alan Reynolds and Bruce Bartlett in a readable form that allowed any Republican candidate to destroy a Democrat who lied about what happened to inflation, jobs, debt, and growth in the 1980's.

But the Left was not only wrong about economics.

The Cold War Seen Clearly

They were wrong, and Ronald Reagan was right for 50 years on the issue central to the survival of America: the intentions and capabilities of the Soviet Empire.

Alexander Solzhenitsyn was quoted in the *New Yorker* Magazine explaining "The Cold War was essentially won by Ronald Reagan when he embarked on the 'star wars' [SDI] program, and the Soviet Union understood that it could not take this next step. Ending the Cold War had nothing to do with Gorbachev's generosity; he was compelled to end it. He had no choice but to disarm."

Paul Gigot of the *Wall Street Journal* quoted Vladimir Lukin, a Boris Yeltsin foreign policy advisor, to the effect that such policies as the Reagan Doctrine and SDI "accelerated our economic convulsions by perhaps five years".

In February 1993, former Soviet foreign minister Alexandr Bessmertnykh, meeting with former Secretary of State George Shultz at Princeton University, confirmed that SDI was decisive in breaking the Soviet Union.

The Establishment Left has lost the ability to control our collective memory of the past. It tried very hard to rewrite the history of the 1980's in economics and foreign policy, but reality and a hard hitting response stopped it. When, in 1994, Clinton urged Americans to choose between him and Reagan, they knew how to vote.

But the Left's collapse is not limited to its failure in the 1980's.

Today, the opened files of the Soviet Union show that the Left was wrong about the 1950's as well. The concern of Republicans about Soviet espionage, the guilt of the traitor Alger Hiss, Julius and Ethel Rosenberg and Soviet intentions around the globe were valid. Republicans, the files of the KGB now show, were right. Hiss was guilty, despite all the efforts by the liberals to protect him. The Rosenbergs were traitors. The nuclear scientists accused during the 1950's of shoveling atomic secrets to the Soviet Union were, it now transpires, doing exactly that. Every day new files tumble open and those liberals still alive must face the fact that they were wrong about foreign policy and about the nature of the Soviet Union and its useful idiots in the United States.

The Left is now losing the 1960's as well. The true nature of the Vietnamese Communists is no secret. The hundreds of thousands murdered by the Cambodian Communists and the re-education camps of the North Vietnamese dictatorship scream out that the American Left lied about Communist intentions in Southeast Asia.

The liberal reporter William Shawcross, who wrote the book *Sideshow*, attacking American policy in Southeast Asia, wrote recently in the *London Times*, "Those of us who opposed the American war in Indochina should be extremely humble in the face of the appalling aftermath: a form of genocide in Cambodia...Looking back on my own coverage, I think I concentrated too easily on the corruption and incompetence of the South Vietnamese and their American allies [and] was too ignorant of the inhuman Hanoi Regime."

David Horowitz, the former editor of *Ramparts*, a New Left leader in the 1970's and now a conservative convert, asked in *My Vietnam Lessons*:

186

Chapter Six

"Why have the passionate advocates of Third World liberation not raised their voices in protest over the rape of Afghanistan or the Cuban-abetted catastrophe to Ethiopia. Not only has the Left failed to make a cause of these Marxist atrocities, it has failed to consider the implications of what we now know about Hanoi's role in South Vietnam's 'civil war'. For North Vietnam's victors have boldly acknowledged that they had infiltrated even more troops into the South than was claimed by the Presidential White Paper which was used to justify America's original commitment of military forces — a White Paper which we leftists scorned at the time as a fiction based on anti-communist paranoia and deception."

Horowitz adds, "My experience has convinced me that historical ignorance and moral blindness are endemic to the American left, necessary conditions of its existence."

The 1960's are coming under further scrutiny as baby boomers have families and children and begin to rethink whether drug abuse and sexual promiscuity are really signs of sophistication and worldliness, or rather self-destructive childish behavior. The hit film "Forrest Gump" makes it clear that Gump is a great deal happier, more decent and, in the end, smarter than his ever-so-sophisticated girl friend who indulges in what the press would have us believe was the reality of the 1960's. Of course, the Establishment press's history of the 1960's is colored. Most American did not abuse drugs. Most did not protest in support of the communists in Vietnam. Most did not drop out, turn on or destroy themselves. Many of those writing about the 1960's did, but they represent an "elite" few. They were not the real America of the 1960's.

It is important for conservatives to set the history record straight, not just on the economics of the 1980's and the American Left's complicity in covering up the crimes of the Soviet Union — from the

Ukraine famines of the 1930's to the genocide in Cambodia — but across the board.

For decades the liberals have attacked the "laissez-faire" rugged individualism of Herbert Hoover, whose free market policies were supposed to have brought on the Great Depression.

As the late economist Murray Rothbard points out in *America's Great Depression*, Hoover was actually an activist, pro-government politician. The stock market collapsed on the day that he endorsed the Smoot-Hawley Tariff Bill. Hoover put into place new spending programs, price supports, wage and price controls, tax hikes, and program after program interfering with the free market.

The Revenue Act of 1932 raised sales taxes on "gasoline, tires, autos, electric energy, malt, toiletries, furs, jewelry. . . [N]ew taxes were levied on bank checks, bond transfers, telephone, telegraph, and radio messages." The personal income tax was raised to a top rate of 75 percent.

Almost every big government program credited to FDR was actually started or advocated by Hoover. It is important that the Republican Party has dropped its once knee-jerk defense of Hoover just as it has refused to defend George Bush's indefensible tax and regulatory record. Some people who call themselves Republicans aren't.

The Nixon years also need revisiting. While his exposure of Alger Hiss as a communist and a traitor earned him the enmity of the Establishment (who would never forgive him for being *right*), his economic policies were a disaster. Nixon greatly increased government spending while president and created scores of new regulatory agencies, spending programs, and McGovernite lunacies that today's Republican Party is trying to eliminate. Nixon took the United States off the gold standard, inflated the currency, and signed treaties with the Soviet Union that undermined America's ability to build a strategic defense. Nixon took the food stamp program from $600 million to

$6.6 billion. He doubled federal spending on education, housing, Medicare, and Social Security, and signed into law the National Environmental Policy Act, which created the Environmental Protection Agency and delivered control of natural resources in the United States into the hands of environmentalists and unelected judges.

It is interesting to note that if the Richard Nixon of 1968-1974 were alive today and a member of Congress, he would be the most liberal Republican in the House of Representatives. Not a Republican in Congress today would vote for wage and price controls, nor for the big-government programs advanced by Nixon.

Newt Gingrich, Speaker of the House, punches his scorecard on the Contract with America as another promise is kept.

CHAPTER SEVEN

CONTRACT WITH AMERICA

During the 1994 election campaign, 367 Republican candidates, incumbents, and challengers assembled on the steps of the Capitol in Washington, D.C., to pledge their support for a Contract with America, a detailed platform of reforms to be brought up and voted on in the first 100 days of the 104th Congress. The language indented below is quoted directly from the Contract. Commentary follows, for clarity and emphasis, and to bring the reader as up to date on progress as is possible.

> *"As Republican Members of the House Representatives and as citizens seeking to join that body we propose not just to change its policies, but even more important, to restore the bonds of trust between the people and their elected representatives. That is why, in this era of official evasion and posturing, we offer instead a detailed agenda for national renewal, a written commitment with no fine print."*

> *This year's election offers the chance, after four decades of one-party control, to bring to the House a new majority that will transform the way Congress works. That historic*

change would be the end of government that is too big, too intrusive, and too easy with the public's money. It can be the beginning of a Congress that respects the values and shares the faith of the American family.

Like Lincoln, our first Republican president, we intend to act with "firmness in the right, as God gives us to see the right". To restore accountability to Congress. To end its cycle of scandal and disgrace. To make us all proud again of the way free people govern themselves.

On the first day of the 104th Congress, the new Republican majority will immediately pass the following major reforms, aimed at restoring the faith and trust of the American people in their government:

1. *Require all laws that apply to the rest of the country also apply equally to Congress;*
2. *Select a major independent auditing firm to conduct a comprehensive audit of Congress for waste, fraud, or abuse;*
3. *Cut the number of House committees, and cut committee staff by one third;*
4. *Limit the terms of all committee chairs;*
5. *Ban the casting of proxy votes in committee;*
6. *Require committee meetings to be open to the public.*
7. *Require a three-fifths majority vote to pass a tax increase;*
8. *Guarantee an honest accounting of our federal budget by implementing zero baseline budgeting.*

Thereafter, within the first hundred days of the 104th Congress, we shall bring to the House floor the following bills, each to be given full and open debate, each to be given a clear and fair vote, and each to be immediately available this day for public inspection and scrutiny.

The Fiscal Responsibility Act
● *A balanced budget/tax limitation amendment and a legislative line-item veto to restore fiscal responsibility to an out-of-control Congress, requiring them to live under the same budget constraints as families and businesses.*

The Taking Back Our Streets Act
●*An anti-crime package including stronger truth in sentencing, "good faith" exclusionary rule exemptions, effective death penalty provisions, and cuts in social spending from this summer's [1994] crime bill to fund prison construction and additional law enforcement to keep people secure in their neighborhoods and kids safe in their schools.*

The Personal Responsibility Act
●*Discourage illegitimacy and teen pregnancy by prohibiting welfare to minor mothers and denying increased AFDC [Aid to Families with Dependent Children] for additional children while on welfare, cut spending for welfare programs, and enact a tough two-years-and-out provision with work requirements to promote individual responsibility.*

The Family Reinforcement Act
● *Child support enforcement, tax incentive for adoption, strengthening rights of parents in their children's education, stronger child pornography laws, and an elderly dependent care tax credit to reinforce the central role of families in American society.*

The American Dream Restoration Act
● *A $500-per-child tax credit, begin repeal of the marriage tax penalty, and creation of American Dream Savings Accounts to provide middle-class tax relief.*

The National Security Restoration Act
● *No U.S. troops under UN command and restoration of the essential parts of our national security funding to strengthen our national defense and maintain our credibility around the world.*

The Senior Citizens Fairness Act
● *Raise the Social Security earnings limit, which currently forces seniors out of the workforce, repeal the 1993 tax hikes on Social Security benefits, and provide tax incentives for private long-term care insurance to let older Americans keep more of what they have earned over the years.*

The Job Creation and Wage Enhancement Act
● *Small business incentives, capital gains cut and indexation, neutral cost recovery, risk assessment/cost-benefit analysis, strengthening of the Regulatory Flexibility Act and unfunded mandate reform to create jobs and raise worker wages.*

The Common Sense Legal Reforms Act
● *"Loser pays" laws, reasonable limits on punitive damages, and reform of product liability laws to stem the endless tide of litigation.*

The Citizen Legislature Act
● *A first-ever vote on term limits to replace career politicians with citizen legislators.*

Further, we will instruct the House Budget Committee to report to the floor, and we will work to enact additional budget savings, beyond the budget cuts specifically included in the legislation described above, to ensure that the federal budget deficit will be less than it would have been without the enactment of these bills.

Respecting the judgment of our fellow citizens as we seek their mandate for reform, we hereby pledge our names to this Contract with America.

* * * * *

COMMENTS ON ELEMENTS OF THE CONTRACT WITH AMERICA

1. Fiscal Responsibility Act

Almost every state requires a balanced budget, and 43 states give their governors the line-item veto. While these two measures have certainly not stopped the growth of state governments, they have just as certainly served as a restraint on that growth. When citizens elect strong, pro-taxpayer governors willing to use the line-item veto, such as Tommy Thompson of Wisconsin, those governors have been able use the line-item veto to trim back pork barrel spending.

The line-item veto (which President Clinton claims to support) also makes the president or governor a responsible party in any government spending decision. Reagan would have liked to cut out much of the government spending that happened during his presidency, but when the entire budget is folded into a single reconciliation bill, or entire multi-hundred-billion dollar departments are financed in a single bill, vetoing the entire bill in order to kill a single wasteful or harmful program can be politically difficult.

A president armed with a line-item veto would be involved in every government spending decision. He would be stripped of the excuse — valid or not — that he was "forced" to sign entire bills.

The balanced budget and line-item veto constitutional amendments proposed will make the president and Congress more accountable for what they do. But alone they will not keep spending low.

A requirement for a supermajority of 60 percent (three-fifths) or 66 percent (two-thirds) to raise taxes would be an important limit on the power of government to spend. Because taxes are almost as permanent as constitutional amendments, one could argue that they should require a higher hurdle for enactment than other legislation. The decision to permanently transfer more resources from the American people to the government should not be taken lightly.

The Republicans promised in the Contract to have an up-or-down vote on a constitutional amendment to require a balanced budget, including a requirement for a 60 percent supermajority to raise the debt limit, borrow money, or raise taxes.

On January 25, 1995, the House of Representatives did indeed vote on the Barton Amendment, which met exactly those requirements. Joe Barton, a Republican from Texas, received 253 votes for his measure to 173 against. This total was less than the 290 votes (or two-thirds of the House) needed to pass a constitutional amendment. The House then passed a weaker version of the balanced budget amendment, one without a supermajority requirement for tax increases. This weak balanced budget amendment passed 300 to 132.

In the following list, Republicans are shown in italics; Democrats in roman type. Bernie Sanders of Vermont was elected as a Socialist, but he votes with the Democrats in caucus.

Chapter Seven

Members voting against a supermajority and for a weak amendment.

Abercrombie (HI-1)
Ackerman (NY-5)
Baldacci (ME-2)
Barrett (WI-5)
Bateman (VA-1)
Becerra (CA-30)
Beilenson (CA-24)
Bentsen (TX-25)
Bereuter (NE-1)
Berman (CA-26)
Boehlert (NY-23)
Bonior (MI-10)
Borski (PA-3)
Boucher (VA-9)
Brown (FL-3)
Bryant (TX-5)
Cardin (MD-3)
Clay (MO-1)
Clayton (NC-1)
Clyburn (SC-6)
Coleman (TX-16)
Collins (IL-7)
Collins (MI-15)
Conyers (MI-14)
Costello (IL-12)
Coyne (PA-14)
DeFazio (OR-4)
DeLauro (CT-3)
Dellums (CA-9)
Deutsch (FL-20)
Dicks (WA-6)
Dingell (MI-16)
Dixon (CA-32)
Doggett (TX-20)
Doyle (PA-18)
Durbin (IL-20)
Engel (NY-17)
Eshoo (CA-14)
Evans (IL-17)
Farr (CA-17)
Fattah (PA-2)
Fazio (CA-3)
Filner (CA-50)
Flake (NY-6)

Foglietta (PA-1)
Ford (TN-9)
Frank (MA-4)
Frost (TX-24)
Furse (OR-1)
Gejdenson (CT-2)
Gephardt (MO-3)
Gibbons (FL-11)
Gonzalez (TX-20)
Greene (TX-29)
Gutierrez (IL-4)
Hall (OH-30)
Hamilton (IN-9)
Hastings (FL-23)
Hefner (NC-8)
Hilliard (AL-7)
Hinchey (NY-26)
Holden (PA-6)
Hostettler (IN-8)
Houghton (NY-31)
Hoyer (MD-5)
Jackson-Lee (TX-18)
Jacobs (IN-10)
Johnson (CT-6)
Johnson (SD-AL)
Johnson, (TX-30)
Johnston (FL-19)
Kanjorski (PA-11)
Kaptur (OH-9)
Kennedy (MA-8)
Kennedy (RI-1)
Kennelly (CT-1)
Kildee (MI-9)
Kleczka (WI-4)
LaFalce (NY-29)
Lantos (CA-12)
Levin (MI-12)
Lewis (GA-5)
Lipinski (IL-3)
Lofgren (CA-16)
Lowey (NY-18)
Luther (MN-6)
Maloney (NY-14)

Manton (NY-7)
Markey (MA-7)
Martinez (CA-31)
Mascara (PA-20)
McCarthy (MO-5)
McDermott (WA-7)
McHale (PA-15)
McKinney (GA-11)
McNulty (NY-21)
Meehan (MA-5)
Meek (FL-17)
Menendez (NJ-13)
Mfume (MD-7)
Miller (CA-7)
Mineta (CA-15)
Minge (MN-2)
Mink (HI-2)
Moakley (MA-9)
Mollohan (WV-1)
Moran (VA-8)
Murtha (PA-12)
Nadler (NY-8)
Neal (MA-2)
Oberstar (MN-8)
Obey (WI-7)
Olver (MA-1)
Ortiz (TX-27)
Owens (NY-11)
Pastor (AZ-2)
Payne (NJ-10)
Payne (VA-5)
Pelosi (CA-8)
Peterson (FL-2)
Pickett (VA-2)
Pomeroy (ND-AL)
Porter (IL-10)
Rahall (WV-3)
Rangel (NY-15)
Reed (RI-2)
Reynolds (IL-2)
Richardson (NM-3)
Rivers (MI-13)
Rose (NC-7)

Roukema (NJ-5)
Roybal-Allard (CA-33)
Sabo (MN-5)
SANDERS (VT-AL)*
Sawyer (OH-14)
Schroeder (CO-1)
Schumer (NY-9)
Scott (VA-3)
Serrano (NY-16)
Sisisky (VA-4)
Skaggs (CO-2)
Slaughter (NY-28)
Spratt (SC-5)
Stark (CA-13)
Stenholm (TX-17)
Stokes (OH-11)
Studds (MA-10)
Stupak (MI-1)
Tanner (TN-8)
Tejeda (TX-28)
Thompson (MN-2)
Thornton (AR-2)
Thurman (FL-5)
Torres (CA-34)
Torricelli (NJ-9)
Traficant (OH-17)
Tucker (CA-37)
Velasquez (NY-12)
Vento (MN-4)
Visclosky (IN-1)
Volkmer (MO-9)
Ward (KY-3)
Waters (CA-35)
Watt (NC-12)
Waxman (CA-29)
Williams (MT-AL)
Wilson (TX-2)
Wise (WV-2)
Woolsey (CA-6)
Wyden (OR-3)
Wynn (MD-4)
Yates (IL-9)

Rock the House

Some members wanted to appear to be for fiscal restraint while actually favoring higher taxes. They behaved as though the old order still held, and that they could vote one way for the cameras and another way when it mattered. The following list is those members of Congress who voted first *against* requiring a supermajority to raise taxes and then *for* the weaker balanced budget amendment. They are no friends of the taxpayer.

Bateman (VA-1)	Kennedy (MA-8)	Payne (VA-5)
Bereuter (NE-1)	LaFalce (NY-29)	Peterson (FL-2)
Boehlert (NY-23)	Lipinski (IL-3)	*Porter (IL-16)*
Bryant (TX-5)	Luther (MN-6)	Richardson (NM-3)
Clyburn (SC-6)	Martinez (CA-31)	Rose (NC-7)
Costello (IL-12)	Mascara (PA-20)	*Roukema* (NJ-5)
DeFazio (OR-4)	McCarthy (MO-5)	Stenholm (TX-17)
Doyle (PA-18)	McHale (PA-15)	Tanner (TN-8)
Frost (TX-24)	McNulty (NY-21)	Torricelli (NJ-9)
Hefner (NC-8)	Meehan (MA-5)	Visclosky (IN-1)
Johnson (CT-6)	Minge (MN-2)	Volkmer (MO-9)
Johnson (SD-AL)	Moran (VA-8)	
Johnston (FL-19)	Ortiz (TX-27)	

The day after the House failed to pass the Barton Amendment, Speaker Newt Gingrich joined Joe Barton and the freshman class, led by John Shadegg of Arizona and Linda Smith of Washington state to announce a new drive to build support for a constitutional amendment to require a three-fifths vote for any tax increase. The vote in the House on this new effort will be held on April 15, 1996. Any member who fails to support that amendment will have to face the voters on November 5, 1996. Gingrich and the Republicans promised at the press conference that, if necessary, they will force a third vote for the supermajority requirement to raise taxes on April 15, 1997 and that this time there will be enough Republicans to pass the amendment. In the words of freshman Shadegg, "We'll be in their faces, in their districts, and if they vote against the taxpayers, we'll be in their seats!"

That is fulfilling the Contract.

2. Taking Back Our Streets Act

Bill Clinton got his "crime bill" passed in August of 1994 by a vote of 235-195 in the House of Representatives. That was the bill with more than $5 billion in pork barrel social welfare spending. Republicans did stop Clinton from including the "Racial Justice Act" which would have put racial quotas on the death penalty.

By February 14, 1995, House Republicans, led by Bill McCollum of Florida, had passed all six provisions of the "Take Back Our Streets" proposal. Republicans killed $3.9 billion in social welfare spending authorized by the Clinton "crime" bill of 1994. Congress voted 238-192 to give $10 billion in block grants to local authorities to use to fight crime. Half of this money is promised to states that enact truth-in-sentencing laws requiring prisoners to serve a minimum of 85 percent of their sentences. The Contract crime provisions as passed by the House will speed up trials, limit the abuse of the appeals process, and focus on punishing criminals and protecting victims.

Bill Clinton is upset that his phony crime bill of the summer of 1994 is being exposed to the light of day, and that the pork barrel spending is being cut out. Clinton claims he wants to keep his promise of "100,000 new police officers", but even the *Washington Post* has pointed out that "100,000 cops on the beat" was always a dishonest number. It was, in fact, an unfunded mandate, requiring cities and states to pay most of the cost for the new police. The price tag to taxpayers would have been $20 billion.

Clinton's attempt to "move to the center" on the crime issue has collapsed. Clinton may veto the Republican Party's "tough on crime" provisions, but that will unmask his true agenda.

3. Personal Responsibility Act

During the 1992 election Bill Clinton's biggest applause line was a promise to "end welfare as we know it". It has been two years since Bill Clinton won 43 percent of the vote, and he has not reformed welfare or even put forward a formal reform package. Some liberals have criticized Clinton for leading with a statist health care scheme which Americans rejected out of opposition to bigger government. These liberals explain that if Clinton had led with welfare reform he might have been a successful president.

This is nonsense. Bill and Hillary Clinton's idea of "welfare reform" is even more alien to the American people than their big government health plan. To begin with, the Clinton proposals put forward would all increase the amount of money taken from taxpayers. Spending more on welfare is not reform. It is not ending welfare as we know it. It is more of the same. Clinton knows this, and that is why he led with the relatively sane power grab over the health care of all Americans.

For Bill Clinton and the Democrat coalition, the welfare system is not a failure. It has been a grand success. It did just what it was supposed to do. It kept millions of American families in poverty and ignorance for generations, where they could be mobilized as a voting bloc. Their very government-imposed misery was used as a justification for more government programs to fix the damage done to families by previous government programs. As long as every failure by the government to alleviate poverty could justify more government, the Democrats were on a roll.

The Democrat Party has not forgiven itself for letting millions of European and Asian immigrants escape the poverty of their ancestral lands, work for themselves, get ahead without any "help" from the government, and then move to the suburbs where the big city machines have no control over them. They were determined this would not happen again. They have been very thorough in stamping out all possible avenues of economic independence that might allow the clients of the welfare state to escape. This is why Democrats fought so hard against enterprise zones that would cut taxes and regulations in inner-city areas, allowing the poor to create jobs for themselves. It is also why they have worked to provide entitlements for immigrants, both legal and illegal.

Speaker Newt Gingrich highlighted the damage we all know the welfare state does to its supposed beneficiaries when he asked us to imagine two Korean brothers who arrive in Los Angeles. One is met by a relative who offers him a below-minimum-wage job that requires him to work two jobs, seven days a week, in violation of all relevant labor laws.

The second brother is met by a social worker who explains all the various programs available to the indigent: free food, shelter, welfare, etc.

Gingrich then asks the question that every American knows the answer to: "After ten years, which brother owns his own home, is running his own business, and has money in the bank?"

If we know that the brother who is helped by the welfare state will fail, and the one who "escapes" the help of the government will succeed, why should we continue this destructive welfare state?

Democrats have been adamant in opposing the privatization of government-owned housing. Republicans have argued that it would be cost-effective to simply give government housing to the poor, so they can take care of their own homes, create capital and have a stake in the community. As one Democrat said, "What would happen if one of these poor families bought or was given their government-owned apartment and then fixed it up and sold it for a $70,000 profit?" The answer, of course, is that that person would become a Republican and would no longer need all that "help" from the government that justifies higher taxes.

Since 1965, welfare spending in the United States has cost taxpayers $4.9 trillion dollars in constant 1992 dollars. In 1995, government will spend more than $350 billion on welfare, or almost one billion dollars every day.

The federal government alone runs more than 76 welfare programs. Democrats like to minimize the amount of money spent on welfare by pretending that only the cash assistance of Aid to Families with Dependent Children (AFDC) is welfare. This dishonestly leaves out the $180 billion dollars taken from taxpayers in 1995 alone to pay for Medicaid, the $21.7 billion taken to pay for housing subsidies, the $40.7 billion in "food and nutrition services", and more than a billion dollars in energy aid. And in the government's own dishonest accounting, only 21.6 percent of welfare spending even shows up as reducing the poverty level in America, because, unbelievably, the government doesn't count all the non-cash benefits it pays for. The purpose of this fiction is to allow the Democrats to keep taking more and more money from the middle class, and spend it on their friends and precinct workers, while their statistics show that such transfers have not reduced poverty. Result: we need to raise taxes and spend more to fight poverty!

Increased welfare benefits to mothers who bear children out of wedlock and remain unmarried has had the unsurprising effect of subsidizing and promoting illegitimate births and broken homes without fathers. The increase in illegitimate births correlates closely with higher welfare spending over the past 30 years. In 1970, 15 percent of children under 18 lived outside two-parent households. By 1992 that number had jumped to 29 percent. The federal government has hurt working men and women with its expensive welfare state. It has destroyed families and the lives of the poor with the welfare state. But that is a necessary cost of maintaining the Democrat Party coalition.

The transfer of all welfare to the states, so that 50 different approaches (requiring work, prohibiting payments to minor single mothers, and others) can be tried will stop this war on America's poor on behalf of the Democrat Party's get-out-the-vote machine.

The Democrat Party's misuse of poor Americans through the false compassion of the welfare state has created the underclass, has broken more families, has killed more kids, and has destroyed more black men than the Ku Klux Klan ever did. It destroys self-respect and aspiration more thoroughly than slavery ever could.

And now everyone knows it: the Democrats whose interest groups will not allow the party to change; the Republicans who are determined to end this crime; and poor Americans who understand that they have been used to maintain the power of a corrupt political machine.

4. The Family Reinforcement Act

The Family Reinforcement Act is designed to have the government help protect families and children and to keep the government from encroaching on the privacy and primacy of families.

First, the Act would require parental consent for any child participating in federally-funded surveys that pry into family life. Many parents have been surprised to find that schools have been engaging in social science experiments with their children without parental notification. "Experimental" studies have included having children write their own obituaries, make decisions about which family member they would save last in a fire or toss first from a crowded life raft, and other, no doubt fascinating, questions that are none of the school's business. The schools have also shown an oddly perverse interest in children's sexuality, administering highly explicit sex surveys and questionnaires, sometimes to very young children.

Second, the Act would strengthen requirements that fathers pay child support for their children; **third**, the Act would establish a refundable tax credit of as much as $5,000 for adoption expenses; **fourth,** the Act would provide a $500 tax credit for families that care for a dependent parent or grandparent at home. **Lastly,** the Act would increase sentences for sexual offenses against children and close certain loopholes in federal laws intended to protect children from abuse and child pornography.

5. American Dream Restoration Act

Under Bill Clinton, the marriage penalty in the tax code was increased. With a graduated income tax, two married people often pay higher taxes than they would if they were single or divorced. Life is tough enough without the federal government punishing people for getting married. The Republicans will begin repeal of the marriage penalty tax. This problem, of course, will be solved once and for all when America moves to a real flat tax and all citizens are treated equally.

Expanding *Individual Retirement Accounts* for all Americans would increase America's savings rate, so damaged by the tax-and-spend policies of the Democrat Party. Voters have noticed that whenever the Democrat politicians who argue for a tax structure based on envy and greed call for taxing "the rich", they aim their tax guns on savings and investment. Then, having kneecapped the economy, they demand more spending on government programs to "help" the economy. They have no shame. Just all our money.

Cutting taxes so that every family receives a $500 tax credit for every child under the age of 18 would begin to reduce the damage Clinton's tax policies do to families. It will not restore families, however, to the where position they were in the 1940's. Then, the average family paid only two percent of its income in direct federal income taxes. Today the average family pays more than ten percent income taxes. That does not include Social Security taxes, which now amount to 7.5 percent (and another 7.5 percent contributed by employers); the self-employed get to pay both halves. Most Americans pay more in Social Security taxes than in income tax. And, of course, there are other, hidden federal taxes on goods, services (like the federal subscriber fee on everyone's phone bill), and businesses.

DEFENSE BUDGETS

America's defense budget peaked in 1985 at $377 Billion (all figures are in 1994 dollars). It then fell steadily to around $243 billion in 1995. It is projected to be only $220 billion in 1998.

Defense is now about 16% of total federal spending, down from 55% in 1955. As defense spending has declined, payments to individuals have grown, from 17% of total federal spending in 1955 to 60% today.

These changes have had a serious impact on defense in a still-dangerous world. The Soviet threat has been replaced by regional conflicts and terrorist activities that are sometimes more expensive to counter.

The first casualty of the declining defense budget has been maintenance, leaving the troops with defective and inoperable equipment. Less that 90% of Marine Corps Equipment is battle ready, and hundreds of Navy aircraft and engines are in desperate need of maintenance.

Another factor contributing to the decline in defense capability is the increasing share of the military dollar being devoted to social experimentation, health care programs, and international "peacekeeping". A pregnancy rate of 100% or more among women assigned to ships means expanded social services and health care spending. It also means serious deterioration of combat readiness. Devoting troops to Somalia or Bosnia means fewer available for missions more directly related to U.S. security.

The Clinton Administration seems to regard the military as a great engine for social change, a means for integrating homosexuals into the larger society and making women "equal" to men. The military also can serve as a wonderful backdrop for photographs during political campaigns. The actual defense of the nation appears to take a back seat.

Impact By States of a $500 Per Child Tax Credit

State	No. of Families with Children in Each State	No. of Children Eligible for a $500 Tax Credit	Amount Each State Gets Annually from $500 Per Child Tax Credit
Alabama	607,775	836,486	$418,243,000
Alaska	83,770	134,962	$67,481,000
Arizona	472,805	744,524	$372,262,000
Arkansas	366,520	524,241	$262,120,500
California	4,444,459	6,625,012	$3,312,506,000
Colorado	493,148	737,544	$368,772,000
Connecticut	466,951	723,674	$361,837,000
Delaware	105,034	172,017	$86,008,500
D.C.	63,940	81,195	$40,597,500
Florida	1,698,710	2,233,271	$1,116,635,500
Georgia	909,966	1,226,073	$613,036,500
Hawaii	167,417	295,346	$147,673,000
Idaho	151,431	263,945	$131,972,000
Illinois	1,622,908	2,501,462	$1,250,731,000
Indiana	851,840	1,110,887	$555,443,500
Iowa	383,031	641,094	$320,547,000
Kansas	393,479	651,174	$325,587,000
Kentucky	536,468	648,121	$324,060,500
Louisiana	646,684	868,102	$434,351,000
Maine	156,799	223,255	$111,627,500
Maryland	675,067	1,038,365	$519,182,500
Massachusetts	750,685	1,110,453	$555,226,500
Michigan	1279,610	1,866,891	$933,445,500
Minnesota	570,424	946,639	$473,319,500
Mississippi	425,312	540,359	$270,179,500
Missouri	697,847	981,008	$490,504,000

Impact By States of a $500 Per Child Tax Credit

State	No. of Families with Children in Each State	No. of Children Eligible for a $500 Tax Credit	Amount Each State Gets Annually from $500 Per Child Tax Credit
Montana	124,551	197,938	$98,969,000
Nebraska	237,460	427,724	$213,862,000
Nevada	168,220	247,958	$123,979,000
New Hampshire	158,319	246,361	$123,180,500
New Jersey	1,006,496	1,522,756	$761,378,000
New Mexico	239,867	321,854	$160,927,000
New York	2,494,133	3,575,251	$1,727,625,500
North Carolina	940,231	1,359,138	$679,569,000
North Dakota	87,390	146,786	$73,393,000
Ohio	1,577,405	2,392,172	$1,196,086,000
Oklahoma	456,751	644,733	$322,366,500
Oregon	422,519	607,615	$303,807,500
Pennsylvania	1,568,632	2,507,260	$1,253,630,000
Rhode Island	111,470	159,461	$79,730,500
South Carolina	569,749	777,909	$388,954,500
South Dakota	96,221	158,309	$79,154,500
Tennessee	637,780	829,778	$414,889,000
Texas	2,582,258	3,628,180	$1,814,909,000
Utah	249,945	473,448	$236,724,000
Vermont	81,163	116,058	$58,029,000
Virginia	859,620	1,286,275	$643,137,500
Washington	737,136	1,141,341	$570,670,500
West Virginia	266,844	346,642	$173,321,000
Wisconsin	722,639	1,175,695	$587,847,500
Wyoming	69,514	122,668	$61,334,000

Source: The Heritage Foundation

206

Chapter Seven

If the per child tax deduction had kept pace with inflation a family today would get a deduction of at least $5,000 per child. Today the deduction is only $2,450. The reason the deduction shrank is that the federal government wanted more money and rather than raising taxes directly and honestly, the politicians simply let inflation eat away at the value of every child's deduction. This inflationary gain for the politicians ended only when Reagan insisted on indexing the deduction (and, indeed, all the graduated tax brackets) to protect Americans from the ravages of inflation — which was caused by government in the first place. The state-by-state impact of the $500 per child tax credit is shown in the table on the preceding page.

6. The National Security Restoration Act

Bill Clinton has undone the progress of the Reagan years in restoring America's military strength after Jimmy Carter and the Democrat Congress had given us a "hollow military" subsequent to the Vietnam War. Once again, training is being cut back, spare parts are in short supply, and fully three out of our nation's 12 active duty military divisions were found to be below readiness in the fall of 1994.

Clinton is also hiding pork barrel spending inside the Pentagon budget, weakening America's defense, and putting Americans at risk abroad, while masking the true size of his cuts in defense muscle. The Heritage Foundation estimates that fully $5 billion dollars of spending by the Defense Department in 1994 was really social welfare spending stuck there by Clinton, not really defense spending as promised to the American people. This includes some $50 million of the Kaho'olawe Island Trust Fund and $1 million for Los Angeles Youth Programs. Such pork inside the defense budget has tripled in the past five years.

When Clinton campaigned for president, he said he wanted to reduce defense spending beyond the Bush defense cuts by another $60 billion over five years. What he really did when he got into power was reduce the projected Defense Department budget (already in decline) by fully $165 billion. This has led, among other things, to a 12.8 percent gap between military pay and comparable civilian pay that has driven some 17,000 active duty personnel and their families into eligibility for U.S. government food stamps. The last time this happened was in the Carter years.

And while Clinton is cutting training, readiness, and real defense spending, he is committing American troops overseas at a furious rate. As the Contract notes, by the end of 1994, "Over 70,000 United States troops were serving in such regions as Iraq, Bosnia, Macedonia, the Adriatic Sea, Rwanda, and the Caribbean Sea for missions involving Haiti and Cuba."

The National Security Restoration Act notes that the "United States is also being assessed 31.7 percent of annual United Nations costs for peacekeeping and other United Nations missions. The next highest contributor, Japan, pays only 12.5 percent."

Specific provisions of the NSRA include the following:

● Maintenance of U.S. troops under U.S. command. Republicans, by and large, oppose the tendency to fight the wars of the United Nations, and they are strongly opposed to allowing "U.N. Commanders" to take control of our soldiers.

● A comprehensive review of U.S. defense needs.

● A restoration of budget "firewalls" that prohibit the raiding of the defense budget to pay for new social programs. The firewalls assure that any cuts in the defense budget go to reduce budget deficits.

● A renewed commitment to a "defense that defends" through the use of anti-ballistic missile technology to defend the territory and people of the United States. Contrary to information put out by those whose priority has never been the defense of the United States, a space-based missile defense is both feasible and cheaper than a ground-based system, which would protect only portions of the United States.

- A renewed commitment to maintaining and expanding the North Atlantic Treaty Organization, which has been so effective in keeping the peace in the decades since World War II.

Although the Democrats (and a handful of liberal Republicans) stopped the House from moving ahead with the Strategic Defense Initiative to protect America from ballistic missiles, House Republicans did pass the rest of the bill to begin rebuilding America's defenses.

7. The Senior Citizens Fairness Act

Today there are more than 30 million Americans over the age of 65, making up more than 12 percent of all Americans. Bill Clinton's 1993 tax increase (the one that was only supposed to hit millionaires) increased the federal income tax paid by more than 6.1 million older Americans on Social Security. This tax on Social Security recipients will cost older Americans some $25 billion over the next five years. The Republican Contract promises to repeal this part of Clinton's tax hike on those "millionaire" Americans earning more than $34,000 as singles or $44,000 as couples.

The present law penalizes Americans between the ages of 65 and 69 who wish to continue to work, by taking from them one dollar of promised Social Security benefits for every three dollars they earn above $11,160. This is, of course, a 33 percent surtax on working older Americans, above and beyond all other taxes. The Republican Contract promises to phase in a higher earnings limit of $30,000 rather than the limit now in place.

The Contract also promises to change tax law to make it easier for Americans to buy long-term care health insurance.

8. The Job Creation and Wage Enhancement Act

Present taxes and regulations hobble America's ability to compete internationally and to create jobs. Cost of Government Day, the day until which Americans work just to pay the costs of taxes, government regulations and government spending, was July 10 in 1994. Given the Clinton regulatory explosion and 1993 tax increase, that date will be moving later into the summer unless Republicans can turn things around.

The Job Creation and Wage Enhancement Act is a list of tax cuts and regulatory relief that will get the government out of the way of real job creation and higher wages.

The Act would cut the present capital gains rate from 28 percent to below 20 percent. This would begin to bring America in line with our international competitors. In fast-growing Hong Kong, investors and savers pay no capital gains tax. In Germany, long-term capital gains are not taxed. The same is true of Belgium and the Netherlands. Socialist Sweden only taxes capital gains at 25 percent. Japan taxes capital gains at one percent of sales price or 20 percent of the net gain. In the U.S., the government has been taxing Americans on inflated values and hurting our ability to compete around the globe.

The Act would also reduce the taxes companies are forced to pay on job-creating investments in machinery. And it would clarify the home office deduction so that self-employed Americans can be treated more fairly and consistently.

The Act further would require federal agencies to assess the risks and costs of the regulatory burdens they impose. Every federal agency would publicly declare how much their decisions cost Americans each year. The Act would also check unfunded mandates on states and localities and would provide an honest reporting of their hidden costs. The Act would put some teeth into the constitutional takings provision that forbids government from taking an individual's property, home, or farmland without just compensation.

Chapter Seven

The true costs of regulations are not always found in dollars and cents.

The Corporate Average Fuel Economy (CAFE) standards that require cars to be smaller and lighter in order to get higher gas mileage, as mandated by federal bureaucrats, increase the likelihood that those in the smaller cars will be killed or injured in an accident.

A 1988 study by Brookings senior economist Robert W. Crandall and Harvard public health professor John D. Graham found that producing cars under a 27.5 miles per gallon standard results in 2,200 to 3,900 additional auto deaths each year. That is a policy of blood for oil, more expensive than any war in the Middle East. The Competitive Enterprise Institute, using the Crandall-Graham research, brought suit against the U.S. Department of Transportation and forced DOT to take these increased deaths into account in formulating its CAFE proposals.

The Food and Drug Administration (FDA) is often cited as a model of government regulation, protecting consumers from unsafe drugs and contaminated food. And yet, there are often real costs associated with the bureaucratic timidity that characterizes FDA.

For example, the Competitive Enterprise Institute estimates that needless delay in approving just one anti-cancer drug may have cost as many as 3,500 lives. FDA had the application for approval for three and a half years, during which time the drug was available in France, Denmark, and other European countries, and during which time 35,000 Americans were denied the option of its use.

CEI General Counsel Sam Kazman points out that the drug "was as effective in 1988 as it is today, and kidney cancer is as deadly today as it was in 1988... If the FDA were as serious about saving lives as it is about re-labeling orange juice, this product would have been approved years ago."

Considering that renal cancer is almost always fatal, it is hard to see why patients should not be given the option of using such drugs, especially when they are already approved in other countries.

In December of 1994, the FDA approved six drugs from its "priority" list. Three of these had been available in other countries for years, and in one case, the approval by FDA took decades. And these were "priority" drugs. As *Science* magazine said, "When a regulatory agency that licenses drugs for heart attacks stumbles, it may have not only egg on its face but blood on its hands. . . A drug that dissolves blood clots should no longer have to answer whether such an action prolongs life".

9. The Common Sense Legal Reforms Act

The costs of America's liability crisis have damaged America's international competitiveness, increased state and local taxes, raised the costs of health care, and made a small number of trial lawyers who abuse the system very, very rich.

The number of lawsuits in federal courts alone has swelled from 90,000 in 1960 to more than 250,000 in 1990. Liability crisis expert Peter Huber calculates the total "tort tax" on individuals, businesses, and government at more than $80 billion each year in direct costs such as litigation and increased insurance premiums and a grand total of $300 billion in indirect costs to society. These include the practice of "defensive medicine" and other efforts to avoid being sued. At a cost of $300 billion a year, the present liability crisis costs more than the entire defense budget.

James Lyons has pointed out that the Bureau of Labor Statistics says there were 582,000 Americans engaged in full-time legal practice in 1991. This number has grown rapidly in recent years. Lyons wrote in *Forbes* Magazine,

Chapter Seven

"Between 1870 and 1970, the number of lawyers grew at about 25% per decade, roughly mirroring the growth of the U.S. population. But in the 1970's the number of lawyers nearly doubled. Their ranks grew another 48 percent in the 1980's. Today, there are nearly 600,000 practicing lawyers in this country —nearly three times as many per capita as in any other major industrialized nation...The Commerce Department figures that legal services now generate more 'value added' — an industry's gross receipts, minus purchases made by that industry from other sectors — than the country's steel, textile or even automobile industries generate."

Of course, when Commerce speaks of "value" added, it really means "costs".

In 1994, the Department of Justice reported that there were 30,000 inmate lawsuits filed against prison officials. The vast majority were frivolous and included complaints that the prison canteen supplied "creamy" peanut butter though the inmate preferred "crunchy". One inmate sued claiming his toilet seat was too cold. Reportedly, one-fifth of the entire budget of the New York states attorney general's office is spent on prisoner lawsuits (for which in 1994 there was a backlog of 28,000).

The Common Sense Legal Reforms Act would penalize those who bring frivolous lawsuits that harass their neighbors and tie up the courts by requiring that those who lose such suits must pay the costs of those they sue. The Act also calls for penalties on lawyers involved in such suits.

The Act would also create a uniform product liability law for punitive damages, joint and severable liability, and fault-based liability. And it would reduce the possibility of abusive lawsuits based on phony or "junk" science.

10. The Citizen Legislature Act

Prior to the Republican landslide in November 1994, the Democrats in the House of Representatives refused to allow a vote on term limits. Worse, Speaker Tom Foley actually participated in a lawsuit against his constituents when voters in Washington state voted to limit House members to three terms and senators to two terms. Foley also spent taxpayer funds attacking term limits in Florida.

To date, 22 states have passed term limits on state legislators and on members of the House and Senate at the federal level. Today, 40 percent of the population of the United states lives under term limits.

On page 216 is the list of states that have passed term limits, the dates of enactment and the percentage of the vote supporting term limits, as supplied by U.S. Term Limits. Then on page 217 is a map showing term-limited states.

There are only 23 states which permit citizen initiatives, and 22 of those have already passed term limits in some form, as the table shows. The 23rd initiative state, Mississippi, has certified a term limits initiative for the 1995 state ballot. The U.S. House limit will be three terms. When Mississippi passes term limits in the fall of 1995, every state where the people can limit terms by their own action will have done so. The rest is up to Congress.

The purpose of term limits is to return the government of this country to a citizen legislature where politicians do not see themselves as separate and aloof from the rest of the nation. Republicans in the House took a big step in this direction when they passed the Shays Act on January 4, 1995 to ensure that Congress will live under the same laws the rest of us are forced to live under. The Senate passed the bill on January 12, and it has already been signed into law. (Maybe Congress will come to learn why people talk about living "under" a set of laws.)

Republicans moved, after the 1992 election, to impose term limits on ranking members of House committees. These ranking members, who accumulate power through their seniority, were limited to only three terms as ranking Republican. On January 4, 1994, Republicans honored their Contract and limited the terms of committee chairmen to three terms or six years. Never again can a member of Congress like Dan Rostenkowski or Jack Brooks accumulate so much power by sitting in a chairman's seat for so long. As a famous term limits poster says under a photo of the now-defeated Rostenkowski: "Term Limits Poster Child: 18 terms, 17 indictments".

THE SUPREME COURT AND TERM LIMITS

On May 22, 1995, the Supreme Court struck down the laws of 23 states limiting the terms of members of the United States Congress. By a margin of five to four, the Court struck down an Arkansas constitutional amendment, which had been adopted by voter initiative, limiting Senators to 12 years and House members to 6 years. The decision, written by Associate Justice Stevens, was devoted almost entirely to the policy implications of term limits, not their constitutionality.

In an 88-page dissent, Associate Justice Clarence Thomas, joined by Chief Justice Rehnquist and Justices O'Conner and Scalia, argued that the three qualifications contained in the Constitution (age, citizenship, and state residence) do not bar states from adding others. "Where the Constitution is silent," wrote Thomas "it raises no bar to action by the state or the people."

Thomas pointed out that, at the time of the adoption of the Constitution, Virginia required candidates to be property owners an additional qualification not mentioned in the Constitution. Other states required a period of residency and some still do. The five justices voting to defend the *status quo* had to ignore the 9th and 10th Amendments to the Constitution and American history to give the Washington Establishment the victory it wanted.

With the avenue of state laws now foreclosed by unelected federal judges, those seeking to dismantle the structure of professional politicians will turn to a constitutional amendment, as discussed in the text.

215

22 STATES WITH TERM LIMITS

State	Year Passed	Winning %	Total Votes
Alaska	1994	63%	103,790
Arizona	1992	74%	1,026,830
Arkansas	1992	60%	494,326
California	1992	63%	6,578,637
Colorado*	1994	51%	554,115
Florida	1992	77%	3,625,500
Idaho	1994	59%	232,277
Maine	1994	63%	245,373
Massachusetts	1994	51%	991,205
Michigan	1992	59%	2,323,171
Missouri	1992	74%	1,590,552
Montana	1992	67%	264,174
Nebraska	1994	68%	359,114
Nevada	1994	70%	257,049
North Dakota	1992	55%	162,150
Ohio	1992	66%	2,897,054
Oklahoma	1994	67%	329,244
Oregon	1992	69%	1,003,706
South Dakota	1992	63%	205,074
Utah	1994	*Passed by State Legislature*	
Washington	1992	52%	1,119,985
Wyoming	1992	77%	150,113
AVERAGE/TOTAL		64%	24,513,439

Bold   States with **3 term** U.S. House limits.
Italic   States with *4 term* U.S. House limits.
Plain Text   States with 6 term U.S. House limits.

*Colorado passed term limits in 1994 decreasing the limits set in 1990 of six terms in the U.S. House to three terms and instituting limits on local officials

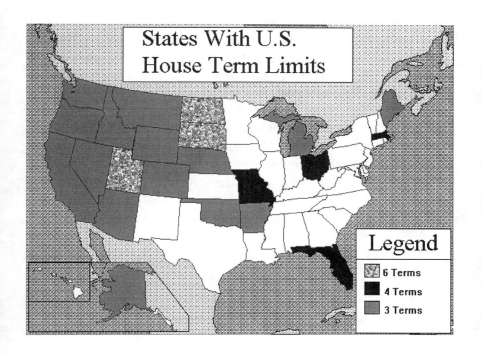

States With U.S.
House Term Limits

Legend

6 Terms
4 Terms
3 Terms

Newt Gingrich has led by example, supporting the request by incoming freshman revolutionaries to limit his term as Speaker to four terms, or eight years. This limit will apply to all future Speakers.

The Supreme Court will rule in late spring of 1995 on the constitutionality of the people's voting through the initiative process to limit the terms of their U.S. senators and representatives. Even the liberals admit that the American people have the right to use the initiative process to limit their state legislators, mayors and school board officials, but Washington once again likes to think of itself as distant from the people and above them. And, the Court may rule in the politicians' favor. After all, every justice on the Supreme Court was appointed by a politician. But the term limit movement is here to stay, and the Republican Party has clearly put itself on the side of term limits at all levels of government. It is only a matter of time before being in the House of Representatives and the Senate is something honest citizens do for a few years at the beginning, middle, or end of a career in the real world, rather than as a career away from the real world.

CHAPTER EIGHT

VOICES OF THE REPUBLICAN FUTURE

While the principles and direction of the Republican coalition are clear, the day-to-day work of dismantling the welfare state and restoring individual liberty for all Americans will be done by men and women of flesh and blood.

Here, in their own words, are the present and future leaders of the Republican Party: representatives, senators, governors, mayors, and businessmen.

Together, their voices — each has chosen 500-1,000 words from a favorite speech or writing — paint an encouraging picture of a Republican Party with a leadership sure of its standing, its vision, and its future.

Undoubtedly among the most influential political figures of the 20th century, Ronald Reagan embodies the ideals of conservatism and supply-side economics. Governor of California from 1967 to 1975 and President of the United States from 1981 to 1989, he was instrumental in, among other things, bringing an end to the Cold War. He is the model which future presidents will have to follow.

In this excerpt from a speech given in 1977, Ronald Reagan presciently outlines the political developments recorded and projected in this book. In light of his foresight and faith, we can only applaud the wisdom of the American people in twice making him president.

"Reshaping the American Political Landscape"
Excerpt from Speech by Ronald Reagan
American Conservative Union Banquet
Washington, D.C.
February 6, 1977

...We know today that the principles and values that lie at the heart of conservatism are shared by the majority.

Despite what some in the press may say, we who are proud to call ourselves "conservative" are not a minority of a minority party; we are part of the great majority of Americans of both major parties and of most of the independents as well.

A Harris poll released September 7, 1975 showed 18 percent identifying themselves as liberal and 31 percent as conservative, with 41 percent as middle of the road. A few months later, on January 5, 1976, by a 43-19 plurality those polled by Harris said they would "prefer to see the country move in a more conservative direction than liberal one".

Last October 24th, the Gallup organization released the result of a poll taken right in the midst of the presidential campaign. Respondents were asked to state where they would place themselves on a scale ranging from "right-of-center" (which was defined as "conservative") to left-of-center (which was defined as "liberal").

- 37 percent viewed themselves as left of center or liberal.
- 12 percent placed themselves in the middle.

- 51 percent said they were right of center, that is, conservative.

What I find interesting about this particular poll is that it offered those polled a range of choices on a left-right continuum. This seems to me to be a more realistic approach than dividing the world into strict left and rights. Most of us, I guess, like to think of ourselves as avoiding both extremes, and the fact that a majority of Americans chose one or the other position on the right end of the spectrum is really impressive.

These polls confirm that most Americans are basically conservative in their outlook. But once we have said this, we conservatives have not *solved* our problems; we have merely stated them clearly. Yes, conservatism is the majority view. But the fact is that conservatism can and does mean different things to those who call themselves conservatives.

You know, as I do, that most commentators make a distinction between what they call "social" conservatism and "economic" conservatism. The so-called social issues — law and order, abortion, busing, quota systems — are usually associated with the blue-collar, ethnic, and religious groups who are traditionally associated with the Democratic Party. The economic issues — inflation, deficit spending, and big government — are usually associated with Republican Party members and independents who concentrate their attention on economic matters.

Now I am willing to accept this view of two major kinds of conservatism or, better still, two different conservative constituencies. But at the same time let me say that the old lines that once clearly divided these two kinds of conservatism are disappearing.

In fact, the time has come to see if it is possible to present a program of action based on political principle that can attract those interested in the so-called "social" issues and those interested in "economic" issues. In short, isn't it possible to combine the two "economic" issues. In short, isn't it possible to combine the two major segments of contemporary American conservatism into one politically effective whole?

I believe the answer is yes; it *is* possible to create a political entity that will reflect the views of the great, conservative majority. We went a long way toward doing it in California. We can do it in America. This is not a dream — a wistful hope. It is and has been a reality. I have seen the conservative future and it works!

Let me say again what I said to our conservative friends from the academic world: What I envision is not simply a melding together of the two branches of American conservatism into a temporary uneasy alliance, but the creation of a new, lasting majority.

This will mean compromise. But not a compromise of basic principle. What will emerge will be something new, something open and vital and dynamic, something the great conservative majority will recognize as its own, because at the heart of this undertaking is principled politics.

I have always been puzzled by the inability of some political and media types to understand exactly what is meant by adherence to political principle. All too often in the press and the television evening news it is treated as a call for "ideological purity". Whatever ideology may mean — and it seems to mean a variety of things, depending upon who is using it — it always conjures up in my mind a picture of a rigid, irrational clinging to abstract theory in the face of reality. We have to recognize that in this country "ideology" is a scare-word. And for good reason. Marxist-Leninism is, to give but one example, an ideology. All the facts of the real world have to be fitted to the Procrustean bed of Marx and Lenin. If the facts don't happen to fit the ideology, the facts are chopped off and discarded.

I consider this to be the complete opposite to principled conservatism. If there is any political viewpoint in this world which is free of slavish adherence to abstraction, it is American conservatism.

Chapter Eight

When a conservative states that the free market is the best mechanism ever devised by the mind of man to meet material needs, he is merely stating what a careful examination of the real world has told him is the truth.

When a conservative says that totalitarian Communism is an absolute enemy of human freedom, he is not theorizing — he is reporting the ugly reality captured so unforgettably in the writings of Alexander Solzhenitsyn.

When a conservative says it is bad for the government to spend more than it takes in, he is simply showing the same common sense that tells him to come in out of the rain.

When a conservative says that busing does not work, he is not appealing to some theory of education — he is merely reporting what he has seen down at the local school.

When a conservative quotes Jefferson that government that is closest to the people is best, it is because he knows that Jefferson risked his life, his fortune, and his sacred honor to make certain that what he and his fellow patriots learned from experience was not crushed by an ideology of empire.

Conservatism is the antithesis of the kind of ideological fanaticism that has brought so much horror and destruction to the world. The common sense and common decency of ordinary men and women, working out their own lives in their own way — this is the heart of American conservatism today. Conservative wisdom and principles are derived from willingness to learn — not just from what is going on *now*, but from what has happened before.

The principles of conservatism are sound because they are based on what men and women have discovered through experience in not just one generation or a dozen, but in all the combined experience of mankind. When we conservatives say that we know something about political affairs, and that what we know can be stated as principles, we are saying that the principles we hold dear are those that have been found, through experience, to be ultimately beneficial for individuals, for families, for communities and for nations — found through the often bitter testing of pain, or sacrifice and sorrow.

One thing that must be made clear in post-Watergate is this: the American new conservative majority we represent is *not* based on abstract theorizing of the kind that turns off the American people, but on common sense, intelligence, reason, hard work, faith in God, and the guts to say yes, there *are* things we do strongly believe in, that we are willing to live for, and, yes, if necessary, to die for. This is not "ideological purity". It is simply what built this country and kept it great.

Let us lay to rest, once and for all, the myth of a small group of ideological purists trying to capture a majority. Replace it with the reality of a majority trying to assert its rights against the tyranny of powerful academics, fashionable left-revolutionaries, some economic illiterates who happen to hold elective office, and the social engineers who dominate the dialogue and set the format in political and social affairs. If there is any ideological fanaticism in American political life, it is to be found among the enemies of freedom on the left and right — those who would sacrifice principle to theory, those who worship only the god of political, social, and economic abstractions, ignoring the realities of everyday life. They are *not* conservatives.

Speaker of the House Newt Gingrich represents the Sixth District of Georgia in the U.S. House of Representatives. Before the Republican victory in 1994 elevated him to the Speakership, he served as House Republican Whip from 1989 to 1994. From 1986 to 1994, he chaired GOPAC, providing training to Republican candidates at the state, local, and federal levels.

Chapter Eight

Before being elected to Congress in 1978, Mr. Gingrich taught History and Environmental Studies at West Georgia College for eight years. Born June 17, 1943 in Harrisburg, Pennsylvania, Congressman Gingrich lives in Marietta, Georgia with his wife, Marianne. He has two married daughters.

Excerpts from Speech by Congressman Newt Gingrich
Washington Research Group Symposium
Washington, D.C.
November 11, 1994

...The best description of me is that I am a conservative futurist. For a long time, I have been friends with Alvin and Heidi Toffler, the authors of *Future Shock* and *The Third Wave*. I really believe it's useful to think about the twenty-first century. On the other hand, I believe the most powerful single doctrine for the leadership of human beings and for their opportunity to pursue happiness are *The Federalist Papers*, Tocqueville's *Democracy in America*, the Declaration of Independence, and the Constitution. I also recommend to all the congressional staffs that they buy Peter Drucker's *The Effective Executive*, study W. Edwards Deming's concepts of quality...I also suggest immersing yourself in the Founding Fathers. These people thought a long time about the nature of being human, about the problems of power, about how to organize a free society so it could sustain freedom. And if you can combine the two, you can begin to create an opportunity for every American to participate in ways that will prove to be quite remarkable.

...We want to get to the twenty-first century, and we want to do so in a way that's effective.

There are...large changes we have to go through...We have to accelerate the transition from a second wave mechanical, bureaucratic society to a third wave information society... Two simple examples:

225

One, imagine the speed and ease with which you use a bank teller card anywhere on the planet and electronically verify your account and get money; second, imagine what happens when you call the federal government about a case. There's no objective reason that institutions of government have to be two or three generations behind the curve in information systems and management, but they are.

...We need to recognize the objective reality of the world market, to realize that we create American jobs through world sales and that we need to make a conscious national decision that we want to have the highest value-added jobs on the planet with the greatest productivity so we can have the highest take-home pay and the greatest range of choices in lifestyles. In order to do that, we have to literally rethink the assumptions that grew up in a self-indulgent national economy; and we have to recognize that litigation, taxation, regulation, welfare, education, the very structure of government, the structure of health — all those things have to be reexamined from the standpoint of what will make us the most competitive society on the planet, the most desirable place to invest to create jobs, and the place with the best-trained and most entrepreneurial work force. . .

...We have to replace the welfare state with an opportunity society. It is impossible to take the Great Society structure of bureaucracy, the redistributionist model of how wealth is acquired, and the counterculture value system that now permeates the way we deal with the poor, and have any hope of fixing them. They are a disaster. They ruin the poor, they create a culture of poverty and a culture of violence which is destructive of this civilization, and they have to be replaced thoroughly from the ground up.

This should be done in cooperation with the poor. The people who have the most to gain from eliminating the culture of poverty and replacing it with a culture of productivity are the people currently trapped in a nightmare, living in public housing projects with no one going to work, living in neighborhoods with no physical safety, their children forced to walk into buildings where there will be no learning, and living in a community where taxes and red tape and regulation destroy their hope of creating new entrepreneurial small businesses and doing what every other generation of poor Americans has done, which is to leave poverty behind by acquiring productivity.

We simply need to reach out and erase the slate and start over; and we need to start with the premise that every American is endowed by their Creator with certain inalienable rights, among which are life, liberty, and the pursuit of happiness; and that extends to the poorest child in Washington, D.C. and the poorest child in West Virginia, and the poorest child in American Indian reservations. And we have been failing all of them because we have lacked the courage to be mentally tough enough to get the job done. I think it can be done, but I think it's very deep and represents a very bold change.

...We have to reestablish...[the Jefferson understanding]...that you had to have limited but effective government precisely in order to liberate people to engage in civic responsibility, and that the larger government grew, the more you would crowd out civic responsibility.

Now, this means that my challenge to the American people is simple. You really want to dramatically reduce power in Washington? You have to be willing to take more responsibility back home. You really want to reduce the bureaucracy of the welfare state? You have to accept greater responsibility back home. We are going to have to be partners. This is going to be a team in which we work together to renew American civilization...

Rock the House

Congressman Dick Armey represents the 26th District of Texas in the U.S. House of Representatives. Before beingelected to the House in 1984, Mr. Armey was a professor of economics at North Texas State University.

One of Congressman Armey's biggest achievements was the military base closing bill. In 1992, he defeated Congressman Jerry Lewis of California for the House Republican Conference chairmanship. After the Democrat majority was ousted in 1994, Congressman Armey's colleagues elected him House Majority Leader. Born July 7, 1940 in Cando, North Dakota, Congressman Armey and his wife Susan live in Cooper Canyon, Texas. They have five children.

Excerpt from Address by Congressman Dick Armey
Conservative Leadership Conference
Washington, D.C.
December 3, 1994

In this first midterm election of the post-Cold War era, Americans made it dramatically clear what they want. They want a return to normalcy. They want a restoration of the good, solid old values that made this country great: limited government, economic opportunity, and personal responsibility. And so we have a clear mandate. We go into this exciting new era with a very clear idea of which values are going to guide our actions.

We also have a clear agenda. The American people expect us to fulfill our end of the Contract with America. And we will. In the first hundred days, we will bring to the floor of the House ten very specific pieces of legislation, debate them, and vote on them in a fair and open process. And let me say, I take this obligation very seriously. I am fully aware that the future of my political party depends on our performance between January 3rd and Good Friday of 1995.

228

Chapter Eight

I've found that, in politics, you can either be a bitter disappointment or a pleasant surprise. Well, we intend to be a pleasant surprise. We intend to produce a persistent, steady stream of good news coming out of Washington for the average American.

Instead of raising taxes, we're going to cut taxes. Instead of writing new regulations, we're going to repeal old ones. Instead of producing more dependency, we're going to encourage self-reliance. Whether the issue is poverty, crime, education, the environment, or even equality of incomes, we believe freedom offers a better solution than does government. My hope is that, as our solutions are enacted, and the good news gets out, it's going to start sinking in. People are going to find themselves looking at one another in amazement and delight and say, "Wow, what's going on up there?"

[Some of you have] expressed concerns that the Contract doesn't go far enough. And if the Contract were the extent of our agenda, I'd say the same thing. But the Contract is just the beginning. I call it the shakedown cruise for the counter-revolution.

After all, the welfare-dependency state took more than a hundred days to build. And replacing it with a conservative opportunity society will also take more than a hundred days. Doubtless there will be setbacks. Sometimes we'll lose a few yards. Sometimes we'll score. Sometimes we'll have to throw long. But with discipline and hard work, day in and day out, I'm confident we'll reach our goal and move beyond big government.

You know, the liberals are already giving away their game plan. They obviously take us for rubes. They think we're going to come in like Attila the Hun and try to sack the place in a massive frontal assault — and, they hope, get ourselves thrown out in '96.

Well, in a former life, I was a marathon runner, and I learned the painful way that sprinters don't finish marathons. A good steady pace wins the prize. So I hate to break the bad news to my liberal colleagues, but we do not view ourselves as a temporary strike force — we are a permanent presence.

We will wage a patient, well-planned, well-coordinated campaign to replace the welfare-dependency state with a conservative opportunity society, not in one futile assault, but brick by brick and stone by stone.

Our source of strength is this. We trust people. We respect the sense and know-how of the American citizen. We trust people to spend their own money and make their own decisions. We trust the typical American family more than we trust a bureaucracy to know what is best for that family. Just look around. Ordinary men and women are capable of extraordinary things, if only we let them. After all, America itself offers the most eloquent proof that free people can do great things.

But just as we respect people's freedom, we also understand that freedom requires personal responsibility. It is character that makes freedom work. And the essence of character is a love for the truth. Truth, honesty, integrity — these things matter. Unfortunately, one of the reasons Americans are so disappointed with their elected officials is that, for too long, Washington has been a city in which powerful people could not be trusted with either words or numbers.

Chapter Eight

Congressman Tom DeLay represents the 22nd District of Texas in the U.S. House of Representatives. A small businessman, he was first elected to the House in 1984. A leader of the Small Business Survival Caucus, Congressman DeLay was elected House Majority Whip by his peers following the 1994 elections. Born April 8, 1947 in Laredo, Texas, Congressman DeLay and his wife Christine live in Sugar Land, Texas. They have one daughter.

Excerpt from Editorial by Congressman Tom DeLay

Last month, in a historic and unprecedented move, more than 300 Republican candidates and incumbents of the U.S. House signed a "Contract With America". We outlined 10 specific bills and several congressional reforms that will downsize the federal government, ease the family tax burden and reduce the deficit; and we signed a covenant that said if Republicans are elected a majority of the House of Representatives, we will vote on these initiatives within the first 100 days of the new Congress.

This was a bold step to take for a Party that many political pundits profess is closer than ever before to winning a majority in the House. We knew this was a risky proposition — it would be much simpler to run against a President with unpopular ideas. But we wanted to give the American people something more than rhetoric and tired promises: we signed a contract, and the American people can hold us accountable. We went out on a limb to lay our cards on the table, ensuring that Americans know exactly what to expect should Republicans gain a majority. In the October 22nd issue of *TV Guide*, Americans will be able to clip that contract and see it for themselves.

Yet poised to poison, the Democrats pounced at their first chance and put their political PR machines in overdrive. They couldn't debate the substance of our proposals; instead, they resorted to

231

attempts to sabotage the contract with critiques unfounded in fact. These attacks demonstrate just how far out of touch they are with grassroots America; they refuse to admit that Republicans can accomplish the contract's agenda without raising taxes or deficit spending.

In fact, Republican Representative John Kasich of Ohio, who has been consistently praised by liberal and conservative media alike for his ability to produce responsible and credible budget proposals, confirms that we can finance our policy initiatives without raising taxes and still reduce the deficit. He says the "cost" of our contract is the Democrats' "Washington budget-speak which really means that American taxpayers would keep $147 billion more of the money they earn instead of turning it over to the Federal government as they would under current tax law". In his "Cut Spending First" budget proposal, Mr. Kasich details $369 billion in specific, detailed spending reductions.

I personally played a large role in writing two of the 10 bills — for welfare and regulatory reform — and neither of them will run up the deficit. Instead, unlike the bills proposed by Bill Clinton in the first two years of his presidency, our bills reflect concepts alien to the Democrats: less government intrusion, less spending, more reform of entitlement programs and extensive infusions of responsibility for those who benefit from the generosity of the American taxpayer. The contract's reception from middle America has been astounding because, unlike legislation proposed by the Democrats, it reflects the kind of government reform that the majority of the American people want in return for their hard-earned tax dollars.

For example, our welfare reform bill proposes a compassionate solution to an urgent problem while requiring recipients to work in return for their benefits, and it pays for this by ending welfare for most non-citizens. And, our regulatory reform proposal — something I have advocated since my first days in the Texas legislature —

proposes infusing some common sense into the regulatory process, thereby allowing for greater, more stable economic growth.

I understand why the Democrats are running scared: they cannot understand how the federal government can operate without spending and taxing more. They do not understand true reform and are gasping and grasping at straws because Republicans have put forth an honest agenda that actually could work if we ever had the opportunity to implement it. And they fear ferociously its impact on their future hold on the majority in Congress.

For more than 40 years Democrats have controlled which bills may be considered for a vote. With a Republican majority, we could finally control the agenda and introduce legislation that will truly ignite economic growth while enabling those less fortunate to get back on their feet and gain independence from the government.

Instead, the Democrat agenda advocates expanding the status-quo by ensuring that certain segments of our society maintain a dependency on federal programs. It is not in the Democrats' best political interest to promote initiatives that free the poor from government programs; maintaining constituencies dependent on Big-Brother government by creating and delivering more and more entitlement programs is the Democrats' ticket to political power. They are not helping the American people; they are empowering themselves to manipulate and control a very vulnerable segment of our society. And through imposing more and more government regulations — few based on scientific fact or economic logic — they are overburdening the very segment of our society that creates jobs and improves all Americans' quality of life. I have faith and confidence in our people; given the opportunities and true incentives, those dependent on federal entitlement programs — which constitute the bulk of government spending — can break free of this vicious cycle.

Democrats, fighting for their political survival, have not voiced one concrete objection to our contract. They can play the numbers game all they want, yet the truth of the matter is that their numbers don't add up. Would Americans prefer to trust the arithmetic of a Democrat White House which claimed that a tax on Social Security recipients was a spending cut? What kind of growth have we seen as a result of the largest tax increase in history, proposed by President Clinton and approved by the Democrat Congress? Was that tax increase on the middle class what President Clinton promised the voters? Was that tax increase the Democrats' answer to jobs creation? I challenge any liberal-minded Democrat to defend that plum for the American taxpayer that passed by only one vote in the House of Representatives.

Economic growth produces more, not less, revenue. And Republican policies, as outlined in the "Contract with America", will give the American people what they demand and deserve — the largest change in the size, scope and direction of the federal government since the 1930's.

Congressman Bill Zeliff represents the First District of New Hampshire in the U.S. House of Representatives and serves as Deputy Majority Whip. He is also Chairman of the Subcommittee on National Security, International Affairs, and Criminal Justice of the Government Reform and Oversight Committee and Chairman of the Small Business Survival Caucus. Born June 12, 1936 in East Orange, New Jersey, Congressman Zeliff and his wife, Sydna, reside in Jackson, New Hampshire. They have three sons.

Chapter Eight

Excerpts from Speech by Congressman Bill Zeliff
John Ashbrook Center for Public Policy
Ohio University
Ashland, Ohio
October 17, 1994

The new Republican Leadership has pledged to reverse the big government trends of the last 40 years. I am committed to that goal. As Chairman of the Small Business Survival Caucus, you can count on me to make sure your voice as an entrepreneur is heard.

My "A to Z" plan is a tool to help Congress cut spending. The rules of the House permit the power elite to control what looks like representative democracy.

They control what bills get to the floor for a vote. They control whether a bill can be amended...and who can offer amendments. They control the whole process. Each year the abuse of that control is more oppressive.

We should get at the pork, waste, and special projects that Congress squanders billions of tax dollars on.

Congressional spending is the heart of the fight over "A to Z". Right now spending bills come to the membership in big bundles. They start with some critical item that no one dares vote against...earthquake relief or small business assistance or something that's truly worthy. Then they load the bill up with pet projects.

A recreation center in the district of a key Congressman. A new building for the Chairman's favorite college.

The power elite can use tax dollars to basically buy votes in Congress. When the bill comes to the floor for debate...everybody talks about earthquake relief. Nobody talks about the pork barrel projects.

"A to Z" would change that system. For one week...for at least 56 hours...the rules would be suspended, and any member could bring

235

up any spending cuts program on its own for debate and a vote. If the program is justified...the vote to cut it fails.

Any program that can't stand on its merit in the light of day gets reduced, or it gets eliminated. That's how to make real cuts in the budget.

Any family in America strapped for money spreads their bills and expenses out on the kitchen table, looks at their checkbook, and figures out what they can pay and where they have to cut back.

They look at their expenses one at a time. It's simple, and it works. That's the "A to Z Spending Cuts Plan". Take up one spending item at a time...figure out what we can afford and where we need to cut. Debate it in the open...vote in the open...make each member accountable.

"A to Z" was never even allowed to come to a vote. They didn't dare. They knew it would pass! They used the same rules that "A to Z" will change to avoid "A to Z"...for the moment.

But next year...after the voters change some of the old faces and give us more members committed to real reform...we'll pass "A to Z" and put it to work.

You probably can tell that I'm a "Man on a Mission" these days...working anywhere in America I can to assure passage of "A to Z".

———————

Chapter Eight

Congressman John Boehner (pronounced "bayner") represents the Eighth District of Ohio in the U.S. House of Representatives. He was first elected to this position in 1990. In 1994, he was voted in as Chairman of the House Republican Conference. In his first term of office, Congressman Boehner was part of the "Gang of Seven", a group of freshman Republicans instrumental in bringing public attention to the congressmen involved in the House Bank and Post Office scandals and to the congressmen who supported the congressional pay raise. Born November 17, 1949 in Cincinnati, Ohio, Congressman Boehner and his wife, Debbie, live in West Chester, Ohio. They have two daughters.

Republican Radio Address to the Nation
by Congressman John Boehner
June 12, 1993

Good morning. I'm Congressman John Boehner of Ohio, and I have the honor this morning of presenting the Republican response to the President's address.

As you heard, the President talked about recent action in Somalia, an issue of importance to the world. However, today, I want to talk to you about an issue critical to each and every American, the President's economic plan being debated on Capitol Hill.

I'm sure you're sick and tired of hearing the same old political rhetoric, the tired name calling that goes on in Washington. I'm convinced that the American people just want someone to talk to them straight and to tell them the truth.

You see, I'm not a life-long politician. I'm a small businessman. I go home every weekend to my wife, two daughters, my neighbors and try to live like everybody else. So, when we get into debates like

237

the one we're having with the President over deficit reduction and cutting spending, I like to hear straight talk, just like you.

When someone tells me they're going to reduce a debt and cut spending, I take that to mean there will be less spending next year than there was this year; pretty simple. The problem is that when people start playing Washington word games, the truth gets lost somewhere in the wash. And while all the arguing is going on, the taxpayers are stuck holding the bag, and we Republicans are relegated to the sidelines, even though we have a solid plan ready to go to reduce the deficit. A plan that calls for no tax increases and true cuts in government spending.

In the meantime, it's not Republicans stopping the President's plan in Congress, but his own party. After begging House Democrats to support him and vote for a huge new energy tax, the President promised them he wouldn't leave them out on a limb. But he did just that in dropping the energy tax for an increase in the gasoline tax, when he needed votes in the Senate.

He makes a deal with conservative Democrats to cut more spending, then breaks it. He makes a deal with liberal Democrats to increase spending and breaks that deal.

First, it's a BTU energy tax, and now it's an increase in the gas tax. He can't even get his own party to support his plan. All because it's hard to believe what he says from day to day, or to know where he stands.

Take the deficit, for example. The President makes the point that his plan calls for $500 billion in deficit reduction over the next five years. You would think that that would mean the government would be spending $500 billion less than it was when the deficit reduction plan started, right? Wrong.

In Washington, this reduction is not in how much the government actually spends, but in the rate of federal spending.

Chapter Eight

Let me make this point a bit clearer by using numbers from the President's own plan. If we were to do nothing and allow the government's out of control spending to continue, we would run a deficit of $400 billion a year over the next five years, adding $2 trillion to the national debt. President Clinton's plan calls for a deficit of $300 billion every year over the next five years, which will end up adding $1.5 trillion to the debt.

Since we'll only go another trillion and a half dollars in the hole, rather than $2 trillion, Bill Clinton calls it deficit reduction. But the truth is, we'll still be increasing the national debt by $1.5 trillion over the next five years.

What seems simple to millions of Americans is, if we really want to cut the debt, we need to quit spending more than what we take in. Every family knows that, and every business knows that.

And it sometimes sounds like even the President knows that, as he talks about reducing the deficit by cutting government spending. But while the whole country is calling for Washington to cut spending first, the President wants to actually increase government spending.

The President has proposed that government spending increase every year, over the next five years. That doesn't seem like less spending in my book. I find it hard to believe that out of thousands of wasteful government programs, the President couldn't find even one to eliminate.

Yes, that's right. The President didn't even eliminate one program.

The President can talk about deficit reduction and spending cuts all he wants. The problem is, that's not what his program is all about.

As a farmer in my district says, "You can call a pig a cow, but that won't make her give milk."

The hard, simple truth is the President is taking us down the path of more taxes, more spending, and bigger government.

Rock the House

If the President continues to avoid talking straight, the people will find it difficult to trust anything he says. That perception is very unhealthy for this nation. The Presidency and the country, itself, are threatened if we cannot trust our leader.

America deserves the truth from its President. It deserves honesty when it comes to the difficult problems that are challenging this nation. Ross Perot's popularity is a testament to the fact that this nation wants to hear the truth, warts and all.

President Clinton must understand that he has to cut spending, for real. He has to reduce the deficit, for real. And level with this nation about the direction he wants to take us in.

If the American people are given a chance to make up their own minds, if given the straight facts, they just might surprise him.

As a Republican, I could take great pleasure at witnessing a Democrat President stumbling, his missteps and declining popularity, but as an American, I cannot do anything but hope and pray that this President recovers his balance and succeeds for the country. Too much is at stake.

Thank you America, and have a great weekend.

With the new Republican majority in the U.S. Senate, Senator Robert Dole of Kansas is now serving his second term as Senate Majority Leader, a post he previously held from 1985 to 1987. Senator Dole has been in Congress as a Republican longer than anyone else, having first been elected to the U.S. House of Representatives in 1960. As a soldier in the Army during World War II, Mr. Dole was gravely wounded in Italy and was twice decorated for heroic achievement. Born July 22, 1923 in Russell, Kansas, where he still resides, Senator Dole is married to Elizabeth Hanford Dole, President of the American Red Cross.

240

Chapter Eight

**Excerpt from Speech on the Meaning of
the November Republican Victory and the
Message of that Election
by Senator Robert Dole
Republican National Committee Winter Meeting
Washington, D.C.
January 21, 1995**

Our mandate must be to rein in our government.

To accomplish that goal, we Republicans will dust off my favorite Amendment — the 10th Amendment — the one that reads, "The powers not delegated to the United States by the Constitution, nor prohibited by it to the States, are reserved to the States, respectively, or to the people." You can find that amendment in the Bill of Rights.

The Democrats seem to discover a new "right" every time they stumble across something that's wrong. They think "rights" are things a government *gives* to the people. But we know that the rights enumerated in our Constitution are the rights of private citizens to be *free from government*, not to be provided things by it.

This is the litmus test: Are you more free if you are guaranteed certain resources that are determined and measured by a governing elite, or are you more free if you are guaranteed that government will not interfere with your ability to pursue what you yourself choose?

We think it is the latter. That's why, in this Congress, we will propose and pass legislation to protect the rights of private property owners and to cut the tangle of red tape forced upon America's small businessmen and women.

And that is why we will cut taxes. The philosophical divide between the parties is especially visible on this issue. President Clinton labels Americans according to "class". But, we must not create factions of Americans competing against one another for the favors of government.

Instead, we should lead by instilling hope and restoring freedom and opportunity for all of our people.

If tax cuts are also to have the effect of limiting government and providing for long-term prosperity, then they also must be matched by real cuts in government spending.

Along with prohibiting unfunded mandates, cutting taxes, and requiring a balanced budget — with an Amendment that requires a three-fifths vote to raise taxes — we have another very effective means of limiting government: cutting government spending.

We will roll back Federal programs, laws and regulations from A to Z — from Amtrak to Zoological studies — working our way through the alphabet soup of government.

Our guide will be this question: Is this program a basic function of limited government, or is it an example of how government has lost its faith in the judgments of our people and the potential of our markets?

Phil Gramm, U.S. Senator from Texas, is a 1996 presidential candidate. A professor of economics, Mr. Gramm was first elected to the U.S. House of Representatives in 1978 as a Democrat. In 1983, after pushing the Reagan-backed marginal tax cuts through the House, he was stripped of his seniority by the Democrat leadership. He resigned from the House, switched parties, and was elected to his old House seat as a Republican. In 1985, his first year as a U.S. senator, and ranking 99th in seniority, Senator Gramm co-sponsored one of the most influential pieces of legislation ever to pass Congress: the Gramm-Rudman-Hollings balanced budget bill.

Born July 8, 1942 in Fort Benning, Georgia, Senator Gramm and his wife, Dr. Wendy Lee Gramm, live in College Station, Texas. They have two college-aged sons.

Chapter Eight

"Rekindling the American Dream"
by Senator Phil Gramm
Excerpt from Keynote Address
103rd Continental Congress of
The Daughters of the American Revolution
Washington, D.C.
April 20, 1994

...I believe that deep down in our hearts we know that there are fundamental problems in our country and that we have to make dramatic changes if we're to preserve the things we love about America. An America where people do not believe their children are going to do better than they have done is *not* the country that I grew up in. Nor is it the country I want my children and grandchildren to grow up in. But where do we find the leadership and courage to change it?

A good place to start searching for the answer is to look to our Founding Fathers. When you look at the problems they faced, they were overwhelming as compared to ours. When you look at the resources they had to deal with those problems, they were very meager as compared to ours.

But they had two things, it seems to me, that we don't have enough of today. They had *faith* and they had *will*. They had faith that God did not set aside this continent for nothing. They had faith that God did not build a society dedicated to freedom and that God did not raise America as a beacon of hope for the world, only to let us fail.

And secondly, they had will, the will to act, the will to make the world over again, the will to risk everything in order to build a country that would be a model for the world.

In closing, I want to leave you with a quote from George Washington. We often think of George Washington's gravest moment as coming at Valley Forge, but it didn't. It took politics to bring Washington's lowest moment. And it occurred during the period of the Articles of Confederation. So much sacrifice had been incurred, yet America was floundering because we didn't have a system that worked. Washington wrote in a letter to Lafayette: "I do not believe that Providence has done so much for nothing. It has always been my creed that we should not be left as an awful monument to prove that mankind was unequal to the task of self-government."

I believe that Washington's creed is as true today as it was then. And if we have faith, if we are willing to act on that faith, I believe we can remake America. Now some people will say that's just a dream, and they're right. It is just a dream, but it's not just any dream. It is the American Dream. I know you hold that dream in your hearts, and so do I.

Senator Trent Lott of Mississippi is now in his second term of office in the U.S. Senate and was elected Senate Majority Whip in December 1994. Senator Lott should feel comfortable in this position, as he was Minority Whip for eight of his sixteen years in the U.S. House of Representatives. In 1988, he gave up a secure House seat to run for the Senate; and in December 1992, he was elected to the Republican leadership as Senate Conference Secretary.

Chapter Eight

Born October 9, 1941 in Grenada, Mississippi, Senator Lott and his wife, Tricia, live in Pascagoula, Mississippi. They have two children.

Excerpt from Speech by Senator Trent Lott
U.S. Chamber of Commerce
Washington, D.C.
January 26, 1995

The election last November 8th was an American Moment, an event that has occurred several times in this great nation's life story.

We can recall American colonists throwing off British rule, GI's defeating Fascism and Communism, and Americans electing Ronald Reagan President as great Moments in our history.

These Moments and others involve Americans choosing to make a change for the better. If you look at it, these great Moments on the whole were great tests and tussles between citizens and the arrogant state. Americans have a natural aversion to an all-powerful government. Fair and limited use of government power is accepted by citizens; arbitrary government action that takes from the many and gives to the few is not.

November 8th, 1994 was another great Moment. That day was the start of a great revolution. We use "revolution" a lot, but the meaning of the word is sometimes skipped over. Revolution is to turn back again. In last year's election, we began to talk again about the scope and size of government. We began to discuss seriously a return to federalism. We began to think again about the relationship between the individual and the state. We began to go back to founding ideals — liberty, responsibility, and equality.

The American people chose to give Republicans a chance to run both houses of the Congress for the first time in over four decades.

The people have suffered from the loss of those founding ideals in Washington, and they want Republicans to restore the balance.

The American people want the federal government out of their lives and out of their pocketbooks. The country has had enough of the caretaker state and wants us to make individuals responsible for their own actions. Americans want to be treated equally and fairly.

All of this is the meaning of the Moment called November 8th, 1994. Republicans have a positive program and a positive view of the future of America. The solutions for tomorrow are in our roots.

Yes, there are many naysayers who believe that change can't or should not be made. The cheerleaders of the status quo — not so cheerful these days — are claiming we Republicans are turning back the clock, turning poor families out on the streets, and turning out to be anti-people ideologues.

The American people know better. Americans sent us here to Washington to do the job of revolution, and I am proud to be a foot soldier in this battle to fulfill the mandate of our recent American Moment.

In one of the most closely contested races in 1992, Paul Coverdell defeated incumbent Senator Wyche Fowler for a Georgia U.S. Senate seat by a 51%-49% margin. Mr. Coverdell, head of the United States Peace Corps during the Bush administration, had been a relative unknown until the senatorial campaign. Previously, he served in the Georgia State Senate, with a 15-year stint as Minority Leader; he was Chairman of the Georgia Republican Party from 1985 to 1987. Senator Coverdell is best known for his management of Republican Senate opposition to the Clinton health care proposal in 1994. Born January 20, 1939 in Des Moines, Iowa, Senator Coverdell and his wife, Nancy Nally Coverdell, live in Atlanta, Georgia.

Chapter Eight

"Substance Defeated Health Care Reform in 1994:
Substance Should Be the Basis of any Effort in 1995"
by Senator Paul Coverdell
Article in the *Washington Times*
October 18, 1994

As Senate Majority Leader George Mitchell brought the gavel down to close the 103rd session of Congress, one could hear the Clinton White House operatives, political pundits and Washington analysts begin the post mortem on how and why health care reform failed in Congress.

We heard Hillary Clinton say it was because the Administration was "misunderstood" in its quest to overhaul 14% of our national economy.

We read in newspapers that it was partisan politics, special interests, or White House miscalculations that brought down the Clinton health care reform plan.

Yet, in all of these reports, as the White House was busy laying blame, one very important reason for their plan's demise was missing. It was substance. Substance.

The health care reform debate in the 103rd Congress was a debate on substance. It was fought on substance, and the White House lost on substance.

President and Mrs. Clinton do not do anyone any favors by suggesting the American people were too uninformed, unable to understand, or taken over by special interest groups in this debate. Instead, the American people heard from Bill and Hillary, Harry and Louise, and everyone in between, and rejected the Clinton version of a government-run health care system in their own right.

In fact, the Clintons should take credit for helping to engage and educate the electorate on health care reform. It was one year ago that Clinton, caretaker of the world's largest pulpit and microphone, came

247

to Congress for a national address on health care reform. What happened over the next 12 months was an intense debate.

The Clintons set out on national tours and bus caravans, and held nationwide town hall meetings and forums. Members of Congress did the same, as did grass roots organizations following this issue. During this year, the *Washington Post* reports "hundreds of town hall meetings, months of Congressional hearings and markups by five committees and days of Senate consideration" were held on health care reform.

At the core of this debate was the issue of how much we wanted the Federal government to dictate every aspect of health care in the United States.

Through a White House task force that privately crafted the President's health care plan, the Clintons attempted an undertaking of moving around the building blocks that comprise 14% of our national economy. The 1400 page proposal submitted by the Clintons laid out a complex plan of national and state boards dictating choices, mandating taxes, and creating new bureaucracies in health care delivery.

The *Washington Post* reports that a legal review team for the White House Health Care Task Force wrote Task Force Chairman Ira Magaziner with the following warning, "There appears to be no precedent for the enactment and implementation of a national reform that alters so many existing statutory, administrative, contractual, private, and moral arrangements as this reform would propose to do."

The Clintons and their advocates, however, persisted. And, in so doing, the public saw more intrusion, massive costs, and more government — precisely the opposite they had been promised in the 1992 elections. What they didn't see was reform, and they objected.

Nothing illustrates the public's objections more clearly than the election results of November 1994. The massive voter shift that was registered throughout the country can only be accurately described as a revolution. For the first time in 40 years, the Republican party claimed control of the House of Representatives. The Senate also changed hands to Republican Control. Two candidates who were among the most clearly identified with health care reform — Harris Wofford, who had run in 1992 as the "health care candidate", and Jim Cooper, author of the "Clinton-Lite" proposal — were both defeated.

No, it wasn't that the public was uninformed in this debate. It was that the White House had tuned out what the public was saying. Following the 1994 elections, pollster Bill McInturff made the following observations in the *New York Times*: "I think health care was enormously pivotal in the elections. Mr. Clinton had proposed a big government plan which helped to strip away his image as a 'New Democrat' among voters in the South and Mountain West."

McInturff said the collapse of the health care plan also fed voters' sense that Washington was in gridlock, and since the Democrats were in charge, they were to blame.

Al From, President of the Democratic Leadership Council, remarked, "It is impossible to overestimate the amount of damage the health care bill did in shaping the image of President Clinton as a big government proponent."

Had the White House listened to what the public was saying during this debate, here is what the Clintons would have heard.

We learned in the 1992 presidential election that the American people are not asking for more government and more taxes. They are not asking for choices to be removed or for bureaucrats and government employees to make decisions about who their doctor will or won't be, or to which hospital they can or can't go.

According to national polling data, eight out of ten Americans are served well and satisfied by our current health care delivery system. Of those two out of ten not served well, some have serious problems, some have concerns less urgent.

These results urge us to ask, is it necessary to overhaul our entire health care system, disrupting and destabilizing the quality of health care of 80% of our families and businesses, in order to reach the 15% to 20% currently not served well? Furthermore, must we look toward turning 100% of our health care system over to the government to reach the 20% of the public currently not served well?

I believe these questions and concerns raised by the voters and lawmakers in Congress should lay the foundation for real reform in the 104th Congress. There is an alternative to the Clinton answer of a massive government overhaul of the health care delivery system. This alternative seeks to implement specific, targeted reforms to preserve the best elements of our existing system while working to improve problem areas. Through an improvement in specific targets we can produce major and significant improvements in the system immediately without destabilizing health care for all Americans.

We can target our attentions toward market reforms and administrative reforms — and we can bring results now, not four years from now. In addition, I believe we should seek to use our states as laboratories for innovation in health care delivery.

For some targets, finding consensus will take time, and we should continue discussion on these areas. Our current problems in the system were 30 to 50 years in the making, and we cannot expect to reform the entire system overnight.

In the meantime, we can target our efforts towards those 2 out of 10 individuals not served well without creating a new government entitlement that encompasses all Americans.

Governor Pete Wilson of California has been involved in politics since he was first elected to the California State Assembly in 1966.

Chapter Eight

*From 1971 to 1983, he served as Mayor of San Diego and in 1982
won a seat in the United States Senate. Elected governor in 1990,
Wilson signed a "Three Strikes and You're Out" bill into law and led
the fight for an initiative to cut off taxpayer-supported services to
illegal immigrants in his first term. His agenda for his second term,
to which he was overwhelmingly elected in 1994, includes education,
welfare, and tax reform. Born August 23, 1933 in Lake Forest,
Illinois, Governor Wilson and his wife, Gayle, live in suburban
Sacramento.*

"California: Forging America's Future"
by Governor Pete Wilson
Excerpts from Second Inaugural Address
Sacramento, California
January 7, 1995

Ours is a generation that cannot take for granted the good life, the
historically generous bounty of California, unless we are prepared to
make dramatic change...

We must choose whether California will be the Golden State —
or a welfare state. It can't be both...

We must be wise enough, tough-minded, and honest enough to
repeal programs that fail their stated noble purpose and fail expen-
sively, incurring fiscal and human costs that are unaffordable.

The people agree. They are out of patience with misfired good
intentions that defy sense or fairness.

They ask: Is it fair that the welfare system taxes working people
who can't afford children and pays people who don't work for having
more children?

They ask: Why should federal law reward illegal immigrants for
violating the law and punish California taxpayers and needy legal
residents?

251

They ask: Why have schools that reward poor teachers for promoting — even graduating — students who can't adequately speak and write English?

And they ask: Why do our laws put dangerous criminals back on our street and put us behind barred windows and locked doors?

The last refuge of those who call these questions unfair is to assert their compassion and to deny ours.

The ultimate compassion is to build an economy that works, one that grows and provides the jobs working Californians need to feed their families, build their homes, and pay their taxes...

So, we will deliberately shrink government to expand opportunity.

We will make clear that welfare is to be a safety net, not a hammock — and absolutely not a permanent way of life.

We will correct our laws to make clear that bringing a child into the world is an awesome personal responsibility for both the mother *and* the father.

The costs are simply too high for society to continue tolerating the promiscuity and irresponsibility that have produced generations of unwed teen mothers...

We will insist that those who receive public assistance earn it. We will give them help and support to escape from dependency to the independence and self-respect of work. We want them to see in the eyes of their children that special look of respect and pride that only working parents can know...

We will demand accountability and personal responsibility. Now the teen predator who does violence to his victim will be prosecuted not as a juvenile, but as an adult...

The fundamental right of every Californian is not to become a crime victim, and it is the first responsibility of government to safeguard that right.

We will do so. Those who commit violent crimes will pay heavily for their brutality...

We must also change our schools....

We must insist on order and discipline in the classroom, or teaching and learning cannot occur...

We must raise our standards high enough to challenge our children to meet the competition they will all too soon encounter in the international marketplace. The standards we enforce must be high and clear, not imprecise and politically correct...

We must reward effort and achievement. We must honor those who work hard, who meet life's test playing by the rules, who respect themselves and the rights of others, who honor their obligations as parents and citizens, who raise their children to obey the law.

And just as we demand that citizens meet these standards of decency and responsibility, we must demand at least as much from government — in Sacramento and in Washington.

California will not submit its destiny to faceless federal bureaucrats or even Congressional barons.

We declare to Washington that California is a proud and sovereign state, not a colony of the federal government...

We will break the bonds of restraint which government has placed on those strong enough to create opportunity and break the chains of dependency on those addicted to government's largesse...

We will make real again the dream of a republic where work is respected and rewarded, where every right is balanced by responsibility, where freedom thrives and opportunity burns bright...

Governor John Engler of Michigan has been one of the most successful governors in cutting state spending. He started his political career in 1970, when he was elected to the Michigan House while still in college. He was later elected to the State Senate. Since being elected Governor of Michigan in 1990, he has cut the state arts budget and abolished general welfare assistance. He has also privatized many public services, despite heavy criticism from public employee unions, and has won approval for the country's most far-reaching charter school legislation. Born October 12, 1948 in Mount Pleasant, Michigan, where he still resides, Governor Engler and his wife Michelle, a practicing attorney, were married in 1990. They have triplet daughters.

"Michigan's Renaissance — America's Hope"
by Governor John Engler
Excerpt from Second Inaugural Address
Lansing, Michigan
January 2, 1995

Four years ago, we started a revolution. Today, Michigan's renaissance is America's hope.

Together, we have transformed Michigan from the broken buckle of America's Rust Belt to a bright beacon of hope for America's families. And last November, this light of change helped bring our nation back home to its founding principles.

Two days from now, a new Congress will be sworn in. We pray they will have the courage to be bold, to follow Michigan's course, to make history just as we have made history. Their mandate is for nothing less than the most sweeping changes in our government since the Great Depression.

This is a defining moment in American history. Overwhelmingly, the American people voted for change in Washington.

Change to cut taxes and help families.

Change to limit government and balance the budget.

Change to restore the American dream and put you — the people — in charge.

Chapter Eight

This incredible chance for change will come only once in our lifetime. It will not be easy, for with major change comes risk and uncertainty.

But as our Michigan experience has taught us, by being bold, by staying the course, by holding fast to our principles, the people will take up the challenge and accomplish great things.

Leadership in the 21st century will be defined by taking risks, not by clinging to the failed policies and ideas of the past.

It is imperative to the people of Michigan that this new Congress succeed. Michigan has already accomplished much, but there is much more to do. In a second term, we seek to build upon our legacy as Michigan continues its quest to lead and innovate.

We will seek to free the power and money that for too long have been held captive in Washington. Not to hoard them in Lansing, but to put your money back in your pocket and to put you back in charge.

This is fundamental. America and Michigan were founded by pioneers seeking the freedom to control their destiny. We have never shied away from a challenge, never given up when times were tough. We have always had faith — in ourselves and in our future.

If we put our hearts, our heads and our hands together, we can do anything we set out to do. That's the Michigan way!

Governor of Massachusetts William Weld was elected in 1990 and surprised citizens in his first year in office when he balanced the budget, cut public spending, and privatized many public services, all without raising taxes. As a matter of fact, he repealed former Governor and presidential candidate Michael Dukakis's state income and estate tax increases. In 1994, he was re-elected with 71 percent of the votes cast.

Rock the House

Born July 31, 1945 in Smithtown, New York, Governor Weld and his wife, Susan Roosevelt Weld, live in Cambridge, Massachusetts with their five children.

Excerpts from Remarks by Governor William F. Weld
Submitted to the House Committee on Ways and Means
Washington, D.C.
January 1995

Government flatters itself when it attempts to match every affliction in society with a program, regulation, or mandate. I do believe that what we have done in Massachusetts asserts the possibility of revolutionary contraction within government and the expansion of freedom outside of government.

When I took over from former Governor Dukakis in 1991, I inherited a $2.6 billion deficit. We closed the deficit without raising taxes. We not only have balanced five subsequent budgets, but we ended last year with a $326 million surplus. We've reduced the state work force by 12 percent, and we've cut taxes nine times. We recently phased out our tax on long-term capital gains. After cutting taxes nine times in four years, we hope our old "Taxachusetts" label is dead and buried.

In the area of crime, we've abolished parole, instituted truth-in-sentencing, reformed our bail laws so judges can consider dangerousness, and enacted legislation allowing violent teenagers to be tried as adults. Our criminal justice system needed an injection of common sense, not an assortment of flaccid "prevention" programs.

Our welfare reform includes a work requirement after 60 days and abolishes the cash grant. We've also overhauled a welfare program known as General Relief that too often gave cash benefits for murky and even bizarre reasons — such as being an ex-convict or a drug addict or over 45 years old, overweight, and without a stable work

256

history. I would have qualified! We drastically scaled back the program, and it now costs $98 million, as opposed to $190 million.

The Republican Party has been properly critical of the Democrats when they seek to extend the long arm of the government where it does not belong. We should be true to that conviction on all issues. If we don't trust the government even to tie its own shoes, why should we trust government to divine solutions to a matter so ethically, theologically, and scientifically complex as abortion? Government ought to stay out of your pocketbook *and* out of your bedroom.

Americans trust Republicans when they focus on their wallets. A majority of Americans trust Democrats when the focus is on social issues. The 1994 elections have given the Republican party an opportunity to transcend those traditional strictures. In my view, we have to seize this opportunity if we are going to capture the White House in 1996 and truly become the majority party in America.

Friedrich Hayek distilled all of this into a "fundamental principle that in the ordering of our affairs we should make as much use as possible of the spontaneous forces of society, and resort as little as possible to coercion". Republicans would do well — will do well — to abide by Hayek's creed.

Wisconsin Governor Tommy G. Thompson is at the forefront of an anti-big-government revolution in the states. Mr. Thompson was first elected to the State Assembly in 1966, where he served as Minority Leader. First elected governor in 1986, he has balanced the budget every year, reduced personal income tax rates, and not raised any major taxes. In 1990, he was re-elected by a landslide vote, winning all but five of Wisconsin's 72 counties.

Between 1987 and 1993, under his leadership, more than 382,000 new jobs were created throughout the state. He spearheaded the Parental School Choice program, the first private school choice program in the country. Born November 19, 1941 in Elroy, Wisconsin, where he still resides, Governor Thompson and his wife, Sue Ann, have three children.

Excerpts from State of the State Address
by Governor Tommy G. Thompson
Wisconsin Assembly Chamber
Madison, Wisconsin
January 25, 1995

We don't just talk about change. We don't just talk about success. We make it happen.

When we say we are going to cut taxes, we do it.

When we say we are going to reform welfare, we do it.

When we say we are going to change education, we do it.

When we say we are going to cut $1 billion off the property taxes, we do it.

Taxes

Eight years ago I told you we were going to cut taxes in this state. And we did.

We cut the income tax. We cut business taxes. We eliminated the inheritance tax. We eliminated the gift tax. We kept the 60% exclusion of the capital gains tax.

And in three weeks I will detail my plan to deliver the largest tax cut in state history, the final step in tax relief for Wisconsin: $1 billion off the property tax bills.

And we are going to do it *without raising other taxes*.

When I say a tax cut, I mean it.

Not raising taxes is greeted by applause tonight in this chamber. I hope all of you remember this in the weeks and the months to come.

Not raising taxes means that programs many of you like will be reduced. Some will be gone.

We are no longer measuring government in dollars and cents. We are measuring it by what we accomplish, by the opportunities we create.

This tax cut gives us a once-in-a-lifetime opportunity to completely re-design and re-define and re-focus what government is, what it does, and what it can do without.

We are ratcheting down on personnel and programs.

And we are gearing up on technology and service.

We are creating a government that is smaller, a government that works better and spends less.

Welfare

Eight years ago we said we were going to change welfare in this state.

And we did it.

Our welfare rolls are at their lowest level in *fifteen years*, down 25% in the last eight years.

Wisconsin changed the dynamics of the welfare debate by laying down the very simple premise that if you accept a check from the state, you will accept certain basic responsibilities in return.

We made it clear that handing out money and expecting absolutely nothing in return is *not* public assistance. It is public apathy.

Not anymore.

Tonight, we are completing the revolution. We are completing the connection between welfare and work.

We are replacing the welfare check with a passport to a better future.

Tonight, I am announcing that we are moving the welfare division from our Social Services Department to a new Department of Industry, Labor and Job Development.

Welfare will no longer exist. It will no longer be part of the vocabulary.

Welfare is going to become a jobs program.

Education

We said we were going to revolutionize education in this state, and we have.

We created the first private school choice program in the country. We have a School-to-Work and Youth Apprenticeship program that is the model for the nation.

Tonight, I am asking teachers, principals, parents and entire communities to join me in creating a new system of public education for the 21st century.

This will mean challenging the status quo. It will mean fighting the gravity pull of those who are afraid to change.

But we are going to do it. We are going to put education *back* where it belongs, back in the hands of our parents, our teachers, and our students.

Our first step in changing education is a complete redefinition of public education in Wisconsin.

From now on in Wisconsin, a public school will mean a school that is *serving the public.*

School choice is part of this new public education.

School choice is more than a program. It is a philosophy.

It is the belief that parents know best when it comes to their own children.

It is the belief that poor parents have the same right to choose as other parents do.

It is the belief that parents will choose the best school for their child.

That's education serving the public.

We are expanding our Milwaukee private school choice program to include more children and all private schools.

If a mother in Milwaukee wants her child to walk to the private school across the street instead of being bused to a public school across town, she's going to have that choice.

If that private school across the street has a religious affiliation, she is still going to have that choice.

Religious values are not our problem. Drop-out rates are.

And private school choice is only part of the solution.

We are going to make *public* choice an option statewide. We are going to make our public schools an excellent choice as well.

Crime

We said we were going to fight crime. And we have.

We passed a three-strikes bill last session. We abolished mandatory release. And we launched the largest prison expansion program in state history.

Statistically, crime is down in Wisconsin. But statistics are no comfort to people who do not feel safe, people who are afraid in their own neighborhoods.

We must be bolder. We must never forget that protecting law-abiding citizens is government's fundamental duty.

My message to violent young criminals is simple: your birthday won't protect you anymore.

To protect our law-abiding citizens from violent crime, we need to keep violent criminals off the streets.

That's why tonight I am proposing the elimination of parole for serious felonies in Wisconsin. From now on, people will serve their full sentences. If you are a violent criminal sentenced to 10 years in prison, you will serve 10 years in prison. No more parole. No more early release. Period.

Rock the House

Mayor Bret Schundler of Jersey City, New Jersey gradu-
ated from Harvard with honors in Sociology, then went to
work as an Executive Assistant to Congressman Roy Dyson of
Maryland. He became a Republican in 1991 and ran for
State Senate, capturing 45% of the vote in a 6% Republican
district. In his second bid for office, in 1992, he was elected
Mayor of Jersey City. As mayor, he has focussed on commu-
nity policing, educational choice, and lower taxes. Born
January 14, 1959 in Westfield, New Jersey, Mayor Schundler
and his wife, Lynn, an attorney, have a two-year-old child.

"A Philosophy of Empowerment"
by Mayor Bret Schundler
Excerpt from Testimony before U.S. Commission on Civil Rights
Ceremonial Court of the U.S. Court of International Trade
New York City, New York
September 19, 1994

When I was elected mayor of Jersey City, New Jersey, I became
the mayor of one of the most diverse cities in America: 30% of our
residents are African American, 25% are Hispanic, and 11% are
Asian. Forty one percent of our residents speak a language other than
English at home, and 14% have immigrated to America within the last
10 years.

I believe this diversity of race, culture, ethnicity, and religion is a
source of our community's strength. But I also know that our
differences have the potential to divide us farther apart, rather than
bring us closer together. That's why I think it is essential that
government enact policies which achieve economic justice by

empowering individuals — economic policies that will help individuals and communities help themselves.

All too often our present system of government highlights our differences as people, and it encourages us to form groups based on these differences to compete for "our proper share" of government benefits. Politicians benefit from this system because they are the gatekeepers who get to decide who receives these benefits. However, this system of special interest politics does not promote harmony among a diverse citizenry because one group's gain often necessitates another's loss.

I would much prefer to see government concentrate on helping every citizen, regardless of his or her racial or ethnic background, gain access to economic opportunity. To help every citizen have a real shot at attaining the American Dream. Naturally, the question then becomes: What type of policies should federal, state, and local governments pursue to help provide such opportunity to all its people? I think the answer to this question is quite simple: government should pursue economic policies which give individuals autonomy, policies which let people decide for themselves what is best for their family, and policies which give people access to the knowledge and capital necessary to be prosperous.

Let me be more specific. I think we all agree that education is a great economic equalizer. A good education can help families drastically improve their economic standing from one generation to the next. However, all too often, the schools of urban America fail to provide our young people with the knowledge they need to succeed in life. That's why I think it is so important that we revolutionize our education system, particularly the school systems located in our urban centers. We need an education system that gives parents a choice of where to send their children to school. A system that encourages parents to become more involved in their children's education.

In addition to knowledge, economic empowerment also requires capital. But given the budgetary pressures that most states and localities face, it is not practical to expect government to have the capacity to provide the funds necessary to redevelop our inner cities. Therefore, as public officials, we must find creative ways to attract capital from the private sector to distressed urban areas.

For example, one of the poorest and most dilapidated sections of Jersey City, Martin Luther King Drive, was once a vibrant shopping district. The city and neighborhood leaders have worked together to create a redevelopment plan that will reinvigorate its retail shopping district and surrounding residential neighborhoods.

This project has a great chance to succeed because, instead of telling the community how their neighborhood should be redeveloped, my predecessors had the foresight to realize that successful redevelopment of MLK Drive required strong support from the community.

Jersey City, like much of urban America, is in the midst of tremendous social change. Our nation is becoming more racially, ethnically, and culturally diverse. These changes present us with new problems, new challenges, and more importantly, a host of new opportunities. If government wants to develop an economic strategy to respond to these social changes, then it should enact policies which empower individuals, policies that help people help themselves.

I think it is time that we discard the word 'entitlement' from our vocabulary, and concentrate on developing innovative ways to help every American gain access to the education and capital necessary to succeed.

Haley Barbour is now in his second term as Chairman of the Republican National Committee. A seventh-generation Mississippi native, Mr. Barbour has had an active career directing many local and national campaigns. As Chairman of the Republican National Committee, he led his party to a takeover of both houses of Congress

Chapter Eight

for the first time in 40 years. Born October 22, 1947 in Yazoo City, Mississippi, where he still resides, Mr. Barbour and his wife, Marsha, have two sons.

**Condensed Version of Remarks
by Republican National Committee Chairman Haley Barbour
Republican National Committee Summer Meeting
Los Angeles, California
July 22, 1994**

When I think back to the first time I spoke to you [RNC Committee Members] in St. Louis, it is stunning how much our mood and outlook have changed. It was a cold winter day, and I had just been elected Chairman in a landslide... on the third ballot.

The media were saying our party was torn apart by divisive social issues, and maybe it was the end of a Republican era.

We have won all nine of the nine biggest elections in the country since Bill Clinton was elected President.

[NRCC Chairman] Bill Paxon advises me that we have more Republican candidates for Congress than ever before. We have more women Republican candidates for Congress. We have more African American [and] Hispanic Republican candidates than ever. The quality of candidates, challengers and all of our incumbents is at a record high level this year.

There is tremendous energy in our party. The grassroots are more active, more alive than I can remember. Our state parties are stronger, better and more self-reliant. That was one of our first goals.

We have rebuilt our small donor fundraising base. We had 50% more contributors in 1993 than in 1992. Three hundred thousand contributors in 1993 did not give to us in 1992. Last year 78% of our contributions came in amounts of $100 or less.

Consistent with our goals, we have put ourselves on the cutting edge in communications. GOP-TV has been a giant hit. Not only are we in over 23 million households on cable or broadcast with our TV show "Rising Tide", but it has been praised by the media, and it makes money.

Our fourth goal for rebuilding our party was to get us back in the policy business. As you see from the briefing papers and issue books we send you, policy drives our political message. We are very involved with our congressional leaders and governors on matters of substance. We all agree issues matter, and the RNC is very issue-oriented.

In St. Louis [at my election as chairman] and ever since, I have talked a lot about unity... If we let any one issue be the litmus test of Republicanism, we need our heads examined... [T]he road to victory is paved with unity. This intolerant, exclusionary, "rule or ruin" stuff is so much barn yard fertilizer, that's B.F. And so is the "take over the party" story. But we shouldn't act as if there are not disagreements in our party. There are, and there always will be. This is not a test. This is a political party, which over the next two years, we intend to make the party of governance in the greatest country in the history of the world. It is a big party.

The road to our victories has been and will be paved with unity. The Democrats know that, and one goal of their Christian bashing is to divide us and drive a wedge between us.

When pro-choice Paul Coverdell defeated a pro-life Republican in a primary so close that they had to have a run-off, did the pro-life Republicans sit on their hands because they disagreed on the issue of abortion? No. Pro-choice Paul Coverdell will tell you that he would not be a Senator today except for the enthusiastic support of pro-life and Christian conservative leaders in Georgia.

The Democrats are forced to play hard-ball with their own members for one simple reason: the rank and file in Congress know

Clinton and his policies are unpopular. So the Democrats are running from Clinton like scalded dogs.

So what does all this tell us? What does this mean to the Republican Party, and more particularly, the Republican National Committee? It means we may have an historic opportunity in November. As I have told you before, I have never seen a better political environment for Republicans; and that environment has produced the largest, strongest field of candidates in my memory.

Our opportunities are as good or better at the state level. There is a real prospect that a majority of states will have Republican governors next year.

We must be for good policy and be against bad policy. And we must never forget the fruits of winning elections must be more support for the good policies and programs that make our nation, our communities and our families more prosperous and safe.

As Ronald Reagan understood, the Republican party's primary goal is not to simply win elections. Our goal is not to build a bigger government. Our goal is to help all Americans reach the life they deserve, for themselves and their kids. Our domestic policy should not be a tool to better government revenues, but a way to better our lives, our businesses, our neighborhoods.

Former Congressman Jack Kemp is co-founder of Empower America, a public policy organization. This former NFL quarterback for the Buffalo Bills served nine terms in the U.S. House of Representatives and seven years as Chairman of the House Republican Conference. Mr. Kemp was the author of the Kemp-Roth tax cuts passed in the first Reagan Administration. He also served as President Bush's Secretary of Housing and Urban Development. Born July 13, 1935 in Los Angeles, California, Mr. Kemp and his wife,

Joanne, live in Bethesda, Maryland. They have four children and eight grandchildren.

"The Politics of the Impossible"
Excerpt from Speech by Jack Kemp
The Heritage Foundation's President's Club
Washington, D.C.
November 15, 1994

Let me share a vision of the American idea, deeply rooted in the conservative vision of the Founders:

Return to people their resources, and they will accept their responsibility.

Return to people power, and they will rebuild the institutions of a free society.

Return to people authority, and they will create the moral capital to help renew our nation.

This begins with some form of bureaucratic birth control. In 1937, a Presidential commission concluded that government programs need "a coroner to pronounce them dead and an undertaker to dispose of the remains". Too many endless, useless public programs remain unburied. If a new Republican Congress can't privatize the NEA, then our mandate will be meaningless. And the NEH and the SBA and the REA and PBS and agricultural subsidies. And while we're at it, we should privatize HUD, the IMF, the World Bank, and on and on.

But that is just the beginning. Our concern is not only for government's cost, but for its role and reach. Einstein said, "A problem can never be solved by thinking on the same level that produced it." We must think on a deeper level — finding ways to reverse the tide of 50 years of impersonal centralization.

Chapter Eight

First, this means relocating government control from the federal level to states and localities close to their own problems.

Problem solving at the federal level means 500 experts, meeting in secret, producing 1,400-page "solutions".

When problems are solved by states, you get a Tommy Thompson promoting school choice for inner city children, a John Engler moving welfare recipients into work and education, a Christie Todd Whitman slashing income tax rates by 25 percent, a Fife Symington eliminating state income and capital gains taxes, and a George Allen empowering residents of public housing to manage their own communities and ultimately own their own homes.

This was the meaning of this election: wisdom lies outside Washington, and we should locate power there as well.

Second, a new conservative philosophy of government should disseminate power beyond government, directly to families and churches and community groups — institutions with spiritual and moral authority denied to federal power.

We should give families control over education and health care.

We should reduce their taxes so they can care for their own needs, be generous to others, and save for the future.

We should provide help to those in need, whenever possible, through private and religious groups experienced at both reform and reformation.

We should provide a safety net below which people should not be allowed to fall but, more important, a ladder of opportunity upon which all people can climb.

This would be a radical change, but it would also be a return to normalcy — to life as lived before American government was centralized by the struggles of our century. It would mean the return to lower taxes, economic growth, stronger communities and families, and a limited federal government — to a stronger era of American life.

An America where the goals of education are set by the PTA, not the NEA.

An America where the debate in Congress is over which taxes to cut, not which taxes to raise, about which government programs to privatize, not which ones to nationalize.

An America where prosperity begins on Main Street and extends to Wall Street, not the other way around.

An America where the character of children is shaped by their parents and grandparents, not by Donna Shalala and Joycelyn Elders.

But conservatives must offer more than a lament for a lost America. We must offer the vision of a new one. We have a responsibility, not just to diagnose what has failed, but to propose what will replace it.

We need a tax code that is flat, fair, and simple — one that rewards work and entrepreneurial risk-taking, that sets economic growth for all as its highest goal, not the redistribution of wealth or soaking the rich.

We need an education system where parents have influence and values have a voice — with school choice for parents in every community.

An anti-poverty agenda based on democratic capitalism, not socialism — on private ownership, not government control. Our definition of compassion is not how many people live on the government welfare plantation, but how many of our people are liberated from government dependence.

Our approach must empower people, not government. It helps men and women without robbing them of their birthright — control over their own lives.

The goal of government is not to secure happiness. It is to secure the God-given inalienable right to pursue happiness, to live our lives in obedience to conscience, not to government.

Chapter Eight

Conservatives must communicate a simple principle: that government governs best that allows us to govern ourselves.

We have stood together since a time when we met in the catacombs, not in conventions. Since a time when conservatism was known as "the forbidden faith" and "the thankless persuasion". We have lived to see conservatism pronounced dead. We have lived to see it survive all of its would-be conquerors. And not just to survive, but to come to this threshold, when dreams become objectives and hopes become plans. It is an historical process that should be familiar: "The stone which the builders rejected has become the chief and cornerstone."

Ladies and gentlemen, it is liberalism that now defends an old, crumbling order — an order maintained by threats and propped up by fear. Now it is conservatism that is the creed of intellectual liberty, of free markets, of faith in people.

We can be proud but not prideful, confident but not content, because our work is not done. It is time to become missionaries for our message in every forgotten corner of the American community. It is time for a new governing conservatism captured by a passion for the possible with a commitment to moving our nation ahead, but, like the Good Shepherd, leaving no one behind.

Characterized by the business community and national press as an innovative insurance marketer and advocate of social causes, Pat Rooney joined Golden Rule Insurance Company out of college. The firm was founded by his father in 1940. Mr. Rooney was elected to the position of chairman and chief executive officer shortly after his father's death in 1976. Under Mr. Rooney, the company embarked on a period of major growth and expansion to become a national firm offering health and life insurance products in 49 states.

by Pat Rooney

We at Golden Rule are interested in solving problems.

Health Care

On health care reform, we have been advocating Medical Savings Accounts (MSA's) because they are the best way to reduce health care spending without doing any harm. Rationing or using a gate-keeper physician to deny services will reduce spending, but will do more harm than good. If you and I had to go to a gatekeeper (with bonus compensation for denial of services) for auto maintenance, we would immediately understand that the gatekeeper would want to avoid major (costly) repairs. Oil changes, but not new transmissions. So it will be with health care if a gatekeeper can earn a bonus for the care that is *not* provided.

MSA's combine a high deductible policy with a savings account out of which the employees pay for routine care. By letting people keep any money that's left, health care spending will be reduced without reducing the quality of care. Before employers and employ-ees can take full advantage of MSA's, a federal change in the tax code is required.

We have offered after-tax MSA's to our employees since May 1993. In those 20 months, Golden Rule employees have personally saved more than $1.2 million. That's their money to keep. This savings represents more than 40% of the total deposits to the accounts. In addition to saving that money, the MSA's have also increased access to preventive care, provided first-dollar coverage, and given the employees an incentive to shop around for medical care. By simply providing that incentive, our company has not had a rate increase for two straight years.

272

Chapter Eight

Education

In addition to helping solve our health care problem, we have been proactive in educational issues. The goal of any educational system should be to produce responsible and contributing citizens. An educator friend of mine says, "The schools need to produce graduates who will pay taxes, not live off other people's taxes." Obviously, there are immense problems with our primary and secondary educational systems, but our colleges (where there is not a government monopoly) work just fine. Many young children are suffering in a system that is not working.

So, four years ago, we established the Educational CHOICE Charitable Trust to pay half the tuition for 500 low-income, inner-city children to go to a non-government school. We see this as a solution for children who need help today. When I visit some of the schools, I see the caring and disciplined environment that makes it easy for children to learn. The program has since grown with the help of other benefactors. Presently 1050 children are in private schools with our help and an additional 800 are on the waiting list.

Stopping Racial Discrimination

In the mid 1970's, we were appalled to learn that large numbers of African Americans could not pass the insurance licensing exam developed by Educational Testing Service and regulated by the Illinois Department of Insurance.

We wanted to end the discrimination. After our arguments with the regulators at the Department and officials at ETS fell on unresponsive ears, we sued ETS and the Illinois Department of Insurance, accusing them of intentional discrimination. (Incidentally, the Department of Insurance regulates us.) The suit went on for eight years, but never went to trial because, we believe, they didn't want the true facts to come out.

Rock the House

As part of the settlement, ETS and the Illinois Department of Insurance had to adhere to new methods of constructing future tests, which were designed to reduce unnecessary racial differences. This new method has become known as the "Golden Rule Method".

As a major employer, we believe we have a responsibility to local, state, and national issues. If there's a problem, we want to get in there and solve it, because it will produce a better society. Then we'll all benefit.

CANADIAN CONTRACT

As always, success breeds imitation. Seeing the success of the Republican Party in the U.S.A., the Conservative Party of Ontario, Canada's richest and most populous province, drew up a social contract of its own to present to the voters. It was modeled closely on the Contract with America, and it produced comparable results.

In elections held June 8, 1995, Conservatives scored their biggest electoral victory since 1955, winning 63% of the seats in the provincial parliament. This feat was all the more impressive as the Conservatives entered the campaign 20 points behind in the polls.

The Conservative platform consisted of a 30% cut in income tax rates, matching spending cuts, workfare in welfare reform, opposition to affirmative action, and reform of laws favoring big labor. The new Conservative Premier pledged to resign if he didn't fulfil his promise, and promised a 50% pay cut for his cabinet if they didn't balance the budget.

The Conservative Party won seats in ethnic neighborhoods and in union strongholds, but lost the financial community. In Canada, as in the United States, the Establishment is liberal, and it includes the financial establishment. Average citizens respond to a clear statement of principles limiting government power, but the Establishment figures it can get along just fine with big government.

Expect to see more "contracts" between candidates and the voters as the voters learn that written promises are worth more than electioneering hot air.

CHAPTER NINE

THE GOP FUTURE: THE CONTRACT WITH AMERICA FOR 1996

What is to be Done?—V.I. Lenin

The Contract with America was the commitment by the Republicans running for Congress in 1994 to the American people that they would enact eight reforms on the first day of Congress and hold votes on ten key pieces of legislation within 100 days. The list of issues to be covered by the Contract was a subject of great debate in the spring and summer of 1994.

Many important reforms of Congress and many reductions in the size, scope and cost of government were not included in the Contract. Speaker Newt Gingrich of Georgia and Majority Leader Dick Armey of Texas have made it clear that the Contract was only a down payment, not the entire reform agenda. This chapter lays out the Republican Agenda beyond the Contract with America — beyond the first 100 days of the 104th Congress. As with the Contract, support for most of this agenda has been building at the local, state and national levels for several years. It enjoys broad support among Republican leaders in and out of government.

Some issues, such as the Flat Tax, are like then-Rep. Jack Kemp's 33 percent tax cut was in 1974: destined to become part of the Republican agenda, but only after a Republican president can join forces with a Republican Congress.

1. Tax And Regulatory Reform

Chief among the items in the extended Republican Agenda is Rep. Dick Armey's campaign for a single-rate income tax (a "flat tax"). This proposal was not included in the Contract despite strong support from many candidates for Congress and hundreds of taxpayer groups around the nation. Rep. Armey himself made this decision, pointing out that his bill would not be ready for legislative action until early 1996, because it would take more than 100 days to build the public support that will be needed to overcome those committed to the status quo.

The flat tax is contained in Rep. Armey's "Freedom and Fairness Restoration Act", which has three parts: Title I, Tax Reduction and Simplification; Title II, Spending Restraint and Budget Reform; Title III, Regulatory Relief. The explanation following is based on material provided by Rep. Armey's office.

* * * * *

Chapter Nine

THE FLAT TAX: THE FREEDOM AND FAIRNESS RESTORATION ACT

Title I: A New, Fair Tax System

Establish a flat income tax rate of 17 percent on all income.

Under the bill, the current complicated tax system is replaced with a low, simple flat tax.

All income will be taxed once — and only once — at a rate of 17 percent (when fully phased in by 1997). Income will be taxed under either the individual wage tax or the business tax.

Individual Wage Tax. Under the individual wage tax, all wages, salaries, and pensions are taxed at the flat 17 percent rate. In 1997, a personal exemption of $13,100 will be permitted for a single person, $17,200 for a single head of household, $26,200 for a married couple filing jointly, and $5,300 for each dependant. For virtually all taxpayers, this will result in a tax cut, especially for families with children. To prevent the double taxation of income, earnings from savings is not included in taxable income, and, therefore, not subject to taxation.

Business Tax. Under the business tax, owners of businesses will pay a 17 percent rate on the difference (if positive) between revenue and expenses. Subject to the business tax are corporate, partnership, professional, farm, and rental profits and royalties. The base for the tax is gross revenue less purchases of goods and services, capital equipment, structures, land, and wages paid to employees. No deductions are permitted for fringe benefits, interest, or payments to owners.

Because the various exemptions, loopholes, complicated depreciation schedules, and targeted tax breaks are eliminated, the tax return is simple enough to be filled out on a postcard, saving taxpayers

277

countless hours and expense filing tax returns. By eliminating the double taxation of savings and allowing complete expensing, the bill will spur investment and economic growth. Because of the generous exemptions, millions of taxpayers are taken off the rolls entirely, and middle-income Americans receive a tax cut.

The doubling of the dependent deduction will provide significant tax relief for families with children.

Minimize the initial static revenue loss by phasing in the 17 percent as spending and the deficit fall.

The Armey bill provides for a new contract with the American people. As federal spending falls and the deficit is lowered, taxes will be correspondingly lowered. Under the bill, the tax rate is set at 20 percent in the first year, providing most Americans a modest tax cut yet limiting revenue loss. In the third year, the rate is lowered to 17 percent, providing additional tax relief. This can be accomplished for two reasons. First, as the economy grows because of the favorable treatment of saving, investment, and low marginal tax rates, revenue to the U.S. Treasury will grow. Second, the spending restraint provided for in the bill (discussed below) will reduce expenditures. Therefore, higher revenue coupled with lower spending will reduce future deficits, freeing up resources to be returned to the American people. That is why the rate is lowered to 17 percent in the third year, providing Americans additional tax relief.

Eliminate the hidden cost of government by ending income tax withholding.

Because most income taxes are taken directly out of Americans' paychecks, the burden of high federal taxes is largely hidden from the American people. By concealing the true cost of government, the political class has built in a bias in favor of larger government.

Under the Armey bill, withholding is eliminated. Because Americans will write a check to the IRS each month when they pay their other bills, they will be able to measure the true cost of government against the benefits.

Title II: Real Spending Restraint

Reinvent government by sunsetting virtually every federal program.

Under the bill, all unearned entitlement and discretionary programs will be sunsetted within the first two years of passage. An "unearned" entitlement is defined as an entitlement not earned in service or paid for in total or in part by assessments or contributions. Social Security, Medicare, veterans' benefits and retirement programs are "earned" entitlements and are not sunsetted. All other programs will be sunsetted within two years of passage of the bill. From that point on, then, all unearned entitlements and discretionary programs will be sunsetted every ten years, after each census.

This provision will genuinely reinvent government by forcing Congress to review virtually every federal program. Sunsetting forces Congress to periodically review the effectiveness of programs, set new priorities, and reduce unnecessary spending.

Place spending caps on the growth of entitlement programs.

The total level of entitlement spending — excluding Social Security — may not exceed the increase in the consumer price index plus the growth in eligible population. If the increase in these programs exceeds this level, an entitlement sequester to eliminate the excess spending will occur on all entitlements except Social Security.

Entitlement spending now accounts for more than half of spending and is the fastest growing portion of the budget. The entitlement sequester will place strong pressure on Congress to make genuine reforms when reauthorizing sunsetted programs.

Establish caps on total federal spending.
The Act will limit the growth in total federal spending after freezing it for one year. If spending exceeds the maximum spending amount established in law, an across-the-board sequester will take effect, allocated at 80 percent from domestic discretionary spending and 20 percent from defense spending until balance is achieved.

The bill also contains a "look-back" sequester. On July 1 of each fiscal year, the Office of Management and Budget (OMB) will be required to determine if the spending cap will be exceeded in the current fiscal year, and if so, by how much. If the limit will be exceeded, a look-back sequester will eliminate the excess spending under the same 80-20 formula.

Capping federal spending with an enforceable sequester is the only way to ensure that federal spending does not exceed a certain level of growth.

Provide for a joint budget resolution.
The bill will provide for a joint budget resolution, replacing the present concurrent resolution, making the president a full participant in the budget process early in the year. Besides making the president a full participant in the drafting of the federal budget from the beginning of the process, this also prevents the House Rules Committee from waiving budget points of order, because a joint budget resolution will now have the force of law.

Chapter Nine

Title III: Open and Honest Regulating.

Protect private property rights.

This provision protects the rights of private property owners by requiring the federal government to compensate landowners when federal regulations have the effect of significantly reducing the value of property.

Many private property owners have had their land essentially seized from them through regulatory takings that prohibit most uses for the land. Requiring the federal government to reimburse property owners for these takings will restore protection for property owners.

Provide for a regulatory budget.

Within one year of passage of the bill, OMB will be required to determine the costs of federal regulations to the American economy. OMB will also be required to calculate the cost of federal regulations to state and local governments. If OMB determines the cost of regulations will exceed the previous year's level, it will be required to submit to Congress proposed changes to existing legislation or regulations which will keep regulatory costs in line with the previous year.

This section of the bill forces Congress and the executive branch, for the first time, to calculate and reveal to the public the economic costs of federal laws and regulations, allowing public officials and the American people to weigh their costs against the expected benefits.

Require cost-benefit analysis and risk assessment for new legislation and regulations.

Just as the budgetary effect of proposed legislation is calculated by the Congressional Budget Office (CBO) before it is considered by the House or Senate, this provision requires a CBO analysis of the economic costs of proposed regulations. For each bill considered by Congress, CBO will determine:

- The degree of risk to public health and safety targeted by the legislation;
- The costs associated with implementing and complying with the measure; and
- The effects on the economy.

OMB will be required to conduct a similar analysis for new regulations.

* * * * *

Merits of the Armey Bill

The *flat tax* is important for several reasons. First, a flat tax treats all Americans equally. It rejects the politics of hate and envy that Bill Clinton and the Democrats have used to divide Americans. If we are to move forward united as a civilization, we cannot allow our politicians to divide us along economic, racial or religious lines. The politics of envy played by House Democrat Leader Dick Gephardt and the racial politics of division played by Alabama Governor George Wallace are the same politics of divide and conquer.

The true purpose of the graduated or progressive income tax structure is to divide taxpayers into groups that can be attacked one by one. Bill Clinton made this strategy explicit when he told Americans, "Don't worry, my 1993 tax hike will only affect the top one or two percent of Americans." In reality, the tax hike hits everyone who buys gas or is a consumer of goods produced by companies small or large. But dividing taxpayers did fool some Americans into believing that they were not going to be affected.

In Massachusetts, the Establishment Left has tried five times to change the commonwealth's constitution that mandates a flat tax. The advocates of larger government know that if they have to raise everyone's taxes at once, they cannot win. In the 1994 election, Barbara Anderson and Chip Faulkner of Citizens for Limited Taxation in Massachusetts produced a 69-percent majority against putting a progressive income tax in the state constitution. The voters firmly rejected the "divide and conquer" ploy. In fact, under Governor Bill Weld, from 1991 to 1994 the flat rate income tax has actually been brought down from 6.25 percent to 5.95 percent.

If everyone benefits from a flat rate tax cut, and everyone is hurt by a flat rate tax being increased, then all taxpayers have the same interest in cutting taxes, reducing spending, and opposing spending increases and the tax increases that follow. A flat tax unites taxpayers; a graduated income tax divides taxpayers. Politicians prefer to have taxpayers divided into groups that can be singled out, mugged and then told to sit back down and shut up while the politicians turn to the next group of taxpayers, who had stood idly by while the first group was hit.

This division of taxpayers into more vulnerable small groups reminds one of the poetic observation of Pastor Martin Niemöller, who said of the National Socialists, "In Germany they came first for the Communists, and I didn't speak up because I wasn't a Communist. Then they came for the Jews, and I didn't speak up because I wasn't a Jew. Then they came for the trade unionists, and I didn't speak up because I wasn't a trade unionist. Then they came for the Catholics, and I didn't speak up because I was a Protestant. Then they came for me, and by that time there was no one left to speak up."

* * * * *

Figure 1: DICK ARMEY FLAT TAX FORM

Form 1 — Individual Wage Tax — 1997

Your first name and initial (if joint return, also give spouse's name and initial)

Your Social Security Number

Present home address (number and street including apartment number or rural route)

Spouse's Social Security Number

City, Town, or Post Office, State and ZIP Code

Your occupation

Spouse's occupation

1. Wages, Salary and Pensions... 1
2. Personal allowance
   a. $26,200 for married filing jointly... 2a
   b. $13,100 for single... 2b
   c. $17,200 for single head of household... 2c
3. Number of dependents, not including spouse... 3
4. Personal allowances for dependents (line 3 multiplied by $5300).................... 4
5. Total personal allowances (line 2 plus line 4).. 5
6. Taxable wages (line 1 less line 5, if positive, otherwise zero)....................... 6
7. Tax (17% of line 6).. 7
8. Tax already paid.. 8
9. Tax due (line 7 less line 8, if positive).. 9
10. Refund due (line 8 less line 7, if positive).. 10

Chapter Nine

Eliminating income tax withholding is equally important. Withholding—interestingly, the brainchild of the otherwise praiseworthy economist Milton Friedman during World War II — hides the true cost of government. The taxpayers' movement began with a property tax revolt, not because property taxes are somehow less just or more onerous than sales taxes, income taxes, social security taxes or inheritance taxes, but because taxpayers actually have to sit down and write out checks every three or six months to pay them. The real cost of local government is more visible than the silent withholding of the income tax from a paycheck. Many Americans think only of their after-tax income, not even considering the pre-tax income to be real. Milton Friedman now strongly supports efforts to repeal withholding for just this reason.

Sunsetting federal programs, as provided for in the Armey Bill, would require each program to justify itself within the next two years, and then to a new generation of congressmen every ten years after that. Today, some programs for which initial sponsors and rationale are long gone are kept simply through inertia. The military budget of the United States sunsets every two years because the Founding Fathers feared a permanent military budget that would become an entitlement. Imagine how they would feel about the pork barrel spending that continues unchecked and unexamined year after year after year. The Constitutional two-year sunset of all military spending is one reason that old spending programs in the military are eliminated to make way for new weapons systems. In social welfare spending, however, new ideas are often piled onto old programs like a barnacle-encrusted ship that is never scraped clean.

Protecting property rights and limiting regulations would rein in two favorite ploys of the politicians to hide the costs of their programs. Just as Rep. Armey's flat tax would make the cost of taxes painfully obvious to all, so too would the banning of unreimbursed takings stop politicians from taking the property of Americans through regulations. And the regulatory budget would highlight the total costs of regulations, so that Americans could make intelligent and informed decisions about whether some regulations are worth the cost.

The Armey Flat Tax and the entire Freedom and Fairness Restoration Act is the Kemp-Roth Act of the 1990's, a bill which has virtues and importance that are clear to all Republicans and can be easily understood by voters. This bill will pass in 1997 when the Republicans control the White House as well as the House and Senate. It will create strong barriers to the future growth of government and strong pressures to bring down the total cost of Washington.

2. Supermajority Requirement for All Tax Increases

The Republican Contract with America promised a vote on a balanced budget amendment that also requires a supermajority (60-percent or more) to either borrow money or raise taxes. Such a requirement would make it more difficult for politicians to put future generations of Americans into debt and make it equally difficult to raise taxes. The goal is to force Congress into the spending cuts needed to bring the budget into balance by the year 2002.

On January 25, 1995, 166 Democrats in the House voted against the Balanced Budget Amendment with a three-fifths supermajority, as introduced by Rep. Joe Barton (R-TX). Barton got 253 votes, or 59 percent of the House, but not the two-thirds (290 votes) required by the Constitution for an amendment. The House then passed (by a vote of 300-132) a simple Balanced Budget Amendment put forward by Rep. Dan Schaefer of Colorado.

Therefore, a requirement that any tax increase receive a supermajority of the House and Senate before it becomes law will not be in any balanced budget amendment Congress passes in 1995.

However, the drive for supermajority votes for tax increases continues. At the state level, taxpayer organizations are successfully pushing to change their state constitutions to require a two-thirds vote of both houses to raise taxes. This was part of Proposition 13 in California, passed in 1978. In Arizona, a constitutional amendment that requires tax hikes to receive a two-thirds vote of the legislature was put on the ballot by a citizen initiative led by taxpayer activist Sydney Hoff-Hay and now-Representative John Shadegg. It passed in November 1992. In 1994, Sam Gibbons, a state legislator from Nevada led an initiative campaign to amend that state's constitution to require a two-thirds vote for tax hikes. It passed on November 8, 1994. Nevada's constitution requires that amendments proposed by the people must be voted on in two different elections separated by an election cycle, so the final vote for the two-thirds Gibbons amendment will be in November 1996.

Oklahoma taxpayers, led by the Oklahoma Taxpayers Union, passed an initiative in 1992 that requires a three-fourths vote for the legislature to pass an *emergency* tax increase (*i.e.*, one that is not subject to a citizen referendum). Colorado taxpayers, led by the Colorado Union of Taxpayers, passed a constitutional amendment which requires that any tax increase be voted on by the people of the state of Colorado. The amendment also requires that any local tax in Colorado be put on the ballot of the town or county for a vote of the citizens. In 1993, now-Representative Linda Smith led a successful initiative effort in Washington state for a three-fifths supermajority requirement to raise any tax.

Activists in Montana, Ohio, Florida, and a dozen other states are considering campaigns to have similar initiative votes on statewide ballots in 1995 and 1996. Across the nation, taxpayers are awakening to the fact that tax increases tend to be as permanent as constitutional amendments and treaties, and that therefore they should have to pass a higher threshold than is required for simple spending programs or run-of-the-mill legislation. The goal is to make it very difficult to raise taxes so that the politicians are forced to think first of spending restraint rather than raising taxes to cover revenue "shortfalls".

At the federal level, constitutional amendments to require two-thirds of the Congress to raise taxes will be reintroduced in both the U.S. Senate and the House of Representatives. As discussed in Chapter Seven, a vote on such an amendment is already scheduled in the House for April 15, 1996 and another (if needed) for April 15, 1997. This will build on the very important change in House rules instituted by Republicans on January 4, 1995 requiring a sixty-percent vote for any income tax increase.

The tax issue is the central divide between the Republican and Democrat parties. Tax policy preferences signal the disposition of the parties to grow or shrink government power, which has policy implications in every other area.

The growing taxpayer demand for a two-thirds vote for tax increases will clearly continue at the federal, state and local levels.

3. School Choice

School choice, the principle that parents should be able to choose the schools their children attend rather than some federal judge, state bureaucrat, or school board, is an idea whose time has come.

Giving parents a voucher or tax credit or scholarship worth the average amount spent per child by the government on public education would empower parents to take that voucher or scholarship to the school of the *their* choice — not some bureaucrat's — and use it to pay for all or part of the costs of that school. Some parents will want to send their children to the local government-owned and operated school, while others will wish to have their children attend Catholic parochial schools, Jewish day schools, Christian schools, or Afro-centric schools.

288

Chapter Nine

School choice would end many of the debates that have long divided Americans. School prayer would cease to be an issue. As long as all Americans have their tax dollars taken from them to pay for government-owned and operated schools and the law requires them to send their children to those schools for six hours a day for 180 or so days a year, then parents will quite understandably fight over whether their children are allowed (or required) to pray in school. Fights will naturally erupt over the kinds of prayers. But if all parents can choose their children's school, religious or secular, government-run or independent, then the parent can choose whether there is prayer in school or not for *their* children.

Some parents have expressed concern about certain books in the government school curriculum, objecting to books they view as racist or pornographic. In the government school system, parents must sign petitions, drive to long evening meetings, write letters to the editor, and argue with those holding the opposite view.

In a parental-choice system, the parents could call the teacher and if an offending book cannot be changed or other arrangements made for the child, the parents can find another school that honors their concerns.

School choice unites all the coalition members of the Republican Party. Free-market libertarians support school choice because they know that when the government runs six percent of the economy — and that is the size of the present kindergarten-through-high school, government-run and owned system — the government will provide a poor product, ignore consumer wishes, and charge twice as much as a competitive system would.

Social conservatives, parents and traditional values conservatives know that the present Supreme Court rulings demand the divorce of education in a government-run school from all moral and religious values. Individuals can only ensure that their children are taught right from wrong and to respect their religious traditions and values in a private non-government-run school.

School choice is also a very important issue for Republicans desiring to reach out to minority voters. Americans of all races, when polled, support educational choice overwhelmingly. Frank Luntz polled California voters and found support for choice among parents running at 70 to 30 percent. But black and Hispanic parents are even more strongly in support, for the understandable reason that theirs are often the children forced to attend schools run by corrupt big-city political machines more dedicated to the political interests of the Democrat Party and the labor union leaders than to children or parents. Black inner-city parents, who are expected to faithfully vote Democrat anyway, find that their voices are ignored when they try to complain about the poor quality of education their children are receiving.

In Jersey City in northern New Jersey, where minorities constitute a majority of the population, Republican Bret Schundler won election as mayor in November of 1992 and again in May of 1993 by stressing his support for school choice. He won 40 percent of the black vote largely because of this support for school choice. And when Christine Todd Whitman ran for governor of New Jersey in 1993, she received fully 25 percent of the black vote after the National Education Association, a teachers' union, sent out mass faxes and posters attacking her for her support of school choice.

After her election, Governor Whitman repeated her commitment to Mayor Schundler's school choice plan in her inaugural address. New Jersey blacks are now watching to see if Governor Whitman keeps her word to them on educational choice.

In Arizona, the battle for school choice raged in 1993. Led by state representative Lisa Graham, state senate president Tom Patterson, and Governor Fife Symington, a full school choice plan guaranteeing a $1,500 voucher for each school child passed the

Chapter Nine

Arizona House of Representatives and fell only three votes short of passage in the state Senate. It was opposed by the teachers' unions and some Republicans to whom the teachers' unions had given campaign contributions.

In 1994, Lisa Graham ran for Arizona state superintendent of public instruction and was viciously attacked by the teachers' unions for her support of parental choice. Still, Arizona voters went to the polls on November 8th and elected her with a strong 58 percent of the vote. They also re-elected pro-choice-in-education Governor Fife Symington and Republican majorities in the House and Senate.

In Pennsylvania, voters elected Tom Ridge, the Republican gubernatorial candidate who campaigned on a strong choice-in-education platform. Majorities of both state legislative houses have committed to supporting choice in education. Two years ago choice passed the state Senate 28 to 22, but failed in the state house 29-114 in the face of constitutional questions about a particular form of the proposal.

In Wisconsin, Governor Tommy Thompson has worked with Democrat State Representative Polly Williams to pass a school choice program limited to lower-income students in the city of Milwaukee. The program has been such a great success that now Thompson and Williams are working to expand the choices available for parents and to increase the number of parents who may participate.

The most important "primary state" in the nation in choosing a Republican presidential or vice-presidential candidate may not be New Hampshire or Iowa, but rather that state which first passes complete choice in education. That would put the governor of that state on the short list of national Republican leaders willing to take on the labor union bosses and the public education bureaucracy in defense of America's children.

4. The Parental Rights Amendment

The struggle for parental choice in education is the largest fight the Republicans will carry on against the failed welfare state and those who profit from the status quo. The issue of parental rights, however, is even broader than school choice.

The "Parental Rights Amendment", a simple two-sentence Constitutional Amendment, was introduced in 20 states in 1994 and will be advanced in all 50 states by 1996. It is already a central rallying cry for the Republican state and federal policy agenda for 1996. The amendment reads:

1. *The right of parents to direct the upbringing of their children shall not be infringed.*
2. *The legislature shall have power to enforce, by appropriate legislation, the provisions of this article.*

This language comes straight from Supreme Court decisions upholding the rights of parents. The importance of this amendment at the state level is that it will strengthen parents in fights with state and local bureaucrats who wish to expand the welfare state at the expense of parental control over children. The language of the amendment continues to give police the authority to stop child abuse, of course, but it will help parents defend themselves against some of the more intrusive sex education "courses" schools have employed—those that supply condoms and do psychological testing and experiments with small children without informing parents.

The Republican coalition of taxpayers, homeowners, small businessmen and women, gun owners, and individualists is greatly strengthened by the growing participation of parents in this coalition. A *Reader's Digest* poll in 1992 found that 50 percent of single Americans under the age of 35 considered themselves "liberal", while 43 percent said they were "conservative".

For married couples under 35 but with children, fully 67 percent considered themselves "conservative", and only 25 percent considered themselves "liberal". And of the 161 million Americans who are 25 years old or older, fully 57 percent are married with children. Eight percent are married without children.

Married couples with children are a voting bloc of 92 million Americans. And, of course, older couples whose children have left home — often only to return with grandchildren — share many of the concerns and needs of parents with children in the home.

Parents and their concerns will become an increasing part of the growing Republican coalition. Recognition that parents with children are more conservative than singles or parents who do not yet have children helps Republican leaders understand why liberal Democrats have been so wrong in projecting into the future the beliefs or even voting patterns of 20-year-olds.

Democrats have hoped, believed, even acted on the idea that if today's 20-year-olds are hostile to traditional values, religion, or even patriotism, then this world view would become the dominant one in 20 years when they attained age 40. Fortunately, experience, time, and perhaps most important of all, parenthood, change that.

Much of the Religious Right might be also understood as the "Parenthood Right". And in terms of building a governing Republican majority, it is well to remember that there are more parents than there are Southern Baptists.

5. Medical Savings Accounts

Bill Clinton used the rising costs of health care in America and the fact that some individuals do not have health insurance to argue for having the government take over the medical industry and control everyone's life-and-death medical decisions. This idea was not popular with Americans.

Still, it is true that government interference in the marketplace for health care has driven up the costs of health care. (Everything the government touches increases in price, while its quality declines. And if you disagree, send your arguments in with the eight-cent stamp that sufficed for first class mail in 1973, and see if it gets here in two days, as was once promised.)

Pat Rooney, the entrepreneur who brought school choice to life and gave it a human face in his successful, privately-funded tuition grant program in Indianapolis, took advantage of Clinton's grab for power to put forward an idea that actually does lower the cost of health care, saves money which then benefits individuals, and gives power to Americans, not to bureaucrats. Bill Clinton and the Left are going to be sorry they started the debate over how much government should interfere in health decisions, because Pat Rooney's invention of the Medical Savings Account means the answer is going to be "less and less".

A Medical Savings Account (MSA) is modeled on the individual retirement account (IRA). The IRA allows every taxpayer to save up to $2,000 each year towards retirement. The accumulated interest paid on that $2,000 investment is not taxed by the federal or state governments. Therefore the investment grows rapidly so that, at retirement, a 25-year-old who has saved $2,000 each year in an IRA will have at age 65 a nest egg of $208,000, assuming a four percent real rate of return. (That rate is just over half the average return earned by investments over the last 70 years, so the amount accumulated could be almost twice that.) At that same four percent, this nest egg alone would produce about $8,000 a year.

If your Social Security taxes were put into such an IRA and invested, and you worked from age 25 to 65, all the while paying the maximum Social Security tax into your IRA rather than to the government, you would retire with an investment of about $1 million in today's dollars, again assuming a four percent rate of return.

Chapter Nine

That amount would pay $40,000 a year, about one-third more than Social Security pays today, out of the interest alone. You would still have the one million to leave to your children or other heirs.

The medical savings account works as follows. If the costs of your present health insurance, paid by an employer or by yourself, for a family of four, come to $4,500 a year, you find that you can use as much health care as you like, and you pay essentially nothing. Therefore, you have an incentive to go to the doctor frequently, and no incentive to shop around for lower-priced services. Since "the insurance company pays for everything", no savings made by smart shopping flow to you or your family.

The MSA would allow you to put $3,000 of that $4,500 into a Medical Savings Account that works just like an IRA. Money could be withdrawn without penalty to be used to meet routine health care costs, at your discretion. The $1,500 remaining would be spent to purchase a catastrophic health insurance policy to pay for any health care costs above $3,000 per year. So you would pay the first $3,000 of health care costs out of your MSA. If you were hit by a bus and had high costs one year, all costs above the $3,000 would be covered by the insurance policy. On the other hand, if you spent less than $3,000 in any given year on health care, the money left over would be saved — by you. You could roll it over into the MSA for future years to cover other costs, or save it for retirement.

This plan makes every consumer a truly price-conscious consumer. Doctors and hospitals would have to compete on price for your business. It does not demand that every patient become a health care expert any more than shoppers at the supermarket need to be experts on beef or vegetables. Knowing that all stores have to compete on price, consumers can walk into a store and benefit from the smart shopping practices of others.

Dozens of Medical Savings Accounts bills have been introduced in Congress, with about 250 members sponsoring one or more of them. MSA's are the single most popular step that could be taken towards the genuine "reform" of health care.

As with school choice, policy entrepreneur Pat Rooney decided that the best way to demonstrate a good idea is not to talk to politicians about a theory — however sound — but to show them the policy in action. In 1993, Rooney's Golden Rule Insurance Company offered a version of the Medical Savings Account to its own workers. This MSA is handicapped by not having the tax-free status legislation would provide, but still its power in changing consumer habits and keeping costs down has been staggering.

The 730 employees of Golden Rule Insurance in Indiana saved $734,037, or more than $1,000 per employee in 1994. And remember that the money saved becomes the property of the employees. One worker tells the story of how she needed some elective surgery, and the doctor quoted a price of almost $10,000. When she said she was paying for it from her own pocket, the price fell by $3,797. When that example is repeated a million times a month (and Golden Rule employees discuss these experiences in the company cafeterias and parking lots), the health care cost "crisis" created by big government will begin to come to an end.

Forbes magazine, run by the entrepreneur Steve Forbes, did a similar experiment with the Medical Savings Account, with similar results.

6. Implement the *Beck* Decision

Since the 1930's the Democrat Party has claimed to be the party of working Americans, while its political leaders have actually been serving the interests of the leaders of the labor unions at the expense of the majority of workers.

Chapter Nine

Democrats fought to allow the Teamsters to mishandle the pensions of transportation workers. Democrats pushed protectionist policies that raised the costs of products for all consumers while "saving" a few jobs that were of importance to union leaders because of the union dues paid. Democrats have repeatedly increased the minimum wage, even though they knew that it priced teenagers out of their first jobs and had a disproportionate impact on black unemployment. The Davis-Bacon Act, long championed by the Democrats, was explicitly passed with the object of pricing blacks out of the labor market, thus protecting the higher-paid union jobs.

The entire U.S. Labor Department serves the interests of labor union bosses making six-figure salaries while the $35 billion cost of the Department is paid by taxpayers, who really *are* laborers. Ripping off the many to benefit the few in the name of the many could be the unofficial slogan of the U.S. Department of Labor.

The Supreme Court of the United States ruled in 1988, in *Beck* v. *Communications Workers of America*, that labor unions could not take money from working men and women in compulsory union dues and spend it on anything other than labor negotiations and maintenance of the labor union contracts of those workers. In the majority opinion, written by liberal Justice William Brennan, the Court ruled that workers had rights that the union bosses had to recognize. It was unconstitutional, the Court ruled, for the communication workers union — which collects dues from one million working men and women — to spend that money on things other than "performing the duties of an exclusive representative of the employees in dealing with the employer on labor-management issues".

The CWA had been spending some of that money — a great deal of that money — supporting liberal politicians that Harry Beck and dozens of his fellow workers objected to. The labor bosses did not care; they told Harry Beck to sit down and shut up and pay his compulsory dues or lose his job. With the support of Reed Larson and the National Right to Work Legal Foundation, Beck and others filed suit in 1976 to get back that part of their dues that was being misused.

The Supreme Court ruled that fully 79 percent of the dues taken by force from Harry Beck and other members of the CWA was being used for things that had nothing to do with their contract negotiations. Some was spent to force workers in other regions to pay dues. Some was given to left-wing Democrat candidates. Some was given to liberal interest groups.

This is a battle where Republicans can fight to protect the rights—fully recognized by the Supreme Court — of workers against the thievery of the labor union bosses. And the Democrat Party is forced by its financial dependence on big labor to spit on the workers and support the union bosses.

Bill Clinton did just this when, in the middle of the night, he revoked the executive order of President George Bush implementing the Beck Decision. Late in his administration, Bush had said, "I will enforce the Supreme Court's decision about the rights of workers." As discussed in Chapter Four, Bill Clinton had a different idea. He said, in effect, "My government will refuse to protect workers and will not respect their rights not to have their money sent to the Democrat Party against their wishes."

With the *Beck* decision, we have a Democrat president whose political needs cancel out the rights of Americans. Clinton had to choose between workers and the union bosses, and he did not hesitate for a moment. He stood with the bosses who give his party millions of dollars each election cycle, dollars taken by force from workers against their will. In 1988, the labor unions spent $388 million in "soft money" in support of Democrat candidates, money taken from compulsory union dues. That year, fully 42 percent of union members voted for George Bush. The labor unions take money from voters who oppose the Democrat Party and syphon it off to Democrat candidates and the Democrat Party.

Republican congressional leaders have announced that they will insist that the *Beck* decision be honored and implemented. This is an important part of any campaign finance reform, for as Thomas Jefferson wrote, it is "sinful and tyrannical" to compel a man to furnish funds for a cause in which he does not believe.

Republicans will introduce legislation to enforce the *Beck* decision, but it will almost certainly be vetoed by President Clinton, who always stands with the elites who give him money rather than with the workers whose money is taken. It will take a Republican president to restore the presidential executive order protecting workers from having the Democrats take their money.

7. Protecting Victims; Punishing Criminals

Now that 23 states have passed measures guaranteeing that victims will be heard during the trials of their attackers, this right of victims will continue to spread to all 50 states and to the federal government. Led by CrimeStrike, a victims' rights group supported by the National Rifle Association, victims will have the right to testify at the trial of their *alleged* attackers and to be present when a parole board thinks about letting a criminal out of prison.

"Tough on crime" initiatives, like the "Three Strikes, You're Out" measure in California and Washington state, will spread to every state. Washington state, which passed the first "Three Strikes, You're Out" measure (which requires criminals convicted of a third violent offense to go to prison for life), can point to its success. In the first six months of 1994, compared with 1993, the number of murders fell 10.9 percent, after increasing 18.9 percent from 1992 to 1993; rapes fell 17.9 percent; robberies fell 3.3 percent; aggravated assaults were down 3.4 percent; burglaries fell 8.6 percent. Overall, violent crime fell 5.3 percent, even though the population was increasing over the period.

This was not the continuation of a trend, but the reversal of one. Car theft, for example, a crime not covered by the "three strikes" law, rose 3.7 percent.

Tougher sentencing works. If a criminal is in jail, he can't commit a crime on the street. It is common sense for most Americans, but anathema to the liberal elite who wish to blame the victims of crime and to raise taxes to pay for "services" for criminals rather than cold prison beds.

Yes, building prisons is expensive. But so are active criminals. On average, it costs $25,000 to keep a criminal in prison for a year; but if that career criminal were left on the street and continuing his life of crime, he would cost society $430,000 each year. Releasing dangerous criminals is the truly costly solution.

Protecting and insisting on the rights of victims and insisting on serious, certain, and strong prison time again divides the Republican Party from the Democrats, who oppose the American people on both issues.

8. Defund the Left

Billions of dollars of taxpayers money are given every day to individuals and groups which turn around and lobby for the Democrat Party's legislative agenda and candidates. Without these funds the Democrat Establishment in the United States would either cease to exist or be forced to become something other than the European-style, left-wing party the Democrat Party is now. The best estimate today is that fully 75 percent of the Democrat Party is government-funded. When one walks through a Democrat national convention, three out of every four persons one meets are government workers, politicians, or those paid from federal, state, or local taxes, sometimes laundered through foundations, contracts, or universities.

Chapter Nine

The Republican Party in 1994 committed itself to stopping the abuse of taxpayer monies being used for political purposes. This is easy for the Republican Party, as it does not receive much of this taxpayer largesse. Republican activists know that every budget cut reduces the number of Democrat precinct workers.

There are several particularly egregious examples of government funding of the Establishment Left. So-called Public Television and National Public Radio always like to pretend that they are "viewer-supported", but they receive hundreds of millions of dollars each year from the taxpayers. The Left used to argue that the small number of television channels meant that taxpayers had to fund opera and left-wing documentaries for the elite. There are today dozens of radio stations and television channels. The liberal bias in National Public Radio is so pronounced that in Washington, D.C. it is called "National Proletariat Radio".

The Legal Services Corporation is another outrageous example of politicians taking hundreds of millions of dollars from the taxpayers to finance left-wing political activity. The LSC now spends $400 million each year for such purposes as hiring left-wing lawyers to sue the government — which conveniently funds them — to require the taxpayers to pay for higher welfare benefits for those who refuse to work.

The National Endowment for the Arts and the National Endowment for the Humanities were also created by the Democrats as funnels for money to support politicized art and cultural propaganda that could not get private sector support.

Most recently, the "Gender Equity Act" has served as a way to have taxpayer funds finance the politics of the Left. The act authorizes some $5 million in fiscal year 1995 to be used to promote feminist politics. It is the policy of the interest groups of the Left to have the Democrats reach into the pockets of the taxpayers to finance the political activities of the Democrat Party's front groups.

The National Council of Senior Citizens is another political organization largely funded with taxpayer dollars engaging in partisan political activity. The NCSC was formed by the labor unions in 1960 as "Senior Citizens for Kennedy-Johnson". It assumed its present form in 1961, during the political campaigns to fund Medicare. Over the years it has been run by and for labor union bosses, present and retired.

From July 1, 1992 to July 1, 1993, the NCSC reported "contributions" from the government of $68,843,321. The American Conservative Union found, using the government's own data, that the NCSC received more than one billion dollars in taxpayer monies between 1961 and 1994. The money is supposed to go for "meals on wheels" and seniors' employment programs, but it is not awarded by competitive bid, there has never been a government audit, and the overhead paid for by the government grants allows a lot of room for politicking by NCSC staff.

For example, on October 27, 1994, Mr. Lawrence Smedley, the executive director of the NCSC, along with other NCSC "members", held a press conference with Senator Charles Robb (D-VA) at Senator Robb's Northern Virginia campaign headquarters. Mr. Smedley, according to an FEC complaint filed against the NCSC, then endorsed Senator Robb in his re-election bid.

Press reports show that the NCSC also endorsed Democrat Senator Harris Wofford of Pennsylvania; Democrat Senate candidate Joel Hyatt of Ohio; Jack Mudd, Democrat candidate for the U.S. Senate in Montana; Democrat Senator Dianne Feinstein; Democrat Rep. Tom Andrews, running for U.S. Senate in Maine; and Ron Sims, the Democrat candidate for a U.S. Senate seat in Washington.

All the incumbents endorsed by the NCSC had voted for taxpayer money to be given to NCSC. How convenient. Dozens of such subterfuges are used to funnel the tax dollars of Americans to the

302

campaigns and political efforts of the Democrat Party directly and to its front groups.

A Republican Party determined to stop the misuse and waste of the tax dollars of working men and women in America will also find that every day it is making its opponents on the left a little smaller and poorer.

Honest governing is good politics.

9. Stopping Voter Fraud

David Wilhelm, the Chairman of the Democratic National Committee (DNC), spoke to the entire DNC on Saturday January 21, 1995, his final speech as outgoing chairman. He began by joking that his seven-month-old son, Kyle, had already voted seven times in the upcoming Chicago elections. The crowd of professional Democrat activists cheered. But voter fraud is no joke. It is an obscenity. There is no moral difference between the Democrat Party's previous history of intimidating blacks to keep them from voting in the South and the present practice of negating their votes in Northern cities like Chicago through vote fraud.

The most vulnerable individuals are often the most abused by voter fraud, as was shown by the *Philadelphia Inquirer* in the 1993 election campaign between Republican Bruce Marks and Democrat William Stinson. On election day, Marks had a 562-vote margin in the voting machines.

But there was an unusually large number of absentee ballots supposedly cast, more than 1,900 out of a total of 40,000 votes. Fully 1,391 of those ballots were cast for the Democrat, Stinson, and only 366 for the Republican, Marks. So Stinson was seated.

The *Inquirer* found that a large number of Hispanic voters had been approached by Democrats and told, contrary to law, that there was a "nueva forma de votar", or new way of voting. They were then furnished with absentee ballots and "instructed" on how to use them.

Absentee ballots, however, may only be legally cast in Pennsylvania by those physically unable to reach the polls, not as a way to vote before election day. The corruption was so obvious and widespread that a federal judge removed Stinson from office and seated Marks instead.

Two elections in November 1994 guarantee that the new Republican majorities will revisit the question of election fraud. In California, a close election between Republican Michael Huffington and Democrat Dianne Feinstein for Senate may well have been won only through vote fraud. The non-partisan Voter Fraud Task Force released a preliminary study on January 3, 1995, the results of which indicate that at least 170,000 fraudulent votes were cast in the election held November 8, 1994.

In just two days of looking, the task force verified that 17 dead people voted in Fresno County, 30 in Orange County, and 20 in Alameda County. The response by the Democrats to this exposed vote fraud has been to argue that there was not *enough* voter fraud to actually change the election result. Republicans have taken the position that any vote fraud is wrong and must be stopped.

The Senate seated Ms. Feinstein with the caveat that it would revisit this action as more information on voter fraud in the 1994 California election comes in.

In Maryland, the governor's race was "won" by Democrat Parris Glendening though thousands of questionable ballots came in late in the evening from Baltimore County, where the rolls had not been purged of dead or moved voters for the past five years. (A favorite voter fraud technique is to "vote" for those known to have died or moved, but who are still on the voting rolls. It is a little more risky, but still quite possible to vote for those who simply fail to vote on election day. Without a requirement of identification, anyone can walk in and vote, using another person's name.)

Chapter Nine

Voter fraud can be fought. The United States sends poll watchers and election experts to help run fair elections in the formerly communist nations of eastern Europe and the former Soviet Empire. International observers and somewhat fair rules stopped the communists from "winning" the election in Nicaragua. Alec Poitevint, the Republican Party national committeeman from Georgia who has observed elections in Russia, Romania, Bulgaria, and Azerbaijan, points out that the rules preventing voter fraud insisted on by the international community are not met in elections held in Democrat-controlled counties in Georgia. "The counting process in many Third World countries is more open and honest than in rural Democratic-controlled counties in the Southern U.S. There is no reason Americans cannot have elections as fair and honest and open as those in Albania," he says.

The Democrat "Motor Voter" bill that passed in 1993 as a top priority of the Clinton Administration not only encourages voter registration of everyone on welfare, but also opens the door wide to voter fraud and the registration of non-citizens. This was not a mistake. It was a purposeful decision to employ voter fraud to save a shrinking party that knows it cannot win fair, open, and transparent elections.

During the debate on "Motor Voter", Wyoming Senator Alan Simpson introduced an amendment that would have terminated mail-in registration and agency-based registration requirements if it were found that non-citizens comprised more than three percent of all registered voters in certain states. The amendment asked the Attorney General to sample three states to see if fraudulent registration of non-citizens was happening. Action would occur only if fully three percent of voters were illegal. Every single Democrat in the Senate voted against checking to see if illegal aliens were registered to vote and against revisiting the rules if the fraud were above three percent — making it clear that the purpose of "Motor Voter" was to facilitate voter fraud. Naturally, Senator Dianne Feinstein voted to protect such fraud from investigation. By substantially party-line votes, Democrats in the House also defeated repeated amendments designed to prevent illegal aliens from registering to vote under " Motor Voter".

Michael Huffington, who gave up his House seat to run for the Senate in California against the well-funded incumbent, Dianne Feinstein, was a major reason Republicans could focus their attention on other races for Senate and House, as Mr. Huffington's personal resources allowed him to finance his own campaign to compete with Ms. Feinstein's access to corporate and union PAC's. But Mr. Huffington's largest contribution to the Republican Party may be the long-overdue focus on the crime of voter fraud in the United States. Despite the joking of the Democratic National Committee chairman, voter fraud is not funny. It is a crime.

The California-based Voter Fraud Task Force suggests a five-point plan to reclaim the integrity of the process.

1. Require identification at the time of voter registration.
2. Require identification to be shown at the polls when voting.
3. Ban all "bounty hunting", where people are paid to register voters.
4. Eliminate registering to vote by mail.
5. Purge the state's voter rolls of dead wood — if someone hasn't voted in one of the last two general elections, drop his or her name from the rolls. This removes those who have died or moved from the voting rolls, and they can no longer be "voted" by the Democrat machines.

10. Term Limits Everywhere

The Republican Party first endorsed term limits in the 1988 Republican Platform. Since then, term limits have been passed in 22 states where over 40 percent of the American population lives. Mississippi will vote on term limits in November 1995, and when they pass in Mississippi, it will mean that every state with the initiative process will have adopted term limits.

In addition, at least 250 cities and towns have term-limited their local elected officials. It is clear that the idea of limiting the number of terms that a politician can serve in one office is as close to a consensus issue as exists in a free society. Frank Luntz's polling has shown consistent support among voters for term limits. At the federal level most Americans — 76 percent of all voters — want to see senators limited to two terms and representatives limited to three terms. Already the president is limited to two four-year terms.

Republican members of Congress took the lead on term limits, beginning in 1992. After the 1992 election, there was a great deal of talk about freshman members being agents of change. While both Democrat and Republican freshmen talked boldly about confronting Washington's Establishment, it was the Republican freshmen who actually introduced and won a limit of three terms (six years) that any Republican could serve as the ranking Republican on a committee. The Democrat freshmen told everyone they would do the same, but their leadership beat them into submission, and the motion was not even introduced in the Democrat caucus, let alone passed.

In 1994, the 71 incoming Republican freshmen joined sophomores from the 1992 election and successfully worked to limit the terms of committee chairmen to six years (three terms). This would have been unheard of only a few years ago, or even today among Democrats. When the Democrats controlled Congress, only a few congressional "barons" made all the key decisions, and they kept freshmen and those without seniority away from all real power. ("Baron" is an appropriate title, for when politicians usurp power, they fancy themselves European-style nobility.) They worked hard to keep power in their own hands and away from the people or their representatives. A majority of Democrats could have taken this "seniority" power away from the few at any time, but they were afraid to buck the system or hopeful of enjoying its spoils. The Republican Party has shown itself to be truly a different party with different leaders in Congress.

There will never again be a John Dingell or a Dan Rostenkowski or a Jack Brooks who will misuse the seniority system to accumulate power and then abuse it. Every six years the chairman of every committee must do something else.

In contrast with the Democrats of the past 60 years, Congressman Newt Gingrich supported a freshman class initiative to limit the Speaker of the House to eight years (*i.e.*, four terms), the same length of time as the president's term limit.

Term limits is an idea whose time has come. A Republican Party confident that it is in step with the American people has destroyed the seniority system in the House by limiting terms of committee chairmen and the Speaker. This is a silent revolution with an importance that has largely been missed by the national Establishment, but not missed by the American people who can now be confident that they can trust these new members, fresh from the real America, to govern.

The Contract with America promised voters that the Republican Party would bring term limits up for at least two votes. The first would limit representatives to three terms and senators to two. This is the limit now in place in 15 states. A second vote will be to limit representatives to six terms (or twelve years) and Senators to two six-year terms.

All leading national term limit support groups in the United States support "Three-Two-Two": three terms for the House, two for the Senate and two for the presidency. However, the most important task for Congress is to protect the wishes of the voters in the 22 states which have already passed term limits on their congressmen. George Nethercutt (R-WA) in the House and Hank Brown (R-CO) in the Senate have already introduced legislation respecting the decisions of the states.

As this is written in February 1995, the Democrat Party's opposition to term limits makes it unlikely that the Republicans will be able to pass a constitutional amendment limiting terms of federal office holders. Republicans and an organization called U.S. Term Limits remind the Democrats that "we'll be back" in 1996 and 1997. And in the meantime, the drive goes on for term limits in the states.

As Howie Rich, the founder of U.S. Term Limits, says: "The American people want term limits. We are going to have term limits. We may need to change many members of Congress, but we're not going to rest until every state has real term limits. We're going to win."

11. Colorblind Society

The Republican Party and conservatives are taking up the challenge of Dr. Martin Luther King, Jr., expressed in his dream of a nation where people are judged by the content of their character and not the color of their skin — a truly colorblind society with no government discrimination against any individual or group based on race, religion or national origin. As President Theodore Roosevelt said at the turn of the century, "There are no hyphenated Americans."

Since the 1960's, the Democrat Party has become the party of racial quotas, government contract set asides to be awarded based on political and racial rationales rather than the best interests of the taxpayers, and government-required discrimination by universities, companies, and local governments.

Americans have rightly rejected this racism by the Democrats as immoral, evil, and wrong. It is yet again another attempt by a faltering political Establishment to keep power by dividing Americans against each other. It will not succeed in America.

California, which began the taxpayer revolt with Proposition 13, is now leading the nation in the drive to wipe out all government racism. The California Civil Rights Initiative will be on the ballot in March of 1996. Glynn Custred and Thomas Wood have put together a coalition of Californians who are gathering more than one million signatures to put the CCRI on the ballot. More than ten other states have begun to plan to put a similar measure on their ballots in 1995 and 1996. As with the term limits movement of 1992 and 1994, the states are taking the lead in putting an issue on the national agenda.

The CCRI, when passed — and it will pass, since rejection of quotas and government racism has always enjoyed majority support of Americans of all colors and backgrounds — will prohibit California and any of its cities and towns from discriminating based on "race, sex, color, ethnicity, or national origin".

The complete text of the California Civil Rights Initiative reads as follows:

a) Neither the State of California nor any of its political subdivisions or agents shall use race, sex, color, ethnicity or national origin as a criterion for either discriminating against, or granting preferential treatment to, any individual or group in the operation of the State's system of public employment, public education or public contracting.

b) This section shall apply only to state action taken after the effective date of this section.

c) Allowable remedies for violations of this section shall include normal and customary attorney's fees.

d) Nothing in this section shall be interpreted as prohibiting classifications based on sex which are reasonably necessary to the normal operation of the State's system of public employment or public education.

e) Nothing in this section shall be interpreted as invalidating any court order or consent decree which is in force as of the effective date of this section.

f) Nothing in this section shall be interpreted as prohibiting state action which is necessary to establish or maintain eligibility for any federal program, where ineligibility would result in a loss of federal funds to the State.

g) If any part or parts of this section are found to be in conflict with federal law or with the United States Constitution, the section shall be implemented to the maximum extent that federal law and the United States Constitution permit. Any provision held invalid shall be severable from the remaining portions of this section.

Republicans are leading efforts to stop the continued racist politics of the Clinton Administration, which has employed a rigid quota system in its own hiring and has supported, through the U.S. Department of Justice, racist decisions to hire by quota. The Clinton Administration has actually demanded that the agencies that regulate banks ask all applicants for loans to assign a sex and race to the owners of the borrowing company.

The following is what appears on the actual form promulgated by the Clinton regulators on September 27, 1994:

Indicate in the boxes following the percentage of the business or farm that is owned by individuals in each of the racial and ethnic groups listed. The percentages for the different racial and ethnic categories should total 100 percent.

Also indicate the percentage of the business or farm that is owned by female individuals and the percentage that is owned by male individuals. The female and male percentages should total 100 percent.

Race or National Origin	% Ownership
1--American Indian or Alaskan Native	
2--Asian or Pacific Islander	
3--Black (not of Hispanic origin)	
4--Hispanic	
5--White (not of Hispanic origin)	
6--Other	
Gender	**% Ownership**
1--Female	
2--Male	

If you ever wanted to know the sex and race of your local dry cleaning operators, Bill Clinton will ensure that you can find out.

Racism has no place in America. The Republican Party will ensure that the federal, state, and local governments reject the Democrats' and Clinton's policies of racism, quotas, and government-funded bigotry.

12. Adoption

Governor William Weld of Massachusetts, working with the Institute for Children in Cambridge run by Conna Craig, began an initiative in November of 1993 called Assignment Adoption — A Home for Every Child. This project increased the number of children freed from foster care and actually adopted into loving families from 725 in 1993 to 1,068 in 1994. This was a 47 percent increase in one year.

Chapter Nine

Across the nation, Republicans are working to help the 50,000 children in foster care who are legally eligible for adoption but who remain in foster care through the incompetence and counter-productive nature of the welfare state. Sadly, many bureaucrats keep children in foster care as wards of the state in order to protect the jobs and perks of social welfare workers. The current system serves the interests of the bureaucrats rather than the best interests of the children who want families, or of the families who can offer love and a home to such children. There are as many as two million couples willing to adopt and more than 450,000 children in foster care in the United States. Thousands of Americans are going to Eastern Europe, South America, or Asia and paying thousands of dollars to adopt children while there are children here in America who need adoptive homes. Only a government mouthing the rhetoric of caring while practicing the reality of bureaucratic greed and self-dealing could keep these children and families apart.

Adoption, like education, is an area where Republicans must fight against the unionized bureaucracies of the welfare state — the teachers' unions and the social workers' unions — in order to help and protect the children. Democrats are forced to choose the needs of the unions and ignore and trample on the needs of children to be adopted and educated. Republicans have no such political constraints.

Americans know why teachers' unions want to keep children in failed public schools that do not teach or even provide safety: the union dues of teachers in those schools that fund the Democrat Party. The foster care system is a small, but still lucrative business. Taxpayers shell out $10 billion each year to fund the foster care system. Much of this money could be saved if it were made easier, rather than more difficult, for children to be adopted. Too many Americans know the truth — that it is often easier to adopt a foreign child than to battle against the welfare workers of a given state to place a child in a loving home.

Republicans know that caring families are better than bureaucracies at raising children. Democrats know this also, but caring families do not pay union dues or work precincts for the Democrat Party, so they come second to the needs of the Democrat Party's financial and political requirements.

13. Victims of Communism Memorial

In December of 1993, Rep. Dana Rohrabacher (R-CA) and Senator Jesse Helms (R-NC) led the fight to pass a law authorizing the National Captive Nations Committee to organize an independent "Victims of Communism Memorial Foundation" which will build a museum on the Mall in Washington, D.C. to memorialize those 100 million men and women killed by the communists in the Soviet Empire, China, and Cuba. This Foundation is headed by veteran anti-communist activists Ambassador Lev Dobriansky and Lee Edwards.

Republicans will lead the effort to support the construction of this museum to stop the efforts of revisionist historians of the Left to deny, justify, or minimize these crimes.

Such a museum will also become the focal point of studies of the Communist Era and inspire other nations to create similar museums, that the crimes of Lenin, Stalin, Gorbachev, Mao, and Castro may never be forgotten.

14. Everything Clinton Vetoes

Bill Clinton will flesh out the Republican Agenda for 1996. The Republicans will be back with anything Clinton vetoes or anything that requires 290 votes (the two-thirds needed to pass a constitutional amendment or override a veto) in the U.S. House of Representatives, or 60 votes (the three-fifths needed to break a filibuster) in the U.S. Senate. If "conservative" Democrats will not help override vetoes or pass constitutional amendments, America will replace them in the

Chapter Nine

1996 election, and then America will swiftly get the entire Contract, signed, sealed, and delivered.

* * * * *

POSTSCRIPT

As this book is sent to the printer, we have completed the 100 days of the Contract with America. As promised, the House Republicans enacted their eight reforms on the first day of the 104th Congress and added term limits on the Speaker of the House for good measure. At this point, all but one of the ten bills promised by the Contract have passed the House, including the Balanced Budget Amendment, the line item veto, tough crime legislation, a ban on unfunded mandates, and a strengthening of America's defenses. Only term limits failed in the House, getting a majority, but falling short of the two-thirds vote it needed.

Republicans fulfilled the Contract with America, holding free and fair votes on all ten planks of the Contract by April 8, 1995. While the Democrats have certainly prevented the passage of a constitutional amendment for term limits, they cannot stop the drive for term limits at the state and local levels, a drive that has been endorsed by the Republican Party and leadership.

It is a good day to finish the book. We have completed the Republican Revolution in the House. This book discusses the 40-year struggle of a conservative nation to overthrow a liberal Establishment which controlled the House and the nation. Political success might not have meant automatic success in governing; timidity might have led Republicans away from the fray. But the die has been cast for revolutionary change and for strong leadership in the House. Any

315

hesitation that might have lurked in the hearts of this House majority has been pushed back and conquered.

It is easier to look ahead, towards a future of stronger and larger Republican majorities in the House, and even the Senate. Bill Bennett has observed that, in politics as in football, a team is either on offense or defense. Newt Gingrich, Dick Armey, and the Republican freshmen chose to fulfill the Contract, and that meant a strong and unrelenting offense. Not just for the first 100 days, but for the next two years, and even the next twenty.

APPENDIX

Dick Armey, House Majority Leader

APPENDEX   A

TAXPAYER PROTECTION PLEDGE

(L) Grover G. Norquist
(R) Senator Robert Dole

Taxpayer Protection Pledge

I, _____, pledge to the taxpayers of the _____ district

of the state of _____, and to the American people that I will

ONE, oppose any and all efforts to increase the marginal income tax
rates for individuals and/or businesses; and

TWO, oppose any further reduction or elimination of deductions and
credits, unless matched dollar for dollar by further reducing tax rates.

_____   _____
Signature   *Date*

_____   _____
Witness   *Witness*

Pledges must be signed, dated, witnessed and returned to:
Americans for Tax Reform
1320 18th Street, N.W., Suite 200
Washington, D.C. 20036

PHONE 202/785-0266 & FAX 202/785-0261

321

(L) Newt Gingrich, Speaker of the House
(R) Grover G. Norquist

APPENDIX B

TAXPAYER PROTECTION PLEDGE TAKERS

APPENDIX B

AMERICANS FOR TAX REFORM

Taxpayer Protection Pledge
The Pledge Takers for the 104th Congress
as of July 18, 1995 (1:18pm)
Senators in Italics

AK-AL	Don Young	CA-39	Ed Royce
AL-01	Sonny Callahan	CA-40	Jerry Lewis
AL-02	Terry Everett	CA-41	Jay Kim
AL-06	Spencer Bachus	CA-43	Ken Calvert
ALSen	*Dick Shelby*	CA-44	Sonny Bono
AR-03	Tim Hutchinson	CA-45	Dana Rohrabacher
AR-04	Jay Dickey	CA-46	Bob Dornan
AZ-01	Matt Salmon	CA-47	Chris Cox
AZ-03	Bob Stump	CA-48	Ron Packard
AZ-04	John Shadegg	CA-49	Brian Bilbray
AZ-05	Jim Kolbe	CA-51	Duke Cunningham
AZ-06	J. D. Hayworth	CA-52	Duncan Hunter
AZSen	*John McCain*	CO-03	Scott McInnis
AZSen	*Jon Kyl*	CO-04	Wayne Allard
CA-01	Frank Riggs	CO-05	Joel Hefley
CA-02	Wally Herger	CO-06	Dan Schaefer
CA-04	John Doolittle	*COSen*	*Hank Brown*
CA-10	Bill Baker	CT-05	Gary Franks
CA-11	Richard Pombo	*DESen*	*Bill Roth*
CA-19	George Radanovich	FL-01	Joe Scarborough
CA-22	Andrea Seastrand	FL-04	Tillie Fowler
CA-23	Elton Gallegly	FL-06	Cliff Stearns
CA-25	Buck McKeon	FL-07	John Mica
CA-27	Carlos Moorhead	FL-08	Bill McCollum
CA-28	David Dreier	FL-09	Mike Bilirakis
CA-38	Stephen Horn	FL-10	Bill Young

325

FL-12	Charles Canady	IN-06	Dan Burton
FL-13	Dan Miller	IN-07	John Myers
FL-14	Porter Goss	IN-08	John Hostettler
FL-15	Dave Weldon	*INSen*	*Dan Coats*
FL-16	Mark Foley	KS-01	Pat Roberts
FL-21	Lincoln Diaz-Balart	KS-02	Sam Brownback
FL-22	Clay Shaw	KS-03	Jan Meyers
FLSen	*Connie Mack*	KS-04	Todd Tiahrt
GA-01	Jack Kingston	*KSSen*	*Bob Dole*
GA-03	Mac Collins	KY-01	Ed Whitfield
GA-04	John Linder	KY-02	Ron Lewis
GA-06	Newt Gingrich	KY-03	Michael Ward
GA-07	Bob Barr	KY-04	Jim Bunning
GA-08	Saxby Chambliss	LA-01	Bob Livingston
GA-10	Charlie Norwood	LA-06	Richard Baker
GASen	*Paul Coverdell*	LA-07	Jimmy Hayes
IA-02	Jim Nussle	MA-03	Peter Blute
IA-03	Jim Lightfoot	MA-06	Pete Torkildsen
IA-04	Greg Ganske	ME-01	Jim Longley
IA-05	Tom Latham	MD-01	Wayne Gilchrest
ID-01	Helen Chenoweth	MD-02	Robert Ehrlich
ID-02	Mike Crapo	MD-06	Roscoe Bartlett
IDSen	*Dirk Kempthorne*	MI-02	Pete Hoekstra
IDSen	*Larry Craig*	MI-04	Dave Camp
IL-05	Michael Flanagan	MI-06	Fred Upton
IL-06	Henry Hyde	MI-08	Dick Chrysler
IL-08	Phil Crane	MI-11	Joe Knollenberg
IL-10	John Porter	*MISen*	*Spence Abraham*
IL-11	Jerry Weller	MN-01	Gil Gutknecht
IL-13	Harris Fawell	MN-03	Jim Ramstad
IL-14	Denny Hastert	MO-02	Jim Talent
IL-15	Tom Ewing	MO-07	Mel Hancock
IL-16	Don Manzullo	MO-08	Bill Emerson
IL-18	Ray LaHood	*MOSen*	*Kit Bond*
IN-02	David McIntosh	*MOSen*	*John Ashcroft*
IN-04	Mark Souder	MS-01	Roger Wicker

Appendix B

MSSen	*Trent Lott*	OH-10	Martin Hoke
MSSen	*Conrad Burns*	OH-12	John Kasich
NC-02	David Funderburk	OH-15	Deborah Pryce
NC-03	Walter B. Jones, Jr.	OH-18	Bob Ney
NC-04	Fred Heineman	OH-19	Steve LaTourette
NC-05	Richard Burr	OK-01	Steve Largent
NC-06	Howard Coble	OK-02	Tom Coburn
NC-09	Sue Myrick	OK-04	J.C. Watts
NC-10	Cass Ballenger	OK-05	Ernest Istook
NC-11	Charles Taylor	OK-06	Frank Lucas
NCSen	*Jesse Helms*	*OKSen*	*Don Nickles*
NCSen	*Lauch Faircloth*	*OKSen*	*Jim Inhofe*
NE-02	Jon Christensen	OR-02	Wes Cooley
NH-01	Bill Zeliff	OR-05	Jim Bunn
NH-02	Charlie Bass	PA-05	Bill Clinger
NHSen	*Bob Smith*	PA-08	Jim Greenwood
NJ-01	Robert Andrews	PA-09	Bud Shuster
NJ-02	Frank LoBiondo	PA-13	Jon Fox
NJ-03	Jim Saxton	PA-16	Bob Walker
NJ-04	Chris Smith	PA-17	George Gekas
NJ-12	Dick Zimmer	PA-19	Bill Goodling
NY-01	Michael Forbes	PA-21	Phil English
NY-03	Peter King	*PASen*	*Rick Santorum*
NY-04	Dan Frisa	*PASen*	*Arlen Specter*
NY-13	Susan Molinari	SC-01	Mark Sanford
NY-19	Sue Kelly	SC-02	Floyd Spence
NY-20	Benjamin A. Gilman	SC-03	Lindsey Graham
NY-22	Jerry Solomon	SC-04	Bob Inglis
NY-27	Bill Paxon	TN-01	Jimmy Quillen
NY-30	Jack Quinn	TN-02	John Duncan
NYSen	*Al D'Amato*	TN-03	Zach Wamp
NV-02	Barbara Vucanovich	TN-04	Van Hilleary
OH-01	Steve Chabot	TN-07	Ed Bryant
OH-04	Mike Oxley	*TNSen*	*Bill Frist*
OH-06	Frank Cremeans	TX-03	Sam Johnson
OH-08	John Boehner	TX-04	Ralph Hall

Rock the House

TX-06	Joe Barton	WA-02	Jack Metcalf
TX-08	Jack Fields	WA-03	Linda Smith
TX-09	Steve Stockman	WA-04	Doc Hastings
TX-13	Mac Thornberry	WA-05	George Nethercutt
TX-15	Kika de la Garza	WA-08	Jennifer Dunn
TX-19	Larry Combest	WA-09	Randy Tate
TX-21	Lamar Smith	*WASen*	*Slade Gorton*
TX-22	Tom DeLay	WI-01	Mark Neumann
TX-23	Henry Bonilla	WI-03	Steve Gunderson
TX-26	Dick Armey	WI-06	Tom Petri
TXSen	*Kay Bailey Hutchison*	WI-08	Toby Roth
TXSen	*Phil Gramm*	WI-09	Jim Sensenbrenner
UT-01	James Hansen	WYAL	Barbara Cubin
UT-02	Enid Waldholtz	*WYSen*	*Craig Thomas*
UTSen	*Bob Bennett*		
UTSen	*Orrin Hatch*	229 Total House and Senate	
VA-06	Bob Goodlatte	31 U.S. Senators	
VA-07	Tom Bliley	198 U.S. Representatives	
VA-11	Tom Davis		

APPENDIX C

ANTI "VAT" PLEDGE
AND
CAUCUS

AMERICANS FOR TAX REFORM

Anti-Value Added Tax Pledge

I, _____, PLEDGE TO THE TAXPAYERS OF THE STATE OF _____, AND TO THE AMERICAN PEOPLE THAT I WILL OPPOSE ANY AND ALL EFFORTS TO PASS A NATIONAL SALES TAX OR A VALUE ADDED TAX.

SIGNATURE   DATE

WITNESS   WITNESS

Pledges must be signed, dated, witnessed and returned to:
1320 18th St. NW Suite 200
Washington, DC 20036
Phone (202) 785-0266/Fax (202) 785-0261

331

APPENDIX C

Citizens Against A National Sales Tax
═══ Value Added Tax ═══

Members of the Anti-VAT Caucus--104th Congress
Hon. Dick Armey   Hon. Tom DeLay   Co-Chairmen
List as of July 14, 1995   2:47pm *Senators in Italics*

AL-01	Sonny Callahan	CA-52	Duncan Hunter
AL-06	Spencer Bachus	CO-03	Scott McInnis
AR-03	Tim Hutchinson	CO-04	Wayne Allard
AR-04	Jay Dickey	CO-05	Joel Hefley
AZ-01	Matt Salmon	CO-06	Dan Schaefer
AZ-03	Bob Stump	*COSen*	*Hank Brown*
AZ-04	John Shadegg	CT-05	Gary Franks
AZSen	*John McCain*	*DESen*	*Bill Roth*
CA-01	Frank Riggs	FL-01	Joe Scarborough
CA-02	Wally Herger	FL-04	Tillie Fowler
CA-04	John Doolittle	FL-06	Cliff Stearns
CA-10	Bill Baker	FL-07	John Mica
CA-11	Richard Pombo	FL-08	Bill McCollum
CA-19	George Radanovich	FL-10	Bill Young
CA-22	Andrea Seastrand	FL-12	Charles Canady
CA-23	Elton Gallegly	FL-13	Dan Miller
CA-25	Buck McKeon	FL-14	Porter Goss
CA-39	Ed Royce	FL-15	Dave Weldon
CA-40	Jerry Lewis	FL-21	Lincoln Diaz-Balart
CA-40	Ken Calvert	*FLSen*	*Connie Mack*
CA-41	Jay Kim	GA-01	Jack Kingston
CA-44	Sonny Bono	GA-03	Mac Collins
CA-45	Dana Rohrabacher	GA-06	Newt Gingrich
CA-46	Bob Dornan	GA-07	Bob Barr
CA-47	Chris Cox	*GASen*	*Paul Coverdell*
CA-48	Ron Packard	IA-03	Jim Lightfoot
CA-51	Duke Cunningham	IA-04	Greg Ganske

333

IA-05	Tom Lantham	MN-03	Jim Ramstad
ID-01	Helen Chenowith	*MNSen*	*Rod Grams*
ID-02	Mike Crapo	MO-02	Jim Talent
IDSen	*Dirk Kempthorne*	MO-07	Mel Hancock
IDSen	*Larry Craig*	MO-08	Bill Emerson
IL-05	Michael Flanagan	*MSSen*	*Trent Lott*
IL-06	Henry Hyde	*MTSen*	*Conrad Burns*
IL-08	Phil Crane	NC-02	David Funderburk
IL-11	Jerry Weller	NC-03	Walter B. Jones, Jr.
IL-13	Harris Fawell	NC-04	Fred Heineman
IL-14	Denny Hastert	NC-06	Howard Coble
IL-15	Tom Ewing	NC-11	Charles Taylor
IL-16	Don Manzullo	*NCSen*	*Jesse Helms*
IL-18	Ray LaHood	NH-01	Bill Zeliff
IN-02	David McIntosh	*NHSen*	*Bob Smith*
IN-04	Mark Souder	NJ-02	Frank LoBiando
IN-06	Dan Burton	NJ-03	Jim Saxton
IN-08	John Hostettler	NJ-06	Frank Pallone
INSen	*Dan Coats*	NJ-12	Dick Zimmer
KS-01	Pat Roberts	NY-01	Michael Forbes
KS-02	Sam Brownback	NY-02	Rick Lazio
KS-03	Jan Meyers	NY-03	Peter King
KS-04	Todd Tiahrt	NY-13	Susan Molinari
KY-01	Ed Whitfield	NY-19	Sue Kelly
KY-02	Ron Lewis	NY-22	Jerry Solomon
LaA-01	Bob Livingston	NY-27	Bill Paxon
LA-06	Richard Baker	NY-30	Jack Quinn
LA-07	Jimmy Hayes	NY-31	Amo Houghton
MA-03	Peter Blute	*NYSen*	*Al D'Amato*
ME-01	Jim Longley	NE-02	Jon Christensen
MD-01	Wayne Gilchrest	NE-03	Bill Barrett
MD-02	Robert Ehrlich	NV-02	Barbara Vucanovich
MD-06	Roscoe Bartlett	OH-01	Steve Chabot
MI-04	Dave Camp	OH-06	Frank Cremeans
MI-11	Joe Knollenberg	OH-10	Martin Hoke
MN-01	Gil Gutknecht	OH-12	John Kasich

APPENDIX C

OH-18	Bob Ney	TX-21	Lamar Smith
OH-19	Steve LaTourette	TX-22	Tom DeLay
OK-01	Steve Largent	TX-23	Henry Bonilla
OK-04	J.C. Watts	TX-26	Dick Armey
OK-05	Ernest Istook	*TXSen*	*Kay Bailey Hutchison*
OK-06	Frank Lucas	*TXSen*	*Phil Gramm*
OKSen	*Don Nickles*	UT-01	James Hansen
OKSen	*Jim Inhofe*	UT-02	Enid Waldholtz
OR-02	Wes Cooley	*UTSen*	*Orrin Hatch*
OR-04	Peter DeFazio	VA-06	Bob Goodlatte
OR-05	Jim Bunn	VA-07	Tom Bliley
PA08	Jim Greenwood	VA-11	Tom Davis
PA13	Jon Fox	WA-02	Jack Metcalf
PA-16	Bob Walker	WA-04	Doc Hastings
SC-02	Floyd Spence	WA-05	George Nethercutt
SC-03	Lindsey Graham	WA-08	Jennifer Dunn
TN-01	Jimmy Quillen	WA-09	Randy Tate
TN-02	John Duncan	WI-01	Mark Neumann
TN-03	Zach Wamp	WI-03	Steve Gunderson
TN-04	Van Hilleary	WI-08	Toby Roth
TN-07	Ed Bryant	WI-09	Jim Sensenbrenner
TNSen	*Bill Frist*	WYAL	Barbara Cubin
TX-03	Sam Johnson	*WYSen*	*Craig Thomas*
TX-04	Ralph Hall		
TX-08	Jack Fields	178 Total	
TX-09	Steve Stockman	18 U.S. Senators	
TX-13	Mac Thornberry	160 U.S. Representatives	
TX-16	Ron Coleman		

Rock the House

APPENDIX D

CONSERVATIVE ORGANIZATIONS

(L) Senator Paul Coverdell (R-GA)
(C) Grover G. Norquist
(R) Carl Parks, Legal Counsel

Conservative Organizations

Accuracy in Media, Inc.
4455 Connecticut Ave N.W.
Washington D.C. 20008
Phone: 202-364-4401
Fax: 202-364-4098
Toll Free Membership Information: 1-800-787-0044

Accuracy in Media, a media watchdog group, was founded in 1969 by Reed Irvine. A national membership organization, it monitors the media for fairness, accuracy, objectivity and thoroughness. AIM's major publication is the AIM Report, which goes to 15,000 members twice each month. The AIM-Allied Educational Foundation Speakers Bureau provides speakers to groups throughout the country at little or no cost, and its officers, staff and speakers are frequent guests on radio and television talk shows and are sought out as interview sources on subjects concerning the media.

American Conservative Union
1007 Cameron St.
Alexandria, VA 22314
Phone: 703-836-8602
Fax: 703-836-8606

The American Conservative Union is the nation's oldest conservative lobbying organization. ACU's purpose is to effectively communicate and advance the goals and principles of conservatism through one multi-issue, umbrella organization.

The Statement of Principles makes clear ACU's support of capitalism, belief in the doctrine of original issues of the framers of the Constitution, confidence in traditional moral values, and commitment to a strong national defense.

American Legislative Exchange Council
910 17th St. N.W.
Fifth Floor
Washington D.C. 20006
Phone: 202-466-3800
Fax: 202-466-3801

The American Legislative Exchange Council (ALEC) was founded in 1973 by a small group of Democrat and Republican state legislators who shared a common commitment of the Jeffersonian principles of free markets, free enterprise, limited government and individual liberty.

Today, ALEC has grown to become the nation's largest bipartisan, individual membership organization of state legislators, with 2,400 members throughout the 50 states, Puerto Rico and Guam. Nearly one-third of ALEC's members hold leadership positions in their legislatures. ALEC's goal is to ensure that our legislative members are fully armed with the information, research and ideas they need to win in the legislative arena.

Cato Institute
1000 Massachusetts Ave. N.W.
Washington D.C. 20001
Phone: 202-842-0200
Fax: 202-842-3490

The Cato Institute was founded in 1977 by Ed Crane and businessman Charles Koch, and moved from San Francisco to Washington in 1981. They publish 6 to 10 books a year as well as a variety of other publications including *Cato Journal*, *Regulation* magazine, and *Cato Policy Report*. Unlike many policy groups, Cato has always focused more on changing the broad public debate than on directly influencing policy makers. Their books and studies are written for a broad audience and are given further circulation through a vigorous op-ed program. The Institute has tried to stick to principle and examine long-run policy problems.

Center for Security Policy
1250 24th St. N.W.
Suite 350
Washington D.C. 20037
Phone: 202-466-0515
Fax: 202-466-0518

The Center exists as a non-profit, non-partisan organization to stimulate and inform the national and international debate about all aspects of security policy, notably those policies bearing on the foreign, defense, economic, financial and technology interests of the United States.

The Center relies heavily upon the active participation of a distinguished board of Advisors. By drawing on the experience, judgment and insights of these accomplished policy-practitioners, it is able to maximize the quality of its inputs into the security policy-making process. This structure also permits the Center to operate with an extremely small core staff and great cost-effectiveness.

Christian Coalition
1801-L Sara Drive
Chesapeake, VA 23320
Phone: 804-424-2630
Fax: 804-424-9068

The Christian Coalition:
- Represents Christians before legislative bodies
- Speaks out in the public arena and in the media
- Trains Christians to be effective leaders
- Informs Christians about issues and legislation
- Protests anti-Christian bigotry

Implementing Christian Coalition's objectives will return America to a country where religious freedoms are guaranteed, where individual liberty is proclaimed, and where the government truly is of the people, by the people and for the people.

Citizens for a Sound Economy
1250 H St. N.W.
Suite 700
Washington D.C. 20005-3908
Phone: 202-783-3870
Fax: 202-783-4687

Citizens for a Sound Economy (CSE) is a 250,000 member advocacy group that promotes market-based policy solutions. CSE identifies and mobilizes constituencies that can benefit from policies that advance or preserve economic freedom. Demonstrating the power of free markets through research, analysis, and the experiences of people allows CSE to increase policy makers' and individuals' understanding of how economic freedom solves everyday problems. Citizens for a Sound Economy Foundation (CSE Foundation), CSE's research and education affiliate, develops private-sector solutions to promote economic growth.

Citizens United
11094 D Lee Highway
Suite 200
Fairfax, VA 22030
Phone: 703-352-4788
Fax: 703-591-2505

Citizens United helped break the Whitewater story wide open in November of 1993 when it conducted an exclusive interview with Judge David Hale, who publicly exposed for the first time that Bill Clinton, as governor of Arkansas, had influenced Judge Hale to make an illegal loan to Clinton's partner in Whitewater Development Company, Susan McDougal. This story was later covered extensively in the major media.

Citizens United also provided regular Whitewater updates by transmitting over 3,000 faxes daily to the major media, talk radio programs, and Members of Congress.

Competitive Enterprise Institute
1001 Connecticut Ave. N.W.
Washington D.C. 20036
Phone: 202-331-1010
Fax: 202-331-0640

The Competitive Enterprise Institute (CEI) is a pro-market, public policy group committed to advancing the principles of free enterprise and limited government. Founded in 1984 by Fred L. Smith, Jr., CEI emphasizes the marketing and implementation of classical liberal ideals. CEI utilizes a five-point management approach to affecting public policy: analysis, education, coalition building, advocacy and litigation. Its purpose is to advance the free-market agenda, believing limited government and competition best serve the public interest.

Conservative Campaign Fund
8321 Old Courthouse Rd. Suite 215
Vienna, VA 22182
Phone: 703-448-0360
Fax: 703-448-8341

CCF is a political action committee supporting low taxes, a strong defense and Congressional reform. CCF identifies with the populist wing of the Republican Party. CCF has no hesitancy to back challengers or GOP candidates prior to the Republican primary. Their goal is to support conservatives who will be conservative leaders if they are elected.

Defenders of Property Rights
6235 33rd St. N.W.
Washington D.C. 20015
Phone: 202-686-4197
Fax: 202-686-0240

Defenders of Property Rights was organized in 1991 for the purposes of serving as a national public interest law foundation whereby private property owners can obtain relief from governmental actions which have deprived them through regulation, legislation or other bureaucratic activities of their property. When it is determined to be in the public interest, Defenders will initiate or participate in legal or administrative actions affecting private property rights.

Eagle Forum
316 Pennsylvania Ave. S.E.
Washington D.C. 20003
Phone: 202-544-0353

Founded in 1972, Eagle Forum, led by Phyllis Schlafly, is one of the most effective grassroots organizations in the nation.

The Eagle Forum single-handedly defeated the so-called Equal Rights Amendment. Active in defense, economic and family issues, Eagle Forum has activists in every state and major city.

Family Research Council
700 13th St. N.W.
Suite 500
Washington D.C. 20005
Phone: 202-393-2100
Fax: 202-393-2134

Family Research Council was organized in 1983. Today, FRC maintains a staff of nearly 50 in Washington and Holland, Michigan. FRC has played a key role in many of the critical debates of recent times. The organization contributed to the grassroots opposition to a big-government health care plan. FRC also played a role urging the removal of Surgeon General Joycelyn Elders. Its position papers, *Insight*, *Family Policy*, and *Perspective*, are used by legislators and pro-family activists nationwide. FRC President Bauer has been a guest on CNN's Cross-Fire, PBS' MacNeil-Lehrer Newshour, and numerous other television and radio interview shows. His column appears in the monthly magazine, *Citizen*, a publication of Focus on the Family.

The Federalist Society
1700 K St. N.W.
Washington D.C. 20006
Phone: 202-822-8138
Fax: 202-296-8061

The Federalist Society for Law and Public Policy Studies is a non-profit group of conservatives and libertarians interested in the current state of the legal order. It is founded on the principles that the state exists to preserve freedom, that the separation of powers is central to our Constitution, and that it is emphatically the province of the judiciary to say what the law is, not what it should be.

Golden Rule Insurance Company
7440 Woodland Dr.
Indianapolis, IN 46278-1719
Phone: 317-297-4123
Fax: 317-297-0908

Golden Rule Insurance Company is an advocate of the Medical Savings Account (MSA's). They have offered after-tax MSA's to their employees since May of 1993. In 20 months, Golden Rule employees have personally saved more than $1.2 million. This savings represent more than 40% of the total deposits to the accounts. In addition to saving that money, the MSA's have also increased access to preventive care, provided first-dollar coverage, and given the employees an incentive to shop around for medical care. By simply providing that incentive, Golden Rule has not had a rate increase for two straight years.

GOPAC
440 First St. N.W., Suite 400
Washington D.C. 20001
Phone: 202-484-2282
Fax: 202-783-3306
In 1979 when former Delaware Governor Pete duPont founded GOPAC, the primary focus and goal was to begin to build a "farm team" of elected officials at local levels who could then run for higher office. As GOPAC and the farm team grew, so too did the need to expand the programs. In 1988 when then Presidential candidate Pete du Pont asked Congressman Newt Gingrich (R-GA) to take over as general Chairman, a broader approach was established to teach and educate the candidates, making use of technological advances and mass distribution methods.

The Heritage Foundation
214 Massachusetts Ave. N.E.
Washington D.C. 20002
Phone: 202-546-4400
Fax: 202-546-8328

The Heritage Foundation is one of the country's leading public policy research institutes. With offices just two blocks from the United States Capitol, The Heritage Foundation's research and studies programs are designed to make the voices of responsible conservatism heard in Washington, D.C., throughout the United States, and in the capitals of the world. The Heritage Foundation was established in 1973 as a non-partisan, tax-exempt policy research institute dedicated to the principles of free competitive enterprise, limited government, individual liberty, and a strong national defense.

Independent Women's Forum
1319 18th St. N.W.
Washington D.C. 20036
Phone: 202-833-4553
Fax: 202-833-4543

The Independent Women's Forum was formed to challenge the conventional wisdom about what women think. IWF exposes the misrepresentation of the feminist left and their influence over culture. Beyond simply challenging the facile, gender-based political culture, they advocate the positive social values of personal responsibility, strong families, and equal opportunity to pursue rewards for hard work and individual merit. In just over two years, relying on volunteer efforts, they have compiled a remarkable record of accomplishments.

Institute for Children
4 Brattle St.
Suite 211
Cambridge, Mass. 02138
Phone: 617-491-4614
Fax: 617-491-4673

The Institute for Children is the only national organization in America wholly devoted to reshaping "the system" of state-run substitute care -- a system in desperate need of repair, as its current design causes a great deal of human suffering. The Institute's mission is to stop and then reverse the huge growth of state-run, state-funded foster care and to rehabilitate private adoption. The Institute's researchers synthesize available data and put action-oriented recommendations into the hands of people who can galvanize change.

The Institute for Justice
1001 Pennsylvania Ave. N.W.
Suite 200 South
Washington D.C. 20004
Phone: 202-457-4240
Fax: 202-457-8574

The Institute for Justice advances a rule of law under which individuals control their destinies as free and responsible members of society. Through strategic litigation, training, and outreach, the Institute secures greater protection for individual liberty, challenges the scope and ideology of the Regulatory Welfare State, and illustrates and extends the benefits of freedom to those whose full enjoyment of liberty is denied by government.

The Leadership Institute
8001 Braddock Rd.
Suite 502
Springfield, VA 22151
Phone: 703-321-8580
Fax: 70-321-7194

The Leadership Institute was founded in 1979 to identify, recruit, train, and place conservatives in the public policy process. Since then, Institute schools have attracted more than 10,000 conservative activists and helped them obtain positions of influence in government and private organizations. Founder and president Morton C. Blackwell is a long-time conservative activist and worked for three years as Special Assistant to President Reagan as his liaison to conservative, veteran, and religious groups.

Media Research Center
113 South West St,
Alexandria, VA 22314
Phone: 703-683-9733
Fax: 703-683-9736

Established in 1987, the Media Research Center is a conservative research and education foundation dedicated to bringing political balance to the media. The MRC monitors all news and prime time entertainment programming and major print publications for evidence of bias and trends of bias in the media. The programs are stored in the MRC Archive, the largest library of its kind in existence, and which now includes over 13,000 tapes and 70,000 hours of programming dating back to 1987.

National Center for Policy Analysis
12655 N. Central Expy.
Suite 720
Dallas, TX 75243-1739
Phone: 214-386-6272
Fax: 214-386-0924

The National Center for Policy Analysis is a nonprofit, nonpartisan, public policy research institute founded in 1983. Major policy areas on which the NCPA concentrates include welfare, health care, tax, environment, crime, and social security. Many of the pro-growth economic ideas are ones which the NCPA has analyzed and promoted since 1989. Additionally, the NCPA developed the idea of Medical Savings Accounts which was included in 25 bills, with bipartisan support of more than 230 cosponsors, during the 103rd Congress.

National Empowerment Television
717 Second St. N.W.
Washington D.C. 20002-4368
Phone: 202-544-3200
Fax: 202-544-2819

NET was established December 6, 1993, following three and a half years of narrowcasting and experimental broadcasting shows. NET is a full-time cable/satellite channel which as of the election reached 11 million homes. NET originates eight hours of news/talk style shows on policy and politics each day, but with repeats broadcast 24 hours a day, 7 days a week.

National Legal and Policy Center
8321 Old Courthouse Rd.
Vienna, VA 22182
Phone: 703-847-3088

NLPC promotes ethics in government through distribution of the "Code of Ethics for Government Service," and through research, education and legal action. NLPC was founded in late 1991 following the release of the Senate Ethics Committee report whitewashing the Keating Five, in order to help give the Code the visibility it deserves

National Right to Life Committee, Inc.
419 7th St., N.W.
Suite 500
Washington D.C. 20004-2293
Phone: 202-626-8800
Fax: 202-737-9189

National Right to Life, the nation's largest pro-life group, works to protect innocent human lives threatened by abortion, infanticide and euthanasia. NRLC was founded in 1973 as a non-partisan, non-sectarian federation of 50 state right-to-life groups, made up of approximately 3,000 local chapters.

National Right to Work Committee
8001 Braddock Rd.
Springfield, VA 22160
Phone: 703-321-9820/800-325-7892
Fax: 703-321-7342

The National Right to Work Committee, established in 1955, is a nonprofit, nonpartisan, single purpose citizens' organization dedicated to the principle that all "Americans must have the right but not be compelled to join labor unions."

The National Right to Work Committee combats compulsory unionism through an aggressive program designed to make the public aware of the evils of compulsory unionism and, at the same time, encourage their support of Right to Work legislation. The NRWC is one of the largest public-interest groups in America. The Committee has over 1.7 million supporters nationwide. Studies have shown, moreover, that 75% of all Americans sympathize with the objectives of the Committee and oppose forced union membership.

National Rifle Association
Institute for Legislative Action
11250 Waples Mill Road
Fairfax, VA 22030
Phone: 703-267-1000

Founded by ex-military men in 1871, the NRA is the oldest sportsmen's organization in America. With 3.6 million members it remains an active grassroots organization dedicated to the right of the individual citizen to own and use firearms for defense and recreation. The political arm of NRA, the Institute for Legislative Action was founded in 1974 to work pro-actively through the legislative and electoral process to protect the freedoms secured by the Bill of Rights.

Progress & Freedom Foundation
1250 H Street N.W.
Suite 550
Washington D.C. 20005
Phone: 202-484-2312
Fax: 202-484-9326

The Progress & Freedom Foundation is a private, non-profit, non-partisan idea center established in 1993 to create a positive vision of America's future founded on our nation's historic principles. It brings together a diverse group of thinkers and policy experts and shares their work with the American people through seminars, conferences, publications and broadcasts. The Foundation believes that conflicting ideologies now are engaged in a very real battle to define America's future, and that an ideology of progress and freedom can and should win that competition.

Reason Foundation
3415 S. Sepulveda Blvd. Ste. 400
Los Angeles, CA 90034
Phone: 310-391-2245
Fax: 310-391-4395

Founded in 1978 and based in Los Angeles, California the Reason Foundation has earned a reputation for sound economic research and a how-to approach that benefits policy makers and elected officials who require practical solutions. Specializing in a variety of policy areas including the environment, education, transportation, and privatization, the Reason Foundation is a leader on the issues that matter most to those outside Washington. *Reason* is a leading social and political commentary magazine that goes beyond the new to deliver insightful and distinctive information and analysis.

The Seniors Coalition
11166 Main St.
Suite 302
Fairfax, VA 22030
Phone: 703-591-0663

The Seniors Coalition is an advocacy organization which represents the mainstream thinking of America's senior citizens. Their goal as a grassroots lobbying organization is to advocate the concerns and interests of senior citizens while utilizing their knowledge and experience. They were founded during the fight to repeal catastrophic care legislation in 1989. Since then, The Seniors Coalition has grown from 200,000 members to more than two million members and supporters. On average, they have 4,500 members per Congressional district. The mission of The Seniors Coalition is to promote and protect the economic well being and the quality of life for America's senior citizens without negatively affecting younger Americans.

Small Business Survival Committee
1337 Connecticut Ave. N.W.
Suite 200
Washington D.C. 20036
Phone: 202-785-0238
Fax: 202-822-8118

The Small Business Survival Committee (SBSC) is a 40,000-member nonpartisan, nonprofit advocacy organization fighting against the growing burden of taxes and regulation on American business and individuals. SBSC produces a series of publications including *Small Business and the Economy, Small Business Tax Watch* and *The Deregulator* to keep its membership, the media and Members of Congress up-to-date on how legislative proposals and current laws effect small business and free enterprise. SBSC rates Congress on many small business issues, and mobilizes its grassroots membership and associated members on legislation before Congress on these issues.

Toward Tradition
P.O. Box 58
Mercer Island, WA 98040
Phone: 206-236-3046
Fax: 206-236-3288

Toward Tradition was founded in 1991 by Rabbi Daniel Lapin along with other Jewish and Christian leaders around the country. It is dedicated to unifying Christians and Jews politically by means of a shared vision of religiously rooted conservatism. Educational rather than overtly political, it publishes articles, produces newspaper announcements and audio cassettes, sponsors conferences and seminars, and provides speakers on the intrinsic morality of conservatism. Toward Tradition focuses on economic issues such as taxation, social issues including welfare, criminal justice, and education.

Traditional Values Coalition
Address:
Phone: California: 714-821-4500
       Washington: 202-547-8570
Fax: California: 714-821-9609
     Washington: 202-546-6403

Traditional Values Coalition (TVC) is the largest non-denominational, conservative grassroots lobby in America, representing over 31,000 churches. Rev. Louis P. Sheldon founded TVC in 1981 in response to the growing needs of pastors to become educated and activated on issues in the public policy arena. TVC believes that its strength is in its churches. The church is society's only stable institution with an infrastructure for disseminating information and organizing people. What makes TVC unique is its multi-racial membership made up of various denominations and socio-economic backgrounds. TVC's varied membership has worked at many levels to fight the increasing attacks on our Judeo-Christian heritage.

U.S. Term Limits
1511 K St. N.W.
Washington D.C. 20005
Phone: 202-393-6440
Fax: 202-393-6434

Founded in 1992, U.S. Term Limits leads the national movement to limit politicians' terms at the federal, state, and local level. To achieve this goal, the organization works with activists across the nation either to place term limit ballot initiatives before the voters or to assist in legislative lobbying efforts. U.S. Term Limits has more than 70,000 members and publishes issue papers, the "Term Limits Outlook Series," and a monthly newsletter, "No Uncertain Terms." Key figures in the group are its President, Howard Rich, Executive Director Paul Jacob, Congressional Affairs Director Ron Nehring and Foundation Director Norman Leahy.

APPENDIX E

STATE POLICY ORGANIZATIONS

(L) Sonny Bono, Congressman CA
(R) Dana Rohrabacher

APPENDIX E

State Policy Organizations

Alabama
Gary Palmer
The Alabama Family Alliance
PO Box 59468
Birmingham, AL 35259
(P) 205-870-9900/(F) 205-870-4407

Arizona
Michael Sanera
Arizona Institute
7000 N. 16th St., #120-420
Phoenix, AZ 85020
(P) 602-277-8682/(F) 602-277-8563

Jeff Flake
Goldwater Institute
Bank One Center - Concourse
201 N. Central Ave.
Phoenix, AZ 85004
(P) 602-256-7018/(F) 602-256-7045

California
Charles Heatherly
Golden State Center
2012 H. St., Suite 101
Sacramento, CA 95814
(P) 916-446-7924/(F) 916-446-7990

Colorado
Tom Tancredo
Independence Institute
14142 Denver West Pkwy., #101
Golden, CO 80401-3134
(P) 303-279-6536/(F) 303-279-4176

Connecticut
Laurence Cohen
The Yankee Institute
117 New London Turnpike
Glastonbury, CT 06033
(P) 203-633-8188/(F) 203-657-9444

Delaware
John Lopez
Center for Innovative Government
PO Box 513
Montchanin, DE 19710
(P) 302-658-7638/(F) 302-658-8869

Florida
Peter Schweizer
The James Madison Institute
PO Box 13894
Tallahassee, FL 32317-3894
(P) 904-386-3131/(F) 904-386-1807

Georgia
Griff Doyle
Georgia Public Policy Foundation
2900 Chamblee-Tucker Rd., Bldg. Six
Atlanta, GA 30341-4128
(P) 404-455-7600/(F) 404-455-7600

Illinois
Michael Finch
The Heartland Institute - Illinois
800 East Northwest Hwy., Suite 1080
Palatine, IL 60067-6516
(P) 708-202-3060/(F) 708-202-9799

Indiana
Thomas D. Hession
Indiana Policy Review Foundation
320 N. Meridian St., Suite 904
Indianapolis, IN 46204-1725
(P) 317-236-7360/(F) 317-236-7370

Iowa
Dale G. Bails
Public Interest Institute
600 N. Jackson St.
Mt. Pleasant, IA 52641
(P) 319-385-3462/(F) 319-385-3799

Massachusetts
David Tuerck
The Beacon Hill Institute
Suffolk University
8 Ashburton Place
Boston, MA 02108-2770
(P) 617-573-8750/(F) 617-720-4272

James A. Peyser
Pioneer Institute
85 Devonshire St., 8th Floor
Boston, MA 02109
(P) 617-723-2277/(F) 617-723-1880

Michigan
Lawrence Reed
The Mackinac Center
PO Box 568
Midland, MI 48640
(P) 517-631-0900/(F) 517-631-0964

Minnesota
Mitchell Pearlstein
Center for the American Experiment
2342 Plaza VII
45 S. 7th St.
Minneapolis, MN 55402
(P) 612-338-3605/(F) 612-338-3621

Nebraska
Richard Thayer
Constitutional Heritage Institute
608 N. 108th Court
Omaha, NE 68154
(P) 402-493-9155/(F) 402-493-7084

Nevada
Judy Cresanta
Nevada Policy Research Institute
PO Box 20312
Reno, NV 89515-0312
(P) 702-786-9600/(F) 702-786-9604

New Hampshire
Emily Mead
The Josiah Bartlett Center
PO Box 897
Concord, NH 03302-0897
(P) 603-224-4450/(F) 603-224-4329

New Jersey
Robert McGee
The Dumont Institute
236 Johnson Ave.
Dumont, NJ 07628
(P) 201-387-1456/(F) 201-387-0744

New York
Thomas Carroll
The Empire Foundation
130 Washington Ave., Suite 1000
Albany, NY 12210
(P) 518-432-4444/(F) 518-432-6617

North Carolina
Marc Rotterman
The Jon Locke Foundation
PO Box 17822
Raleigh, NC 27619

Ohio
Andrew Little
The Buckeye Center
131 N. Ludlow St., Suite 308
Dayton, OH 45402
(P) 513-224-8352/(F) 513-224-8457

Oklahoma
David Dunn
Resource Institute of Oklahoma
5101 N. Classen Blvd., Suite 307
Oklahoma City, OK 73118-4433
(P) 405-840-4920/(F) 405-840-4925

Brett Magbee
Oklahoma Council of Public Affairs
100 W. Wilshire, C-3
Oklahoma City, OK 73116
(P) 405-840-4920/(F) 405-840-4925

Oregon
Steve Buckstein
Cascade Policy Institute
813 SW Alder, Suite 707
Portland, OR 97205
(P) 503-242-0900/(F) 503-242-3822

Pennsylvania
Don Eberly
The Commonwealth Foundation
600 N. 2nd St., Suite 300
Harrisburg, PA 17101-1032
(P) 717-231-4850/(F) 717-231-4854

South Carolina
Edward McMullen, Jr.
South Carolina Policy Council
1419 Pendleton St.
Columbia, SC 29201
(P) 803-779-5022/(F) 803-779-4953

Tennessee
Nelson Griswold III
Andrew Jackson Institute
511 Union St., Suite 1004
Nashville, TN 37219
(P) 615-726-0247

Texas
Jeff Judson
Texas Public Policy Foundation
8122 Datapoint Dr., #910
San Antonio, TX 78229
(P) 210-614-0080/(F) 210-614-2649

Vermont
John McClaughry
Ethan Allen Institute
RFD 1
Concord, VT 05824
(P) 802-695-2555/(F) 802-695-2555

Virginia
Walter Curt
The Commonwealth Foundation of
Virginia
6405 Arbor Landing Dr.
Chester, VA 23831
(P) 804-796-3272/(F) 804-796-3282

Washington
Bob Williams
Evergreen Freedom Foundation
PO Box 552 Olympia, WA 98507

Della Newman
Washington Institute
999 Third Ave. Suite 1060
Seallte, WA 98104
(P) 206 956-3482 (F) 206 467-0910

Wisconsin
James Miller
Wisconsin Policy Research Institute
3107 North Shepard Ave.
Milwaukee, WI 53211
(P) 414-963-0600/(F) 414-963-4230

APPENDIX F

STATE TERM LIMITS LEADERS

State Term Limits Leaders

Alaska

Portia Babcock
Alaskans for Constitutional Reform
716 W. 4th Ave. Suite 540
Anchorage, AK 99501
(907) 465-3762; FX: (907) 465-3805

Dick Randolph
Alaskans for Constitutional Reform
610 12th St.
Fairbanks, AK 997-1
(907) 456-7787; FX (907) 456-5766

Arkansas

Tim Jacob
1200 Barrow Road Suite 214
Little Rock, AR 72205
(501) 223-8408; FX (501) 223-8408

Steve Munn
Orkansans for Governmental Reform
P.O. Box 1447
Little Rock, AR 72203
(501) 661-8699; FX (501) 372-7004

California

Jane Armstrong and Lee Phelps
Alliance for CA Taxpayers
443 Rio Del Mar Blvd.
Aptos, CA 95003
(408) 688-8896; FX (408) 662-9138

Susan Whitman
Citizens for Term Limits
612 Lighthouse Ave #101
Pacific Grove, CA 93950
FX (408) 646-0181

Colorado

Dennis Polhill
Colorado Term Limits Coalition
14142 Denver W. Parkway Ste 185
Golden, CO 80401
(303) 986-8948; FX (303) 238-7931

Tom Tancredo
Colorado Term Limits
14142 Denver W. Parkway #101
Golden, CO 80401
(303) 279-6536; FX (303) 279-4176

Connecticut

Tom Durso
Connecticut Term Limits
Box 571
10 Golf View Dr.
Watertown, CT 06795
(203) 274-4650; FX (203) 274-3825

District of Columbia

R. David Hall
DC Coalition for Citizen
Empowerment
1315 Q Street, N.W.
Washington, D.C. 20009
(800) 374-6904

Georgia

Patrick Gartland
Georgia Term Limits
4167 Chadds Crossing
Marietta, GA 30062
(404) 977-8049; FX (404) 973-8015

Iowa
Sondoe Walker
Iowans for Term Limits
2740 25th Ave.
Marion, IA 52302-1309
(319) 377-0819

Idaho
Beau Parent
Idahoans for Term Limits
817 West Franklin Ste B-105
Boise, ID 83702
(208) 336-6986; FX (208) 338-9748

Illinois
Tom Colgan & Patrick Quinn
Eight is Enough
676 No. LaSalle St. #326
Chicago, IL 60610
(312) 654-0088; FX (312) 654-0087

Indiana
Gregg Gaylord
Indiana Term Limits
230 Camden Dr.
Zionsville, IN 46077
(317) 929-8876

Kansas
Jim Cates
Term Limit Coalition for Kansas
6850 Allesbury
Topeka, KS 66610
(913) 272-7616

Kentucky
Ernie McAfee
Kentucky Term Limits
149 Adams Lane
Richmond, KY 40475-8765
(606) 266-2247; FX (606) 269-8461

Louisiana
Peter Devine
Louisiana 96
1 Seine Ct. Suite 200
New Orleans, LA 70144
(504) 364-0122; FX (504) 364-6198

Billy Hankins & Trey Mannheim
Louisiana for Term Limits
9550 Interline Blvd.
Baton Rouge, LA 70809
(504) 923-2999; FX (504) 927-0195

Maryland
Nelson Warfield
Marylanders for Term Limits
9725 Connecticut Ave.
Kensington, MD 20895
(301) 933-2203

Maine
John Michael
Congressional Term Limits
P.O. Box 233
Auburn, ME 04212
(207) 782-8975; FX (207) 786-8123

Scott Simonds
12 Lucille St.
Saco, ME 04072
(207) 283-1252

Lowell Weeks
Suite 202--Windham Crossing
744 Roosevelt Trail
Windham, ME 04062
(207) 892-2253

Michigan
Allan Schmid
Taxpayer United for Term Limits
255 No. Center
Saginaw, MI 48603
(517) 799-4641; FX (517) 799-6850

Minnesota
Patti Awada
Minnesota Term Limits
444 Cedar St. Suite 810
St. Paul, MN 55101
(612) 221-4043; FX (612) 222-7625

Missouri
John Thompson
P.O. Box 5
Marshfield, MO 65706
(417) 468-5428; FX (417) 468-7577

Greg Upchurch
763 South New Ballas Suite 160
St. Louis, MO 64141
(314) 872-8118; FX (314) 991-2178

Mississippi
Mississippi Term Limits
P.O. Box 2524
Madison, MS 39130
(601) 936-7750; FX (601) 936-7750

North Carolina
Scott Rasmussen
N.C. Term Limits
2915 Providence Road
Charlotte, NC 28111
(800) 554-6487; FX (704) 365-0615

North Dakota
Ralph Muecke
N.D. Term Limits
HCO 1, Box 14
Gladstone, ND 58630-9509
(701) 225-8568

Nebraska
Guy Curtis
601 Broadway St.
Imperial NE 69033
(308) 882-4215

Ed Jaksha
Nebraskans for Term Limits
13406 Shirley
Omaha, NE 68144
(402) 333-2912; FX (402) 333-7384

Ally Milder
9568 Louis Drive
Omaha, NE 68114
(402) 392-1172; FX (402) 393-5739

New Hampshire
Mike Biundo
N.H. Citizens for Term Limits
18 Hughey St.
Nashua, NH 03060
(603) 881-3347; FX (603) 595-2962

New Jersey
N.J. Term Limits Coalition
45 No. Broad St.
Ridgewood, NJ 07450
(201) 652-5600; FX (201) 652-4266

New Mexico
Angela Whately
N.M. Term Limits
6821 Montgomery, N.E.
Albuquerque, NM 87109
(505) 837-2737; FX (505) 837-1033

Nevada
Sig Rogich
Nevadans for Term Limits
8110 Castle Pine
Las Vegas, NV 89113
(702) 228-0222; FX (702) 873-0976

New York
John Butarazzi
New Yorkers for Term Limits
1290 Avenue of the Americas # 1508
New York, NY 10104
(800) 378-8376; FX (212) 265-2003

Oklahoma
Gary Gardenshire
Oklahoma Term Limits
629 24th Avenue, S.W.
Norman, OK 73069
(405) 360-9700; FX (405) 360-7902

Oregon
Paul Farago
2815 SW Patton Lane
Portland, OR 97201
(503) 274-0441; FX (503) 274-1062

Rhode Island
Charles Silverman
454 Paddock Lane
Bristol, RI 02809-1566
(401) 253-5868; FX (401) 253-5868

South Dakota
Pam Hughes
Route 2, Box 221-A
Custer, SD 57730
(605) 673-3021;FX (605) 341-9175

Tennessee
Tennessee Term Limits
Alan Lindsay
4437 Kingston Pike #2204
Knoxville, TN 37917
(615) 281-9230; FX (615) 689-3233

Texas
Mark Sanders
Texans for Term Limitations
7901 Cold Stream Dr.
Austin, TX 78748
(512) 280-3202; FX (512) 280-2804

Utah
Bart Grant
Utah Term Limits
1247 Wasatch Ave.
Salt Lake City, Utah 84104
(801) 538-3482; FX (801) 596-1058

Virginia
Richard Sincere
Virginians for Term Limits
P.O. Box 522
Arlington, VA 22216
(202) 862-3900; FX (202) 862-5500

Vermont
Janice Gambro
Vermont Term Limits
11 Taft Street
Essex Junction VT
(802) 879-3848

Wisconsin
Mike Riley
Wisconsin Term Limits
W55 N774 Cedar Ridge Dr.
Cedarburg, WI 53012-1565
(414) 375-4953; FX (414) 375-4953

West Virginia
Lou Allen
Concerned Citizens for W.V.
101 Laurel Ridge Road
Scott Depot, WV 25560
(304) 757-7224

Wyoming
Jack Adsit
Wyoming Citizens for Responsible
Gov't.
73 Metz Rd.
Sheridan, WY 82801
(307) 674-4983

APPENDIX G

STATE TAX ACTIVISTS

State Tax Activists

Barbara Anderson, President
Citizens for Limited Taxation
18 Tremont St Room #608
Boston, MA 02108
617-248-0022
202-248-0270

Bill Baldwin, President
WA Institute for Policy Studies
999 Third Avenue, Suite 1060
Seattle, WA 98104
206-467-9561
206-467-0910

Joseph L. Bast, President
The Heartland Institute-IL
800 E Northwest Hwy. Suite 1080
Palatine, IL 60067
708-202-3060

David Biddulph, Chairman
Tax Cap Committee
P.O. Box 193
New Smyrna Beach, FL 32170
904-423-4744
904-426-1785

Steve Buckstein, President
Cascade Policy Institute
813 SW Adler, Suite 707
Portland, OR 97205
503-242-0900
503-242-3822

Mike Ciamarra, Projects Director
Alabamians Against Government
Waste
3608 River Ridge Rd
Birmingham, AL 35259
205-969-3678

Pat Cooksey
True Blue Patriots
PO Box 62404
Cincinnati, OH 45262
513-777-8120
513-777-8140

Judy Cresanta, President
Nevada Policy Research Institute
P.O. Box 20312
Reno, NV 89515
702-786-9600
702-786-9604

Griff Doyle
Georgia Public Policy Foundation
2900 Chamblee-Tucker Road, Bldg 6
Atlanta, GA 303414128
404-455-7600
404-455-4355

Sean Duffy, Executive Director
Pennsylvania Leadership Council
223 State Street
Harrisburg, PA 17101
717-232-5919
717-237-1186

Pete du Pont
Delaware Public Policy Institute
One Commerce Center, Suite 200
Wilmington, DE 19801
302-655-7221
303-654-0691

Joel Fox, President
Howard Jarvis Taxpayers Assoc.
621 South Westmoreland, Ste. 202
Los Angeles, CA 90005
213-384-9656
213-384-9870

Sydney Hay, President
The Lincoln Caucus
2907 North 2nd St
Phoenix, AZ 85012
602-248-0139
602-263-7790

Ed Jaksha, President
Nebraska Taxpayers Assoc., Inc.
13406 Shirley
Omaha, NE 68144
402-333-2912
402-333-7384

Grant Malloy, President
Ctrl FL Taxpayer's Action Network
1821 Blaine Terrace
Winter Park, FL 32792
407-896-0196

Dave Murray, Executive Director
NC Taxpayers United
3901 Barrett Dr , Suite 100
Raleigh, NC 27609
919-571-1441

John McClaughry, President
Institute for Liberty and Community
RR 1
Concord, VT 05824
802-695-2555

Ed McMullen, Exec Vice President
South Carolina Policy Council
1419 Pendleton Street
Columbia, SC 29201
803 779-5022
FAX/803-779-4953

Sam Perelli, President
United Taxpayers of New Jersey
P.O. Box 103
Cedar Grove, NJ 07009
201-890-0271
201-890-1917

Karl Peterjohn, Executive Director
Kansas Taxpayers Network
Box 20050
Wichita, KS 67208
316-684-0082
316-684-7527

Lawrence Reed
The Mackinac Center
119 Ashman , PO Box 568
Midland, MI 48640
517 631-0900
FAX/517-631-0964

Michael Riley, President
Wisconsin Taxpayers Network
W55N774 Cedar Ridge Dr
Cedar Berg, WI 53012
414-375-4953

Marc Rotterman, President
John Locke Foundation
6512 Six Forks Rd, Suite 203-B
Raleigh, NC 27619
919-847-2690
Fax/847-8371

David Stanley, President
Iowans for Tax Relief
P.O. Box 747
Muscatine, IA 52761
319-264-8080
319-264-3363

Oscar Stilley
Arkansans For School Choice
516 Central Mall Pl 5111 Rogers Ave
Fort Smith, AR 72903
501-452-3714
501-484-5632

C.A. Stubbs, President
TACT
6322 Sovereign Bldg. 1 Rm.
San Antonio, TX 78229
210-340-8298

James Tobin, President
United Taxpayers of Illinois
223 W. Jackson, St. 1202
Chicago, IL 60606
312-427-5128
312-427-5129

Gordon Webb, President
New York Taxpayers Alliance
PO Box 3224
Kingston, NY 12401
914-338-8334
914-339-8209

APPENDIX H

SMALL BUSINESS
SURVIVAL CAUCUS

Small Business Survival Caucus
Rep. Bill Zeliff, *chairman*

"American Dream Restoration Pledge" Signers
updated 3/22/95
total current membership: 47

Rep. Cass Ballenger	(R-NC)	Rep. Sue Kelly	(R-NY)
Rep. Roscoe Bartlett	(R-MD)	Rep. Steve Largent	(R-OK)
Rep. Charles Bass	(R-NH)	Rep. Steve LaTourette	(R-OH)
Rep. John Boehner	(R-OH)	Rep. John Linder	(R-GA)
Rep. Steve Chabot	(R-OH)	Rep. Frank LoBiondo	(R-NJ)
Rep. Helen Chenoweth	(R-ID)	Rep. James Longley	(R-ME)
Rep. Howard Coble	(R-NC)	Rep. Buck McKeon	(R-CA)
Rep. Tom Coburn	(R-OK)	Rep. Jack Metcalf	(R-WA)
Rep. Mac Collins	(R-GA)	Rep. John Mica	(R-FL)
Rep. Gary Condit	(R-CA)	Rep. Charlie Norwood	(R-GA)
Rep. Tom DeLay	(R-TX)	Rep. Richard Pombo	(R-CA)
Rep. Phil English	(R-PA)	Rep. Jim Saxton	(R-NJ)
Rep. Michael Flanagan	(R-IL)	Rep. Dan Schafer	(R-CO)
Rep. Mark Foley	(R-FL)	Rep. Andrea Seastrand	(R-CA)
Rep. Michael Forbes	(R-NY)	Rep. John Shadegg	(R-AZ)
Rep. Jon Fox	(R-PA)	Rep. Lamar Smith	(R-TX)
Rep. Paul Gilmor	(R-OH)	Rep. Mark Souder	(R-IN)
Rep. Bob Goodlatte	(R-VA)	Rep. Cliff Stearns	(R-FL)
Rep. Pete Green	(R-TX)	Rep. Randy Tate	(R-WA)
Rep. Denny Hastert	(R-IL)	Rep. Charles Taylor	(R-NC)
Rep. Joel Hefley	(R-CO)	Rep. Jerry Weller	(R-IL)
Rep. Wally Herger	(R-CA)	Rep. Roger Wicker	(R-MS)
Rep. David Hobson	(R-OH)	Rep. Bill Zeliff, *chairman*	(R-NH)
Rep. Tim Hutchinson	(R-AR)		

APPENDIX I

AMERICAN DREAM
RESTORATION PLEDGE

The Small Business Survival Caucus

American Dream Restoration Pledge

Whereas, small business represents the backbone of the American economy;

Whereas, increased taxation hurts the economy, kills jobs, reduces individual freedom and strips away the fundamental free enterprise principle called risk and reward;

Whereas, government-imposed mandates and regulation are strangling American business, slowing national economic growth and leading to higher prices for consumers;

Whereas, government interference and overregulation has jeopardized everything from free enterprise to private property rights protected by the Constitution;

In recognition of the "American Dream" and the entrepreneurial spirit that lives in the small businessmen and women of America;

I pledge to fight against government taxation, overregulation, and over spending in order to allow Americans to be the decision-markers, and restore the American Dream. And I pledge to support the entrepreneurial spirit and America's small businesses.

_____
Member of Congress

_____
Bill Zeliff, Chairman SBSC

APPENDIX J

CONTRACT WITH AMERICA CHECKLIST

APPENDIX J

Republican House candidates pledged, in writing, to vote on these 10 common-sense reforms:

Contract with America

- -

We've listened to your concerns, and we hear you loud and clear. On the first day of Congress, a **Republican House** will:

- Force Congress to live under the same laws as every other American.
- Cut one out of every three congressional committee staffers
- Cut the congressional budget.

Then, in the first 100 days, we will vote on the following 10 bills:

☐ **1. Balanced budget amendment and line-item veto**: It's time to force the government to live within its means and to restore accountability to the budget in Washington.

☐ **2. Stop violent criminals**: Let's get tough with an effective, believable and timely death penalty for violent offenders. Let's also reduce crime by building more prisons, making sentences longer and putting more police on the streets.

☐ **3. Welfare reform**: The government should encourage people to work, not to have children out of wedlock.

☐ **4. Protect our kids**: We must strengthen families by giving parents greater control over education, enforcing child support payments and getting tough on child pornography.

☐ **5. Tax cuts for families**: Let's make it easier to achieve the American Dream, save money, buy a home and send the kids to college.

☐ **6. Strong national defense**: We need to ensure a strong national defense by restoring the essential parts of our national security funding.

☐ **7. Raise the senior citizen's earning limit**: We can put an end to government age discrimination that discourages seniors from working if they choose.

☐ **8. Roll back government regulations**: Let's slash regulations that strangle small businesses, and let's make it easier for people to invest in order to create jobs and increase wages.

☐ **9. Common-sense legal reform**: We can finally stop excessive legal claims, frivolous lawsuits and overzealous lawyers.

☐ **10. Congressional term limits**: Let's replace career politicians with citizen legislators. After all, politics shouldn't be a lifetime job.

After these 10 bills, we'll tackle issues such as common sense health care reform, tax rate reductions and improvements in our children's education.

387

APPENDIX K

"CONTRACT" SCORECARD

APPENDIX K

"CONTRACT" SCORECARD

Congressional Reforms:

- Congressional coverage of other laws:
  Passed 1/4/95, 429-0. (R 225-0; D 23-178)

- Institute "truth in budgeting" measures:
  Passed 1/4/95, 421-6. (R 225-0; D 196-6)

- Impose term limits for Speaker and Committee Chairmen:
  Passed 1/4/95, 355-74. (R 228-0; D 127-74)

- Ban proxy "ghost" voting in committee:
  Passed 1/4/95, 418-13. (R 228-0; D 190-13)

- Open committee meetings to public and press:
  Passed 1/4/95, 431-0. (R 227-0; D 204-0)

- Require 3/5 vote for tax increases:
  Passed 1/4/95, 279-152. (R 227-0; D 52-152)

- Require audit of House of Representatives spending:
  Passed 1/4/95, 430-1. (R 228-0; D 202-1)

- Cut congressional committee staff and budget:
  Passed 1/4/95, 426-12. (R 224-0; D 192-12)

Contract Item #1:

- Balanced Budget Amendment:
  Passed 1/26/95, 4310). (R 228-0; D 72-130)

- Line-item veto:
  Passed 2/6/95, 294-134. (R 223-4; D 71-130)

Contract Item #2:

- Victim restitution: Passed 2/7/95, 431-0. (R 229-0; D 202-0)

- Exclusionary rule reform: Passed 2/8/95, 289-142. (R 220-7; D 69-135)

- Death penalty reform: Passed 2/8/95, 289-142. (R 226-1; D 164-19)

- Prison construction: Passed 2/10/95, 2650156. (R 206-20; D 59-136)

- Criminal alien deportation:
  Passed 2/10/95, 380-20. (R 216-1; D 164-19)

- Anti-crime block grants: Passed 2/14/95, 238-192. (R 220-9; D 18-183)

Contract Item #3:

- Welfare reform: Passed 2/24/95, 234-199. (R225-5; D 9-193)

Contract Item #4:

- Family privacy protection: Passed 4/4/95, 418-7. (R 225-0; D 193-7)

- Sex crimes against children: Passed 4/4/95, 417-0. (R 225-0; D 192-0)

Contract Item #5:

- $500 per child tax credit; "marriage penalty" relief; American Dream
  Savings Accounts; adoption tax credit; elder care tax credit:
  Passsed 4/5/95, 246-188. (R 219-11; D 27-177)

Contract Item #6:

- National security revitalization:
  Passed 2/6/95, 241-181. (R 223-4; D 18-177)

Contract Item #7:

- Social Security benefits tax repeal; earning limitation reform; long-term care insurance tax reform:
  Passed 4/5/95, 2460188. (R 219-11; D 27-177)

- Housing for older persons: Passed 2/6/95, 424-5. (R 228-0; D 196-5)

Contract Item #8:

- Unfunded mandate reform: Passed 2/1/95, 360-74. (R 230-0; D 130-73)

- Paperwork reduction act: Passed 2/22/95, 418-0. (R 228-0; D 190-0)

- Risk Assessment and cost-benefit analysis:
  Passed 2/28/95, 286-141. (R 226-2; D 60-139)

- Regulatory reform and relief:
  Passed 3/1/95, 415-15. (R 228-0; D 187-15)

- Private property protection:
  Passed 3/3/95, 277-148. (R 205-23; D 72-125)

- Tax incentives for job creation:
  Passed 3/14/95, 246-188. (R 219-11; D 27-177)

Contract Item #9:

- Attorney accountability: Passed 3/7/95, 232-193. (R 216-11; D 16-182)

- Securities litigation reform: Passed 3/8/95, 325-99. (R 226-0; D 99-99)

- Product liability and legal reform:
  Passed 3/10/95, 265-161. (R 220-6; D 45-155)

Contract Item #10:

- Congressional term limits: Received 227-204 majority 3/29/95 but did not achieve the 290 votes required for a constitutional amendment.

393

BIBLIOGRAPHY

396

Bibliography

Introduction

Dr. Seuss [pseud]. *Horton Hatches the Egg.* New York: Random House. 1940.

Chapter 1

Republican National Committee. *1994 Chairman's Report.*

Ladd, Everett Carll, ed. *America at the Polls.* Roper Center for Public Opinion Research. 1994.

Chapter 2

Adams, Charles. *For Good and Evil* Lanham, Maryland: Madison Books. 1993.

Alinsky, Saul D. *Rules for Radicals.* New York: Vintage Books. 1971.

Asay, Chuck, and Sharon Cooper. *Taxpayers' Tea Party.* Riverdale, New York: Baen Publishing. 1994.

"Democrat upset in Oklahoma." *Washington Times.* September 2, 1994.

Barnes, Fred. "The Family Gap." *Reader's Digest.* July 1992.

Barone, Michael, and Grant Ujifusa. *The Almanac of American Politics 1994.* Washington D.C.: National Journal. 1994.

Bell, Jeff. *Populism and Elitism.* Washington D.C.: Regnery Gateway. 1992.

Birnbaum, Jeffrey H. "Recent Gingrich Moves Give Democrats Villain They Need in Election Year." *Wall Street Journal.* October 17, 1994.

Folsom, Burton W., Jr. *Entrepreneurs vs. The State.* Reston, VA: Young America's Foundation. 1987.

Fund, John. "We are All Pundits Now." *Wall Street Journal.* November

Fund, John. "The Revolution of 1993." *Wall Street Journal.* October 19, 1994.

Gingrich, Newt. *Window of Opportunity.* New York: TOR Books. 1984.

Kleck, Gary. "The Good Side of Guns." *Social Problems.* Vol. 35, No. 1. February 1988.

LaPierre, Wayne. *Guns, Crime, and Freedom.* Washington D.C.: Regnery Publishing. 1994.

MacDonald, John. "Effect of Halving PAC Donation Cap Would." *Washington Post.* June 13, 1994.

Nock, Albert Jay. *Our Enemy the State.* New York: Libertarian Review Foundation. 1989.

Perry, James M., and Jeffrey H. Birnbaum. "Tactic of Campaigning Against the President is Taken to Extremes, Even in Local, State Races." *Wall Street Journal.* October 17, 1994.

Phillips, Kevin B. *The Emerging Republican Majority.* Garden City, New York: Doubleday. 1970.

Pirie, Madsen. *Blueprint for a Revolution.* Adam Smith Institute. 1992.

Reed, Ralph, Jr. "Casting a Wider Net." *Policy Review.* Summer 1993.

Thomas, Cal. " 'God' Supports Crime Bill?" *Christian American.* October 1994.

Wanniski, Jude. *The Way the World Works.* New York: Touchstone. 1978.

Whitley, David S., ed. *The Conservative Directory.* Costa Mesa, Calif.: Conservative Concepts. 1994.

Lane, Rose Wilder. *The Discovery of Freedom.* New York: Laissez Faire Books. 1984.

Chapters 3 and 4

Barr, Stephen. "OPM Spells Out Un-Hatched Political Acts." *New York Times*. September 22, 1994.

Beichman, Arnold. "Be all their quotes remembered." *Washington Times*. December 14, 1994.

Bennett, James. "The Myth of Union Decline." *Roll Call*. October 14, 1991.

Bennett, James. "Unions: Shrinking, but Richer Than Ever." *Wall Street Journal*. January 13, 1992.

Bozell, Brent. "Pooh-poohing Election Results." *Washington Times*.

Bozell, Brent. "Playing 'gotcha' with facts." *Washington Times*. January 12, 1994.

Brown, Peter. *Minority Party*. Washington D.C.: Regnery Gateway. 1991.

Butler, Stuart. "Health Care Debate Talking Points #8: Impact of the Mitchell Bill's Individual Mandate on the Middle Class." *F.Y.I.*, Heritage Foundation, August 17, 1994.

Casse, Daniel. "Shades of Carter in Clinton Health Plan." *Wall Street Journal*. October 21, 1993.

" 'Health Fairy' Tales." *Wall Street Journal*. May 5, 1994.

Edmonds, Thomas N., and Raymond J. Keating. *D.C. By the Numbers*. Lanham, Maryland: University Press. 1995.

Ehrlich, Paul R. *The Population Bomb*. New York: Ballantine Books. 1968

Glassman, James. "Is the Government's Health Care Cure Really Needed?." *Washington Post*. January 9, 1994.

"Six Reasons Why Bill Clinton's National Service Program is a Bad Idea." *Issue Bulletin*. Heritage Foundation, June 23, 1993.

Horowitz, David. "My Vietnam Lessons." Accuracy in Media Pamphlet.

House Republican Conference, "Clinton's War on the West."
Issue Brief. May 26, 1994.

House Republican Conference, "The Clinton Democrats' Attack on Religion."
Issue Brief. June 29, 1994.

Hull, Tupper. "Wilson suit mounts serious challenge to motor-voter law."
Washington Times. December 22, 1994.

Irvine, Reed, Joseph C. Goulden, and Cliff Kincaid. *The News Manipulators.*
Smithtown, New York: Book Distributors Inc.. 1993.

Jacoby, Mary. "Conservatives Slate Freshman Orientation Seminar to Compete
With One at Harvard." *Roll Call.* October 12, 1992.

Johnson, Paul. *Intellectuals,* New York: Harper & Row. 1988.

Kamen, Al. "For Freshman, No Harvard."
Washington Post. November 23, 1994.

Klein, Joe. "An Awful Year." *Newsweek,* November 14, 1994.

Lowry, Rich. "Fax Populi." *National Review.* November 7, 1994.

McCaughey, Elizabeth. "No Exit." *The New Republic.* February 7, 1994.

"The Best Notable Quotables of 1994." *Notable Quotables.*
Media Research Center, December 19, 1994.

Murray, Charles. *Losing Ground.* New York: Basic Books Inc.. 1984.

O'Sullivan, John. "To Hell and Back." *National Review.* January 23, 1995.

Pines, Burton Yale. *Out of Focus.* Washington D.C.: Regnery Publishing. 1994.

Pressler, Hon. Larry, U.S.S. *Statement Before the United States House of
Representatives Appropriations Committee Regarding the Corporation for Public
Broadcasting.*

Sabato, Larry J., and S. Robert Lichter. *When Should the Watchdogs Bark?* Washington D.C.: The Center for Media and Public Affairs. 1994.

Schmults, Robert. "A Coup from Within? Democrats Suspected of House Power Play." *Insight.* January 25, 1993.

Small Business Survival Committee, "Nationwide Polling Results of 500 Small Business Owners." 1994.

Steffens, Lincoln. *The Autobiography of Lincoln Steffens.* Vol. 1. New York: Harcourt, Brace, and Jovanovich. 1958.

Waldman, Steven, and Bob Cohn. "The Lost Chance." *Newsweek.* September 19, 1994.

Will, George. "Un-Hatching a Monster." *Washington Post.* August 1, 1993.

Williams, Walter E. *South Africa's War Against Capitalism.* New York: Praeger. 1989.

Wines, Michael. "President Grows a Money Tree." *New York Times.* October 4, 1994.

Chapter 5

"For Gorbachev, Timely Advice From Bush." *Money.* October 26, 1992.

"Flip-Flops and Photo Ops." *The Sierra Club Bulletin.* August 1992.

"State and Local Elections." *USA Today.* November 4, 1992.

"Clinton For President." *The New Republic.* November 9, 1992.

"Bush Slaps Right to Work in the Face." *National Right to Work Newsletter.* September 1992.

Brookes, Warren. "Dead Wrong Again." *National Review.* October 7, 1991.

Bush, George. "Agenda for American Renewal."
Bush-Quayle '92 General Committee.

Duffy. Michael. "The Perfect Spy." *Time.* November 5, 1990.

Frum, David. *Dead Right.* New York: Basic Books Inc.. 1994.

Helprin, Mark. "Baker Should Resign." *Wall Street Journal.* April 15, 1992.

Kolb, Charles. *White House Daze.* New York: The Free Press. 1994.

Krauthammer, Charles. "Bush: Two Great Challenges Met." *Washington Post.*
November 23, 1992.

Moore, Stephen. "Done in by a deal." *Washington Times.* October 21, 1992.

Noonan, Peggy. "Why Bush Failed." *New York Times.* November 5, 1992.

Reed, Ralph, Jr. "Survey shows election was a referendum on the economy."
Christian Coalition Press Release. November 4, 1992.

Safire, William. "Bush's Gamble." *New York Times Magazine.*
October 18, 1992.

Toner, Robin. "Critical Moments." *New York Times.* October 11, 1992.

Woodward, Bob. "Origin of the Tax Pledge." *Washington Post.* October 4, 1994.

Woodward, Bob. "No-Tax Vow Scuttled Anti-Deficit Mission."
Washington Post. October 5, 1992.

Chapter 6

"'Star Wars' Victory." *The Shield.* March/April 1994.

Anderson, Martin. "The Reagan Boom — Greatest Ever."
New York Times. January 17, 1990.

Anderson, Martin. *Revolution: The Reagan Legacy.*
Stanford, Calif: Hoover Press. 1990.

Aslund, Anders. *Gorbachev's Struggle for Economic Reform.*
Ithaca, New York: Cornell University Press. 1989

Boaz, David. *Assessing the Reagan Years.* Washington D.C.:
The Cato Institute. 1988.

Daxon, Thomas. "Shrinking Mortgage." *Policy Review.* Winter 1992.

Ferrara, Peter, ed. *Issues '94.* Washington D.C.: The Heritage Foundation. 1994.

Gaffney, Frank. "Decisive trump forsaken?" *Washington Times.* March 4, 1993.

Gigot, Paul. "Gates's Opponents Blame Him For Being Right."
Wall Street Journal. October 4, 1991.

Grenier, Richard. *Capturing the Culture.* Washington D.C.: Ethics and Public
Policy Center. 1991.

"I.F. Stone Outed." *AIM Report.* August-B, 1994.

"The Real Men of the Decade." *AIM Report.* January-A, 1990.

Johnson, Bryan T., & Thomas P. Sheehy. *The Index of Economic Freedom.*
Washington D.C.: The Heritage Foundation. 1995.

Johnson, Paul. *Modern Times.* New York: Harper Perennial. 1983.

Bartley, Robert L. *The Seven Fat Years,* New York: The Free Press. 1992.

McKenzie, Richard B. *What Went Right in the 1980's.*
San Francisco, Pacific Research Institute for Public Policy. 1994.

Noonan, Peggy. *What I Saw at the Revolution.* New York: Random House. 1990.

Reynolds, Alan. "Marginal Tax Rates."
Fortune Encyclopedia of Economics. 1993.

Rothbard, Murray. *America's Great Depression.*
Kansas City: Sheed & Ward. 1975.

Rubenstein, Edwin. *The Right Data.* New York: National Review. 1994.

Rosenfeld, Stephen S. "The Hard-Liners Had It Right."
Washington Post. January 20, 1995.

Samuel, Peter. "Barbarians Within?" *National Review.* August 31, 1992.

Sowell, Thomas. *Inside American Education.* New York: The Free Press. 1993.

Stein, Robert. "Nixon's 'Economic Touchstones'."
Investor's Business Daily. April 29, 1994.

Thomas, Cal. "The Sixties are Dead: Long Live the Nineties." *Imprimis.*
January, 1995.

Walker, Simon, ed. *Rogernomics.* Auckland: CP Books. 1989.

Chapter 7

"Summary of H.R. 3: The Taking Back Our Streets Act of 1995."
Subcommittee on Crime.

American Council for Capital Formation Center for Policy Research. "An
International Survey of Saving Rates and the Taxation of Personal Saving."
Special Report. May, 1993.

American Tort Reform Association. *Polls on Tort Reform,* 1993.

Armor, John. *Why Term Limits?.* Ottawa, Illinois: Jameson Books. 1994.

Bovard, James. *Lost Rights,* New York: St. Martin's Press. 1994.

Bovard, James. *The Farm Fiasco.* San Francisco: ICS Press. 1989.

Bray, Anna. "Civil Justice & Common Sense." *Investor's Business Daily.*
December 30, 1994.

Bray, Anna. "Why Have Tort Costs Exploded?." *Investor's Business Daily.*
January 20, 1995.

Brimelow, Peter, and Leslie Spencer. "The plaintiff attorneys' great honey rush." *Forbes*. October 16, 1989.

Brimelow, Peter, and Leslie Spencer. "Ralph Nader, Inc." *Forbes*. September 17, 1990.

Coyne, James K., and John H. Fund. *Cleaning House*. Washington D.C.: Regnery Gateway. 1992.

Galloway, Lowell, and Richard Vedder. "Waiting for Welfare Reform." *Issue Brief: Institute for Policy Innovation*. October 1994.

Gingrich, Newt, Dick Armey, and the House Republicans. *The Contract with America* New York: Times Books. 1994.

Crane, Edward H., and Roger Pilon, eds. *The Politics and Law of Term Limits*. Washington D.C.: The Cato Institute. 1994.

Publius [James Madison, Alexander Hamilton, and John Jay]. *The Federalist Papers*

Harris, John. "Clinton Meets With Backers from the Military." *Washington Post*. January 13, 1995.

"H.R. 7 — The National Security Restoration Act: Congress's Defense Contract with America." *Issue Bulletin*. Heritage Foundation, January 19, 1995.

House Republican Conference. "Clinton's Hollowing of the Military?." *Issue Brief*. November 7, 1994.

Murphy, Daniel J. "Bellying up to Plaintiffs' Bar." *Investor's Business Daily*. October 12, 1994.

Lippman, Thomas. "Military Readiness." *Dallas Morning News*. December 26, 1994.

Lyons, James. "It's not a wonderful situation" *Forbes*, February 4, 1991.

National Committee for Adoption. *Adoption Factbook*, Washington D.C.: National Committee for Adoption. 1989.

Naylor, Sean. "Ready to go? 4 divisions fail the test." *Army Times*. November 20, 1994.

NRA CrimeStrike. "The Clinton Crime Bill: A Guide for Congressional Candidates." 1994.

Shepherd. Chuck, and Jim Sweeney. "News of the Weird." *Washington City Paper*. November 18, 1994.

Sperry, Paul. "Why Reforming Welfare is Key." *Investor's Business Daily*. June 29, 1994.

Symms, Steve, and Larry Grupp. *The Citizen's Guide to Fighting Government*. Ottawa, Illinois: Jameson Books. 1994.

Chapter 9

Armey, Dick. "The Freedom and Fairness Restoration Act." 1995.

Banks, Howard. "Politics as Usual." *Forbes*. October 10, 1994.

Berlau, John. "The Quota Paradox." *Policy Review*. Spring 1994.

California Voter Fraud Task Force. "Huffington Files Election Contest." *Report from California Voter Fraud Task Force*. January 4, 1995

Charen, Mona. "Absence Makes the Vote Grow Stronger." *Washington Times*. December 3, 1995.

Custred, Glynn. "California's Government-Sponsored Racism." *CPR Update*. Summer 1993.

"A Union's Due." *Washington Times*. August 6, 1991.

"Why Resist the 'Motor Voter' Law?" *Washington Post*. January 25, 1995.

Institute for Children. *Foster Care Fact Sheet*, 1994.

Lindsey, Lawrence. "Remarks before the Board of the Federal Reserve System." September 26. 1994.

Olson, Walter K. *The Litigation Explosion*. New York: Dutton. 1991.

Palmeri, Christopher. "A Conflict of Ambitions." *Forbes*. October 10, 1994.

Republican Policy Committee. "Motor Voter/Partial Sunset if 3% Fraud Rate", *Senate Record Vote Analysis*, March 17, 1993.

"Jackson Calls Conservatives Fascists, Racists." Reuters. December 26, 1994.

"Dues-Payers' Revolt." *Wall Street Journal*. August 27, 1991.

Stein, Robert. "Clinton's Civil Rights Approach." *Investor's Business Daily*. October 19, 1994.

Voter Fraud Task Force. "Evidence of Voter Fraud Released." *Report from Voter Fraud Task Force*. January 3, 1995.

Will, George. "Clinton Shows His Core Values." *Washington Post*. December 15, 1994.

General

Liberal Republicans

Barber, Noel. *The Week France Fell*. New York: Stein and Day. 1976

Conservative Democrats

Bulfinch, Thomas. *Bulfinch's Mythology*. New York: Gramercy Books. 1979

INDEX

ABC, 10, 56, 11, 114, 118, 120
abortion , 168
   and Reagan, 55
   and New Deal coalition, 46
   and term limits, 309
Abramson, Jill, 88
Aburto, Mario, 130
Accuracy in Media, 82
adoption, 204,312
   in Family Reinforcement Act,
      193
   tax credit for, 204
Adriatic Sea, 111, 208
Afghanistan, x, 147
Africa, 172
Afrikaaners, 32
Afro-centric schools, 288
Ahmanson Foundation, 84
Aid to Families with Dependent
     Children, 202
   in Personal Responsibility Act,
     193
Al From, 249
Alabama, 110, 283
   poll on trial lawyers, 105
   trial lawyer contributions, 103
Alameda County, Calif., 304

Alaska, 3
   and gun ownership, 30
   and "victims' rights", 30
   term limits, 28
Albania, 111
   elections in, 305
Allen, George
   and gun control, 53
   election of, 69
Alternative, The, 112
America
   history is revolution, x
   nation and state distinct, xi
American Association of Christian
     Schools, 77
American Association of University
     Professors, 82
American Conservative Union, 220,
     302
American Enterprise Institute, 81
American Gas Association, on
     gasoline taxes, 136
American Red Cross, 240
American Samoa, delegate from,
     126
American Spectator, 88, 112
American Tort Reform Association,
     103

Americans for Tax Reform, 115
    and Cost of Government Day, 40
    conference calls, 115
    on Internet, 115
    work with local taxpayer groups, 37
Americans with Disabilities Act, 134, 153
    as unfunded mandate, 39
AmeriCorps, 132
Anderson, Barbara, 283
Andrews, Tom
    and gun control, 54
    endorsed by NCSC, 302
Anita Hill, 88
Anschutz Foundation, 84
Anthony, Beryl
    defeated by gun-owner activism, 54, 162
Anti-VAT Caucus, 145
Archer, Bill, 16
Archey, Bill, fired by U.S. Chamber, 139
Arena, The, 86
Arizona, 3, 16, 116, 149, 169, 287, 291
    governor's race, 20
    and school choice, 290
    supermajority requirement, 287
Arkansas, 88, 124
    Lt. Gov. race, 68
    gang from, x
    trial lawyers defended by Clinton in, 105
Arlington House, 113
Armey, Dick, 12-13, 316
    amendment to H.R. 6, 75
    amendment to H.R. 6 passes, 79
    and agricultural subsidies, 138

    and home schoolers, 73
    Anti-VAT Caucus, 145
    Dear Colleague on H.R. 6, 78
    flat tax proposal, 276
    floor amendment to H.R. 6, 76
    Freedom and Fairness Restoration Act, 276
    Freedom and Fairness Restoration Act, 277-282, 277
    on future Contract, 275
    speech, 227-230
Army, homosexuals in, 95
Asia, 172
    and adoption, 313
Aspin, Les, appointed Secretary of Defense, 68
Association of Christian Schools International, 77
Association of Concerned Taxpayers, 86
Association of Trial Lawyers of America, 104
Atlanta Journal Constitution, 62, 65
Attila the Hun, 229
Atwater, Lee, 65, 166
Austin, Jeanie, ran Women Who Win seminars, 23
Avanti!, 171
Ayres, Q. Whitfield, on Coverdell race, 62
Azerbaijan, elections in, 305

Baez, Joan, 98
Baird, Zoë, 130
Baker, James, 158, 159
    distinction between politics and governing, 165
    insensitivity on Yugoslavia, 165

Index

balanced budget amendment, 12,
195
  Congress refused, 177
  Fiscal Responsibility Act, 193
  opposed by Clinton, 50
  supported by Christian Coalition,
72
  with supermajority requirement,
286
balanced budget amendment, xv, 2,
12, 50, 72, 106-107, 109, 177,
196, 286, 315
Balch, Steve, 82
Baltic states , 164-165
Baltimore County, 304
Barbour, Haley, speech, 264-267
Barca, Peter, 68
Barone, Michael, on the Clintons,
146
Barr, Bob, 48,60
Barr, William, former Attorney
General, 48
Barry, Marion, 130
Bartlett, Bruce, in defense of Reagan
record, 185
Bartley, Robert, 114
  in defense of Reagan, 183, 185
Barton, Joe, 286
  balanced budget amendment,
196
  new effort on balanced budget
amendment, 198
Beck v. *Communications Workers of
America*, 127, 162, 296-297
Beck, Harry, 128, 297, 298
Beckel, Bob, 167
Beijing, 165
Belgium, 210
Bennett, William, 159, 316

Benson, Steve, 87
Bentsen, Lloyd, 63, 136
  resignation, 21
Berlin Wall, 32
Bessmertnykh, Alexandr, 185
Beyer, Don, election of, 69
big city machines, part of New Deal
coalition, 91
Big Labor, 127
Billmire, Richard, on Stenholm, 108
Bird, Justice Rose, 115
Black Americans
  and crime, 46
  and school choice, 290
  economic gains under Reagan,
181
  part of New Deal coalition, 91
Blackwell, Ken, 88
Blackwell, Morton, 85
Bloom, Allan, 88
Blue Wolf Network 18
Boaz, David, 83
Boehner, John, 139
  speech, 237-240
Bohan, Jim, 18
Bosnia, 208
Boston, 124
Boston Harbor, 163
Bozell, Brent, 82
Bradley Foundation, 84
Bradley, Bill, 19
Bradley, Tom, gun control and his
defeat, 53
Brady Bill, 161
  public support, 51
Brady Foundation, 84
Brady, Nicholas, and Reagan
economic legacy, 160
Bray, Tom, 114

411

Brennan, Justice William, and Beck
    decision, 297
Brickman, Lester, on trial lawyers,
    105
Brimelow, Peter, article on trial
    lawyers, 104
Brock, David, 88
Brookings Institution, 81, 211
Brookline, Mass., 124
Brookover, Ed, 22
Brooks, David, 114
Brooks, Jack, xi, 10, 14, 17, 215,
    308
Brown, Jerry, opposed Prop 13, 36
Brown, Sen. Hank, and term limits,
    309
Buchanan, Pat, 55
    at Houston convention, 65
    on H.R. 6, 77
Buckley, William F., Jr., 111
Budget deal, 65,66,153-156, 161
Bulgaria, elections in, 305
Bureau of Labor Statistics, 212
Bush Administration
    and Beck rules, 128
Bush campaign
    and William Horton, 49
Bush, Barbara
    friends in the administration, 159
Bush, George, 1, 24, 18, 125, 149,
    173
    1992 loss, 44, 151
    alienated NRA, 161
    and assault rifles, 50
    and *Beck* rules, 162
    and Boston harbor cleanup, 163
    and conviction, 150
    and destruction of USSR, 152
    and Gramm-Rudman, 155

    and Reaganites, 158
    and regulation , 153
    and Religious Right, 163
    and taxes, 21, 49, 146, 153
    and the economy, 150
    and the Reagan legacy, 151
    and the veto, 157
    budget deal compromise, 156
    calls Clinton a bozo, 166
    Darman's first victim, 65
    dealt only with leaders, 166
    defense cuts, 207
    distinction between politics and
        governing, 165
    implementation of *Beck*, 298
    in Maryland in 1988, 54
    loss of NRA support, 50
    lost Georgia, 57
    lost support of NRTWC, 59
    on L.A. riots, 164
    poll standings at his nomination,
        65
    refused Reagan credit for Cold
        War, 160
    signed minimum wage increase,
        134
    Taxpayer Protection Pledge, 37
    treatment of Reagan, 160
business PAC contributions
    are bipartisan, 135
    go to incumbents, 135

California, 3, 9, 70, 114-115, 130,
    139, 149, 168-169, 287, 299,
    306
    and gun control issue in 1982,
        53
    and Proposition 13, 36
    and school choice, 290

Index

and voter fraud, 304
civil rights initiative, 310
gasoline tax, 29
health care, 29
initiative, 30
prison reform, 48
supermajority requirement, 287
trial lawyer contributions, 103
California Civil Rights Initiative,
   text of, 310
Cambodia, 86, 188
communism in, 98
nature of communists in, 186
Cambridge, Mass., 124
Campbell, Ben Nighthorse, 2
Canada, 143, 144, 168
Canada's "Contract", 274
candidate recruitment, 22
capital gains taxes, 166, 210
capital investments, taxes on, 210
Capturing the Culture: Film, Art, and
   Politics, 172
Caribbean Sea, 208
Carnegie Foundation, captured by
   the Left, 140
Carter, Jimmy, 15, 44, 85, 110, 123,
   150, 161
1976 election, 110, 111
defense decline under, 207
moral equivalent of war, 143
regulatory excesses, 153
Carville, James, 14, 65
and tax issue, 19
Castro, Fidel
crimes of, 314
ruled Cuba since 1959, 1
Catholic Conference
silent on H.R. 6, 78
Catholic parochial schools, 288

Catholic voters, 17
Catholics, 67-68, 164, 169, 284
and H.R. 6, 74
part of New Deal coalition, 91
Cato Institute, 83, 115, 127
CBS, 10, 111, 114, 117, 118, 120
Ceausescu, Nicolae, 182
Center for Individual Rights, 82
Center for Media and Public Affairs
analysis of election coverage,
   120
Chamber of Commerce of U.S., 137
and Clinton health care, 138
opposed Bush's tax increase,
   138
opposed Reagan's tax increase,
   138
seduced by Clinton, 133
size and membership, 53
Chenoweth, Helen, election of, 70
Chicago, Ill., 303
child support, 204
child tax credit, in American Dream
   Restoration Act, 194
Chile, 182
China, 1, 314
Choice, Not an Echo, A, 149
Christensen, Jon, election of, 70
Christian Coalition, 16-17, 62, 72,
   81
and Coverdell race, 61
and NYC school board elections,
   68
Christian Right, 56
Christian schools, 288
Chung, Connie, 35
Citizens for Limited Taxation, 37,
   283
Civil Rights Initiative, 310

Clancy, Dean, staff to Dick Armey, 73
Clark, Senator Joe, defeat by gun issue, 53
Class Warfare, 67
Clean Air Act, 134, 153
  and 1992 election, 44
  as unfunded mandate, 39
Clift, Eleanor, advice on abortion issue, 64
Clinton Administration
  action against home schoolers, 79
  and racial quotas, 311
Clinton, Bill, 12, 13, 15, 18, 21, 89, 150, 161, 185, 299, 126, 127, 294
  1992 election, 123
  1992 fundraising, 27
  1993 budget, 107
  1993 tax increase, 38
  and Cold War, 44
  and corporate fundraising, 26
  and crime bill, 199
  and cultural Left, 163
  and NAFTA, 50
  and 1994 proposed regulations 41
  and stimulus package, 101
  and tax hikes, 146
  and trial lawyers, 46
  appoints Bentsen to Treasury, 63
  appoints Les Aspin Secretary of Defense, 68
  benefited from collapse of USSR, 44
  Brady Bill, 50
  business fundraising, 131

campaign to repeal Taft-Hartley, 163
campaigned for Fowler, 58
carried Georgia, 57
disavows VAT, 145
dupe of Soviets, 166
effect on candidate recruitment, 23
effort to rebuild Democrat coalition, 124
electoral base disappearing, 95
energy tax, 19, 31
failed Socialist coup, 147
got conservative votes, 151
gun control, 50
health care fears, 293
learned nothing from 1994 defeat, 31
marriage penalty increased, 204
miscalculation of number of homosexuals, 96
misread Reagan record, 184
no mandate for, 168
not New Democrat, 142
on FOCA, 66
on ideas, 168
on volunteers, 131
on welfare reform, 200
outreach to captive nations vote, 165
payoff to mayors, 97
plans for America, 71
politics of envy, 283
poll standing, 65
preferred to Bush, 151
revoked Beck rules, 128, 298
saw gun control as popular, 50
signed bill limiting legal fees, 105

Index

signed family leave bill, 134
support for line-item veto, 195
supported NAFTA and GATT, 94
his tax increase compared to H.R. 6, 74
tax increase on seniors, 209
unelectable before 1992, 45
use of regulatory agencies, 27
use of state troopers, 88
Clinton, Hillary
 calls for a VAT, 145
 health care plan, 133
 health care program, 143
Closing of the American Mind, The, 88
Coalitions, factor in 1994 win, 16
Coelho, Tony, 14, 125
 and corporate fundraising, 27
 efforts to seduce business, 141
 misread Reagan record, 184
 resignation of, 104
Cohen, Richard, 87
Cold War, 151, 160, 169, 185
 and the conservative coalition, 43
 as unifying issue, 44
Coleman, Tom, defeated by gun ownership advocate, 162
Colorado, 169, 286
 cigarette tax, 29
 crime initiative, 30
 supermajority requirement, 287
 term limits, 28
Colorado Union of Taxpayers, 287
Colosio, Luis Donaldo, 130
Commentary, 112, 118, 172, 183, 191
Commerce Department, 213

Committee for a Pro-Life Congress, 61
Communications Workers of America, use of union dues, 128
Communism, importance to voters, 44
Communist Party, 99, 111
Communists, 284
 aggression of, 45
Competitive Enterprise Institute, 115
 on CAFE, 211
 on FDA, 211
CompuServe, 115
Confederacy, 3
Connecticut, 16, 88, 169
 1994 governor's race, 20
 attack on home schoolers, 79
Conservative Book Club, 113
Conservative Opportunity Society, on U.S. Chamber of Commerce, 139
Constitution, 144
Contract With America, 12, 18, 184, 191
 American Dream Restoration Act, 194, 204
 and committee staff, 9
 and tax increases, 38
 and term limits. 308
 Citizen Legislature Act, 195, 214
 Common Sense Legal Reforms Act, 194, 212
 completed, 315
 Congressional reform, 191, 192
 Family Reinforcement Act, 193, 203

Fiscal Responsibility Act, 193, 195
   for the future, 275
   Job Creation and Wage
      Enhancement Act, 194, 210
   National Security Restoration
      Act, 194, 207
   nationalized campaign, 11
   Personal Responsibility Act,
      193, 200
   Senior Citizens Fairness Act,
      194, 209
   Taking Back Our Streets Act,
      193, 199
   unfunded mandates, 40
Contras, supported by Stenholm,
   108
Coors Foundation, 84
Copps, Sheila, Deputy Prime
   Minister of Canada, 144
Coriolanus, 165
Corporate Average Fuel Economy
   (CAFE), 211
   opposed by family groups, 137
Cost of Government Day, 40, 210
Cox, 139
Coverdell, Paul
   election of, 56-60, 62, 66
   favored right-to-work laws, 58
   friend of gun owners, 58
   pro-choice, 60
   gun control in election of, 52
   speech, 246-250
   supported Bush over Buchanan,
      60
   supported Bush over Reagan, 60
   supported Bush over Robertson,
      60
   supports *Roe* v. *Wade*, 60
Craig, Conna, on adoption, 312

Crandall, Robert, 211
Crane, Ed, 83
crime, 47, 96
   and New Deal coalition, 46
   and racism, 49
   and the states, 46
   replaces Cold War as issue, 44
   Safe Streets Alliance, 47
CrimeStrike, 299
   NRA, 47
Croatian-Americans, 165
C-SPAN, 111, 113, 116
Cuba, 208, 314
   and Ethiopia, 187
   nature of Castro's, 99
Cuban-Americans, 165
   and Castro, 42, 45, 96
Cummings, Norm, 22
Cuomo, Mario, 9, 20
Custred, Glynn, 310
cyberjockeys, conservative nature of,
   18

Dalton, John, and gun control issue
   in Virginia, 53
Darman, Richard, 66
   and Reagan economic legacy,
      160
   distinction between politics and
      governing, 165
   on tax pledge, 155
   sold Bush on budget deal, 156
   wrong budget projections, 154
Dartmouth Review, 86-87
Davidson, James Dale, organized
   National Taxpayers Union, 36
Davis-Bacon Act, 297
de Codevilla, Angelo, 86

Index

de Tocqueville, Alexis
    on volunteerism, 132
De-Foley-ate Congress (DF8), 18
Deal, Nathan, 110
death by regulation
    CAFE, 211
    FDA, 211
Declaration of Independence, 144
Delaware, 84
DeLay, Tom, 16, 139
    Anti-VAT Caucus, 145
    speech, 231-234, 231
DeLay-Wallop Bill, 156
Democrat coalition, 67
Democrat Party
    75% government-funded, 300
    and crime, 46
    and gun control, 49
    and immigrants, 200
    and Soviet threat, 46
    election of Roosevelt, 2
    erroneous predictions of, 182
    has controlled Washington, 10
    learned nothing from 1994
        defeat, 31
    one-party control, 1
    opposes school choice, 290
    party of racial quotas, 309
    position on victim's rights, 300
Democratic Congressional
    Campaign Committee, 67, 141
Democratic Leadership Council, 249
Democratic National Committee,
    136
    compared to trial lawyers, 103
Denmark, 211
Department of Education, and home
    schoolers, 73

Department of Justice, and racial
    quotas, 311
Department of Labor, and Beck
    rules, 128
Department of Transportation, and
    CAFE standards, 211
dependent care credit, 204
Detroit, Mich., declining population,
    96
Detroit Economic Club hears Bush
    economic speech, 158
Deukmejian, George, and gun
    control in California, 53
Dewey, Thomas, 149
Dingell, John, 27, 308
District of Columbia, delegate from,
    126
Dobriansky, Ambassador Lev, 314
Dobson, James, and H.R. 6, 76
Dole, Elizabeth, 162
Dole, Robert
    filibuster against Clinton
        stimulus package, 107
    inauguration, 32
    Senate majority leader
    speech, 240-242
Donaldson, Sam, on Evil Empire, 99
Douglas, Chuck, on Stenholm and
    balanced budget amendment,
    109
D'Souza, Dinesh, 86
du Pont, Pete, 84-85
Dukakis, Michael, 123, 124, 161
    1988 fundraising, 27
    and furlough program, 49
    beaten by Bush in 1988, 167
    compared to General Patton, 45
    goal of disarming the public, 50

417

on Points of Light, 132
"Taxachusetts," 29
Dulles, John Foster, 164
Dutschke, Rudi, 171
Dyson, Roy, 262

Eagle Forum, 84
Earhart Foundation, 84
Eastern Europe, 98
   and adoption, 313
economics, 98
Edwards, Lee, 314
Effective Executive, The, 225
Eisenhower, Dwight, 1, 149
Elders, Joycelyn, and drug
   legalization, 50
Elementary and Secondary
   Education Act, H.R. 6, and home
   schoolers, 73
Empower America, freshman
   orientation, 114
energy (BTU) tax, 18, 145
energy taxes, 31
Engler, John, 16
   speech, 253-255
English, Glenn, resignation, 22
environmental activists, allied to
   Vice-President Al Gore, 142
Environmental Protection Agency,
   153, 189
environmentalists, part of Democrat
   coalition, 91
Equal Rights Amendment, 84, 137
   in Vermont, 115
Establishment, xi, 116
   and Bill Clinton, 88
   and government funding, 300
   denied the Reagan record, 183
   in shock and disbelief, 32

learned nothing from 1994
   defeat, 31
on Nixon, 188
opposes term limits, 308
rejected, 121
Establishment Left, 185, 283
   and gun control, 55
   and presidential politics, 43
   broken in America, x
   lashing out at Newt Gingrich, x
   no longer monopolizes
      communications, 117
   on Limbaugh, 116
Establishment media, 72
   and David Brock, 88
   and Washington power structure,
      118
   hid Congress's actions, x
   on Religious Right, 64
   on social issues, 64
Estonia, 43, 182
Estonian-Americans, 164
Ethiopia, 187
Europe, 145
evangelicals, 55, 169

Fabrizio McLaughlin and
   Associates, 12
Family Research Council, freshman
   orientation, 121
Farris, Mike
   700 Club interview; H.R. 6, 76
   defeat of, 69
   Home School Legal Defense
      Assn., 73
   interview on Dobson radio show
      on H.R. 6, 76
   interview on Pat Buchanan radio
      show, 77

Index

on organization of home
schoolers, 79
on the number of home
schoolers, 74
Faulkner, Chip, 283
Fazio, Vic
and 1994 elections, 70
attacks on Religious Right, 67
Chairman, DCCC, 67
failed strategy of, 71
Federal Bureau of Investigations,
155
Federal Communications
Commission, alleged attack on
religious radio, 72
Federalist Society, 85
Feinstein, Sen. Dianne, 304, 306
endorsed by NCSC, 302
feminists, part of Democrat
coalition, 91
Ferguson, Tim, 114
Ferrara, Peter, 83
insatiably brilliant, 184
Feulner, Edwin J., 83, 86
filibuster, 57, 62, 107, 127, 129,
314
Fiscal Responsibility Act, 193
Flanagan, Mike, defeated Dan
Rostenkowski, 14
Flat Tax, 276
treats all equally, 283
Florida, 3, 199, 214
and gun control issue in 1986,
53
supermajority proposal, 287
tax limitations, 31
Florio, Jim
and tax issue, 19

assault weapons., 52
NRA, 52
Focus on the Family, 61
Foley, Tom, ix, xi, 10, 14, 16-18,
118
action on special orders, 127
and gun issue, 54
on Clinton budget, 107
sued his constituents over term
limits, 214
supported NAFTA and GATT,
94
support for Armey on H.R. 6, 77
Fonda, Jane, 98
and Vietnam, 42
wrong about communism, 98
food stamps, 188
Food and Drug Administration, 212
Forbes
article on trial lawyers, 104-105
MSA experiment, 296
poll on Clinton, 141
Forbes, Mary Lou, 112
Forbes, Steve, 296
And Whitman campaign, 20
Ford Foundation, captured by Left,
140
Ford, Gerald
1976 election, 110
and the veto, 157
impact of gun control issue 1976
election, 53
Ford, William, compromise on H.R.
6 unacceptable, 78
Fortune 500 companies, hired
Democrats, 10
Fossedal, Greg, 86
Foundation for Economic Education,
81

Founding Fathers, 285
Fowler, Wyche
    Darman's second victim, 66
    defeat of, 56-60, 62, 66
    defends tax vote, 65
    gun-grabber, 58
    supported by unions, 58
France, 211
Frank, Barney, 125
Franks, Gary, 88
Free Congress Foundation, 82
    freshman orientation, 121
free trade, 158
Free World, 151
Freedom of Choice Act, 61, 66
    focus of pro-life groups, 66
Frenze, Christopher, in defense of
    Reagan record, 185
Fresno County, Calif., 304
Friedman, Milton, creator of
    withholding, 285
Frohnmeyer, John, defended by
    White House, 164
Fund, John, 114

Galbraith, John Kenneth, wrong
    about communism, 98
Gallup polls
    on gun control, 51
    on Clinton, 141
Gann, Paul, 36
Garland, Pat, 61-62
Gaylord, Joe, 22
Gender Equity Act, 301
General Agreement on Tariffs and
    Trade (GATT), 93
General Motors, 59
Georgetown, 184
Georgia, 110, 275, 305

1992 Senate race, 55-60, 66, 68
crime initiative, 30
home schoolers from, lobby on
    H.R. 6, 77
import of special election, 65
NRA members in, 52
Georgia Christian Coalition, 61
Gephardt, Dick, politics of envy, 283
Germany, 94, 151, 168, 210, 284
    model for ClintonCare, 133
Germany, East, 182
gerrymandering, 9, 23, 43, 126
Gettysburg, Battle of, 147
    compared to H.R. 6, 74
    like Contract, 14
Gibbons, Sam, of Nevada, 287
Gigot, Paul, 114
    on U.S. Chamber of Commerce,
        139
    quoting Vladimir Lukin, 185
Gilder, George, 100
Gingrich, Marianne, 225
Gingrich, Newt, 12, 85, 201, 316
    and tax pledge, 38
    Democrat Party attack on, 104
    election night 1994, ix
    inauguration, 32
    on balanced budget amendment,
        198
    on C-SPAN, 116
    on Clinton radicalism, 142
    on future Contract, 275
    on Stenholm, 108
    on term limits, 308
    speech, 224-227
    supported terms limits on
        chairmen and Speaker, 218
    use of special orders, 127

Index

Glendening, Parris, 304
  and tax issue, 20
gold standard, 188
Golden Rule Insurance Company,
  and MSAs, 296
Goldwater, Barry, 149
Goodling, Bill, defends Miller on
  H.R. 6, 77
Goodman, John, 83
GOP-TV, 265
GOPAC, 85
  audio tapes, 115
  conference calls, 116
Gorbachev, Mikhail, 147, 151, 169
  crimes of, 314
  forced to disarm, 185
  supported by Bush, 164
Gore, Al, 126, 142
  business fundraising, 131
  campaigned for Fowler, 58
government workers, part of
Democrat coalition, 91
Graham, John D., on CAFE
standards, 211
Graham, Lisa, 290-291
Gramm, Phil
  disciplined for opposing
    leadership, 109
  speech, 242-244
Gramm-Rudman, 155
Gramsci, Antonio, Italian leftist, 171
Gray, Bill, resignation of, 104
Great Depression, 188
Great Society, 57
Greenberg, Stan, 14
Grenier, Richard, 172
Greve, Michael, 82
Grover Hermann Foundation, 84
Guam, delegate from, 126

Gulf War, 166
  masked Bush unpopularity, 156
  reporting of, 117
Gumbel, Bryant, 116, 117
  misinformation on Reagan
    record, 184
gun control issue
  and polls, 50, 51
  and the Democrat Party, 49
  Brady Bill, 50
  lost by Bush in 1992, 161
gun control v. crime, 48
Gun Owners of America, 17
Guttmacher Institute, on number of
  homosexuals, 95

Hafif, Herb, trial lawyer, 104
Haiti, 208
Handgun Control Inc., size and
  membership, 53
Harlem Globetrotters, 109
Harris poll, on Brady Bill, 51
Hart, Ben, 86
Hart, Gary, 85
Hartman, Richard and Mary, and
  Foley Campaign, 18
Harvard University, 81, 98, 100,
  211
  freshman orientation, 121
Hatch Act, repeal, 129
Hatch, Orrin G.
  striker replacement, 129
  use of audio tapes, 115
Hayek, Friedrich, 257
Hayes, Jimmy, 110
health care, 31, 50
  and the middle class, 143
  business support for, 133
health care reform, 142-143

Heinz Foundation, captured by the Left, 140
Helms, Jesse, 314
Herblock, 87
Heritage Foundation, The, 81, 83, 86, 115, 127, 184, 207
    freshman orientation, 114, 121
    Town Hall, 115
Heston, Charlton, campaigned for Coverdell, 58
Hilleary, Van, election of, 70
Hirschman, Susan, 84
Hispanics, and school choice, 290
Hiss, Alger, 186
    and Nixon, 188
Hitler, 166
Hoff-Hay, Sydney, 287
Hollywood, 171
Home School Legal Defense Association, newsletter on H.R. 6, 75
Home School Legal Defense Fund, 82
home schooling, 72, 74-75, 77-80
homosexual activists, part of Democrat coalition, 91
homosexuals
    and New Deal Coalition, 46
    percentage of electorate, 95
Honnecker, Erich, 182
Honest Graft, 27
Hong Kong, 210
Hoover Institution, 86
Hoover, Herbert, exponent of big government, 188
Horn, Joan Kelly, defeated by gun ownership advocate, 162
Horowitz, David, 82, 186
Horton, William

ad not defended by Bush, 167
    and Bush campaign, 49
House of Lords, 126
House of Representatives, controlled by Democrats since 1955, 1
House Post Office, 125
Huber, Peter, on tort costs, 212
Huckabee, Mike, elected Lt. Gov., 68
Hudson, Jim, Georgia Senate candidate, 57
Huffington, Michael, 304, 306
Human Events, 81, 112
Human Life Amendments, 66
Hungarian freedom fighters, 99
Hungary, 99
Hussein, Saddam, 164
Hutchinson, Barry, 22
Hutchison, Kay Bailey, 66, 68
    1993 special election, 21
    election of, 63
    supported by the Religious Right, 68
Hyatt, Joel, endorsed by NCSC, 302

Idaho, 70
    and "victims' rights", 30
    property tax limitation, 37
    term limits, 28
illegitimacy and the Personal Responsibility Act, 193
Illinois, 164
    redistricting, 28
immigrants, part of New Deal coalition, 91
income tax withholding, elimination of, 285
Indiana, 70, 296

Index

Individual Retirement Accounts (IRAs), 204
  model for MSAs, 294
Individual Rights Foundation, 82
Indochina, 186
Ingraham, Laura, 86
initiatives and referenda
  and crime issue, 46
  in 1994, 28
  tax hikes defeated by, 56
  Tough on Crime bills, 56
Institute for Children, 312
Institute for Justice, 82
Intercollegiate Review, 86
Intercollegiate Studies Institute, 81, 86
Internal Revenue Service, attack on religious schools, 71
Internet, 18
Investor's Business Daily, 114
Iowa, 114, 291
Iowans for Tax Relief, 37
Iraq, 208
Irvine, Reed, 82
Israel, and U.S. military weakness, 43
Italy, 145

Jackson, Brooks, 27
Japan, 210
  and the U.N., 208
Jarvis, Howard, and Proposition 13, 36
Jeffords, Jim, liberal voting patterns of, 57
Jennings, Peter, 184
  misinformation on Reagan record, 184
  on 1994 elections, 118

Jersey City, NJ, has Republican mayor, 97
Jewish day schools, 288
Jews, 284
Johnson, Lyndon B., use of FCC, 72
Johnson, Paul, in defense of Reagan, 183
Joint Chiefs of Staff, on homosexuals in the military, 95
Joint Economic Committee, on regulation, 153
Jones, Gordon S., 86
Joyce, Mike, 84

Kaho'olawe Island Trust Fund, 207
Kansas, 149
  1992 crime initiative, 45
Kasich, John, 50, 232
Kazman, Sam, on FDA, 211
Kemp, Jack, 159, 276
  and tax issue, 21
  speech, 267-271
Kemp-Roth Act, 286
Kennedy School of Government, freshman orientation, 121
Kennedy, David, 84
Kennedy, John F., use of FCC, 72
Kennedy, Paul, 182
Kennedy, Ted, 85
  faith in Democrat dogma, 32
Kentucky
  1994 special House race, 21-22
  special House election, 70
Kerrigan, Karen, 42, 82, 141
  on U.S. Chamber of Commerce, 139
Keyes, Alan, 88
KGB, new files of, 186
Khmer Rouge, 86

Kiev, 164
Kildee, Dale, and Catholic
    Conference on H.R. 6, 78
King, Dr. Martin Luther, Jr., 309
Kinsey Report, 95
Kirkpatrick, Jeanne, 88
Kirkpatrick, Melanie, 114
Klaas, Polly, 30-
Klein, Joe, on 1994 elections, 119
Knox, Neal, 53
Koch Foundation, 84
Kohl, Helmut, 168
Korea, 160
Kosovo, 165
Krieble Institute, The, 83
Krieble, Bob, 83, 84
    on U.S. Chamber of Commerce,
    139
Krueger, Bob, defeated by
    Hutchison, 68
Ku Klux Klan, 203
Kudlow, Larry, and Whitman
    campaign, 20

Labor Department, 85, 162, 297
labor unions, part of Democrat
    coalition, 91
Laos, communism in, 98
LaPierre, Wayne, 17
Larry, Dick, 84
Larson, Reed, and *Beck* decision,
    297
Latin America, 172
Latvia, 43, 182
Latvian-Americans, 164
Leadership Institute, 85
Leave us Alone Coalition, includes
    Christian Right, 71
Lee, Robert E., 147

Left, 171-172
    and the 1960s, 186
    apologists for Soviet
        imperialism, 160
    on Marxist atrocities in Ethiopia,
        187
    view of business, 134
    wrong on more than economics,
        185
left-wing intellectuals, part of
    Democrat coalition, 91
Legal Services Corporation, 301
Lenin, V.I., 275
    and scientific socialism, 99
    crimes of, 314
Lesher, Richard, 138
    and Phyllis Schlafly, 137
Levin, Fred, trial lawyer, 104
Lewis, Anthony, 87
Lewis, Flora, 87
Lewis, Jerry, 228
Lewis, Ron, election of, 70
Libertarian Party, endorsed
    Coverdell, 60
libertarians
    and Republican coalition, 55
    and school choice, 289
Liberty Fund, 84
Liddy, G. Gordon, 114, 116
    listenership, 114
Limbaugh Letter, The, 114
Limbaugh, Rush, 116
    gun control ads on, 52
    keynote speaker at freshman
        orientation, 114
    on H.R. 6, 77
    talk radio show, 113
Lincoln, Abraham, first
    Republican president, 192

Index

Lindberg, Tod, 112
line-item veto, 195
Lithuania, x, 43, 182
Lithuanian-Americans, 164
Lobo Azul, 18
Loctite Corporation, 139
Los Angeles, Calif., 94, 164
    1993 mayoral race, 21
    elects Republican mayor, 68
    Republican mayor, 97
Los Angeles World Affairs Council, 165
Los Angeles Youth Programs, 207
Losing Ground, 100
Lott, Sen. Trent, speech, 244-246
Louisiana 110
    poll on trial lawyers, 105
    redistricting, 28
Lukin, Vladimir, quoted in *WSJ,* 185
Luntz, Frank
    on gun control polls, 51
    poll on school choice, 290
    poll on talk radio, 120
    polling on term limits, 307
Luntz Research, 13
Lyons, James
    on lawyers, 212

MacArthur Foundation, captured by the Left, 140
Macedonia, 208
MacNelly, Jeff, 87
Maddoux, Marlin, on H.R. 6, 76
Magaziner, Ira, health care plan, 133
Maginot Line, 116
Maine, 2, 302
    and gun issue, 54
    gun control in 1990, 54
    term limits in, 28

Major, John, 168
Maloney, Pat, trial lawyer, 104
Malveaux, Julianna, on Clarence Thomas, 119
mandates, in lieu of taxes, 38
Mandela, Nelson, 32
Mann, Judy, 87
Mao Tse-tung, crimes of, 314
Markey, Ed, 27
Marks, Bruce, 303
marriage penalty, 204
Martin, Lynn, 162
Martinez, Bob, and gun control issue in Florida, 53
Marx, Claude, 114
Marx, Karl, 171
Marxism, 171
Maryland, 16
    1994 governor's race, 20
    and voter fraud, 304
    impact of gun control on Bush campaign in 1988, 54
Massachusetts, 16, 124, 169, 312
    and furlough program, 49
    and gun control in 1976, 53
    and rent control, 29
    graduated income tax, 29
    home schoolers put pressure on Moakley, 78
    keeps flat tax, 283
    Kennedy re-election, 32
    property tax limitation, 37
    term limits, 28
Mayer, Jane, 88
Mattingly, Mack, 57
McCaffrey, Neil, Jr., 113
McCardle, Tom, 114
McInturff, Bill, 249

McCollum, Bill, 16
    on crime bill, 199
McDonald, Michael, 82
McDonalds, suit against, 103
McGovern, George, 15
    and Massachusetts, 29
McKenzie, Richard
    in defense of Reagan, 183-185
    on charitable giving, 181
McPhail, Evelyn, campaign training, 22
Media Research Center, 82
Medicaid, 202
Medical Savings Accounts, 293
Medicare, 189, 302
Merline, John, 114
Mexico, 1, 126, 151
Meyer, Eugene, 85
Meyerson, Adam, 114
Michigan, 3, 16, 164
Middle East, 211
military budget, 285
Miller, George
    amendment to H.R. 6, 73
    Dear Colleague on H.R. 6, 77
    opposes Armey amendment to H.R. 6, 75
Milne, A.A., 113
Milwaukee, Wisc., 291
minimum wage, 297
minority voters, and school choice, 290
misery index, 178
Mississippi, 214
    poll on trial lawyers, 105
Missouri, 25,-26, 31, 45, 77
    home schoolers from, lobby on H.R. 6, 77
Mitchell, George, 14

and gun issue, 54
    supported NAFTA, GATT, 94
Moakley, Joe, action on H.R. 6, 78
Modern Times, 183
Mondale, Walter, 44, 85, 123, 124
    and compassion, 102
Montana, 302
    attack on home schoolers in, 79
    supermajority proposal, 287
    tax increases, 29
Moscow, 164
Moss, Frank, defeated by Orrin G. Hatch, 115
Motor Voter Bill, 130, 131, 305
    and illegal aliens, 306
Mudd, Jack, endorsed by NCSC, 302
Mulroney, Brian, 168
Murray, Charles, 100
My Vietnam Lessons, 186

Nader, Ralph
    campaign against Gingrich, 104
    supported by trial lawyers, 104
Natcher, William, death of, 22
National Abortion and Reproductive Rights Action League (NARRAL), and FOCA, 66
National Association of Scholars, 82
National Center for Home Education, and H.R. 6, 73-74
National Center for Policy Analysis, 81, 83
    crime report, 47
National Council of Senior Citizens, 302
National Education Association
    action against home schoolers, 79

Index

attack on religious schools, 71
attack on home schooling, 73
attacked Whitman on school
   choice, 290
membership of, 104
National Empowerment Television,
   71, 82, 139
National Endowment for the Arts,
   163, 301
and religious conservatives, 163
National Endowment for the
   Humanities, 301
National Environmental Policy Act,
   signed by Nixon, 189
National Federation of Independent
   Business (NFIB), 133
active in Georgia Senate race, 59
National Institute for Justice
   crime study, 48
   gun control study, 49
National Lawyers Guild, 85
National Opinion Research Center,
   on number of homosexuals, 96
National Organization for Women
   (NOW), and FOCA, 66
National Public Radio, 301
National Republican Congressional
   Committee, 15-16, 52
and candidate training, 22
National Republican Senatorial
   Committee, 52
and candidate training, 22
National Retail Federation, hired
   Democrat staffer, 136
National Review, 81
established in 1955, 111
National Rifle Association, 17, 81,
   299
and CrimeStrike, 47

and Whitman election, 52
denied support to Bush, 59
in Georgia Senate race, 58
inaction in 1992 election, 50
size and membership, 53
National Right to Work Committee,
   81, 162-163
denied support to Bush, 59
in Georgia Senate race, 58
National Right to Work Legal
   Foundation, and *Beck* decision,
   297
National Rural Electric Cooperative
   Association, 22
national sales tax, 39
National Socialist Germany, an
   aberration, 99
National Socialists, 284
National Taxpayers Union, 115
NBC, 10, 111, 117-118, 120
Nebraska, 2, 70
   rights of gunowners, 54
   term limits, 28
Nelson, Lisa, 85
Nethercutt, George, and term limits,
   309
Netherlands, 210
Neumann, Mark, and the Religious
   Right, 68-69
Nevada, 3, 287
   supermajority requirement, 287
   tax increases, 29
   term limits, 28
New Deal coalition, 91
New Democrat, pose abandoned, 50
New Hampshire, 291
New Jersey, 3, 16, 20, 97, 116
   1993 election, 19, 20-21
   and gun control, 52

and school choice, 290
impact of governor loss on
   Clinton, 52
New Left, wrong about communism,
   98
New Mexico
   1992 crime initiative, 45
   patronage losses in, 10
New Orleans, La., 1988 Republican
   Convention, 38
New World Order, 166
New York, 16, 97, 149, 168
   1994 governor's race, 20
   patronage losses, 10
   redistricting, 28
New York City
   1993 mayoral race, 21
   declining population, 96
   elects Republican mayor, 68
   has Republican mayor, 97
New York Times, 72, 81, 96, 116-
   117
New Yorker, 98
Newark, NJ, 94
Newsweek, 64
Nicaragua, 305
Niemöller, Pastor Martin, 284
Niskanen, Bill, 83
Nixon years reconsidered, 188
Nixon, Richard, 1, 11, 15, 84, 149,
   189
   disastrous economic policies,
      188
   regulatory excesses, 153
Noonan, Peggy, 132
North American Free Trade
   Agreement (NAFTA), 50, 93
   compared to H.R. 6, 74

North Atlantic Treaty Organization,
   151, 209
North Carolina, 97
   and gun crontol in 1976, 53
   redistricting, 28
North Dakota, and gunowners, 54
North Korea, 1
North Vietnamese, terrorism, 98

Office of Management and Budget,
   154
Ohio, 11, 88, 149, 164, 302
   and "victims' rights", 30
   soft drink tax, 29
   supermajority proposal, 287
Oklahoma, 17, 88, 287
   1994 special House race, 21, 22
   gun control in 1992, 54
   special House election, 70
   supermajority requirement, 287
   term limits, 28
Oklahoma Taxpayers Union, 287
Olin Foundation, 84
Orange County, Calif., 304
Oregon, 57
   and tax increases, 31
Orthodox Jews, 67, 68, 92
Orton, Bill, 110
Oxford University, 124, 166
O'Connor, Cardinal John and NYC
   school board elections, 68
O'Neill, Joe, National Retail
   Federation, 136
O'Neill, Tip, 11, 14
   and Harvard seminar, 121
O'Rourke, P.J., on William Horton,
   167

Pacific Legal Foundation, 82

Index

Pacifica Radio, 119
Packwood, Bob, pressures on, 57
Panama Canal Treaties, electoral impact of, 66
parental notification, 203
Parental Rights Amendment, 292
parents, part of conservative coalition, 292
Pataki, George, and tax issue, 20
Patricelli, Robert, resigned from U.S. Chamber board, 140
patronage, 9, 10
Patterson, Tom, 290
Patton, George, 45
Paxon, Bill
  and tax pledge, 38
  NRCC Chairman, 15
  party builder, 16
  view of 1994 candidates, 22
Payne, James, on congressional testimony, 129
peace activists, part of Democrat coalition, 91
Peace Corps, 132
Pennsylvania, 17, 127, 164, 302
  absentee ballots, 304
  and school choice, 291
  home schoolers from, lobby on H.R. 6, 77
  redistricting, 28
Penny-Kasich legislation, 50
Perdue, Tom, Coverdell's campaign manager, 65
Perot, Ross
  got conservative vote, 151
  organization active in Georgia Senate race, 60
Persian Gulf, 152
Personal Responsibility Act, 193

Pew Memorial Trust, captured by the Left, 140
Philadelphia, Pa., 104
Philadelphia Inquirer, 303
Philby, Kim, compared to Charlie Stenholm, 106
Phillips Publishing, and *Human Events*, 112
Phillips, Doug, home school leader, 76
Pierson, Jim, 84
Pines, Burton Yale, 82
Planned Parenthood, 95
Poitevint, Alec, 305
Polish freedom fighters, 99
Polish-Americans, 164
Polish-Americans, 45
  and Soviet occupation, 44
Politæa, 86
political machines, 91
Porlier, Vic, 84
pornography and school choice, 289
pornography., 204
Powell, Gen. Colin, on homosexuals in the military, 95
Prather, Joe, defeat of, 70
Princeton University, 86, 185
prison construction, 193
Prison Notebooks, 171
prisons, cheaper than criminals, 300
Pritchett, Kevin, 86
pro-life position, 17, 55, 60-61, 63-64, 66, 68-70, 266
property rights, 285
Proposition 2½, 37
Proposition 13, 287
  used in Idaho, 37
Protestants, 67, 284
Pruden, Wes, 112

Public Broadcasting System, 119
Public Television, 301
Puerto Rico, Resident
    Commissioner, 127
Quayle, Dan, 159
racism, 309
    and school choice, 289
Rahn, Richard, on U.S. Chamber of
    Commerce, 139
Raleigh, NC, has Republican mayor,
    97
Ramparts, 186
Rand Corporation, 81
    crime study, 48
Rather, Dan, 35, 116, 117
Reagan Administration, 125
Reagan coalition
    in Georgia Senate race, 58
    resented Bush's treatment, 160
    survived end of Cold War, 44
Reagan Democrats, 164
    abandoned Bush, 151
Reagan Doctrine
    contribution to demise of USSR,
    185
Reagan, Michael, 116
    listenership, 114
Reagan, Ronald, 1, 11, 14, 15, 53,
    83, 84, 88, 112, 151, 172
    and compassion, 102
    and the Evil Empire, 99
    and gerrymandering, 9
    and Stenholm, 108
    and the tax burden, 175
    and tax cuts, 146
    and the veto, 157
    at Houston convention, 65
    economic boom, 178
    firmness in foreign policy, 182

impact of gun control issue in
    1976 and 1980, 53
impact on 1980 Georgia Senate
    race, 57
legacy to Bush, 150
NRA member, 53
reached out to moderate
    Republicans, 159
right on Soviet empire, 185
speech, 219-224
takes Bush as vice president, 149
talked with people, 166
tensions in coalition, 67
Reaganomics, 178
Real Anita Hill, The, 88
Reason Foundation, 81
recycling bill, rejected, 169
Red Chinese, nature of, 99
redistricting, 9
    impact in 1996, 27
Reed, Amy, 84
Reed, Ralph, 17, 62, 81
    of Christian Coalition, 72
Regnery, Al, 113
Regnery, Henry, 113
Regnery-Gateway, 113
regulation
    moratorium, 41
    reduced by Reagan, 172
regulatory reform, 12, 210
regulatory takings, 40
Reilly, William, appointed by Bush
    to EPA, 153
Religious Right, 62, 63
    and 1994 elections, 70
    and home schoolers, 72
    as parenthood right, 293
    as threat to Republican coalition,
    55

Index

attacked by Fazio, 67
supported Hutchison, 68
Reno, Janet
call for gun registration, 51
on criminal v. victim's rights, 46
Republican coalition
and gun control, 55
and traditional values, 55
Republican Majority Coalition, 63
Republican National Coalition for
Life, 61
Republican National Committee, 52
and candidate training, 22
compared to trial lawyers, 103
Republican Party, ix, 11
and school choice, 289
and tax issue, 21
and the crime issue, 48
capture of the House, x
committed to term limits, 308
control over redistricting, 9
dropped defense of Hoover, 188
election of Lincoln, 2
in the post-Reagan era, 12
national party, 3
now majority party, ix, 1
party of term limits, 218
position on victim's rights, 300
seven reasons for 1994 gains, 11
vehicle for conservatism, x
wholly conservative, 150
won control of House, 1
Resource Conservation and
Recovery Act, 40
Revenue Act of 1932, Hoover tax
increase, 188
Reynolds, Alan
in defense of Reagan record, 185
on marginal tax rates, 174

Reynolds, Morgan, crime report for
NCPA, 47
Rhoads, Paul, 84
Rich, Howie, 309
Richards, Ann, supported by trial
lawyers, 104
Richardson, Bill, use of video tapes,
115
Ridge, Governor Tom, 291
Right Data, The, 183
Riordan, Richard, accused of
religious extremism, 68
Rise and Fall of Great Powers, The,
182
risk assessment, 194, 282
Robb, Sen. Chuck, and NCSC, 302
Robert Wood Johnson Foundation,
captured by the Left, 140
Roberts, Paul Craig
in defense of Reagan, 183
on indexation of capital gains,
157
Roberts, Steve, on 1994 elections,
119
Robertson, Pat, 17, 55, 56
at Houston convention, 65
in Virginia, 69
on H.R. 6, 76
Robinson, Peter, 86
Robinson, Randall, 88
Rockefeller Foundation, captured by
the Left, 140
Rockefeller, Nelson, 149
Roe Foundation, 84
Roe v. Wade
weakening of, 55
not impetus for Religious Right,
71
Roff, Peter, tax activist, 108

Rohrabacher, Dana, 314
Roll Call, on H.R. 6, 74
Romania, 182, elections in, 305
Rooney, Pat
    and MSAs, 294
    implementation of MSAs, 296
    speech, 271-274, 271
Roosevelt, Franklin D., 2, 92, 161
    blamed for Yalta, 164
    coalition of, 67
Roosevelt, Theodore, on hyphenated
    Americans, 309
Rooseveltian model, 19
Rosenberg, Julius and Ethel, 186
Rostenkowski, Dan, xi, 10, 14, 118,
    215, 308
    defeated, 97
    on Stenholm budget
        compromise, 108
Rothbard, Murray, on Hoover, 188
Rove, Karl, on trial lawyers in
    Texas, 104
Rowland, John, and tax issue, 20
Rubenstein, Ed
    in defense of Reagan record,
        183, 185
    on black economic progress, 181
Rules Committee, action on H.R. 6,
    78
Russia, elections in, 305
Rutherford Institute, 82
Rwanda, 208
Ryskind, Allan, 112

Safe Drinking Water Act, impact on
    rural communities, 40
Safe Streets Alliance
    and crime, 47
    and truth-in-sentencing, 47

Safire, William, 87
Salt Lake City, Utah, 115
Samuelson, Paul, 98
Sanders, Bernie, 196
Sarajevo, 165
Saturday Night Live, parody of news
    media, 118
Saudi Arabia, 133
Sauerbrey, Ellen, and tax issue, 20
Scaife, Foundation, 84
Scanlon, Heidi, 81
Schaefer, Dan, 286
Schlafly, Phyllis, 55, 84, 149
    and Coverdell, 61
    use of video tapes, 115
school choice, 116, 166, 288
    opposed by teachers' unions, 92
School prayer, 289
    school choice impact on, 289
Schundler, Mayor Bret
    and school choice, 290
    speech, 262-264, 262
Schwartz, Victor, on trial lawyers,
    105
Seastrand, Andrea, election of, 70
self-employed, 210
Serbia, 165
Seven Fat Years, The, 183
Shadegg, John, 287, and balanced
    budget amendment, 198
Shalala, Donna, 270
Shawcross, William, on communism
    in Vietnam, 186
Shays Act, 214
Shlaes, Amity, 114
Shultz, George, 185
Simon, Bill, 84
Simon, Senator Paul, and balanced
    budget amendment, 50

Index

Simpson, Sen. Alan, amendment to
Motor Voter, 305
Sims, Ron, endorsed by NCSC, 302
Skinner, Samuel, purged Reaganites,
158
Slovenia, 165
Small Business Survival Caucus,
231, 234-235
Small Business Survival Committee,
82, 141
and regulatory takings, 42
cost of Clinton tax hike, 145
on U.S. Chamber of Commerce,
139
small businessmen, 92
Smedley, Lawrence, 302
Smith Richardson Foundation, 84
Smith, Denny, and crime initiative,
45
Smith, Linda, 287
new effort on balanced budget
amendment, 198
Smoot-Hawley Tariff Bill, 188
Sobran, Joe, 87, 183
social conservatives, 42, 168, 289
and school choice, 289
Social Security, 189
and IRAs, 294
earnings limit, 194
recipients part of New Deal
coalition, 91
Senior Citizens Fairness Act,
194
taxes, 205
Socialism, failure of, 97
Socialist Russia, an aberration, 99
Solzhenitsyn, Alexander, credits
Reagan on Cold War, 185
Souder, Mark, election of, 70

South Africa, 32, 165
South America, and adoption, 313
South Korea, 100
Southeast Asia, 43
Southern Baptist Convention, 68
Southern Baptists, 293
Southern whites, part of New Deal
coalition, 91
Soviet Empire, 185, 314
collapse hurt liberalism, 97
compared to criminal behavior,
48
Soviet imperialism, 32, 45
in Southeast Asia, 98
replaced by crime as issue, 45
Soviet Politburo, 126
Soviet Union, 151, 172, 182, 188
breach in the Berlin Wall, x
couldn't match Star Wars, 185
crimes of, 187
files on the 1950s, 186
Lithuania and Afghanistan, x
loss in Cold War, 43
nature of, 99
view of business, 134
Sowell, Thomas, 87
Spence, B.B., on trial lawyers, 104
Spencer, Leslie, article on trial
lawyers, 104
Stalin, Josef, crimes of, 314
Stanford University, 86
Stanley, David, 37
Stanley, Jean, 37
State Department, 85, 100
Steffens, Lincoln, 97
Stein, Bob, 114
Stenholm, Charlie
compared to Washington
Generals, 109

false flag conservative
Democrat, 106
given post of Deputy Whip, 109
on balanced budget amendment,
107
on Clinton budget, 107
Stinson, William, 303
Stockman, Steve, defeated Jack
Brooks, 14
Stone, Roger, 63
strategic defense, 188
Strategic Defense Initiative, 172,
182, 209
Striker Replacement, 129
Studds, Gerry, 125
sunsetting, 285
Sununu, John, 138, 159, 165
distinction between politics and
governing, 165
supermajority requirement for tax
increases, 196, 286
in the states, 287
Supreme Court, 163
and abortion, 55
and *Beck* decision, 127-128,
297, 298
and school choice, 289
decisions on parental rights, 292
on term limits, 218
Sweden, 145, 210
Symington, Fife
and school choice, 290
and taxes, 20
Synar, Mike, and gun control, 54

Taft, Robert, 149
Taft-Hartley Act, 162-163
Taiwan, 100
Taking Back Our Streets Act, 193

Talmadge, Senator Herman, ethics
charges against, 57, 58
Tammen, Melanie, on the *Wall
Street Journal*, 114
Tanzania, 100
Tauzin, Billy, 110
tax credit for children, 204
tax cuts, 210
for families, 12
Tax Foundation, Tax Freedom Day,
36
taxes, 18, 21, 96
cut by Reagan, 172
tax reform
supported by Christian Coalition,
72
Taxpayer Protection Pledge, 20, 37-
38, 154-156, 161
signed by 43% of House
members, 38
teachers' unions, part of Democrat
coalition, 91
Teamsters Union, 297
Tennessee, 70
term limits, 12, 17, 166, 168, 214,
307
Citizen Legislature Act, 195
in 1994, 28
on committee chairmen, 307
on Ranking Republicans in
Congress, 307
on Speaker of the House, 308
on state and local officials, 307
role in Georgia Senate race, 59,
60
supported by Christian Coalition,
72
Terry, Mary Sue, defeated in
Virginia, 69

Index

Texas, 9, 11, 18, 139, 145, 275
    1992 Senate race, 63, 68
    1993 special election, 21
    Dallas rally in support of home
        schooling, 77
    Dallas, home of NCPA, 83
    import of special election, 65
    poll on trial lawyers, 105
    redistricting, 28
    trial lawyer contributions, 103
Texas Democrat Party, supported by
    trial lawyers, 104
Third Wave, The, 225
Thomas, Clarence, 87
Thomas, Evan, on 1994 elections,
    119
Thompson, Gov. Tommy
    and school choice, 291
    speech, 257-261, 257
    use of line-item veto, 195
Time, 82
Toffler, Alvin and Heidi, 225
TransAfrica, 88
trial lawyers, 212
    campaign against Gingrich, 104
    contributors to Democrat Party,
        103
    part of Democrat coalition, 91
Truman, Harry S, 92
    and the veto, 157
    built on FDR, 161
TV Guide, 231
Tydings, Joseph, defeat by gun issue,
    53
Tyrell, R. Emmett, 112
U.S. Term Limits, 214, 309
Ukraine, 164, 182
Ukraine famines, 188
Ukrainian-Americans, 164

Ulm, Gene, on trial lawyers, 104
unionized workers, part of New Deal
    coalition, 91
United Auto Workers, 94
United Nations, 88, 101
    peacekeeping costs, 208
United Steel Workers, 94
University of Indiana, 112
Unruh, Jesse, on lobbyists, 135
U.S. News and World Report, 119,
    146
USA Today, 119
Utah, 3, 110
    rights of gunowners, 54
    term limits, 28
value added tax (VAT), 39, 145
Vance, Cyrus, 85
Vermont, 57, 115, 196
veterans, 95, 96
Victims of Communism Memorial,
    314
victim's rights, 299
Vietnam, 160, 187
    communism in, 98
    nature of communists in, 186
Vietnam War, 207
    reporting of, 117
Vietnamese Communists, 99
Vietnamese-Americans, 42
Virginia
    1993 governor's race, 21
    home schoolers from, lobby on
        H.R. 6, 77
    and gun control in 1977, 52-53
    and the Religious Right, 69
volunteer activity, during Reagan-
    Bush years, 132
Von Kannon, John, 112

vote fraud, 21, 303
    in Chicago, 97
    in New York, 97
Voter Fraud Task Force, 304
    recommendations of, 306
Voter Research and Surveys (VRS),
    poll on abortion, 64

Wagner Act, 93
Walker, Bob, 16
    use of special orders, 127
Wall Street Journal, 27, 114
Wallace, George, racial politics, 283
Wamp, Zack, election of, 70
Wanniski, Jude, 114
Warner, Senator John, attacks on
    Mike Farris, 69
Washington state, 17, 198, 299, 302
    supermajority requirement in,
    287
Washington Generals, compared to
    Stenholm, 109
Washington Legal Foundation, 82
Washington Post, 87-88, 111-112,
    116
    poll after Houston convention,
    65
Washington Star, 112
Washington Times, 112
Washington, D.C., 96, 130
    declining population, 96
    statehood for, 127
    term limits, 28
Watergate Babies, 125
Watts, J.C., 88
Ways and Means Committee, 10
Wealth and Poverty, 100
Weicker, Lowell, and taxes, 20

Weld, Gov. William, 16
    on adoption, 312
    reduced tax rates, 283
    speech, 255-257
welfare reform, 50, 200
    Personal Responsibility Act, 193
    supported by Christian Coalition,
    72
West Virginia, home schoolers from,
    lobby on H.R. 6, 77
wetlands, 42
Weyrich, Paul, 82, 83
    on creation of Religious Right,
    71
What Went Right in the 1980s, 183
Whitman, Christine Todd, 16
    and Brady Bill, 52
    and NRA, 52
    and school choice, 290
    and tax issue, 19, 21
    assault weapon, 52
Wilhelm, David, jokes about voter
    fraud, 303
Wilhelm, Kyl, 303
Will, George, 87
    on government isolation, 129
Williams, Dick, Atlanta Journal, 65
Williams, Polly, and school choice,
    291
Willkie, Wendell, 64
Wilson, Gov. Pete, speech, 250-253,
    250
Winters, Tom, 112
Wirthlin Group, 13
    poll on abortion, 63
Wisconsin, 68
    and school choice, 291
Wittmann, Marshall, 81

Index

Wofford, Sen. Harris, endorsed by
    NCSC, 302
women, and crime, 46
Woo, Michael. attacks Religious
    Right, 68
Wood, Thomas, 310
Wooster, Martin, 114
work requirements, Personal
    Responsibility Act, 193
Wright, Jim, 125
    on business support for
        Republicans, 141
    resignation of, 104

Wyoming, 10, 305
    crime initiative, 30

Yale Law School, and crime, 47
Yale University, 81, 124
Yalta, 164
Yeltsin, Boris, 185
Yeshiva University, 105
Yugoslavia, 165

Zeliff, Bill
    A to Z Bill, 234
    speech, 234-236

438

Contact Grover G. Norquist
On the Internet

Join Americans for Tax Reform and become a Taxpayer Activist! You can meet Grover on the Internet and do much, much more!

Get the latest news on tax reform! Stop wasteful government spending! Organize a Taxpayers' Day of Outrage! Find other taxpayer activists in your area! Bring the Initiative and Referendum process to your state! Learn about Cost of Government Day! Stop sales tax increases! Defeat the Value-Added Tax! Find out about term limits and school choice! Demand a supermajority or vote of the people for any new tax or tax increase! See how bloated government is squashing your retirement income! Figure your taxes on Dick Armey's Flat Tax form!

Americans for Tax Reform maintains a wealth of information on the ATR homepage, including who among federal elected officials has signed the ATR Taxpayer Protection Pledge and who has not. If you can access the World Wide Web, sign on to **http://www.emerald.net/ATR/**. Additional homepages are coming soon, including one at **http://www.townhall.com**. Otherwise, email to **AmTxReform@aol.com**.

You can become part of a political revolution as the taxpayers' movement presses forward in all fifty states this year and next. State-level issues and initiatives are driving national politics to an unprecedented degree. Even local issues matter — remember Spokane voters were passing a city-wide term limits measure the day they rejected former House Speaker Tom Foley. So, tune into talk radio, watch C-SPAN, and chat with other taxpayers in cyberspace. Then bring the ATR message to your community!

ALSO AVAILABLE FROM

VYTIS PRESS, INC.
AUDIO

ROCK THE HOUSE©
by
GROVER G. NORQUIST

PROLOGUE
by
Newt Gingrich, Speaker of the House of Representatives

ISBN   0-9645786-3-8

$12.95 / Two cassettes

VYTIS Press, Inc.
5100 N. Federal Highway Suite 102
Ft. Lauderdale, FL 33308
1 (305) 772-1236
*

Distributed by
BOOKWORLD Services, Inc.
1933 Whitfield Park Loop
Sarasota, FL 34243

Americans for Tax Reform
1320 18th Street, N.W., Suite 200
Washington, D.C. 20036

Charter Membership
Acceptance

☐ YES, I want to join as a Charter Member of Americans for Tax Reform and actively support your all-out battle to stop further Clinton tax increases.

I understand that with my support today, Americans for Tax Reform will accelerate its already aggressive campaign to obtain signed and public commitments from members of Congress pledging them to oppose any further Clinton tax rate increases.

ATR has already persuaded 140 members of Congress, both Republicans and Democrats, to sign this firm commitment that there will be no more Clinton taxes.

With my support as a Charter Member of ATR, the goal of this remarkable campaign is to collect enough signatures to block any further Clinton taxes.

THIS ATR ANTI-TAX PLEDGE CAMPAIGN IS THE BEST PROTECTION I HAVE AGAINST ADDITIONAL CLINTON TAXES.

To enable ATR to recruit tens of thousands of additional Americans to this anti-tax campaign and build on your success of this all important campaign I am enclosing a special Charter Membership contribution in the amount of:

/ /$25   / /$35   / /$50

/ /$75   / /$100   / /$_____other

_____
Name

_____
Address

_____
City   State   Zip

Please make check payable to ATR. Contributions are tax-deductible to the extent permitted by law.

ABOUT THE AUTHOR

GROVER G. NORQUIST

*

Mr. Norquist, a native of Massachusetts, has been one of Washington's premier issues management strategists for over a decade. Speaker of the House Newt Gingrich described Mr. Norquist as, "the person who I regard as the most innovative, creative, courageous and entrepreneurial leader of the anti-tax efforts and of conservative grassroots activism in America . . . and he has truly made a difference and has truly changed American history."

Mr. Norquist presently serves as President of Americans for Tax Reform (ATR), a coalition of individuals, taxpayer groups and businesses concerned with federal tax policy. The primary project of ATR is the "Taxpayer Protection Pledge", committing candidates for office to opposing any effort to increase personal or corporate income taxes. Mr. Norquist also serves as President of Citizens Against a National Sales Tax/VAT, a national coalition of businesses and tax groups opposed to a Value Added Tax (VAT) in the United States. Mr. Norquist writes a monthly column, "On Politics", for the American Spectator, a monthly review of politics and opinion. Mr. Norquist also serves as co-host of the National Empowerment Network (NET) program Empowerment Outreach Live, broadcast monthly to groups of activists all across America.

Mr. Norquist was an adviser to the Bush/Quayle campaign on crime and tax issues and served as staff to the 1988 and 1992 Republican Platform committees. He holds a Master of Business Administration Degree and a Bachelor of Arts in Economics Degree from Harvard University. Mr. Norquist lives in Washington, DC.

ADDITIONAL EXCLUSIVE, NEW PUBLICATION FROM
VYTIS PRESS, INC.

RONALD REAGAN'S CRUSADE
by
Norman Wymbs

A biography with depth and deep respect of a man whose life has been a crusade for America . It looks at his family background and the parental influence that so molded his childhood and all of his subsequent formative years. Instilling in him the strong Christian beliefs and moral dedication that would propel him into the office of the President of the United States and into the history books as one of, if not the greatest, political leaders of the twentieth century.

(Hardcover - $25.00, U.S.D. plus shipping and handling)

To be released: Fall 1995

NOTE: All books published by:
VYTIS PRESS, INC. are available at quantity discounts with bulk purchase for educational, business or sales promotional use. For information, please write, FAX or phone:
Special Sales Department
VYTIS PRESS, INC.
Phone: (305) 772-1236
FAX: (305) 772-8707
*

Distributed by
BOOKWORLD Services, Inc.
1933 Whitfield Park Loop
Sarasota, FL 34243

RONALD REAGAN'S CRUSADE
by
Norman Wymbs

To Harriett and Norm Wymbs
With best wishes,

Ronald Reagan

RONALD REAGAN'S CRUSADE ©

In 1980 when Ronald Reagan won the nomination for the U.S. Presidency from the Republican Party, his enthusiastic partisans showed little doubt they really understood their charismatic candidate. His campaign speeches and every public expression struck them as clear and understandable, leaving no question as to his position on every political issue. His opposition, every bit as fervent and positive as his supporters, were just as sure there was nothing there and they showed real puzzlement over his appeal. Reagan, in the opinion of both sides, was not a complex man. He appeared so uncomplicated, in fact, that few who met or heard him could retain any pretense of neutrality. With Ronald Reagan, the American people did not have to strain their intellects. It was an instant love or hate reaction!

Although he had served two reasonably successful terms as Governor of California, little was known nationally of his accomplishments or failures in leading that giant state government. In addition his strong support of the unsuccessful Goldwater campaign for the Presidency, as well as his own personal losing effort to wrest the GOP Presidential nomination from Gerald Ford in 1976, left no lasting impression as to his qualifications to lead the country.

Politically murky though he may have been to most observers before his later successful campaigns, there was one facet of his background which everyone felt fully qualified to evaluate, his career in Hollywood. Even casual followers of the glamorous motion picture industry were well aware of the handsome young man who appeared in so many glitzy, if unremarkable, offerings of the movie capital of the world. Of the dozens of eminently forgettable motion pictures featuring Ronald Reagan, a few did stand out sufficiently to etch an image of the star on the public consciousness.

ROCK THE HOUSE©

by

GROVER G. NORQUIST

PROLOGUE

by

Newt Gingrich, Speaker of the House of Representatives

Soon to be released in hardcover
(Collector Quality)

$25.00

ISBN 0-9645786-2-X

VYTIS Press, Inc.
5100 N. Federal Highway Suite 102
Ft. Lauderdale, FL 33308
Phone: 1 (305) 772-1236   FAX: 1 (305) 772-8707
*
Distributed by
BOOKWORLD Services, Inc.
1933 Whitfield Park Loop
Sarasota, FL 34243

ORDERING INFORMATION

ROCK THE HOUSE

PLEASE CALL, WRITE OR FAX TO:

VYTIS Press, Inc.
5100 North Federal Highway
Ft. Lauderdale, FL 33308
PHONE: (305) 772-1236
FAX: (305) 772-8707
*

Distributed by
BOOKWORLD Services, Inc.
1933 Whitfield Park Loop
Sarasota, FL 34243
1-800 444-2524

PRICE (EACH)	$13.95 USD
NUMBER OF BOOKS	_____
TOTAL	_____
SALES TAX - FL RESIDENTS (6%)	_____
S / H ($1.50 PER BOOK)	_____
TOTAL	_____

WE ACCEPT

MONEY ORDER (U.S.D.)
MASTER CARD OR VISA (U.S. BANK)